11/07 nn

Postminimalism into Maximalism
American Art, 1966–1986

Studies in the Fine Arts: Criticism, No. 22

Donald B. Kuspit, Series Editor

Professor of Art History
State University of New York at Stony Brook

Other Titles in This Series

Postminimalism into Maximalism
American Art, 1966–1986

by
Robert Pincus-Witten

 U·M·I Research Press

Ann Arbor, Michigan

Produced and distributed by
UMI Research Press
an imprint of
University Microfilms, Inc.
Ann Arbor, Michigan 48106

Library of Congress Cataloging in Publication Data

Pincus-Witten, Robert.
  Postminimalism into maximalism.

  (Studies in the fine arts. Criticism ; 22)
  "A revised and expanded version of the two previously
published books "Postminimalism : American art of the
decade" "Entries (Maximalism) : art at the turn of the
decade" "
  Includes index.
  1. Art, American—Themes, motives. 2. Art, Modern—
20th century—United States—Themes, motives. 3. Avant-
garde (Aesthetics)—United States—History—20th century—
Themes, motives. I. Title. II. Series.
N6512.P493 1987   700'.973   86-24925
ISBN 0-8357-1928-6 (pbk.)

For Ileana Sonnabend

7 January 1986

*A revelation during lunch with Ileana Sonnabend and Antonio Homem: Ileana =
il y en a, French for whatever there is to be had, there is. Antonio scoffs, but I
think it goes far in explaining Ileana's generous spirit however much she scorns
popular psychology.*

30 March 1986

*Antonio jokes at the scarcity of my recent writing about Ileana's choice of artists:
"Everybody must think we are paying you not to write about the gallery."*

—"Yes," I go on. "In your pocket, buying my silence."

Contents

Postminimalism

Maximalism

The New Irascibles

Figures

Introduction:
Postminimalism into Maximalism

Odd, how a term tossed off the top of one's head should catch on. That's what happened to the rubric "Postminimalism," coined to denote the shift in sensibility away from the frozen and hierarchical academy of American abstract painting in the 1960s and to characterize the radical nature of new efforts. These attempts embraced open and unstable modes, forms not only beautiful in themselves despite their unfamiliarity—beautiful on the level of unmediated sensation—but forms that also called into question the stabilized appearance of the day's abstraction.

Granting the stressful climate of the time—dominated by the horror of the Vietnam War or the adventurism of the subsequent Nixon years—to call to mind yet another vexing issue, younger artists would have been hard pressed indeed not to regard the wafting of skillfully colored silken banners by way of casting the illusion of art as little more than an empty mandarin conjury—which is, of course, what happened and what it was.

The formalist concentration on the pictorial elements of a work of art, and the dialectical reflexivity underlying this materialist reductiveness eventually, inevitably, drew attention to the verbal conditions of a work of art. Ironically, Clement Greenberg, the pioneer critic of Abstract Expressionism who adumbrated these necessities of modernism, adjured the Conceptual developments derived from his emphasis on the pre-executive aspects of abstract painting. Throughout his long life as a critic, dating back to the Great Depression, Greenberg always claimed the superiority of Realism over Abstraction, adding the rueful caveat that despite his predisposition, modernist painting had never found a realist voice of comparative quality to the abstract tenor. Still, had he his druthers. . . .

In The Meanwhile, younger artists, excluded from a golden circle of elect painters and sculptors and repulsed by an agenda based in modernist self-referentiality, came to view a reflexive formalism and the gallery system that sponsored it as alien and pernicious. In short, the academy of abstraction became The Enemy and the activities covered by the term Postminimalism emerged. This opposition continued on from the 1960s into the 1970s with the conflation of Conceptualism and Minimalism. When that occurred, the cognomen Postminimalism began to take on its own life and the idea that there was this thing out there, this style called Postminimalism, gained ground, reified.

Reification: a process of hardening, induration and objectification of an idea, of a notion. We recognize the fruits of the process well after the fact as when, for example, we speak of Impressionism or of the Rococo. Clearly there are no such "things" as Impressionism or the Rococo; consensus opinion has simply come to govern their meaning and the usage of their names. Conversation progresses without wondering just what it was that the speaker meant when the terms were appealed to.

One could, I suppose, natter on about Impressionism as not only manifesting and "early," "late," "mannered," or even a "post-" phase, but also as a totality, chock-a-block Impressionism. Thus the movement would be seen as one big cultural impulse careening through history, capital-I Impressionism—as when we talk, say, of The Renaissance as a kind of force of nature that traces its own organic momentum. Postminimalism could be seen to stand in that relationship to Minimalism, as so naturally continuous with it that it may be regarded as part of the same impulse. Similarly, Postminimalism also strikes me as continuous with Maximalism; Minimalism into Postminimalism and on into Maximalism, all part of the same continuum, especially if we consider in the immense role played by a growing historicist impulse during this same period, a revision and revival part and parcel of the so-called Post Modern debate.

In the case of Postminimalism some of the reification process is still easily traceable. For example, Roberta Smith notes the following in her introduction to the first retrospective of Joel Shapiro's sculpture held at the Whitney Museum in the Winter of 1982:

> Robert Pincus-Witten . . . made the most ambitious attempt to order the proceedings, gathering these tendencies and various unassigned artists under the rubric Post-Minimalism. He focused attention on the work of such artists as Mel Bochner, Dorothea Rockburne, Richard Serra, Vito Acconci, and particularly Eva Hesse. But Pincus-Witten may not have extended his designation far enough. It seems to me that the entire decade of the 1970s might be labeled Post-Minimal and that, in addition to the "official" Post-Minimalists, there is a second "unofficial" group contemporary in age with the first, which must also be considered, and which includes such artists as Joe Zucker, Jennifer Bartlett, Scott Burton, and Jonathan Borofsky.

In fact an essay on Burton does appear in *Postminimalism* (1977), a detail which should have rendered him "official"; another in *Maximalism* (1983) along with one on Shapiro. My point is not about petty rectifications but to show that a spontaneous intuition had fallen on responsive critical/historical ground. Postminimalism suddenly sprouted into stylistic fact; indeed, had so clearly reified that a respected critic/historian could reasonably speak to an "official" versus an "unofficial" Postminimalism and still be understood. That was gratifying.

What is equally fascinating is to note the degree to which this idea of a double-value also caught on and in doing so further reified the notion of the Postminimalist

style. We read, for example, the following excursus in Deborah Emont-Scott's introduction to the Alan Shields catalogue for an exhibition held in 1983 at the Memphis
Brooks Museum of Art:

> Robert Pincus-Witten in his book *Postminimalism,* describes this time, the years 1966 to 1970,
> as a watershed in American art when many paths radiated from Minimalism's stylistic nexus. Some,
> he explains, adhered to the strict geometry intrinsic to Minimalism, while others deviated on paths
> seemingly at odds with its basic ideals . . . Roberta Smith more recently suggests that the entire
> decade of the 1970s might be labeled Post-Minimal and that another group of artists . . . should
> be considered with Pincus-Witten's list of "official" Post-Minimalists as "unofficial" Post-
> Minimalists. . . . When reviewing Alan Shields's career, it becomes clear that he shares characteristics
> of both Post-Minimalist groups.

So now there were two sides, recto and verso of the Postminimalism
phenomenon. Happily the bibliography of the latter catalogue points out my
December 1969 review of Shields's work in *Artforum* as virtually the earliest. This
sense of scruple seems to have eluded the organizers of an exhibition held in Madrid
between May and July of 1986 that accepts Postminimalism as " . . . this decade's
common description. . . . " The term is found throughout the introduction to *Entre
la Geometria y el Gesto, Escultura Norte Americana, 1965–1975,* without indicating
where the term originated, an oversight that perhaps speaks to the fact that, by
now, the style has become a household name. Similarly, the just-published third edition of H. H. Arnason's *History of Modern Art* assumes the term as generic to
the seventies, as is seen in the chapter devoted to conceptual art and public monument called "The Post-Minimal Seventies."

While one saw the term Postminimalism repeatedly in the art press or often
heard it in studio chatter, Maximalism—admittedly a shock-value journalistic term
set to powerfully contrast against the Minimalist predispositions of the day—had a
harder time of it, especially in the face of a so-called Post Modern sensibility that
in its ironic distancing sustains comparison with the cool strategems of Pop Art.

Back in the 1970s, the Post Modern was first argued for in an architectural
context by a new sort of architect who, though thoroughly steeped in modernist
values, temporarily felt a fatigue with the bland technological Utopianism that
dominated advanced architectural practice up to the 1960s. Excited by an architecture vivified by an ornament first justified on the grounds of a specious Pop
enthusiasm—intellectual slumming that is always fun—these younger architects embraced ornamentation and structural detail as a means of ironic revival. Then the
dean of American architects, Philip Johnson, took up the standard. The modernist
belief in the ethical criminality of ornament was rejected. Suddenly we were awash
in an architectural history ransacked for all manner of reference and motif.

The initial intention was decorative enough though the collegiate apologist, hitch-
ing these evolutions to earlier French intellectual authority, began to claim that these
architectural modifications and, latterly, pictorial ones as well, embodied a critical
semiotic, the signifiers of a "deconstructive" mode. By the 1980s "deconstruction"

and "appropriation" had become architectural and graduate school cliché. Throughout all of this, the hidden agenda of "deconstruction"—its anti-capitalist bias—was underplayed by the American epigones, perhaps as a way to cover the tracks of preferred artists whose work very quickly commodified in ways presumably at odds with the arguments used to sustain their works in the first place. The Agora—seminar room and market place—was suddenly at sixes and sevens.

This recent evolution must be rehearsed a bit if only to clarify the tenor of certain of the essays and entries in Maximalism and to illuminate and hopefully simplify the complexity of the situation of the recent turn of the decade.

Quite as Abstract Formalism was entering its period of greatest credibility in the United States, many Europeans preferred the view that the wresting of Modernism from the grasp of the French by the New York School during the Second World War and on into the 1950s had really served to screen the political forces of the Right that come to mind when one hears the name McCarthy invoked or recalls such phrases as The Red Scare. Serge Guilbaut's famous *How New York Stole The Idea of The Modern,* to cite perhaps the best known revisionist study (published in 1983), sits easily in a background cushioned by the pieties of a European Left ever bitter over the Miraculous Transfer of the House of Modernism from Paris to New York. This levitation was made possible, according to the Leftist view of things, by dirty hands, laundered money, bad faith, CIA and MoMA collusion, media support, etc.—consumer privileges in short supply in a Europe felled by the Second World War but in which the Ugly Americans were rich.

More recent chapters in American politics further hardened received opinion. Vietnam and the Nixon years, let alone the manipulative appeals of an egregious Reagan policy in Central America or the umbrella of Star Wars, while adding fire to the political debate, only continued to carry coals to Newcastle so far as the European Left (especially in France) regarded international developments in the arts.

Modernism is a function of the dialectical principles perceived by German Romantic Idealists and reduced to bald mechanics in Marx: thesis, antithesis, synthesis. The grandest achievement of the dialectic was to have been the abolition of the class system and the foundation of a classless world state. This illusion begins in the October of the Revolution and dies with the Hitler/Stalin pact. That stretch, from the end of the First World War to the beginning of the Second, is, in brief, the Modernist Period, assassinated by its own internal forces, the Fascism implicit to the self-service of totalitarian wills to power, wills often enough Socialist in origin. Small wonder the recent Left has embraced the intellectual despair of the Post Modern. How else could it integrate a grief generated by the very internal disparities and discrepancies of its very own position?

In art, the dialectical principle underscored the paradox of a theory of perpetual revolution, one that lead not to the end of style, to stylessness or artlessness—as the dialectic in action was to have led to classlessness—but to the notion of an inescapable succession of Style as its most cogent expression. Style is the bourgeois word for history. Style reinforces a bourgeois notion of history even as it conspires to transform the work of art into commodity. Style, above all else, allows for the alchemical transformation of art into capital. Bourgeois is such an odd word, permissible when appealing to refrigerated and academic class distinctions but ambiguous for all of that. Think of middle class, urbane, public, municipal, philistine, civic. How astonishingly different all their meanings are. Yet they share a common sector of overlap, the bourgeois itself.

The grandest irony of all is that the continuity of the modernist dialectic assumes as a given the continued prosperity of a middle class—a bourgeoisie—suppressed by Aristocratic or Proletarian absolutism. Yet neither of those latter classes recognize as art a production that does not expressly glorify them. By contrast, the bourgeoisie can allow for such an imaginative leap and bounds with alacrity when such criticism is also a stylistic *dernier cri*. The bourgeoisie recognizes as art even those cultural manifestations that are severely critical of its perquisites, let alone the fruits of its often grave wrongdoing, especially when such a critique is situated at the cutting edge of style shift. Neither titled birth nor lumpen clay is capable of that imaginativeness, though to note this in no way exonerates or exculpates bourgeois criminality.

Workers may have lost their chains but artists remain bound by an endless linkage of stylistic successiveness—styles, one after the other—a modernism to come even after the passing of the Post Modern. For surely this style shall pass, just as Futurism has passed despite its egregious claim on the Eternal, to being futuristic. Seen this way, the Post Modern thus becomes yet another phase in the modernist stylistic sequence despite its claim on the turf of all the "posts" to come. It is itself just another modernist style.

Unexpectedly, the Conceptualist/Minimalist mode was taken up by European theorists, especially so as semiotics allowed for a deconstruction of Capitalist ideology. The systems worked out in the Post Existential years were coincidental to the ascendance of American abstraction—Derrida, Barthes, Foucault, Baudrillard, etc.—adding to their contributions the Freudian/Marxist twist of Lacan and, unexpectedly, the premonitory cultural analyses of the German Walter Benjamin and the linguistics of the Russian Roman Jakobson. Marxicism and Marxicists. The mix was complete. Suddenly, the work of art existed not in its objective condition but as a text in which one read the indices of Post Modern ambiguity and alienation from the bourgeois value.

How could one fail to read them this way? The modernist object of transcendence that neutralizes all irony or bolting sense of paradox was replaced by the broad field of equivocation and temperamental dissociation. The utopian indices that resolved all clash and ambivalence in the transcendent work of art of early modernism now only pointed to, as the college kids are fond of saying, the separation of the signifier and the signified and the thrillingly provocative ambience of doubt and irresolution of the Post Modern. Still, when the "criticality" abates, works emblematic of the new critical position (even if argued as embodying ambiguity) will be as seen as forthright, authoritative and unequivocal (even of the conditions of ambiguity) as any works come down to us in the modernist canon. As is always the case, while the arguments for contemporary art are forgotten, discourse reifies into a notion of period style and the work appears, just like that of earlier style, as if it demanded no more discourse. On To The Next.

This recognition goes far in inflecting the despair deemed Post Modern on which Maximalism formed a crust of journalist aperçues. By the mid 1980s the atmosphere was marked by a nostalgia for the transcendent Object of Radicality characteristic of the early modern period even as the careerism which also characterizes the decade came into full play.

Even faced with the attractiveness of the Post Modern ethos, Maximalism as a journalistic grabber gained some ground, as when, for example, shortly after publication of *(Entries) Maximalism* in 1983 an exhibition using the term was mounted in New Jersey by a group of expressionist artists who ran the gamut from the entrenched figures of contemporary art such as Lucas Samaras and Kes Zapkus to just-emerging talents who would shortly be associated with the renascent East Village scene. Or, in the Winter 1986 issue of *Effects,* a "Magazine for New Art Theory" (edited by Tricia Collins and Richard Milazzo, Post Modern apologists so arch they appear as virtual parodists of the critical mode they espouse), one finds a paean to "Maximal Artists, Maximal Art."

By the term Maximalism I intended to describe the pluralist tendencies that followed hard upon Postminimalism, when the often puritanical sense of discretion that marked Abstract Formalism, Minimalism and Conceptualism gave way to an unrepentant Expressionist volubility. It was then that another paradox arose; the congestion and the open typologies of Postminimalism reverted to an art of fixed conventions, the time-honored vehicles of painting and sculpture. As I noted in the original introduction, "Maximalism, despite its brave name, is perhaps a more conservative artistic consciousness—let's say it, style—than its predecessor."

New York, Spring 1986

Postminimalism

Introduction to Postminimalism

This collection of essays postulates a history of American art of the decade between 1966 and 1976. Written as independent acts of critical advocacy, they form the history of a shifting temper in the appreciation of formal values in America. At least I hope so.

The pinched scholarly mode of the earlier essays reflects the mandarin tone characteristic of critical writing in the sixties, especially at *Artforum* (where most of the earlier essays of the present volume first appeared).

The early-to-mid-sixties was marked by a striving academically oriented critical style epitomized by the younger school of Harvard critics, notably Michael Fried. That tone—often inflated to the pompous—corresponded to a closed formalist machine of judgment from which personal reference and biography were omitted. This occurred not only because formalist critics imposed an apersonal, hermetic value system on their writing, but because the artists insisted on it as well. Formalism became, at its crudest, an elaborate Wölfflinian discussion of self-evident, visual priorities. Equally apparent today is the style that I characterize as Postminimalism, one that actively rejects the high formalist cult of impersonality.

By the end of the sixties it was clear that formalist abstraction had been challenged by a new set of formal and moral values, imperatives tempered by despair over the conduct of American politics (Vietnam, Watergate, etc.), and energized by the insurgency and success of the Women's Movement. High formalist art seemed to have become the objective correlative, a fitting decor to the glass and steel-enclosed corporate complexes that profited from the war (though "seeming" and "being" are not necessarily the same.)

What formalist sensibility would have considered eccentric processes, substances and colorations, were assimilated to emerging social and aesthetic imperatives. More recent artistic emphasis is almost directly opposed to the formalist values of the mid-sixties. It is revealed in those art activities stressing autobiography, the artistic persona and psyche, stripped bare as it were, layer by layer.

Despite this apparent reversal of values, an essential constancy of modern art—the uniqueness of personality—persists, though no longer manifested through facture, the individuality of touch, but through an unrepentant autobiographical confession or fantasy concerning those areas of human activity in which the artists are most singularly personal—their literally private lives.

As they stood, the earlier essays were either double-bound or doubled-blessed (depending on one's vantage); couched in a formalist jargon, they championed an anti-formalist art. For the most part the essays dealing with the later, more conceptually-oriented aspects of Postminimalism reflect a shift from a jargonized and opaque writing to one more accessible to the reader. In part this resulted from the fact that opacity and jargon were no longer central critical desirables, a position concomitant with that of the artists who no longer insisted on formalist impersonality.

But to re-edit the earlier essays to correspond to more immediate inflections of speech in critical writing would falsify the historical typology of critical writing itself. Thus, this anthology reveals two histories—one that identifies major figures and shifts in artistic values; the other that duplicates in art criticism these very same shifts in artistic priorities, from an inert withholding stolidity to a more ingathering declamatory mode.

To this end, perhaps, a rough scheme of the decade will be helpful. The years 1966–70 mark a watershed in American art, ending the decade that derived its options, by and large, from a still earlier parent style, Minimalism. Minimalist forms reflected a geometric abstract style based on a "pre-executive inner necessity." What the phrase means is that the rigorous external geometry of Minimalism attempts to be congruent with the logic of the style, a logic concluded even before the paintings were begun or the sculptures made. Of course it is obvious that to think through an argument is not the same as to make an object; the actual doing of things provokes myriad formal interventions and discontinuities upon engaging concrete matter. Such encounters constantly alter and redirect the act of making: thus where painting or sculpting may lead can never be where the argument had gone. Numerous paths radiated from Minimalism's stylistic nexus: some maintained the fixed, reduced geometry innate to Minimalism; others moved off in paths seemingly at odds with the style of the matrix.

A simple comparison: between 1880 and 1900, there developed in parallel avenues (though one might think of them as osmotic laminations) the classicizing Divisionism of Seurat, the proto-Cubist spatial ambiguities of Cézanne, the Symbolism of Gauguin, and the Expressionist options of Van Gogh. These trends huddle together beneath the blanket term Postimpressionism. The derivation of some of them from Impressionism is easily perceived; in other instances, less immediately so; yet all derive from the formal inquiries posed by Impressionism. Certain aspects of Postminimalism are also readily seen to derive from Minimalism's essential reductive and analytical character, others less immediately so. The term, then, is useful in a broad way—the way the term "Post Impressionism" is useful—a term covering a multitude of stylistic resolutions preceded and posited by an apparent generative style.

The first phase of Postminimalism is marked by an expressionist revival of painterly issues. This was occasioned by a reaction to the taciturn inexpressivity and absence of chromatic appeal typical of Minimalism. Equally striking was the application of this expressive painterliness, not only to painting itself, but to sculpture. Such manifestations then may be said to mark a revival of gestural Abstract Expressionist attitudes after a long hiatus during the fifties and early sixties. This expressive painterliness was accompanied by a refreshed focus on personality and colorism, and on a highly eccentric dematerialized, or open form. These are features, say, of a work of Eva Hesse, Lynda Benglis or early Barry Le Va and Keith Sonnier. Often the eccentricity of the substances they used was a means whereby the artist could be identified, a "signature substance"; Serra's lead, Sonnier's neon, Benglis' foam, Le Va's felt.

The new style's relationship to the women's movement cannot be overly stressed; many of its formal attitudes and properties, not to mention its exemplars, derive from methods and substances that hitherto had been sexistically tagged as female or feminine, whether or not the work had been made by women.

This early phase peaked in 1968–70 and is here referred to as "pictorial/sculptural." I noted its emphasis on the process of making, a process so emphatic as to be seen as the primary content of the work itself, hence the term "process art." When this occurred, as it did in the lead tossings of Richard Serra, or in *The Drawings That Make Themselves* by Dorothea Rockburne, to cite but two examples, the virtual content of the art became that of the spectator's intellectual re-creation of the actions used by the artist to realize the work in the first place.

The nerve center of Minimalism was its attachment to the "pre-executive," the intellectual. This rationalistic strain maintained and generated an ever more sharply honed, up-front intensification of the theoretical and analytical bases of art. In certain cases, such theories led to the production of visible or tangible forms, whose primary content maintained parity with an analytical logic, be it linguistic, mathematical or philosophical. Sol LeWitt and Mel Bochner are noteworthy examples. In others, theory appeared to usurp the visual, to become, as it were, the formal embodiment itself. Here art and language grew interchangeable.

The grand intuition of this strain of Postminimalism was the adumbration of new methods of composition that were no longer based on the Realist's mirror of nature, or the Expressionist's empathetic distortion, or the Surrealist's gestural automatism, but rather on organizational principles derived from information-centered theories of knowledge (theories "out there" in the world), from epistemology.

Thus there emerged, around 1970, an information-oriented abstraction, one that loosely honored, say, mathematical set theory, 0 to 9 formulas, Fibonacci series, "Golden Sections" or spectrum-based color sequences with their contingent analytical systems emphasizing red-yellow-blue primaries (rather than a sensibility-based choice of color). In this, the work of Sol LeWitt, Mel Bochner and Dorothea Rockburne are exemplary—although earlier, Ellsworth Kelly and Jasper Johns formed bridges between the Abstract Expressionist generation and the postminimalists. Mondrian, Malevitch and Barnett Newman were newly reassessed as models.

The epistemological trend paralleled a widespread invocation of the role of language either in terms of its own science—linguistics—or, somewhat later, as a kind of loosely applied metaphor. The stress on the role of language triggered wide reaches of the conceptual movement, a name by which the broad front of the art of the early seventies is now known. Aspects of the conceptual movement addressed art wholly as a function of linguistic systems replete with philosophical and political ramifications. This tendency has now splintered into subsequent evolutions instigated by neo-Marxist critiques of capitalist culture, or lured by extremely individualistic confrontations between word and image. (The typology most often encountered today might be described as an extended captioned photograph).

The epistemological examination of "pure knowledge" continues apace; however, work produced as a function of such closed systems may be said to be, by this moment, less an urgent matter than it once was. First theory was honored; then it was honored in the breach. Honor in the breach, especially in terms of its broad-front appeal today, indicates the receding interest in a purely theoretically-based art. Then again, honor in the breach is itself a Romantic update of a theory of art—one leading to a revived interest today in sensibility.

The rejection of "epistemology" was met from the very first—from 1968 on—in terms of a revival of Dada principles first broadcast in New York City by Duchamp, Picabia and Man Ray around 1915. Paraphrasing New York Dada's ontological concerns, many aspects of Postminimalism emphasized temporality and a theatrical cult of maneristic personality in which the artists themselves became the malleable raw material of their art, as well as their own myths and products. A reinvigoration of temporal and theatrical issues led to the development of the conceptual theatre—Body Art and the like as seen in later Benglis, Chris Burden, Dennis Oppenheim and Vito Acconci.

Thus, an extremely spare scheme of the last decade can be read as (1) the advent of the "pictorial/sculptural" mode; (2) the emergence of an abstract, information-based epistemology; and (3) its counterpoises, body art and conceptual theatre.

I hope this brief scheme will simplify matters, providing the reader a framework within which to place the individual examples to be discussed, a generalized model to which the work of the individuals may be referred. The issues are perhaps better stated in their initial presentation, in the essays themselves; to further elaborate here skirts redundancy. By and large, the essays are reproduced as they first appeared. When small excisions occur, it was done to avoid reiteration.

New York, April 1977

Postminimalism

Pictorial/Sculptural

Richard Serra: Slow Information

I

Although our social relations were almost entirely limited to chance encounters at Queens College (we were both members of the art department), I recall once meeting Richard Serra at the Guggenheim Museum at the time of the Sculpture International in 1967. I was examining the works in preparation for a review and we toured the exhibition together. The idea of Serra's which struck me most was his observation that Robert Morris' untitled floor piece[1] was an extension of a Cubistic grid idea—a notion regarding the principles of serial structure and Minimalist ontology that is now generally accepted. At this point I still had no idea what Serra himself was up to as an artist although I was well aware of the nature of his teaching. I now regard this part of his career as an important pedagogical contribution.

Serra's teaching is neither directive nor judgmental. It deals with an elementarist analysis of the physical properties germane to any given material. It minimizes—almost to extinction—any valorized finished product, but instead stresses those issues and procedures which are central to the execution of any specific act, or set of acts, in as clear and didactic a way as possible. Since the stress is on the executive act and programmatic clarity, the resultant experiences tend to be simple, and frequently repetitive. The implication of this in terms of many of the features of Serra's own works is self-evident.

Serra's teaching, at least at first, seemed at odds with the studio methods then fostered. These methods tend to be post-Cézanne-like in character, stressing dimensional forms in locatable spaces; post-Hofmann-like, asserting the "push and pull" of color areas; and post-Albers-like, emphasizing a "less is more" color-scientism. And, of course, there is an emphasis too on a more or less direct transcription of nature. I think, in fact, that such a characterization holds true for all art schools throughout the country at the moment and it is not my intention here to disqualify such principles. I only mean to indicate that Serra's indirection and elementarism

This article originally appeared in *Artforum*, September 1969.

was, at the time, at odds with the highly evolved and final object-oriented nature
of prevailing teaching practice. The object orientation of such teaching implies that
an evaluation of student work is both desirable and feasible because it is related
to a determinable quotient, one based on previously achieved standards.

I was grateful that Serra's courses were accessible to the students, if only because
they were "antidotic" to the esthetic predeterminism which, of necessity, emerges
out of the evolutionary teaching method which I have so briefly characterized. I
recall several chance meetings with Serra's students' work, in which basic pictorial
and structural properties appeared to be the "subject" of primary importance: images
of stroking, counting, forms which leaned, forms which fell, scatterings, mural scale
compositions of pasted paper in which at each moment that a focal center "appeared"
so was it "displaced"; student films in which moving objects were shot so that they
appeared to be still while the static environments appeared to move. I cite these
only as memories of things representative of the work done in Serra's classes.

A critical problem is brought into play by Serra's teaching, namely, that all such
exercises tend to look equally "good" (though this is, in fact, untrue). The reason
for this is, I imagine, because no a priori criterion is in evidence. Such exercises were
"bad" or "good" or "indifferent" only within an evaluative scale predicated on the
conditions of the problem it sought to solve, one which may or may not be in evidence
when faced with the final thing one is regarding. In the end, too, "elementarism"
can itself become an "imitable" style. Since there was no "perfect" model against
which the student production could be gauged, a radical aspect of Serra's teaching
was that the notion of "Excellent," "Good," "Fair," or "Failing" was expunged. In
short, the entire notion of "Art" did not arise.

What appears to have happened is that Serra realized that his teaching was,
in fact, being used "antidotically" within an established pedagogical situation—that
is, it became, in a short while, another a priori option and therefore, another standard
academic tool. Recognizing that the strength of his radical teaching may have been
weakened by its absorption within an academic setup, Serra has, at least for the
moment, abandoned teaching (although the necessity of team assistance in the
execution of his most recent work will, in some way, ultimately affect the thinking
of his assistants, as it only recently profoundly marked a restrained and very fortunate
body of students).

II

In my view, the earliest problem of sculpture was to reproduce the verticality of
the human being in contrast to the horizontality of the earth. I don't mean to say
that the problem was to reproduce the human image, although our first great
sculptures, the "Venus" fetishes, the Pharaoh portraits and the Greek Kouroi, do
so. What I am trying to get at is that they are vertical—not that they are anthropomorphic. An urge toward verticality which characterizes the history of sculpture
became further energized through such intermediary assists as bases or through

technological processes, such as bronze casting or metal forging or new plastics, which permit heavy masses to be supported at elevated heights upon slender shafts, as our legs carry our torsos. By extension, sculptures which are supported by architectural elements other than the floor are by their sheer perversity a testimony to the traumatic grip of the pervasiveness of the idea of verticality and its correlative dependence upon the floor. What then of horizontality? We have seen, in the past two years particularly, an almost concerted assault on the axiomatic verticality of sculpture in favor of horizontality. There is, of course, a kind of familiar horizontal form which, although not called by the name of sculpture, has always insisted on certain sculptural qualities—furniture. When Brancusi made horizontal sculpture, he justified himself by regarding the results not as "sculpture" but as "furniture," calling such sculptural artifacts "Bench," or "Table," stressing by such appellations a functional rather than horizontal connotation.

In this respect, that Carl Andre's floor-bound square modules should be called "rugs" seems less fortuitous than may appear at first hearing. Carl Andre, perhaps, may be regarded as an intermediary between Brancusi and Serra in that his work stresses a furniture-like horizontality and focuses on elemental material properties, both features shared by Serra. Andre's works are admittedly a case apart. He is taken to be a figure central to Minimal and geometrical sensibility. Yet, there is a "dumbness and "inertness" in his work that somehow marked him as different from the general run of antiseptic purveyors of three-dimensional geometric propositions. His most recent exhibition at the Dwan Gallery, presenting grid configurations of elemental metals selected from the chart of atomic valences, indicated that we were meant to compare the differences, visual and extra-visual, between elemental substances in identical figurations. Serra's relationship to Andre is one of focusing on the properties of the material. Andre appears to be interested in the inert surface qualities of the material and Serra in the intrinsic structural potential of the material. However, the modular characteristics of Andre's work disaffiliate him from Serra and link Andre to the prevailing geometry which is a cardinal feature of the Minimal mode against which Serra and numerous associates can only, at this moment, appear to be pitted, whether or not this is their stated intention. The Minimalist's source is the module, the unit, the one; Serra's is the verb form.

It would be tempting to erect an analogical structure comparing the aims of Serra and those of Ludwig Wittgenstein, about whom Serra often spoke, Such a method is bound to fail from the outset as the dynamics of one species of inquiry are hardly interchangeable with those of another. The most abject art criticism has traditionally been predicated on the dynamics of poetry: *ut pictura poesis*. But a certain harmony of interest is evident, especially in Serra's early work. In a memoir on Wittgenstein, written by one of the rare intimates of the philosopher, is the following characterization of Wittgenstein's quest:

> According to him, complex propositional forms are merely functions of simple propositions, and therefore cannot express anything not already stated by the latter. The existence of causal or

teleological relations between the facts, however, transcends the realm of facts and cannot, therefore, be expressed in meaningful propositions.[2]

Serra is involved with the elementary components or the processes of building, as distinguished from the expression, visual or otherwise, of a finely turned pun. The impetus to work derives from a simple proposition of a verb form: to roll, to tear, to splash. On the bluntest level, Serra is interested in the problem of what sculptural properties may encompass. The problems Serra attacks are structural in nature, problems which have scarcely any linguistic correlation, except possibly as highly extenuated syntactical or grammatical analogies.

The first body of Serra's pieces seen in New York City were exhibited by Richard Bellamy in February, 1968. He appeared in a group show with Walter de Maria and Mark di Suvero (who, for many years, was Serra's neighbor in California). The works shown were largely made of rubber materials and neon tubing. The contrast of material partly impressed me because the tubing exploited both the coloristic immateriality of light and the hard, cold surfaces of glass. The rubber was used either bluntly as a broad surface, hung into swags of crumpled, kneaded erasers or as lengths of belt-like harnesses, which, although flaccid, were joined into fixed positions by bent industrial staples[3] (fig. 1).

Subsequent to the rubber and neon pieces and as party to a broad offensive against verticality, Serra undertook numerous exercises in horizontality, in "floorness." The piece that I am going to characterize as "bench-like" (over Serra's reservations), is *Candlepiece,* shown in the St. Louis *Here & Now* exhibition of January 1969. It consisted of a length of timber drilled at equidistant intervals along a horizontal axis. Into these apertures were set a row of ten burning plumber's candles. The unfinished surfaces, the thick candles, the constant equidistant holes are all related to a kind of physicality that one recognizes as a central characteristic of Serra's work, as it was long before in Brancusi's wood carvings. In this sense, the *Candlepiece* conveyed many of Serra's basic interests. As to what Serra has called a "time piece," however, the work later struck him as "illustratively simple-minded." Clearly in this work there are several "clock-like" clues. As we shall see, other apparently formal conceptions are often shot through with a relationship to the problem of time. This piece "fails" for Serra in that it remained primarily "an on-going visually illustrational process which smacks of the permissiveness of Happening and Theater."

In the same exhibition, a vast expanse of floor itself was covered by three loosely overlaid rubber sheets. The surface of these sheets was formed by spreading a layer of latex rubber mixed with orange paint across the face of corrugated roofing from which the sheets were then lifted and spread upon the floor. The corrugated surface was a device used to "hold the expanse to the floor," as was the orange color. For Serra, it was incidental that the orange color is the color of anti-rust paint, or that corrugated construction siding is itself a common and offensive structural material (at least insofar as it has generally been employed by the American middle class).

III

At the same time that the horizontal floor pieces were undertaken, Serra was attracted by the possibilities of lead, a material which he employed for its weight, malleability, entropy, inelegant lack of sheen and other properties which one recognizes as directly opposed to the chromium steel and polished glass which has dominated "good taste" for at least three decades.

Among the activities Serra investigated were tearing exercises such as the methodical ripping away, by hand, of successive edges of a lead square (fig. 2). One is tempted to point to the square, concentrically structured paintings by Frank Stella of the early 1960s for the "diagrams" of Serra's exercises—although, for Serra, they are parallel to "the concerns of Anton Ehrenzweig, such as 'dedifferentiation,' 'scanning,' 'scattering,' and 'synchronistic vision.'" The formulation of the image of Stella's painting assumes its total meaning when an inevitable sequence, adumbrated by the support, has been carried to its completion and becomes itself the final image. Serra's lead sculptures, on the other hand, reject the final image, for, were the work carried to its inevitable conclusion, it would arrive at a point and an instant in time beyond which further tearing is impossible. Serra brings our attention to both this sense of time-shift and to the physical procedure itself. The inevitable sequence of the "tearings" is also very much akin to the sequence of constant chamfers in Brancusi's *Endless Column*. Both works are marked by constant repetitive and artisanal actions. "The many versions Brancusi carved of *Endless Column* make it clear that the motif had a special place in his affections . . . Once the proportions are established it is only necessary to lay them out on the beam of wood and proceed almost automatically; the work goes on like a litany, with no need for invention. Every new *Column*'—like each new tear piece—'seems to develop its own individuality. From a relatively small effort there is here a great poetic yield."[4]

What then is important: the statement of the process (place, time, procedure), or the accruing pile of crumpled lead "tearings" which accumulate during the execution of the piece? It would seem that the answer is both of these, or, as Serra states, quoting Whitehead, "process and existence pre-suppose each other." The crumpled "tears" of lead in their chaotic accumulation, were also related to the subsequent lead splashings, though certainly the molten condition of lead (by its very familiarity) would have suggested itself as an expressive means to Serra, quite independently of the "tearings."[5]

The first lead splashing was seen at the Castelli *Warehouse Show* of December, 1968. The spattering of lead, which had been tossed into the juncture of floor and wall, was made again at the Kunsthalle in Bern, in front of the Stedelijk Museum in Amsterdam and received still further elaboration at the *Anti-Illusion: Procedures/Materials* exhibition at the Whitney Museum (fig. 3). There, one of Serra's pieces was a floor work of thirteen such tossings, twelve of which, after having cooled and hardened, were pried away from the corner and laid one after the other in sequence. The work affords the possibility of the sequential visual reconstructions of its making, which parallels the purely visual aspects of the piece. In this sense Serra designates such works as "slow information" pieces. The material condition of this sculpture—something which was once molten and is now solid, revealing the potential of the material—reminds one of the earliest neon pieces which dealt with antithesis between luminosity and glossiness. Moreover, the viewer recreating the acts leading to the piece cannot fail to sense the time increments embodied in the twelve tangible"splashes."

The torn lead and splash pieces point to a two-and-one-half minute film made by the artist. The film concentrates on a single image, Serra's right hand attempting to catch and release a piece of lead which was dropped in front of it. One saw neither the source of the falling fragment, nor the pile-up of pieces on the floor; one saw only the artist's hand catching the scrap of lead or missing it, its muscles straining to adjust to this mechanistic role. The film points up the ultimate inability of the hand to function as a tool, for, were it able to have successfully carried out such an *a priori* task, one would have witnessed a theatrical performance. Instead, the film concerns itself with the breakdown of a positivist assumption because the hand after a moment is physically unable to negotiate the predetermined demand. Thus, the value of the film lies in its clear indication that all assumed or received systems—linguistic, esthetic, experiential, formal—are in themselves subject to breakdown. In short, the breakdown is as much a part of the context as the structuring of the experiment.

IV

In my view, Serra's loose lead work can be associated with a shift in modernist sensibility, omnipresent throughout the winter of 1968 and spring of 1969. This was attested by the number of exhibitions devoted to so-called process artists, conceptual artists, earthwork artists, and artists, particularly sculptors, who stress horizontality and "floorness" in their work. This new sensibility tends to be anti-precisionist and anti-geometric. It once again fosters values connected with Abstract Expressionism, that is to say, it sponsors the sensibilities covered by Wölfflin's term *malerisch*. In this respect Serra's lead splashes and "tearings" are almost the *sine qua non* of the new sensibility. But while being related to the widespread revival of painterliness, Serra's pronounced constructivism is also in evidence.

At the same time that splashing was employed as a device, Serra was examining lead for its more obvious structural possibilities. (Seven such preeminently didactic works were exhibited as part of the Theodoron Foundation exhibition at the Guggenheim Museum in June–July, 1969 (fig. 4). Serra was interested in the idea of lead which had been tightly rolled into a column and which in its solid columnar state became the object of elementary building procedures: to roll, to saw, to divide, to rest, to lean, etc. More complexly elaborated works, held by their weight and the pull of gravity, support additional rolls or plates of lead held up flush against the wall. Each solution clarifies the physical limitations of the same material in different situations.

The idea of propping massive forms together by sheer weight and gravitational pull became more visually engrossing when the leaning elements gradually approached the vertical. This was effected through the introduction of additional elements that were supported by the leaning column itself. Gradually, the column was forced to a "vertical" upright by introducing median horizontal "pins" which extended out from the wall and which were supported there as autonomous elements by the slight tilt of the lead column. Eventually broad sheets of thick lead supplanted the rolls in such structural experiments.

In rejecting welding, which he calls "stitching," Serra employed the first method of raising forms from the ground, that of leaning and propping, as a child leans cards one against the other. The device of propping or leaning forms leads to several issues of importance. Through this device Serra is able to indicate an affiliation with David Smith without any concomitant copying; that is, Smith's arrogant cubic forms could be retained without recourse to Smith's oxyacetylene torch, the first tool to which the confirmed Smith imitator would turn. Smith, our greatest sculptor, could vertically raise cubic configurations high in the air, predicated on a "pictorialism" and "false weight" which are virtually impossible without welding (they could, of course, have been carved). Serra raises forms that are only possible through propping. Hidden in this distinction is the time-honored argument surrounding "integrity" and "truth to materials" which, in our time, are almost exclusively associated with Brancusi.

The idea of utilizing the wall as a correlative support was for the moment put aside, and the lead elements were used to support themselves autonomously. The most representative work of this kind is the *One Ton Prop, House of Cards* (fig. 5), shown at the Whitney Anti-Illusion exhibition. Each of the four faces of the sheets is held by a slight incline of the lead plate "arrested" at each corner by a repressed pinwheel configuration. The work was colloquially spoken of as "getting Carl Andre up off the floor," which is to miss the point. For, in both works, the gravity as well as the material is "compressed downward."

While such a notion is in fact extremely simple, its execution is less than easy. This difficulty, however, is not a criterion for its effectiveness as a work of art, while its massiveness and weightiness most certainly are. A film by Robert Fiore (shown, by the way, over Serra's objection), recorded the first studio experiments with such a structure prior to its execution and installation at the Whitney Museum. The film shows Serra and his team dollying the quarter-ton plates across the studio floor and leaning them one into the other until the final aperture was produced. The film records the extra-visual sensation and recalcitrance of the heavy lead, as registered in the physical gestures and responses of the artist and his team.

In this respect such films, like articles or journals or manuscripts or photographs or tape-recordings, may in turn aspire to the condition of works of art. The acceptance of such views tends to render expendable the product on which they are based, so much so that many new works may exist only as literary ideas or possibilities in the artist's mind.

On one hand, it would appear then, that part of the new sensibility is a kind of nihilism, an impulse to supplant a work of art with its own adumbration. Such is the case of artists of more Dadaistic or linguistic turns of mind. The difference between Serra and these parameters and proximities there may be, is that there is no literary focus at all in Serra's work. Therefore, its meaning cannot be supposed on the basis of concomitant documents. For a Dadaist of the new sensibility, such a record will in time become the central emotional repository, which is nothing more than "self-conscious history-making." The art of Richard Serra is not in a snapshot; it is in the viewer's ability to reconstruct, on the basis of the work's clear exposition, the artist's undisguised step-by-step intentions.

Notes

1. The Morris piece is reproduced in exhibition catalog, *Guggenheim International Exhibition, Sculpture From 20 Nations* (New York, 1967).

2. Paul Engleman, *Letters from Ludwig Wittgenstein with a Memoir,* trans. L. Furtmüller (New York: Horizon Press, 1968), p. 105.

3. "New York Reviews," *Artforum,* vol. 8, April 1968, p. 65.

4. Sidney Geist, *Brancusi, A Study of the Sculpture* (New York, Grossman, 1968), p. 73. With regard to the temporal implication of such constantly decremented tearings, again Geist supplies us with deep insight: "A mnemonic system in art that does not imply the world is an ornamental frieze or fretwork, which is a metaphor of memory and its opposite, anticipation. In this respect it is worth noting that the *Endless Column* of Tirgu Jiu (a kind of vertical frieze), is sometimes called "Column of Endless Remembrance" (pp. 174–75).

5. It goes without saying that the piles of lead "tearings" share many characteristics with the work of a broad wave of young artists who are involved in a rudimentary return to the pre-vertical condition of sculpture. I know that the distinctions between each of the following figures are telling, but I cite, only in passing, the sweeping compound and graphite scatterings of Bill Bollinger, the colored mesh unravellings of Alan Saret, the mounds of broken stone of Robert Smithson, the piles of earth and crank grease of Robert Morris, the floor flockings of Keith Sonnier, the random distributions of Barry Le Va, the displays of plasticized containers and sheets of Eva Hesse, the "rungs" of Carl Andre, not to mention the pile of colored rubber strips of Richard Serra himself, shown at the Castelli *Warehouse Show* of December 1968.

    It is perfectly obvious that this list is far from complete and that each of the figures mentioned are working in sculptural areas that can hardly be viewed as congruent either esthetically or qualitatively except insofar as they are all producing antivertical, low-lying experiences. The interrelationships between these figures, particularly with regard to their attitude towards color is especially critical.

Figure 1.   Richard Serra, *Belts*, 1966–67
Vulcanized rubber and neon, 6′ × 24′ × 20″.
(Photo courtesy Leo Castelli Gallery)

Figure 2. Richard Serra, *Tearing Lead from 1:00 to 1:47*, 1968
Lead, 9'×9'.
(Photo courtesy Leo Castelli Gallery)

Figure 3.   Richard Serra, *Casting*, Detail, 1969
Lead, 25′×15′.
(Photo courtesy Leo Castelli Gallery)

Figure 4.   Richard Serra, *Shovel Prop; Closepin Prop*, 1969
Lead.
(Photo courtesy Leo Castelli Gallery)

Figure 5. Richard Serra, *One Ton Prop (House of Cards)*, 1969
Lead, 48″×55″×55″.
(Photo courtesy Leo Castelli Gallery)

Entries: Oedipus Reconciled

In the last years of the past decade, Richard Serra forded two sculptural extremes. One was a blunt, unapologetic investigation of industrial matériel, an orientation akin, at the time, to the work of Carl Andre. This mode most clearly expressed Serra's continuity with Minimalist sensibility. By contrast Serra was also drawn to an expressive gesture that affiliated him with the revival of Abstract Expressionism and a process-orientation equally marked in the period. This side of things came to be recognized as the first type of Postminimalist expression, a refreshed pictorialism in sculpture shared commonly with early Benglis, early Le Va, Eva Hesse, and others.

These extremes, so marked in early Serra, were also bound up with the profound Oedipal syndrome that marks the evolution of American style, a history in which the father is killed, so to speak, as if to acknowledge the paternity all the more. The father totem, in this case—David Smith. Serra, determined to continue the traditions of Smith, rejected Smith's essential tool, the oxyacetylene torch. This allowed the maintenance of the idiom of a Cubist-derived Constructivism while camouflaging, at least for the time, a suppressed, even closeted, commitment to Constructivism, for, in the late 1960s, Constructivism had fallen into a debasement similar to the bankruptcy of latter-day formalist painting. In rejecting the torch of Constructivism's master, Serra came to rely on stresses, pressures, masses, cantilevers, balances, and other natural forces and weights to create a cool, crypto-Constructivist work that encoded simple verb infinitives—to rest, to cut, to lean, to intersect, etc. These direct postulates, of course, could take on more expressive intonations, especially, say, when Serra chose to toss ladlefuls of hot lead or to distribute torn pieces of lead sheeting as functions of his process-related concerns.

As such, Serra seemed a central sculptor of Postminimalism. But one of the truths of the history of style, especially in the twentieth century, is how quickly it is depleted. So while many were drawn to the style that Serra so forcefully inaugurated, he himself was leaving it, reverting back to a Constructivist mode—as Bochner, say, also returned to painting—as early as 1971. In reviewing an exhibition

---

This article originally appeared in *Arts Magazine,* November 1980.

in which Serra participated in that year, I noted the awakening of the Constructivism that had remained dormant the preceding four or five years.

But that Serra may have, at this moment, opted to move outside a proscriptive Postminimalism—then fast shrinking to an exact diagnostic profile—he was also answering needs organic to his own development. His was no accommodation to exterior critical notions, but a necessary response honoring internal exigencies, no matter where they would carry him. And it brought him back to Constructivism, but one of an enormously open field of interest. Not for him the small part-to-part comparison, the glorified paperweight of the confirmed David Smith knock off.

Many possibilities—at least five major ones—asserted themselves this past decade: (1) comparisons made over vast terrain-locked elements; (2) sculptures, the elements of which sparked shifting perceptions (as speculation aimed at mentally imagining [or participating with] components only but hinted at through the use of partial, even fragmentary evidence); (3) enormous, often geographic scale. In all this, (4) Serra bracketed Malevich to Newman, thereby allowing the Suprematist graphic motif to assert itself even more greatly. This may be an additional clue to understanding the close connections in Serra's work between sculpture and the architectural or site-specific drawing. In a certain sense, vast sprawling works continue the romantic and pictorial side of Serra's mind.

Then, too, there was (5) the even greater compaction of industrial substances, more densely compressed molecular structures of steel plates and cubes forged under technological weights hitherto unexamined in sculpture. Such properties can be said to continue the classicizing Minimalist side of the sculptor's sensibility. Even if the 1970s saw Serra's return to the Constructivist mainstream, his version of Constructivism modified and enlarged what the term means—and for precisely those mental and physical qualities from which early on he had distanced himself.

It is egregious to rebroadcast "Slow Information" (1969), an old essay on Serra, but as I glance through my private journals, many stray entries precisely refer to those new Constructivist developments that Serra disclosed this past decade: Fast Information.

17 January 1971

Philip Lieder [then editor of *Artforum* magazine] and I going to the Bronx—183rd Street and Webster Avenue— to see Richard Serra's piece *To Encircle Base Plate Hexagram*, as part of, but not included in, the museum precincts of this year's Whitney Annual. The work is implanted in an asphalt street that slopes up to a heavy stone palisade from the height of which one looks down on the work. This piece is perhaps the most understated kind of monument possible to a neighborhood that resists, it is maintained, the notion of art as high abstraction. Lining the street is the rubble of razed, burned-out tenements. (For a second I thought that certain mounds of brick or broken concrete were meant to be the disingenuous solution to the problem.)

The work designates a flat circular site. It's made of steel, laid like a collar into the asphalt, in the figure of a circle. Half the circle has a wide flange, the other narrow—options open to the facings of a 90° corner-beam forged into a semi-circle. From the overlook, the work suggests that once there may have been something there—a trolley-car turn-table, a water tower—but, like the tenement blocks that had once bordered the site, no longer extant.

There's something about this ringed figure that is both religious and ambiguous. Phil said that when Serra and Carl Andre were in Japan, they were struck by curious structures, pile or mound-like erections of some kind, placed at the ends of little streets. The sense of these structures was neither clearly intentional nor were they accidental or impermanent, like rubble at a building site. And they liked them.

My deepest association concerning Serra's circle is that of Brancusi's *Table of Silence,* but somehow sunk to ground level. Phil thought that the changed flange width of each semi-circle was akin to yin and yang.

10 March 1973

Went to a Serra talk to students held at the Whitney Museum that touched on numerous interesting details. The visit to Japan made a great impression on him. He says he now wants to go to Machu Picchu. (Is his father from Peru?) Japan meant learning to look at things for great lengths of time. When puzzled by something, he always asks "What's that all about?" in a piping voice. From the audience, I inquired after the Bronx circle in the ground. He wants it to be looked at the way the Japanese regard their Buddhist gardens. He spoke of a solid, rather tangible conception of sculpture at odds with the disintegrated, expressionistic lead tossings. Sculpture for him has come to reassert a formal, emotional, psychological meaning—though only the formal can be talked about. He's still interested in Robert Smithson [who was to die tragically four months later], Carl Andre "when he works," and Mel Bochner, "who is, you know, a sculptor."

4 July 1973

I saw the beginning of the actual wall painting of Bochner at the Sonnabend Gallery and remarked that the wall is too long, tending toward a kind of Mannerist distortion of a rectangular space. Yellow rectangles appear to float in the white atmosphere with red and blue rectangles yet to be added. Something about this "control of space" reminds me of the dense metal cubes and extended oblongs [called *Different and Different Again,* 1973] which establish parallel formations (one has to imagine them) in Serra's recent large, shifting installations at the Guggenheim Museum. The parallel bars and cubes of Serra's recent work at the Whitney annual [*Elevation,* 1973] also came to mind, especially as they were widely displaced, elements being set on the floor, distant from one another and quite up close to the wall with a broad plane of "empty space" in between.

4 June 1974

Saw Richard Serra today by chance. He described a new project for Cologne. He attributed the source for the 120-foot sited wall to his recent experience in Peru. The project is an enclosure dealing with perceptual discrepancies occasioned by positioning oneself within an oddly formed four-sided unit. There are two 6-foot entries and several 9-inch breaks in a wall of Corten steel. From certain positions the wide entrances read as thin as the narrow breaks in the wall. Because of the discrepant relationships between the wall sections, persons standing within the piece, equidistant from one another, appear disproportionately larger or smaller in an exaggerated perspectival illusion. Also, though enclosed, the view of the city through the narrow slits is quite complete—a bit like seeing it through snow goggles. He plans to call his work after a Peruvian site.

He at first submitted a project that the city of Cologne is more greatly keen to have. But Serra rightly does not want to do it, as it is very much in line with the logarithmic expansions perhaps too reminiscent of Smithson's early work. [I'm unsure as to the fate of these projects, but aspects of them are maintained in the *Untitled Piece for Bochum* (1977), the tentative project for the Ohio State University (1978–79), as well as the trepanned Cubism of *T.W.U.* (1980), set up on West Broadway between Franklin and Leonard Streets.] Serra, for all his single-mindedness (probably because of it), is perhaps the most "artist artist" I know. Anyway, it's a toss-up between Mel and Richard.

4 June 1978

To Richard Serra's King City, Canada piece just beyond York University in a bucolic field—clouds forming, a jet plane's vapor trail marking our arrival. *Shift* (1970–72), as it is called, is naturally a disappointment—as would be expected—on seeing so legendary and yet so isolated a work. The first effect was to "think deep thoughts." In the rising warmth of the day, swarms of mosquitoes were aroused by our walking through the already high grass drying in the morning sun. On investigation the piece grows beautiful. There's something here of Richard Long become a Don Judd or an Andre. This severe work allows itself one or two aestheticized flourishes. Acute cuts mark the top of the wedge-driven walls, postulating a vague parallel memory of some specific enclosure.

I think of wedge walls in a continuum of wedge shapes from Morris to Judd to the *Seedbed* of Vito Acconci, even Duchamp's *Wedge of Chastity*—though I know that Serra is disinterested in the historical iconography of abstract elements, but rather seeks an enormous physical investigation of, here, more than 1600 feet one way, and that doesn't include the valley between the slopes. Still, iconography determines form—at least in some measure—and it is possible, even reasonable, in the late twentieth century to speak of an "abstract iconography."

Late in the torpid afternoon I met Richard Serra. He is setting up a new piece. At the end of Canal Street there is the Holland Tunnel approach, a wide, swerving island approachable on foot only across an industrial overpass. This traffic island, covered in gravel and a bit of neglected landscaping, falls under the jurisdiction of the Port Authority. Serra got to the agency, said he wanted to site something on the island, and received a go-ahead signal. At the moment there are 12-foot-high poles tipped in yellow, forming an almost perfect quadrant "eyeballed" into the gravel, 90 degrees of a circle that would be, if complete, some 800 feet in diameter. The wall intended to occupy the demarcated curve will be made of Corten steel. One sees how the monumental wall is a function of the curve of driven access. For the motorist, the wall shifts in an ambiguous perspective from the condition of line (that is, vertical edge) to a long curving plane that defies easy, perspectival comprehension.

Richard has studied the site from the windows of the surrounding buildings; he has even seen it from the air in a helicopter. For me, the thing works only in blueprint, as an elegant linear curve. Once the piece is identified as wall, especially steel wall (open to graffiti attack, behind which derelicts live), the project will not be supported. But it is all so typical of Serra; coveting the site, he nonetheless avoids an acceptable solution, that is, a vertical construction which could be seen as a kind of an insignia or emblem, or beacon. I don't want him to do this, but should he, such a proposal would handily succeed. I want him to do what he wants, but what he wants won't pass—not because it's not good or important, but because it will be shouted down owing to sociological anxieties.

Built into Richard's dedication to sculpture is a kind of set-up situation: not to fail (for he cannot fail), but rather one of immensely strained resistance, leading to a heightened sense of failure, or rejection, of grand effort put forth without the concomitant approval he also hopes for.

His hair cropped short is now grizzled. His strong body has grown thickened and squared-off, so that he seems older than he is.

On Thursday last, a reception for Richard Serra, whose great sculptures are now part of New York. The *St. John's Rotary Arc* outside the Holland Tunnel is the curved, horizontal, low-lying counterpart to his vertical piece, *T.W.U.*, in terms of its part-to-part open Cubist Constructivism, symbolizes sculpture itself. The broad face of the *Rotary Arc* symbolizes painting. One could be even more specific: the very edges of the arc enact the "zips" of Newman. The paradigms for these two works are Brancusi's *Table of Silence* and the *Endless Column* at Tirgu Jiu. Sidney Geist once pointed out that the urban monuments that inspired Brancusi at Tirgu Jiu were the *Arc du Caroussel* and the obelisk in the Place de la Concorde. Accepting the connections, Obelisk = *Endless Column* = *T.W.U.* and *Arc du Carousel* = *Table of*

Silence = Rotary Arc, further enlarges the historical ironies implicit in public sculpture. The distance separating *T.W.U.* from the *St. John's Rotary Arc* to the south marks, to the north, its distance too from a dead triviality, a recently erected and inadvertently droll effigy of Juan Pablo Duarte (by a certain Nicola Arrighini). It's as if Serra's pieces argue the symbolic status of painting and sculpture between themselves and the sculptor's relationship to Brancusi, while they also argue against the dead representational traditions of public sculpture by which we've been mostly abused these last few years, viz., the ghastly *Alice in Wonderland* in Central Park and the horrendous Einstein Memorial in Washington, D.C.

4 May 1980

Stroll up from City Hall and pass *T.W.U.* Graffiti commences—a boldly crayoned "Fuck Art"; and someone has tossed a bucket of red paint high on the work so it could dribble down. So it goes.

Keith Sonnier:
Materials and Pictorialism

Keith Sonnier is 28 and was born in Mamou, a French-and-English-speaking town in Louisiana. The unassimilated Frenchness of Sonnier's background—he speaks with no Southern accent—partly made for an unregretted childhood, and one which was open to the arts; at least it was not hostile to personal eccentricity. His father ran a hardware and electrical supply store. At 12 he drove. He went to Mamou High between 1955 and 1959. Nothing deeply disrupted this Southern rural picture except when, at 15, he had an inkling that "there had to be something else."

From high school, Sonnier went to the University of Southwestern Louisiana, 1959 to 1963, where he became the central figure of a small body of art majors.[1] Color slides of Sonnier's student works indicate that they were paintings of high quality revealing an awareness of the 20th-century European tradition. They are marked by a heady sensuality and the easy, natural color of a native painter who was early in control of his color and medium. These canvasses of female nudes, half drawn, half painted, are lyrical and shift in a Soutine-like way from wet impastoes to thin washes of a generally muted, dank tonality.

In 1963, Sonnier went to France, starting out in Normandy—"just another peasant culture, no communication'—and then to Paris, ending in the working class district of Clignancourt in the *rue du Poteau*. He continued to paint between 1963–65 in an erotic "mystical" way, but saw his work slowly transform into something that was "considerably more abstract."

After working in isolation in France he acted on impulse and communicated with the Rutgers University Art Department, where he was offered a teaching assistantship beginning in 1966. The return was critical. Among his colleagues there were Robert Morris, Robert Watts and Gary Kuehn. Through them, Sonnier was introduced into the New York art world, as part of the "Rutgers Group." His medium shifted from paint to vinyl and other prefabricated plastic substances such as vacuum cleaner coils. These materials tended to be comparatively soft. They adopted forms of a loose geometry—hollow rectangular forms, cones, pyramids, supported on the inside by hidden air blowers. Often such forms were set into tables and surfaces

This article originally appeared in *Artforum*, October 1969.

that toppled slightly. The change in the medium was more radical than the shift in the metaphor, which remained sexual in its connotations. The central figure, for better or worse, was Oldenburg, who, at the time, has engendered a wide range of funky, soft sculpture, though Sonnier's pieces were not necessarily imitative of the Pop sources of Oldenburg's imagery.

In the fall of 1966, Lucy Lippard introduced the work of Keith Sonnier in a group show held at the Fischbach Gallery, called "Eccentric Abstraction." It also included the work of Bruce Nauman, Gary Kuehn, Eva Hesse, Frank Lincoln Viner and several other artists who had assembled earlier in the year at the Graham Gallery under the banner of "Abstract Inflationists and Stuffed Expressionists." Lucy Lippard's early essay touched on many serious features of these young artists who were already attracted by a new range of sensibility—one connected both with the idea of procedure ("process art") and ideation ("conceptual art"). Such options as were taken by these artists seemed particularly laughable at that moment, for so much of what was being taken seriously in art was still vitally Minimalist in character. It seems a commendable critical feat that Lippard should have observed that these works were "nonsculptural"; that they presented "indirect affinities with the incongruity and often sexual content of Surrealism"; that the "increased influence and participation of painters has undermined sculptural tradition, producing a nonsculptural or object idiom that looks to formalist painting rather than to previous sculpture for its precedents." Of Sonnier, she observed that he "presents to apparently contradictory states as parts of a single phenomenon. A boxy but soft form slowly inflates and deflates in comparison to its hard, inert counterpart. The rhythm is mechanical and voluptuous, barely active, offering change and subsequent return to the first state until the two become one physical sensation."[2] Works of this nature were also shown at Douglass College, Rutgers University, in 1966.

At this time, Sonnier began to be handled independently by Richard Bellamy of the Goldowsky Gallery. As has been the case with each successive wave of new sensibility, especially since the triumph of Rauschenberg in 1964, the more daring German dealers have endorsed young American artists by creating platforms for them, often long before their being widely shown in this country. In 1967 Rolf Ricke of Cologne gave Keith Sonnier his first one-man show, which was sold out, two works entering German museums.

It is not my intention here to describe Sonnier's career in terms of a "suite of triumphs." What interests me more is that Sonnier's work is central to a broad shift in sensibility, which was marked in the period of 1967–69, and which by the spring of this year had become so pronounced as to be virtually recognized as a distinct new style—yet one so disparate as to defy a single specific cognomen like Pop Art or Minimalism.

Since formalist art tended to be grounded in geometric appearances and permutations (it was an art which stressed "formal" rather than "contentual" values), an anti-geometric bias became visible and endemic in the new sensibility. Of necessity, formalist criticism, which tended to focus on determining the nature of geometric relationships through Aristotelian description, had to have been placed in jeopardy. These rejections, both on the part of artists and critics, were, of course, carried out in many quarters in a vindictive spirit occasioned by the false belief that formalist criticism had become the exclusive mouthpiece of Minimalism. What was overlooked in the new attack on formalism is that formalism as a visual and critical tool has arisen in the late 1930s in the social criticism of Clement Greenberg out of a need to expunge literary issues from the arts—those issues which were either politically slanted or Surrealistically biased. In short, formalist criticism arose out of a need to rid art of the debasing features of late Surrealist poetics and die-hard Stalinist polemics. To achieve this end, Greenberg placed new emphasis on those problems which were immediately bound to artistic procedure and the nature of the medium. He viewed successful solutions to these problems as "formal" and distinguishable from those issues which were either a hangover personality charade or those which had been tied to a deplorable and hypocritical social ethic.

The clear manifestations of new sensibility during these past two years may be divided into three streams, a bifurcated formalist stream, and a literary one. The last stresses "poetical" values and deals with image/word transfer play, which, if it is not Dadaist in nature, is nothing else. Its primary exponent and most vertiginous promoter is Bruce Nauman. The second stream is entirely Constructivist in character. It emphasizes elementary structural issues, that is, problems of joining, standing, raising up. It is clearly a sculptural and architectural style marked by an ambitious scale. Its primary exponent is Richard Serra. As counterpart to the Constructivist stream is a group centered about the issues of color. Their productions are marked by a desire to create forms related to and perhaps which more readily evolve out of painterly issues. Several young artists meet here—though they are yet of unclear positioning—Alan Saret, Bill Bollinger, David Novros, Eva Hesse, and Keith Sonnier.

Throughout 1967 sonnier was attracted by lowlying, floor-bound assemblages which—despite structural premises centered upon long, perverse beams and "links"—also spoke of a new breadth of sensitivity and suggestibility. Sonnier's critical piece along these lines took the form of a thin loaf. It is made of foam rubber padded over a wooden core. The rubber in turn has been covered with glistening pink satin which, because of a fairly equidistant set of "pullings" and "tightenings" formed a sequence of twenty-three units. The divisions were established "by feel" and not based on an *a priori* mathematical ratio. Other works by Sonnier of a similar and equally evocative nature were foam rubber "tubes" resembling satin-covered links, which were then laid over with "blankets" of cheesecloth, a highly modifying, disembodied substance, which in its shroudlike character acts in a way similar to a broad "wash" of color. Several trough-like works were also covered with cheesecloth, or were presented at rest upon such "beds." At this point Sonnier felt that he too "was an artist, not just saying something about myself as an adolescent but saying something to everybody." These would be the last "constructed" sculptures until

1969—although the act of covering such forms with semi-transparent rags brings up considerable issues connected to color as well as "poetical" ones, such as disguising, hiding, covering: covert versus overt.

Before attacking such a problem, let me indicate that the "tiny module" —as Sonnier characterized the diaphaneity of cheesecloth—and the high gloss of the pink satin had its counterpart in several sculptures of 1968, made of window screening. This is a more tensed-up, resistant material, one which was also shiny and composed of minute crosshatchings of wire once again forming "tiny modules." The use of window screening led to several bulging works (now destroyed) of eccentric proportions—long, wall pieces, in which the wiry sheen was stressed, as well as the capacity of the substance to lend itself to *repoussoir.* Other experiments with screening were several floor exercises of elementary pleating and folding. In 1967, Sonnier began to incorporate a further range of materials: rags, torn patches of tinted silks and disembodied, delicately colored remnants.

The new tremulous substances and hesitant colorations led Sonnier to be interested in broad sprawls of latex, often heightened with "flocking" that is, of colored powdered rayon, a substance employed in the manufacture of wallpaper (fig. 6). The act of spreading the latex on the wall or floor has superficial resemblances to the flooding of colors in field painting—think of those by Morris Louis, for example. But the bleeding of thinned out paint into unprimed canvas is much faster, much more flushed than the comparatively resistant stickiness of the thick and pasty liquitex substance. Moreover, there is no absorption into the ground as in the case of thin paint on unprimed canvas. Instead, the spread latex remains on the surface and dries into distinct figure-ground relationships. The dusting, or flocking, is an attempt to modify the color and shape problems caused by a layer of rubber contrasted against the color of the wall. perhaps the use of rubber is similar to Richard Serra's rubber spreads of 1968, although his was used even more thickly and in a more shredded, tire-like fashion. Sonnier instead emphasized the membrane-like nature of rubber and its potential for thinness and fragility.

The flocked latex works measure Sonnier's refined sense of the whole environment, not only because of the coloration and tonality of the pieces themselves but also because they are so affected by the stray elements of the studio; a chair, a wall, a table, an electrical circuit box, a nest of cables. By peeling the latex membrane from the wall other issues were brought into prominence. The latex pulled down halfway in a more or less rectangular sheet related to issues of limpness as well as surface subdivision: arrangements of flocked surface, naked latex underside, the color of the wall, and the smudged original edge of the latex rectangle would result. These were further dilated upon by tying the peeled edges or levels away from the wall and by holding these projections out into space by thin, improbably weak strings or cords, which were sometimes fixed to the floor at some distance from the wall or which were themselves allowed to dangle limply. The tentative sculpture that results is a kind of muted memory of the edges of loose collage or

Cubist grids. The strings tying all these limp substances into twisted rectangles tended to project a collage-like appearance into space, as if palely colored rectangles had been projected off the paper and their edges, now transformed into strings, were tied to the ground, or the floor, or the wall, or simply left to the mercy of gravity.

At this moment, too, the materials employed were enlarged to include neon tubing which was industrially molded after templates fashioned out of copper tubing by the artist. This kind of gestural neon is peculiar and idiosyncratic rather than commercial in character. It may be that Richard Serra's rubber and neon pieces of 1968 helped to confirm Sonnier's decision to introduce luminous and gestural components, although in the latter's work the materiality of the substance was underplayed in favor of its role in the pictorial and coloristic vocabulary.[3] Neon assumed the role of line and gesture in contrast to the flocked latex and rags which were, in this context, identifiable as transparent planes, washes and patches of color. It would be interesting to know to what degree James Rosenquist's *sui generis* "*Tumbleweed*" (1963, fig. 7), a construction of wood, barbed wire and neon, affected both Sonnier and Serra, since both expressed admiration of this work to me.

What I have been trying to show is that the latex, the flocking, the neon, the rags, the cheesecloth, were, in Sonnier's case, substances analogous to the painter's palette, which he superficially appeared to have abandoned at the time of the "inflatable sculptures." These substances mark, then, in 1968, a return toward painterliness and colorism, a rejection of his "sculptural phase" which had been touched by the prevailing Minimalist mode, however eccentric its forms may have appeared. It is evident that Sonnier shared several coloristic premises with a body of young artists working in New York City who gravitated to the Bykert Gallery. Foremost among these were William Bollinger and Alan Saret, the latter particularly. Saret's colored wire sculptures, limp rubber sheetings and mounds of powdered chemicals share with Sonnier both an intense feeling for color, which itself is unusual, as well as a revival of certain features connected with Abstract Expressionism, notably a gestural focus and an allover dispersal of energy. These Abstract Expressionist qualities are more Saret's than Sonnier's, who in all of his work has rejected the Abstract Expressionist infinite screen in favor of a configuration based on a viable internal structure of shifting weights and balances. That is, there is no "figure" in Saret; there is a kind of oriental or calligraphic "figure" in Sonnier. This orientalism is particularly noticeable in the *Neon with Cloth* of 1968.

These coloristic attitudes were especially evident in the "Here & Now" exhibition held at Washington University in January 1969. Commenting on the similarities between Saret and Sonnier I observed at the time that in addition to its relation to Abstract Expressionism, the new colorism possibly may relate

to something older . . . there are qualities relevant to late Monet [I mean after 1890], in the kind of unravelling that one sees in the later paintings of Monet. And this is sensible in the kind of colors that Saret is using, a highly lyrical, perfumed and confectionery range, equally relevant to

> the painting of late Monet. That kind of color is also . . . in the fine color selections that were in the works by Keith Sonnier: pale pinks, pale greys. Utilizing the pale beige of the wall is a very conscious coloristic reference back to issues that deal with late Monet.[4]

It is apparent that the range of color favored by Sonnier is of a wistful, greyed-out range. The emotional tenor of the color, and the insubstantiality of the material in which that color is embodied, led me to a dangerous area of "poetical" speculation, although I am not yet willing to abandon this attitude entirely. At the same panel, I went on to speculate that the kind of forms taken by such limp materials

> enter a very remarkable area of subjectivity . . . that is a kind of funerary, shroud-like, dispiriting . . . association. I think that the shroudiness is perfectly easy to see, or is visible in that enormous pile of dusty rubber . . . by Saret, in a certain sense there is also, in the pink shroud floor piece by Sonnier, a kind of delimited, funerary site, the grey flocking covering an abandoned bed.[5]

The piece I was referring to was specially made for the St. Louis exhibition. It was executed on the beige linoleum tile floor. A "bed" of latex was spread and flocked over with grey. A pink rectangle was fixed along the lateral edge, like a gauzy blanket.

The latex and flocked pieces on which, I would say, the present reputation of Sonnier has been built vacillates between the two poles of an art predicated on fine color plays and insubstantial materials, and a desire for clear, expository effects such as elemental examinations of surface peel. But the latter area, rather than existing for its own end, accompanies the refined, pictorial sensibility to which these remarks have largely been addressed.

Throughout the remainder of 1968 and into 1969, Sonnier's "palette" of materials remained fairly constant. However, in the spring of 1969, when an international interest in the new sensibility had already been stimulated—with many exhibitions held in St. Louis, Bern, German private galleries and the Whitney, for example—a change in Sonnier's work became evident, one which is still very much in the process of realizing itself. Instead of utter bonelessness and depletion, Sonnier's objects are now tending toward a fresh tenseness. This evolution is begin accompanied by a greater reliance on elements of industrial prefabrication, particularly on thick sheets of glass squares or circles. Their role is largely to modulate light and, therefore, they can be related, startlingly enough, to the swathes of cheesecloth of the earlier work. The neon gestures have also been expanded to include specific geometrical elements such as arc-sections and straight "lines." Moreover, "real" elements, such as shaded light bulbs, light sockets, movie and slide projectors, and strobe lights, which had modestly functioned at the "edges" of the earlier assemblages are here being directly incorporated into the "calligraphic figure," with passages of neon tubing "lassoing in," so to speak, such real electrical appliances. Such environmental clues were, in the earliest latex pieces, first experienced tacitly and unapologetically. By now, such material has become almost a special area of exploration. In this sense, the latest works carry in them a heavy residue of Happening, Theater and Environment.

The glass sheets, because of their weight and hardness, demand a more physical and Constructivist interplay and, therefore, are more arduously set into propped and architectural relationships. The neon elements are being placed into more tectonic—vertical, horizontal or parallel—associations, not that gestural neon has been given up entirely. Several of the most recent pieces tend to contrast the transparent geometric glass shapes against rushes of gestural neon. Such contrasts inevitably take into account the glossy modulations of light reflected by the glass surfaces as well as the transparent shadows cast *onto* the studio wall *through* the glass planes themselves. We are still dealing with a highly elaborate coloristic sensibility but it appears that the inert rags and dusty flockings are slowly being moved away from.

Among the loveliest of these recent works is the one in which a gestural yellow diagonal of neon reflects on and through a glass square, or the one shown this June at the Whitney "Anti-Illusion" exhibition, in which a semicircle of fluorescent green neon is reflected into the lower half of a circular glass sheet flushing the clear glass green up to the central horizontal bar. This last work is particularly geometric in character—though all the recent neon pieces need not be. Another remarkable gestural piece is a kind of free "M" (fig. 8), in which an orange neon light encircles five blue neon prongs. The front face of the orange stream has been silvered opaque forcing these passages to read as black strokes, while the orange light is deflected back against the wall.

The purpose of this essay has not been to create an argument on which one may make predictions regarding the future. Whether or not Sonnier retains his pre-eminence in a stream which itself is constantly threatened with evaporation because of its sheer delicacy, is simply beside the point. Instead the manifest excellence of Sonnier's work is the *donnée* which demanded a descriptive analysis.

Notes

1. Sonnier especially recalls the teachings of Calvin Harlan as helpful. Harlan is a New Orleans painter of clear and rigorous color principles, in nature akin to Albers and the Yale Art School and who also had an "in" to what was happening in recent English sculpture.

2. Lucy Lippard, "Eccentric Abstraction," broadside to an exhibition organized for the Fischbach Gallery, New York, Sept. 20–Oct. 8, 1966.

3. Sonnier has acknowledged that Bruce Nauman's neon pieces were instrumental in bringing him to this material.

4. "Here & Now" exhibition, symposium transcript of a panel held in St. Louis on January 12, 1969, p. 4. I would like to extend my appreciation for the copy of the transcript to Joseph Helman, President of Steinberg Art Gallery Associates (SAGA), and Robert T. Buck, Jr., Director of the Washington University Gallery of Art.

5. "Here & Now" exhibition, symposium transcript, *op. cit.*, p. 13.

Figure 6. Keith Sonnier, *Mustee*, 1968
Latex, flocking and string, 12'×6'. Work destroyed.
(Photo courtesy Leo Castelli Gallery)

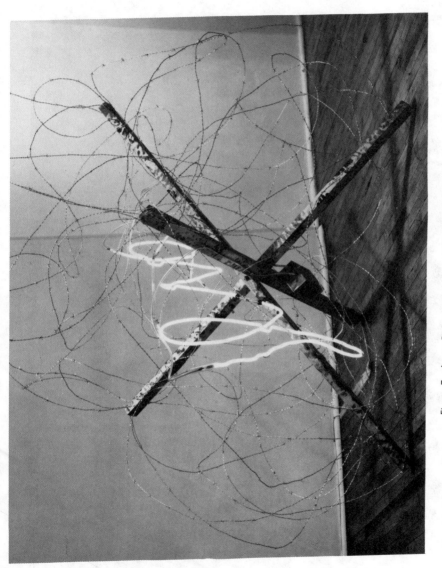

Figure 7. James Rosenquist, *Untitled (Tumbleweed)*, 1963
Neon, barbed wire, mixed media, 76" ×80" ×96".
(Photo courtesy Leo Castelli Gallery)

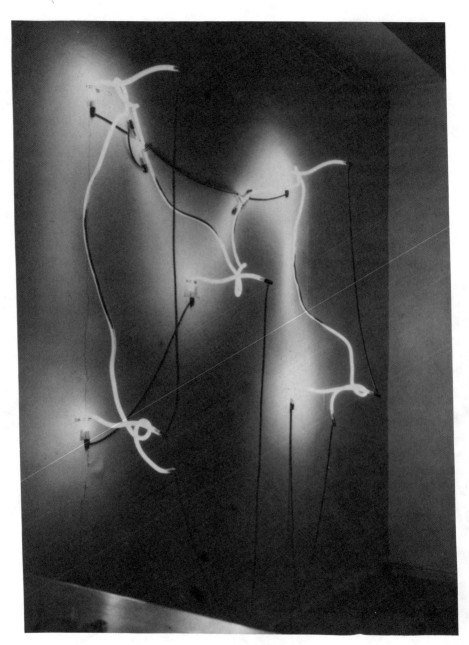

Figure 8. Keith Sonnier, *Untitled*, 1969
Neon, 6'×9'×2'.
(Photo courtesy Leo Castelli Gallery)

Eva Hesse: More Light on the Transition from Postminimalism to the Sublime

Eva Hesse was born in Hamburg, Germany, to a Jewish family on January 11, 1936—in full *Hitlerzeit*. During her infancy, Eva Hesse was separated from her family for a period of three months. In 1939, she went with her father, mother, and sister to New York City where she was raised in Washington Heights, a neighborhood which, since the large emigrations following the First World War, had become largely a German-Jewish enclave in Manhattan's Uptown. Bilinguality was to serve her well, for, shortly after her graduation from the Yale University School of Fine Arts in 1959, she and her husband Tom Doyle went to Germany and remained there for nearly two years. Eva Hesse's first extensive exhibition took place under the tutelage of the Kunstverein für die Rheinlande und Westfalen in Düsseldorf in 1965.

This exhibition was the culmination of a deeper, more internalized quest—the discovery of who she was, through the reconstruction of the facts and fragments pertaining to her family lost during the war. The return to Germany was "a weird search like a secretive mission . . . a new generation seeking a past. I know nothing of my family—my grandparents. Seeking out statistics, establishing losses encountered by the H[esses] . . . never knowing their lives, their never knowing me or mine . . . never having had grandma, grandpa [Moritz and Erna Marcus], life at all the gatherings, house, encouragements, proudnesses. . . ."[1]

Eva Hesse's difficult childhood was further traumatized by the separation of her parents in this country, the remarriage of her father, and the death of her mother. Her diary notations indicate that she identified the intellectual and structural side of her mind with her father—sought, in fact, to conform to what she took to be those sources of pride which he took in her, perhaps as a guarantee that she would never again be abandoned.

A high point of her young career—and of paternal pride—occurred when, in the September 1954 issue of *Seventeen* magazine, Eva Hesse's illustrations were featured as part of the annual competition award, "It's All Yours." Her work had

---

This article originally appeared in *Eva Hesse: A Memorial Exhibition* (Exhibition Catalogue) (New York City, The Solomon R. Guggenheim Museum, December 1972–February 1973).

appeared in a nationally distributed magazine. She had earned $100. "We like to think that we discovered Eva Hesse," wrote Marie McPartland, the editor of the feature, "but actually she came up to *Seventeen* on her own in February of this year, fresh from Pratt Institute . . . We hired her on the spot to work part time on our staff. In the evening she attends the Art Students' League nearby. This month she begins a three-year course in painting, drawing, sculpture, and graphics at Cooper Union in New York City."[2]

In the fall of 1965 Eva Hesse returned from Germany to New York City, where she was to die four years later on May 29, 1970. Her production, therefore, is strikingly compressed. In addition to the works themselves—paintings, sculptures, drawings, and the combined idiom that the artist preferred—Eva Hesse's estate also includes notebooks which range from ledger size to scratch pad in which she had, from adolescence on, recorded impressions, experiences, dreams, stray information, and artist's recipes. At times these were set down with fastidious control; at other times, they were hastily recorded, often in cryptic clues, especially when dealing with aspects of her private life. At the very end, when the intellectual equipment remained, but tortured by physical deterioration, many phrases are left unfinished. Even here there are type-size sheets of manuscript describing this experience.[3]

The history of artistic creation can never be said to be recorded in this way—the growth of a sculptural and pictorial oeuvre answers its own imperatives and not those of literature, even confessional or diaristic literature. Still, in Eva Hesse's case, it would be foolhardy to ignore these notebooks. Art history is richer for them, and they bring into sharp focus those personal and artistic events which shaped the production of a gifted art student, transforming it into one of remarkable power. The most painful notations record the central trauma of individuation provoked by the death of the artist's father in the summer of 1966 and the rupture with her husband which peaked at this time as well, events without which, I believe, Eva Hesse's art might have remained an effort of primarily local interest. These events are also mentioned as a means of introducing certain figures—Sol LeWitt, Mel Bochner, Lucy Lippard, Robert Smithson, and Helen Charash,[4] artists and critics largely, who were to reinforce the vision which these two traumas aided in triggering. The terror and isolation provoked by the death of the artist's father and the withdrawal of her husband from her—instead of forcing incipient madness—provoked the crystal lucidity of original creation. In the summer of 1966, during the complex events and family rituals surrounding the death of her father (in Switzerland, as it happened), Eva Hesse found herself in the unfamiliar serenity of her sister's household, surroundings which intensified a sense of guilt. She had not become the kind of artist which the "It's All Yours" suggested she might have become (neither did Sylvia Plath, who shares this curious coincidence with Eva Hesse). She wrote: "I feel more helpless, insufficient, stupid . . . I want to prove myself. My only weapon is art." In August of 1966 Eva Hesse's life as a mature artist begins.

Even at this short remove it grows difficult to ascertain the individuals who created the movement away from Minimalism and from formalist criticism. Certainly,

Richard Serra, Carl Andre, Keith Sonnier, Robert Smithson, Robert Morris, Sol LeWitt, Mel Bochner and the critic Lucy Lippard must be recalled in this connection; several of the artists listed here had also functioned in the capacity of theorists and critical essayists as well. Eva Hesse also contributed enormously to this shift of sensibility, and her journal notations after 1966 make constant mention of LeWitt, Lippard, Bochner, and Smithson, acknowledging their crucial assistance during a period when otherwise she might have felt herself alone in the making of a new art as well as of a new life. The death of Eva Hesse also makes it possible to regard her production in a way quite different from that of her Postminimalist colleagues. Their careers are still being elaborated. What can only be elaborated now, in Hesse's case, are our changing modes of perceiving what is important in her work.

During 1965 Hesse began to break with the explicit Expressionist and Surrealist clues of her art—those fine ambitions that an extensive art training and long European stay engendered. Biomorphic relief elements announced a fresh attitude toward pictorial-sculptural ambiguity. Some fifty items, drawings and combine paintings, comprise the checklist of the summer run of Eva Hesse's first exhibition, *Materialbilder und Zeichnungen* held at the Studio für Graphik in Düsseldorf from August to October 1965. The front page of the one-fold checklist reproduces a photograph of the artist surround by five works. Although the reliefs are seemingly abstract, their organic inferences will, by the end of the following year, have been further attenuated so that what we now view as a kind of generative abstraction—breast and nipple forms, womblike configurations—will have evolved into a vestigial suggestiveness.

One is impressed by their vigorous biomorphism and sense of craft, as well as their often raucous color. This chromatic plangency is notable because it argues for a rejection of the systematic color theories of Josef Albers, one of the important teachers whose influence the artist underwent at first hand. Unlike her teacher's paintings, Hesse's works are expressionistic in terms of their harsh and obtuse color. Taking note of the generally monochromatic appearance of her work after 1965—a monochromism largely traceable to an appreciation of Jasper Johns' work—I conclude that Eva Hesse was a largely insecure colorist, never comfortable with this emotionally oriented world, despite her successes in Albers' classroom.

Once again in New York City and more self-aware of her ambitions, Eva Hesse found support among a small community of compatible artists. A disparate range of work came into being, resistant to the architectural and sculptural ambitions of Minimalism. These artists, in order to cut through Minimalism's solemn atmosphere, adopted a self-mocking stance. The general levity was viewed as "doing an Oldenburg number." The shifting sensibility was expressed in the growing use of highly colored, emotionally associative materials and through the rejection of the geometrical tradition of Constructivism. The limp, the pliable, the cheap were sought; the hard, the polished, the expensive became suspect. Unanticipated methods of seaming and joining were emphasized—sewing, lacing, grommeting. Rags, vinyl, street detritus came to be choice materials surpassing even welded stainless or Corten steel.

In the late spring of 1966 several artists of this stamp joined together for a group exhibition at the Graham Gallery, calling themselves *Abstract Inflationists and Stuffed Expressionists*. The exhibition was largely construed by the gallery-going public as a tardy Pop put-on, a joke, at worst jejune, at best harmless. This condescension was inescapable when regarded in the context of a larger situation in which Tony Smith, Kenneth Noland, and Frank Stella were taken to be the representative figures of modern art. The reviews of the exhibition were few and terse, equally understandable granting the youth of the participants and the unfamiliar idiom in which they were working. The most salient feature requiring mention went ignored—that such an option should have been adopted by a body of artists in the first place.

The announcement for the *Abstract Inflationists and Stuffed Expressionists* exhibition was a toy balloon, surprinted with the gallery particulars, emphasizing in this way an air of comedy. The good nature of the exhibition led me to write that Eva Hesse's contribution—ironically called *Long Life* (fig. 9)—was a "slapstick ball and chain [that] might easily pass for an anarchist's bomb designed by a color blind obsessive compulsive."[5] I was struck by the process of manufacture—a core of papier-mâché painstakingly bound in gray-painted cord. The relationship of the piece to the early painting of Jasper Johns is notable especially in view of its subject matter—if that term is still a viable one. It can easily be allied with, say, the *Painting with Two Balls*, the gray version, which, like the gray work by Hesse is equally sexually inferential. Although Hesse's work also seems to bear reference to the early Johns-like production of Robert Morris, it seems doubtful to me that Morris' career ever had a decisive influence on Eva Hesse's work despite Morris' essay "Anti-Form" (*Artforum*, April 1968), a position paper to which Hesse's work is appended by virtue of her relationship to the movement Morris is describing.

From 1964 on, there appears in Hesse's work a conscious use of motival configurations. One such figure would be the "ball" and "chain" motif of *Long Life*, a large, round body from which a thin length depends or is extruded. Such a formal predicate remains constant through the remainder of Hesse's short career—perhaps abandoned in the plastic and rope skeinings and ladder-like structures of the last year of her life. Although in some German-period work such motifs are revealed, the "ball" and "chain" motif appears first to have been fully realized in a piece of 1966, *Total Zero*—now destroyed, somewhat inner-tube-like in shape from which a short swirl escapes. The motif is sexually connotative, possibly generative, carrying with it an abortive note inferring both uterine container and slashed umbilicus.

Such sexual metaphors are not introduced into Eva Hesse's work because of an active literary fantasy, but because they take their spur from closely lived experience. They are always a function of the actual events of a life painful from the first, even at its seemingly best moments. The "uterine" motif, for example, is given credence by the notations made in a notebook at the time that Eva Hesse was still a student at the Yale University School of Fine Arts. On November 2, 1960, Eva Hesse noted that "her problems of mysterious pains have been detected and explained . . . A logical explanation and proper steps shall shortly be taken. I will have an operation and the opening at the ovary will be dilated." Later she noted, "Tomorrow I go to hospital. Tues., Operation."

While such innuendos in her art correspond to the troubled personal life of the artist, such a line of inquiry must remain speculative as it falls into the province of trained analysis, if even then. But that Hesse thought along such lines is substantiated throughout the notebooks. Her notations indicate that she was attracted to Freudian analytical patterns—as early as her studies at Yale—because they are so potently simple and seemingly true. In a notebook dated April 1966 (although it covers a broader period of time), the basic statement of the conflicts besetting her were recorded as the "Underlying Theme [of the] conflicting forces inside Eva"—in her notebooks she often refers to herself in the third person—viewed as an opening sadomasochistic multivalence within a Mother–Father polarity:

1. *Mother force: unstable, creative, sexual, threatening my stability, sadistic-aggressive.*

2. *Father, Stepmother force: good little girl, obedient, neat, clean, organized-masochistic.*

Later, through 1967–69, the motif of the trailing cord may be construed in the context of plasma bags and intravenous tubing, although by the period of her life when the surgical readings ought to be most evident, in the last year, this motif had, in fact, been displaced. Still, these motifs are not interesting because they may lend themselves to elaborate extrapolations of meaning but simply because their forms are interesting apart from any thematic obliquity. The forms infer, but they do not depict. Their essential ambiguity attests as well to a stylistic evolution out of Jasper Johns and through him to a still larger distillation of the Surrealist theory and a modern obsessive tradition, combined with, in Hesse's usage, ruggedness, pragmatic resourcefulness and an appreciation for the intrinsic physical properties of her materials.[6]

The compulsive coiling of these early pieces—a kind of pleasure-inducing craftswork—indicates a curious methodology. In this connection, the influence of Lucas Samaras is sensible in the tendency toward pictorializing sculpture which marks the later 1960s and announces the Postminimalist phase. My intuitions are borne out by an important note: "I met Sol [LeWitt]," Hesse wrote, "at the Whitney [Museum of American Art]. Saw recent acquisitions (Held, Johns, Kelly) & Lipman Collection. Lot of mediocrity along with few fine pieces. One beautiful Samaras (2 inferior ones), a fine Morris & Judd. The Samaras I loved was a box covered with pins, cover slightly ajar, with bird's head forcing its way out from under cover. Old cords and rope dropping out from front."[7]

In addition to the dangling, stray appearance of the sculpture, Hesse also responded to the fact that the characteristic surface of a Samaras box is formed by a network of parallel strands of multicolored knitting yarn. The obsessive nature of Samaras' work—both in subject and method—must be emphasized as another means of altering the idiom of Postminimalism. The conjunction of this psychological strain with a less sensuously appealing art sustained by the lucid theoretical positions of her friends Sol LeWitt, Mel Bochner and Robert Smithson, may have accounted for the enormous psychological persuasiveness of Hesse's manipulation of the otherwise spare rigor of Minimalist and serial structures to which she equally was being drawn at this time. LeWitt and Bochner have contributed to our understanding of this evolution. Some of the essential reference works in the movement, say Mel Bochner's "The Serial Attitude" (Artforum, December 1967), include pictorial examples of Hesse's work without specifically illustrating the way in which her more psychologically focused art elucidated the theory.

Taking into account organic inference, mixture of media and the fact that Marisol is a well-known woman artist, one might imagine that Hesse's work was cued in some measure by Marisol's work. Yet, a visit to Marisol's studio is recorded in the April 1966 notebook and the entry makes it clear that while Hesse was struck by the openness of Marisol's attitude regarding the use of odd substances, she had strong reservations as well. "Marisol does all work herself. She will try anything, experiment with any medium, incorporating all things." Here the sense of community ends and Hesse sharply notes that "What she does do is leave too much on the surface— design, decoration. Mystery is lost."

The rejection of Marisol is important to note because of Hesse's strong consciousness of the problems of being a woman artist, sympathies which were at that moment beginning to be explored by the more alert members of the New York art community. As early as 1966, Hesse confessed that "I have this awful trait in competing with male artists, which is to say almost everyone. Then, that's not bad enough, I compete as a 'woman' with women in 'female' areas. It's another major area to be thought about."

The biomorphic frame of reference in Postminimalism had, of course, been discussed since the emergence of Claes Oldenburg's soft sculptures, especially those of ca. 1962–64, when Hesse herself was first being drawn to this metaphor in her German combine paintings. It is in this historical relationship that Hesse emerged in the Eccentric Abstraction exhibition organized for the Fischbach Gallery by one of Eva Hesse's friends, Lucy Lippard. It was at this time that Hesse came to know Donald Droll who was then the director of the gallery.[8]

The Eccentric Abstraction exhibition, held in September and October of 1966, is one of the most influential group exhibitions in recent history. Lippard viewed her exhibition as antithetical to "the solid formal basis demanded of the best current non-objective art." Importantly, she emphasized the "indirect affinities with the incongruity and often sexual content of Surrealism." Lippard noted of Hesse's work that "intricately controlled and tight-bound, paradoxically bulbous forms do not move but their effect is also both fixed and changeable. The finality of their black to gray gradation is countered by an unexpected unfixed space and the mood is both strong and vulnerable, tentative and expansive." Lippard presaged, that "The future of sculpture may well lie in such non-sculptural styles." What was a "non-sculptural" possibility in 1966 has clearly become a sculptural actuality, if not even a stylistic cliché, if one takes into account the number of artists at present working in an idiom immediately dependent upon Eva Hesse's achievements.

An underground was coalescing and emerging. The then unfashionable loft area south of Houston Street—hence SoHo, bordered on the east with the Bowery, where Eva Hesse had her studio—was discovered to be the new bohemia. Eva Hesse's life changed from that of agony and fear into one central to a vital movement. She was valued as never before by artists, colleagues and friends. She had found an important gallery to represent her work—the Fischbach Gallery—although she noted in her journal that she had hoped to be shown at the now defunct Dwan Gallery at which Sol LeWitt was represented, despite the fact that the astringent severity of the general character of the Dwan roster was foreign to the tendencies exploited by Hesse. Perhaps, too, Hesse still wanted to demonstrate to Tom Doyle, who had been shown at Dwan, that she could now stand independently of him, but on his own turf.

The works of this phase of Hesse's career emphasize loaded dangling forms, either presented singly or clustered in groups: the ball of *Long Life,* another, *Vertiginous Detour,* is a black ball caught in a net which hangs from ceiling to floor, a work composed of groups of nets stuffed with crumpled plastic sheeting, *Ingeminate,* the sausagelike elements of *Several*—the last two included in the *Eccentric Abstraction* exhibition. These testiclelike clusters re-enact, in terms of their coloristic neutrality, the lessons of Johns combined with the organic metaphor of Oldenburg, fusing the former's conceptual presentations with the latter's viscerally identifiable soft sculpture. They are unique however, in that they foster an "intelligence" based on natural pressure, an "intelligence" or "rightness" such as we experience in clusters of onions, or sausage links. The tug of gravity, the action of the ground sprawl, the steadying and the support of the wall is always felt, quite unlike the autonomous works of Oldenburg. This remains constant, even in Hesse's seemingly errant pieces, the networks of the last year. These, too, have the natural "intelligence" and "order" that can be found, for example, in the tangled silk snares of certain nongeometric spider webs.

In this way, the visceral punning derived from Oldenburg was displaced in favor of the pictorial/sculptural fundamentalism found in the radical offerings of the day—say, in Richard Serra's lead tossings, an important example of which is dedicated to Eva Hesse, or in Carl Andre's metal "rugs." These presentations argue for the baldest acceptance of the floor and wall and reject as bankrupt the virtual monopoly the monolith isolated upon a plinth had enjoyed for millennia. The frank acceptance of the rudimentary—as directed against the base and therefore against the isolated "art object"—was only one part of the Postminimalist bias apparent in Hesse's work at this moment, since her work for two years more at least, was to give equally strong evidence of Minimalist structure, a style very much in evidence in New York art at that time.

Eventually, Hesse exactly understood her relationship to Oldenburg. In her most artistically exclusive notebook—really a collection of unbound and looseleaf pages, undated, but largely after 1967—Hesse observed of Oldenburg's work: "as eroticism, his work is abstract. The stimuli arise from pure sensation rather than direct association with the objects depicted." These ideas reiterate contentions made in Lucy Lippard's essay "Eros Presumptive" (*The Hudson Review,* Spring 1967) in which the critic attempted to isolate the sexual metaphor in abstract art, an idea which doubtless had been mulled over between critic and artist for some time before publication. In the article Hesse is mentioned, but only in passing, and then, revealingly enough, when bracketed with the name of Lucas Samaras. Lippard observed that Hesse's "black, bound organs" offer an indication wherein "the opposition and eventual union of Eros and Thanatos is one more contradiction to be absorbed by form."[9]

During the emergence of an "Eccentric Abstraction" the abstract-sexual legacy of Oldenburg had been transmuted by the free acceptance of natural forces as well as by an idiosyncratic employment of a formalist bias. This is especially evident in the *Metronomic Irregularities,* one version of which was included in the *Eccentric Abstraction* exhibition. It is clear that from 1966 on Eva Hesse was at pains to answer to the total style of Minimalism. The notebooks begin to record exact mathematical notations, axioms, and definitions. Ultimately these notations will supply her with a repertoire of titles, just as earlier her notes filled with biological and genetic phraseology, had provided the names of many "eccentric" works. Transposing notions of graph, seriality, modularity, and checkerboard structure, Hesse, in the *Metronomic Irregularities,* for example, acted as if she were eviscerating a three-dimensional tic-tac-toe board placing diagrammatic figures one beside the other and then, as if sewing or threading, determining rational junctures for hanging the boards together. This decision combines the firmness of Minimalist ontology with the erratic inconsistency of eccentric interconnection, an impression facilitated by the cotton-covered wires which act as the threading agent.

Hesse's serialist presentations were often string-wrapped semispheric reliefs, first realized in the important *Ishtar* of 1965 (fig. 10), from which dangled at each mound's center, a length of line: the erotic abstraction of the earlier breastlike configurations treated in a protomodular sequence. Such reliefs were worked out in numerous geometrical drawings which emphasized circles deployed one beside the other in grid formation. This kind of delicate drawing continued throughout the remainder of her life, although in the last year the elements are much enlarged and handled more brusquely.[10]

Eva Hesse's drawing during 1966–68 emphasized modular and grid arrangements alluding, in this way, to the high regard in which Agnes Martin was held, although the delicacy of wash application in Hesse's serial composition—as well as the single motif in isolation—equally refers to the target figure in the Jasper Johns encaustic paintings of the mid-1950s.

The controlled gradations of gray in this moment correspond in the artist's mind to an absurdist view of the world—an absurdness of the kind she admitted to experiencing in the work of, among others, Duchamp, Johns, and Andre, an absurdness which had been corroborated by the events of her life. It is tragically ironic, for example, that as a child, Hesse had been destined for German extermination camps, and in 1965 had found her first public there. This kind of world view is expressed throughout an exchange in a taped interview made during a three-day remission in the artist's last days, when Hesse was both aware of her rank as an artist and that her life was draining from her, perhaps the most tragic irony of all. "If something is absurd," she said, "it is much more exaggerated, much more absurd if it's repeated."[11]

The *Eccentric Abstraction* phase is a fertile period, dominated by such masterpieces as *Ennead* and *Hang Up* (fig. 11), the two works which gained in prestige for having been reproduced and exhibited widely. The meandering lengths of string in the *Ennead* refer to a numerical system, an ennead, a term derived from Greek to indicate groups of nine elements, although it also has a subordinate meaning relating to the mythology of the ancients. Moreover, the name carries with it an aural association with the name of Aeneas, Virgil's hero. The confused skeining of gravity-tugged lines suggests his wanderings. But, of course, the primary experience is mathematically based on a grid structure of dark, nipplelike, buttons.

Such mythologizing inferences are not gratuitous. Several works carry classical overtones. The great *Vinculum I* of the last year specifically refers to unifying bonds or links and to the bracketing symbol of compound qualities in a mathematical expression. But it also carries with it the forceful name of Vulcan smashing at his forge and the idea of the vincible (or the invincible) as well. *Laocoön* of 1966 takes the name of the Trojan priest whose warnings against the wooden horse of the Greeks went unheaded, and who was strangled with his sons by the avenging serpents of Athena and Apollo. *Ishtar* of 1965, with its ten double rows of hemispheres ranging from light to dark gray with each dome dangling a length of cord from its center, takes its name from a multibreasted mother goddess of Babylonian worship, the Aphrodite of the Ephesians.

Hesse's journals intersperse mathematical and mythological information, recorded because it corresponded to real working problems. She is an artist for whom the title of the work is deeply considered and exactly to the point.

Ennead was a central achievement for the artist.

It started out perfectly symmetrical at the top and everything was perfectly planned. The strings were gradated in color as well as the board from which they came. Yet it ended up in a jumble of strings. . . . The strings were very soft and each came from one of the circles. Although I wove the strings equally in the back (in the back of the piece you can see how equal they are) and it could be "arranged" to be perfect, since they are all the same length, as soon as they started falling down they went different ways and as they got further to the ground the more chaotic they got.[12]

But the chaos came to be valued as it determined the style of much of the last year's work with its sense of arrested clotting and insect-flight webwork such as we find in *Right After.*

Dearer to Hesse than the *Ennead* was *Hang Up.* The artist identified it as "the most important early statement I made. It was the first time my idea of absurdity of extreme feeling came through."

> It was a huge piece, six feet by seven feet. The construction is really very naive, it is a frame, ostensibly, and it sits on the wall with a very thin, strong but easily bent, rod that comes out of it. The frame is all cord and rope. It's all tied up like a hospital bandage—as if someone broke an arm. The whole thing is absolutely rigid, neat cord around the entire thing. . . . It is extreme and that is why I like it and don't like it. It's so absurd to have that long thin metal rod coming out of that structure. And it comes out a lot, about ten or eleven feet out, and what is it coming out of? It is coming out of this frame, something and yet nothing and—oh, more absurdity!!—it's very, very finely done. The colors on the frame were carefully gradated from light to dark—the whole thing is ludicrous. It is the most ridiculous structure I have ever made and that is why it is really good. It has a kind of depth or soul or absurdity or life or meaning or feeling or intellect that I want to get. . . . I know there is nothing unconnected in this world, but if art can stand by itself, these were really alone and there was no one doing anything like that at the time.[13]

The work was, as well, the focus of a long description in a New York Letter in which Lucy Lippard further commented on the issues of the *Eccentric Abstraction* exhibition:

> Eva Hesse's gray sculptures depart from a . . . fanaticism that has absorbed rather than been conquered by a strong formal sense . . . Her most impressive work is *Hang Up,* an empty six-foot "frame" on the wall, from which emerges a huge narrow loop. Both elements are tightly wrapped, or bandaged, in cloth or cord, and graded, not obviously, from a very light gray at the upper left corner of the frame and a near black toward the right or the loop. Free and confined, regular and irregular, rectangular and unmanageable, the components exist in a peculiar idiosyncratic space. There is a yearning quality of suppression and release as well as pathos and humor to this strange relief that should reach a broad audience.[14]

Despite the biomorphic inferences in Hesse's work she did come to grips with the Minimalist issue—but in a highly peculiar way. Facing up to Minimalism meant that Hesse had to formulate a special view of the cube in sculpture and the square in painting. These elements, while providing a compositional type which employed modular sequences and seriality, nonetheless allowed Hesse to fashion her own vision of counter-Cubist structure. They permitted a composition in which no element functioned preferentially to any other—taste and sensibility being, in Hesse's case, always imbued with biomorphic inferences and the mark of straight natural force.[15] The solution was easy for Hesse. In the *Accession* series of 1967 (fig. 12)—"Accession, increased by something added," she once noted in the "art-notes" —Hesse turned to the conventional cube of Minimalism (cf. LeWitt's modular frames, Smith's hollow *Die,* Andre's daislike platforms or Serra's one-ton lead squares). In the first *Acces-*

sion, Hesse built a galvanized steel frame—this solution is closest to LeWitt (fig. 13)—and laced the five faces up from the base with plastic tubing leaving the uppermost face open. The interior loops were then slashed on the inside in a manner similar to the way that woolen loops are clipped in the manufacture of hooked rugs producing a tactile cube, bumpy yet smooth on the exterior, but brushy within where the cut tubing still projected (fig. 14). The tactile discovery was important and the artist repeated it three times, employing a casing of fiberglass from which the plastic tubing extruded in the subsequent versions. "That huge box I did in 1967, I called it *Accession*. I did it first in metal, then in fiberglass. Outside it takes the form of a square, a perfect square and the outside is very clear. The inside, however, looks amazingly chaotic, although it is the same piece of hose going through . . . It's too beautiful, like a gem, and too right."[16]

Even in Hesse's most serialized conceptions it was the sense of the hand, of making and doing, which took precedence. Compared to more purely theoretical Minimalists ("Solipsists" Mel Bochner called them[17])—LeWitt, Judd, Morris—Hesse's version of seriality and modularity appears more playful, even "incorrect." The smaller pieces often seem little more than primitive checkerboards, games, childlike counting exercises quite unlike the metal and plexiglass monuments which we take to be the shining examples of Minimalism during its sway (fig. 15). In Hesse's work structural continuity is often disguised, rendered insensible despite the serialization. A key work is *Expanded Expansion* of 1969, in which fiberglass and rubberized cheesecloth—industrial materials which allow for the mark of the hand—permit a variation even though each of the elements or screens which compose it is fixed to the other. "I think what confuses people in a piece like this is that it's so silly and yet it is made fairly well. Its ridiculous quality is contradicted by its definite concern about its presentation."[18]

Such spatial concerns, curtainlike possibilities and serial hints remain as well in the rubberized fiberglass work called *Contingent* (fig. 16), shown at the Finch College assembly *Art in Process IV,* held in the winter of 1969 and reproduced on the cover of *Artforum* in May 1970. Writing about the effect that this work had on him, Philip Leider, then the editor of the magazine, observed that it was "probably the only piece in the exhibit that had nothing to scream about, no manifesto to adhere to and no theory to back it. It is Abstract Expressionist sculpture of a higher order than I would have thought possible, an inspiration that I would not have thought available to a younger artist. Her work struck me as being as stumbling and as deeply felt, as expressive and as inchoate as, say, a work like Pollock's *She Wolf.*"[19]

"Sickness" broke the hold of Minimalism and opened Hesse to a more sublime vision, one freed of local theory. It induced the most extreme reaches of Eva Hesse's work. Masterpieces dominate the last year. With the exception of the two versions of *Vinculum,* I think Leider was right in noting that the last phase of Hesse was one which was essentially Abstract Expressionist in its larger premises. Whereas *Vinculum I,* in which unified stretcherlike supports of fiberglass rectangles continue

Minimalist seriality, the most expressive work of Hesse at this time deals with a skeining and intertwining of forms, that in some measure recalls the Abstract Expressionist sculpture of wire and metal tubing made by Claire Falkenstein of the mid-1950s through the early 1960s.[20]

The prototype of Contingent and its eight-part mock-up were included in the Finch College exhibition. Between the execution of the work and its viewing in the winter, Eva Hesse had succumbed to the effects of a tumor discovered to be growing in her brain. A suite of operations began. She was able, however, to attend the opening festivities of the exhibition in December of 1969. "Anyway, did go to Finch— and it was an opening and I was told how great my piece was. I enjoyed myself despite feeling lousy," she noted in the manuscript describing the course of her disease and hospitalization. She also read the ambitious statement she had contributed to the catalogue concerning the Contingent series. In it she describes the experience of going beyond Postminimalism, beyond the local style, beyond art. Her words are only paralleled by the vision of art that was experienced by the first generation of Abstract Expressionists. Anyone who has studied Newman's "The Sublime is Now," Clyfford Still's confession in which he describes the discovery of an art devoid of any distorting premise of Western culture or Ad Reinhardt's statements regarding an iconic art of total placelessness, must be struck by the similarity of voice in Eva Hesse's statement.

> . . . not painting, not sculpture . . .
> I remember I wanted to get to non art, non connotive,
> non anthropomorphic, non geometric, non nothing,
> everything, but of another kind, vision, sort.
> from a total other reference point. is
>   it possible?
> I have learned anything is possible. I know that.
> that vision or concept will come through
>   total risk,
>   freedom, discipline.
> I will do it.
> . . . it's not the new. it is what is yet not known,
> thought, seen, touched but really what is not.
> and that is.[21]

Two options were left to Eva Hesse; one purely physical art, the other an intellectual-mystical art. The latter conjunction is startling, but it is meant in the way that Still's is a mystical-intellectual art, or more clearly, Reinhardt's.

The first option is affecting but, however astonishing the last works are, they still may fall within the purview of the organic evolution of Hesse's career. Mel Bochner is probably correct in thinking, when on seeing Connection in progress in Hesse's studio, the fiberglass over polyethylene was being worked as a kind of physical exercise, squashing, or hand-over-hand manipulation, executed largely as the physical expression still open to the artist at this time. But certainly, as he equally realizes, this is not the central issue. Much of Hesse's work of the final year was accomplished through the direction of student assistants selected from her classes at the School of Visual Arts in New York City. She was a highly admired teacher and was instrumental in formulating what might be called a "School of Visual Arts style." It first received expression in the studios of that institution and, spurred by burgeoning interest in Eva Hesse's work, was quickly absorbed into mainstream vanguardism.

Similarly the untitled work, familiarly called *7 Poles,* was not executed as an act of physical therapy. Its familiar name is revealing: Pollock's *Blue Poles* is the source. In the same way that Pollock was at last able to get past history and culture to a kind of prehistory, the ultimate stylelessness which both Pollock and Newman regarded as the equal, if not the superior of the art of "culture," so too does Hesse's *7 Poles* have the bedrock foundation of paleolithic sources.

The second option projects Abstract Expressionism "all-over" into actual space, a cosmos so to speak, an attitude realized in the *Right After* works (fig. 17). During the creation of the *Contingent* series Hesse had undergone three surgical interventions. After these she returned to a piece that had hung fire in her studio for more than a year, suddenly recognizing in it a number of possibilities that had eluded her before (fig. 18), a work resumed immediately upon her release from the hospital. "The idea totalled before I was sick. The piece was strung in my studio for a whole year . . . I wanted to totally throw myself into a vision that I would have to adjust to and learn to understand."[22]

It was while working on the rope piece that Eva Hesse gained her widest, if unaware, public as she was photographed through this work for *Life* magazine in connection with an article on Postminimalism that was called "Drip Art," acknowledging in this way the resurgence of Abstract Expressionist qualities in much of the newer painting and sculpture of 1968–70.[23]

Eva Hesse was no longer making easy or ingratiating Abstract Expressionist statements—she had moved beyond considerations of style. "The decorative is the only art sin" she once said. *Life* magazine had described the rope version of *Right After* as an unfinished work. Yet in the article Eva Hesse is quoted as saying that "this piece is very ordered . . . Chaos can be as structured as non-chaos. That we know from Jackson Pollock."

". . . I remember I wanted to get to non art, non connotive, non anthropomorphic, non geometric, non nothing, everything, but another kind of vision, sort. . . . " The voice no longer speaks to us, but beyond us. In her last year Eva Hesse discovered the sublime, another place and time at which the critic only guesses and where the historian maps only these superficial paths. She had left her Postminimalist colleagues and friends, and joined Newman, Still, Pollock, and Reinhardt.

Notes

1. From an undated pocket notebook [1964?]. This small notebook records stray hints, addresses, names as well as immediate biographical material which Eva Hesse would need to complete bureaucratic forms and the like, pertinent not only to her stay in Germany, but to her husband's stay as well.

2. "It's All Yours," *Seventeen* magazine, September 1954, p. 140. Eva Hesse's illustrations appeared on pp. 140–41 and p. 161 of the issue.

3. The manuscript is published in my "Eva Hesse: Last Words," *Artforum*, November 1972.

4. The sister of the artist who as possessor of these documents generously allowed me to study them free of any hampering stipulations.

5. *Artforum*, May 1966, p. 54.

6. These last qualities were those of Robert Rauschenberg's work of the period 1958–62, and for a European-minded American artist, Rauschenberg, who carried off the first prize at the Venice *Biennale* in 1964, would certainly be a preoccupation. The doughnutlike apertures of some of Hesse's pieces of 1965–66 point to the automobile tires of Rauschenberg's "combine paintings," the very term which Hesse had used in German—*Materialbilder*—to describe her works on the cover of the brochure for her first one-woman show.

7. The April 1966 notebook. In the same notebook, Eva Hesse once recorded as a compliment an observation made by the surrealizing and obsessive artist, Paul Thek: "He liked my work lots. Said, 'The best he's seen of eccentric fetishistic art compared to Lucas Samaras.' " These ideas are further developed in my "Rosenquist and Samaras: The Obsessive Image and Post-Minimalism."

8. The subsequent relations between the director and the artist were very close. It was at Droll's loft, in the spring of 1969, that Eva Hesse first collapsed. He saw her through her medical attentions. I am indebted to Donald Droll for facilitating my access to Hesse's private papers.

9. The essay gained a broader audience when it was republished in *Minimal Art: A Critical Anthology*, New York, Dutton, 1968, ed. Gregory Battcock. Eventually to view Hesse's work as a fusion of contradictions became the standard way of handling it critically. In the exhibition catalogue, *Anti-Illusion: Procedure/Materials* written by Marcia Tucker and James Monte for the influential exhibition of the same name held at the Whitney Museum of American Art between May and July 1969 (at which Postminimalism was awarded museological and historical prestige after a studio and gallery existence), James Monte wrote of Hesse's work in dualistic terms concluding with the observation that "whether her works are diminutive and intended to be hand-held, or made on a grand scale, her finest sculpture has a unique animus which is anthropomorphic in quality if not in intent. Her work alludes to human characteristics such as the softness of skin, the swell of muscle or the indeterminate color of flesh fading under clothing after exposure to summer sun." Distressed by a facile dualistic argument, Lawrence Alloway observed in the exhibition catalogue, *Tony Delap/Frank Gallo/Eva Hesse: Trio* (Owen-Corning Fiberglass Center, New York City, May–September 1970), that "one of our ingrained habits of thought is to arrange the world dualistically, in such pairs as right and wrong, us and them, North and South. In art, Classical and Romantic is one such pair; geometric and organic form is another. It is a sign of Hesse's originality, and to some people a cause of difficulty, that her sculptures do not conform to the latter pair. For example, the sculptures have a curious way of consisting of modular units, which, even as we recognize their repetition, become knotted and collapsed. John Perrault described her work as "surreal serialism," ["Art," *The Village Voice*, November 28, 1968] a phrase that catches very well the ceaseless play of systematic and organic elements in her work.

10. In April of 1970, while reviewing an exhibition of drawings held at the Fischbach Gallery, Hilton Kramer gathered that the works were "drawn from the structure of windows . . . all soft-focus and atmospheric, at times Whistlerian." (*The New York Times*, April 18, 1970). This return to a broader drawing style may be regarded as a reemergence of the Expressionism of her drawings seen as early as 1961 when, shortly after graduation from the Yale University School of Fine Arts, Hesse joined a three-artists' show with Donald Berry and Harold Jacobs (The John Heller Gallery, New York City, April–May 1961) at which she was represented by a set of gesturally-based drawings.

11. Cindy Nemser, "An Interview with Eva Hesse," *Artforum*, May 1970, p. 62.

12. Ibid.

13. Ibid.

14. Lucy Lippard, "An Impure Situation; New York and Philadelphia Letter," *Art International*, May 1966, p. 64. The issues dealt with in footnote 9 apply here.

15. These ideas, except for the elements of biomorphic inference and the natural force, were worked out in the modular structures of Sol LeWitt whose influence on the Minimalist movement was enormous. When given a retrospective exhibition at the Haags Gemeente Museum, July–August 1970, he honored the memory of his friend Eva Hesse by dedicating the catalogue and exhibition to her.

16. Nemser, *op. cit.*, p. 62.

17. Mel Bochner, "Serial Art Systems: Solipsism," first published in *Arts Magazine*, Summer 1967, republished in Battcock, *op. cit.*

18. Nemser, *op. cit.*, p. 62.

19. *Artforum*, February 1970, p. 70.

20. I also think that Lucio Fontana's savagely rent earthen and metal spheres of the early 1960s were an important influence on Eva Hesse. Since she spent so much time in Europe she could not have failed to be aware of his work. The fiberglass variations of *Repetition 19, III*, with its grouped and clustered scatterings, and the more chaotically organized *Tori* of 1969, made the nine bucketlike units torn on the sides seem to indicate a knowledge of Fontana.

21. Eva Hesse, a catalogue statement for *Art in Process IV*, Finch College Museum of Art, Contemporary Wing, New York City, December 1969–January 1970, n.p. Hesse's catalogue entry was transcribed from a tape recording.

22. Nemser, *op. cit.*, p. 63.

23. "Drip Art," *Life*, February 27, 1970, pp. 62–66. Lynda Benglis, Richard Van Buren and Richard Serra were also included in this photo essay.

Figure 9. Eva Hesse, Studio View, Works 1965–66
(From left to right) Untitled, 1965, Enamel painted cord over wood
or metal and hose; *Ennead,* 1966, Dyed string and papier-mâché,
36′×22″×1-1/2″; *Ingeminate,* 1965, Papier-mâché, cord, enamel
over balloons, surgical hose, 7′×11′×7′; *Vertiginous Detour,* 1966,
Enamel, rope, net plaster, 22″ ball, 40″ circumference; *Untitled,*
1966, Acrylic paint, cord over papier-mâché on wood,
7-1/2″×7-1/2′×4″; *Total Zero,* 1966, Rubber, plastic, epoxy,
acrylic, polyurethane, papier-mâché over inner tube, metal,
2′3″×2′3″×3′, destroyed; *Untitled,* 1966, Enamel paint, cord
over papier-mâché and balloon, string, 31″×26″; *Untitled,* piece
destroyed, no measurements available; *Long Life,* 1965, papier-
mâché, epoxy, cord and enamel over beach ball and hose, 20″
diameter, hose 7′, destroyed; *Untitled,* 1965, Painted iron, wood,
ca. 10′6″ high, destroyed; *Unfinished, Untitled or Not Yet,* 1966,
Nine dyed nets with weights and clear polyethylene, 72′×24″×14′.
(Photo courtesy Xavier Fourcade Gallery)

Figure 10. Eva Hesse, *Ishtar*, 1965
Wood, cord, paint, rubber, 36″ × 7-1/2″ × 2-1/2″.
(Photo courtesy Xavier Fourcade Gallery)

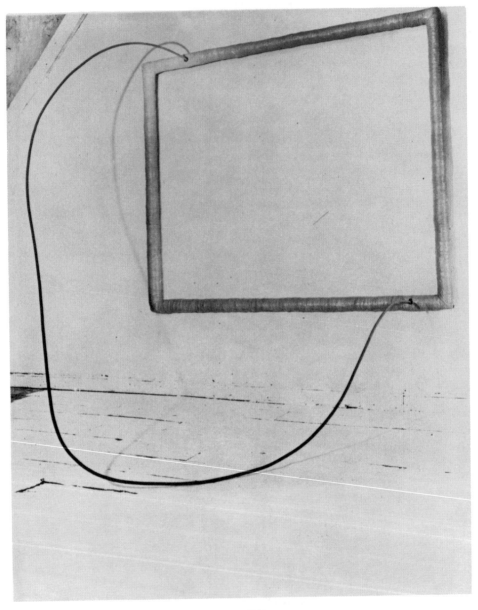

Figure 11.   Eva Hesse, *Hang Up*, 1966
Acrylic on cloth over wood and steel, 72″×84″×78″.
(Photo courtesy Xavier Fourcade Gallery)

Figure 12. Eva Hesse, *Accession*, 1967
Steel and vinyl plastic extrusion, 3'×3'×3'.
(Photo courtesy Xavier Fourcade Gallery)

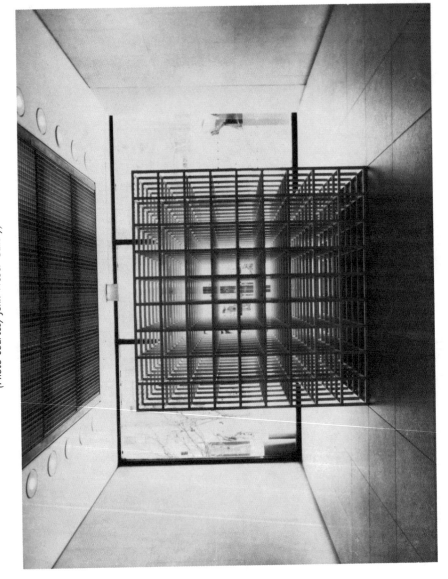

Figure 13. Sol LeWitt, *Nine Part Module Cube*, 1977
Baked enamel on aluminum, 7'2-1/2" ×7'2-1/2" ×7'2-1/2".
(Photo courtesy John Weber Gallery)

Figure 14.   Eva Hesse, *Accession II*, 1967
Detail of interior corner.
(Photo courtesy Xavier Fourcade Gallery)

Figure 15. Eva Hesse, *Iterate*, 1966
Acrylic on woodshavings, glue, string and board, 20″×20″.
(Photo courtesy Xavier Fourcade Gallery)

Figure 16.   Eva Hesse, *Contingent*, 1969
Rubberized cheesecloth, fiberglass, eight units, each ca. 14'×3'.
(Photo courtesy Xavier Fourcade Gallery)

Figure 17. Eva Hesse, *Right After*, 1969
Fiberglass hung with hooks and wires, ca. 6-1/2'×10'×15'.
(Photo courtesy Xavier Fourcade Gallery)

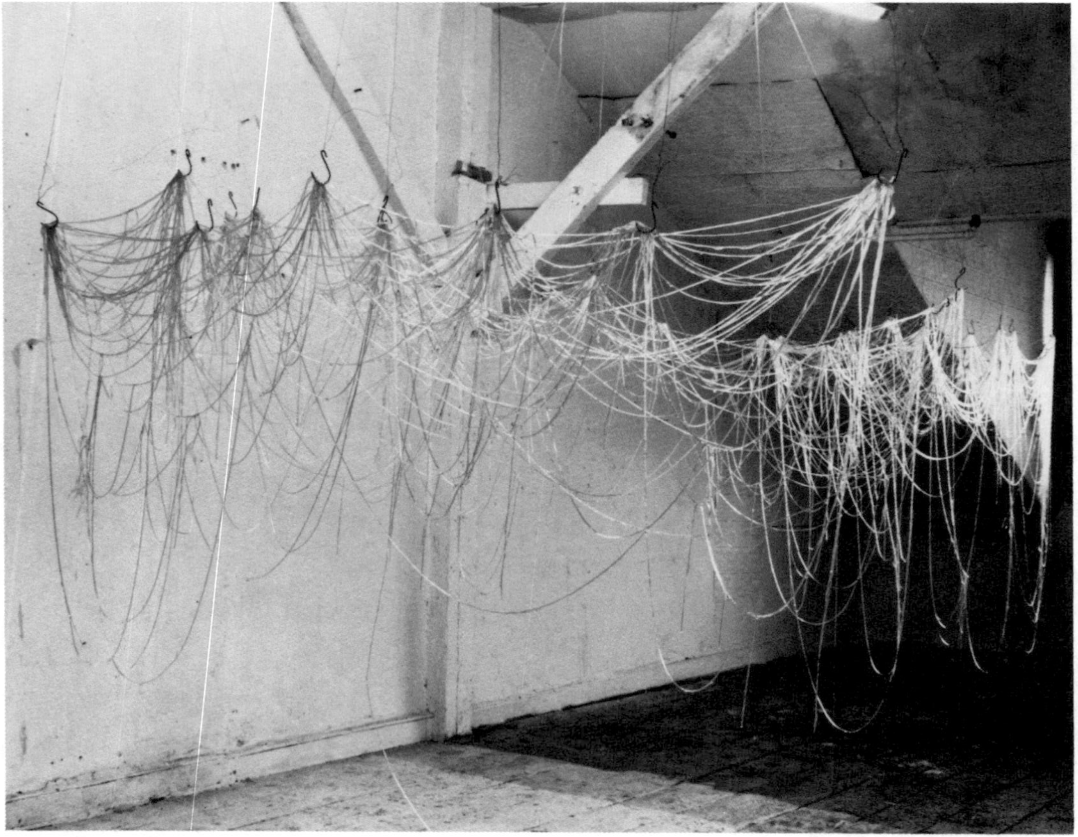

Figure 18. Eva Hesse, *Untitled (Rope)*, 1969
Latex over rope, string, wire, 12'x10-1/2'x7-1/2'.
(Photo courtesy Xavier Fourcade Gallery)

The Art of Richard Tuttle

In 1967 Richard Tuttle dyed a group of irregularly shaped and hemmed canvas octagons in various pots of Tintex. Shortly thereafter, when they had dried and had been hand smoothed, they were limply pinned to the wall or laid upon the floor (fig. 19). It did not matter much in which way they were hung or where on the floor they were spread. (Exhibition photographs taken of the works are inscribed on the back "to be held any way.") The issue at hand was not primarily about figure/ground relationships (an extenuation of Jean Arp's collages "arranged according to the laws of chance"); nor were Tuttle's octagons simply still more artifacts in a long line of Dada-inspired work, although their roots in Dada, and in Arp particularly, cannot be denied.

Serious criticism attempted to locate Tuttle among those artists interested in confounding divisions between sculpture and painting. He was thought of as fusing painting and sculpture into a new polymorph in which sheer tangibility and blunt materiality alluded to sculpture while the character of soaked-in-paint bespoke painting. Some writers assumed that Tuttle derived from an aspect of field painting as it was then known in the work of Frankenthaler, Louis, Noland and Olitski.

One critic, Emily Wasserman, attempted more. In addition to recognizing Tuttle's relationship to field painting, she also referred to an evolution out of the artist's earlier wooden reliefs and indicated in which way Tuttle's peculiar hermeticism—"withdrawn" she said—differed from other equally oblique and factual artists, in particular Brice Marden, David Novros, Don Judd and Carl Andre. In Tuttle's work she observed "a concern for the sensuous and for a kind of chromatic fantasy . . . which are levelly denied by the work and thinking of his colleagues."[1]

For my part, I prefer to regard Tuttle's work in terms of its own organic evolution and the artist's personal experiences. Tuttle was born in Rahway, New Jersey, in 1941. His paternal line traces American roots to the early 17th century. The Tuttles had come here to be small land-owners and originally cultivated farms near where Trinity Church now stands. Some Tuttles prospered. Others, like the artist's branch, did not. Richard Tuttle grew up in Roselle, New Jersey, "a rather poor town," the

This article originally appeared in *Artforum*, February 1970.

second son of four children. He went to Roselle High, part of a class that was unusual only because it was "brighter than most." The family was conservative. His grandmother, on his father's side, set a family tone of fundamentalist Presbyterianism. The artist's grandfather was "something of a dilettante who wrote, drew and experimented." He would make gifts of his drawings to his grandchildren on the condition that they would continue a square-to-square grid enlargement with which the drawing would be accompanied and which had already been begun. At length, Tuttle got to college, Trinity College, Hartford, an Episcopalian school in which the artist found "little outlet for doing any creative work." During Tuttle's student days an exhibition at the Wadsworth Atheneum in Hartford, called "Black, White, and Grey," made a deep impression on the student, as did Agnes Martin, who had gone up to the museum to speak in connection with the exhibition. Shortly thereafter, Tuttle contacted Agnes Martin in New York to ask whether he might purchase one of her drawings. This inquiry marked the beginning of an important friendship. The highly ascetic, Minimalist persuasion of Martin's work is curious to admit in Tuttle at the time, although there may be the dim memory of grandfather's grids in all of this.

Very little remains from Tuttle's student days. He designed sets for student productions of *End Game, Zoo Story* and *American Dream.* (The emphasis on Edward Albee is partly explained by the fact that the author is an alumnus of Trinity.) Tuttle also designed two senior yearbooks. In examining *The Trinity Ivy* of 1963, the year Tuttle graduated and enlisted in the Air Force, one is struck by the nervous and delicate wood-block illustrations; several are full page. They deal in landscape ideas— vortices of solar energy and softer views of streams and border shrubbery. The wood-block illustrations have an expressionizing nostalgia to them that is widespread in semi-abstraction, a nostalgia that is perhaps at odds with the detachment of the cloth octagons—except, perhaps, for the latter's depressed, washed-out range of color.

Tuttle's experience with the Air Force exteriorized a break with the past and the mature person suddenly emerges from this episode. Tuttle describes a training that lasted six weeks. Three were spent as an underclassman, three as an upperclassman. The latter's duties included assisting in the "indoctrination" of the underclassmen. Training was completed by undergoing a machine-scored examination, the answers to which, in Tuttle's view, were "perfect median responses."

After "indoctrination" it was unimaginable to score below 80 although a person of military aptitude might score as high as 83. "I blew the machine. I did it on purpose. I got 2. I was everything for the authorities. Catatonic. They said I never could enter military or civilian employment for the rest of my life." At the end of six weeks of training Tuttle was honorably discharged. He was 22. He returned to New York and found modest employment as an assistant at the Betty Parsons Gallery, where he earned enough on which to subsist and still provide sufficient time to work on his painting.

Between 1963 and 1965 Tuttle began to construct things, "often little things, such as 3-inch paper cubes that fit neatly into the palm of your hand." The paper cubes stressed issues of incision, slotting, folding and cutting—of constructing—but with an oddly infant-like thrust to them quite different from the small, colored celluloid cubes of Lucas Samaras, which were shown during the same period at the now defunct Green Gallery. The 1965 wooden reliefs continued to explore these issues but exaggerated their consciously infantile quotient. The constructions were hollow, perhaps two inches thick. The reliefs were essentially ideograms of landscape or nature, treated in slightly amorphous contours and painted in single colors. They were supported by a nail which entered the work through a small hole in the back. The natural shorthand of the shapes—*Hill, Torso, Water, Fire*—were painted the blunt coloristic equivalent of the sense of the piece. *Water* was blue, *Fire* red, *Hill* grey and so on. In addition to their Arp-like qualities, the pieces also resembled the elements of a child's fitted jigsaw puzzle—large, squat, simplified shapes. The pieces were exhibited at the Betty Parsons Gallery in September, 1965 and several of the works were laid directly on the floor, the most extreme option open to contemporary sculpture working against the tradition of vertical monolith.

Of the motifs, perhaps *Hill* is the most important. It describes a single, rainbow-like arc on the wall. A drawing of 1963, *Elephant*, nervously depicts the arc of a vast and possibly protective elephantine mound or hump. This work is still drawn in terms of the delicate Trinity wood blocks, although its ritualizing "feel" is quite new in Tuttle's work.

The relationship of the 1965 ideogrammatic reliefs to the immensely important sculptural attitudes that were emerging in the 1960s is, of curse, of greater moment. Constructivist practice—the attitude whereby the method of affixing element to element takes precedence over all other considerations in the execution of a work—first arose in Picasso's Synthetic Cubist assemblages of still-life material in 1912–14. The intellectual artists of the Russian Revolution elevated this attitude into a style that came itself to be known as Constructivism. However remarkable the accruings possible to carving and modeling, Constructivist practice made evident the unmodernity of these earlier sculptural attitudes. It was not until the late 1950s and early '60s that a viable alternative to Constructivism came into being, without, it is evident, supplanting it. It is a practice which receives its predicates from pictorial issues, from painting. There are numerous aspects of this radical option. There are, for example, sculptures which take on the color, texture and even the evanescence of painting and collage—Keith Sonnier's, for example. Even more important than this, for Tuttle's work, is the kind of pictorializing sculpture which results when the depicted contour and the real contour of an image are congruent. This may take a representational form—a Flag by Johns—or a non-representational one—a lacquered plank by John McCracken. Such a pictorializing sculptural option—in part the result of Pop, in part the result of Minimalism—corresponds to the ideogrammatic reliefs of Tuttle. Of course there had been antecedents. One of the reasons that Arp is once more so highly esteemed is that his painted wooden reliefs, particularly those made through the 1920s, articulate a similar attitude.[2] The substantive alignment of Tuttle's reliefs of 1965 with the critical sculptural issues of the early 1960s are striking and important. But, in themselves, I find the reliefs facile and disappointing. History, however, inaugurates a kind of *force majeure* and after the experience of the cloth octagons, and now the paper ones, the ideogrammatic reliefs, wall hung, unitary, displaceable at the possessor's discretion, theoretically appear more interesting. Hindsight has added much, particularly with regard to the issues which are still being argued in the cloth and paper pieces. As Tuttle told me, "I started out making thick wood pieces and they got thinner and thinner. They turned into cloth. And now I am doing paper."

I recently visited the artist in his midtown West Side studio, an anonymous neighborhood for New York, nowhere. The studio occupies the top floor of a tenement. It is painted a dingy white and is largely empty except for essentials, a table, a chair. Books and food are stored in the same cupboard.

The cloth and the (newer) paper octagons may be affixed limply to the wall, like garments, and they share formal concerns with the work of Sonnier and Robert Morris. They have less in common with Robert Ryman, with whose work one might be tempted at first to compare them. Ryman's papers emphasize surface; their white brushed surfaces reiterate the nature of the wall and the two-dimensionality of the whole undertaking. In the newer Rymans the urge toward seriality has been replaced by other methods which still conform to emphasizing the nature of the wall-like surface, such as brushing around the square module so that the square shape is negatively expressed by the removal of the square template. There may be some affiliation, however, in the use of masking tape. These support the recent Rymans and they are the necessary, though hidden, support of Tuttle's paper octagons.

The octagons had been cut one after the other. Tuttle considered each new one an improvement over the last. He remembered the sequence. The earlier ones tended to have a more pronounced symmetry and axiality, a familiarness. One could easily suppose which part of the octagon was the bottom. It tended to have longer sides. It was heavier. The later octagons were more eccentric, employing greater numbers of variegated lengths to the sides and more unanticipated interior angles.

"The later ones are better," said Tuttle.

"I don't know if I agree with you, although I admit that they are less familiar."

"I would like to make all six octagons the same. But I'll never do that."

On the mantelpiece of a closed fireplace of what is now the kitchen lay a thin piece of wood through which many nails had carefully been driven, their exposed points spelling TUTTLE.

"Are you going to perforate your signature?"

"I was thinking about it."

"Do you sign pieces?"

"Signing is equal to destroying the piece. It is no longer a piece of paper. It violates its purity. Here, I'll show you." Tuttle wrote his name with a felt-tip pen large across the face of one of the paper octagons.

"Purity" seems, in large measure, to be a function of the viewer rather than of the work. "They (the papers) set the limits of a person's appreciation. They are disposable and not disposable. Even Rembrandts are disposable. It all depends on the limits of a person's appreciation."

In the end, even the purity of the white paper is questionable. "I have a hatred for this white thing. I can't stand the kind of purity that white implies in our environment. But the kind of purity that comes out of the complete electrical functioning of the whole human being—that's the kind of purity I aspire to. To be free of senses and the intellect. I would really like to be ignorant." The Zen overtones in these sentiments are not incidental. After the success of his cloth exhibition, Tuttle went to Japan for a year, visiting the villages rather than the major cities. He plans to return this year; the two books on his mantelpiece were a Japanese-English dictionary and a Japanese grammar. He does not encourage, however, a description of his own artistic ambitions in terms of his involvement in Oriental attitudes. "Any conceptions that Americans can have about Oriental ideas are really still about their own ideas. . . . "

I had copied some inscriptions that Tuttle had made on working drawings for the cloth octagons. One read, "This is a working drawing of a more or less isometric house which made an empty house . . . only seven sides." Another read, "This is a drawing which ended the drawing of the work; the idea came out later in an eight side dull red piece."

"That was a joke," said Tuttle. "They were drawn after the pieces were made. The drawings showed me what I didn't want to know."

Notes

1. Emily Wasserman, "Richard Tuttle," *Artforum*, March 1968, pp. 56–7. Several important catalogs credit me with this perspicacious review. The catalogs *Live In Your Head, When Attitudes Become Form*, Kunsthalle; Bern, March–April 1969, and *Anti-Illusion: Procedures/Materials*, Whitney Museum, 1969, are in error in this respect.

2. Tuttle acknowledges his debt to Arp although he notes that he became aware of Arp only after the reliefs had been made. This cannot deny the derivation, however, since Arp's attitudes have long been subsumed into wide artistic consciousness. Tuttle, therefore, could have assimilated Arp's thinking from thousands of sources, not one of them being Arp himself. Moreover, the Arps at the Museum of Modern Art were known to Tuttle even if he had not thought about them especially.

   There is still another art of the early 1960s to which Tuttle's bears striking resemblance, although in this case it is highly probable that Tuttle was unaware of it. I refer to the singularly important and neglected *Concetti Spaziali* of Lucio Fontana, particularly those reliefs whose surface is but little scored, or lacerated. Fontana was shown at the Martha Jackson Gallery in 1961 although he had been widely exhibited in Europe, with a long career played out in Italy, although he had been born in Argentina. And the similarity of Tuttle's work to that of Ellsworth Kelly is beyond dispute, a connection perhaps emphasized by Agnes Martin's historical association with Kelly when they and several other artists shared an old loft building at Coenties Slip in the late 1950s.

Figure 19.   Richard Tuttle, *Cloth Octagons*, 1967
Ca. 54″ diameter.

Bruce Nauman:
Another Kind of Reasoning

Generally, they were pieces of rubber shower caps, which I cut up and glued together and which had no special shape. At the end of each piece there were strings that one attached to the four corners of the room. Then, when one came in the room, one couldn't walk around, because of the strings! The length of the strings could be varied; the form was ad libitum. That's what interested me. This game lasted three or four years, but the rubber rotted, and it disappeared.

Marcel Duchamp (in conversation with Pierre Cabanne)

Bruce Nauman's career has been based almost exclusively in California. A lack of vigorous firsthand acquaintance with this ambience has made me acutely conscious of—though not necessarily sympathetic to—certain Californian qualities, which I often sense as outlandish. The central Californian characteristic seems to me to be a pervading narcissism expressed through mirroring and colorism predicated in a technically oriented automotive culture and a geographical metaphor. I think this originates and has been intensified by the comparative smallness of the scene, a feature which has tended to a stylistic inbreeding. This is a quality, not necessarily pejorative, historically noted in all regional art centers. It can be said as easily of London art today as of Dutch art at the height of the de Stijl movement.

The chief distinction separating the arts of the two seaboards, at least through the end of the 1960s, appears to be between an art concerned with the *characterological* functionings of its *creators* (California) and the *morphological* processes of *creation* (New York). Tersely, the distinction is between "being" and "doing." Despite the broadness of this distinction, it permits one to close in on Nauman, who, if nothing else, stresses confession, autobiography, and narcissism—certainly in the work after 1966, when Nauman's art seems or seemed primarily to be about the artist's ability to reconstruct himself before an audience. Such a theatrical intention is congruent in many respects with those episodes that have been variously named Process, Phenomenological (Marcia Tucker once punned "pheNAUMAN-

This article originally appeared in *Artforum*, Feburary 1972.

ology") or Conceptual art, and which I group under the umbrella term Postminimalism. But in Nauman's case it is essentially a received art, stemming from Marcel Duchamp and given vitally important refurbishment in the work of Jasper Johns, in whose tradition Nauman continued to be nourished, at least through the end of 1969.

Fidel Danieli, a California critic who wrote the first intelligent article on Nauman, observed that Nauman's work "would appear at first exposure to be a vaguely repulsive caprice."[1] Danieli also affiliated Nauman to Marcel Duchamp (the *Green Box*) and to Jasper Johns (the *Skin Print* drawings). He recognized that Nauman was not above a certain duplicity, citing as an example of "cheating" the knees referred to in the *Wax Block with the Impressions of the Knees of Five Famous Artists*, 1966, which the critic knew to be impressions of the artist's own knees. Nor was Danieli deceived by the arch double-dealing of the title, a problem to which I will return. In a like manner, the romantic and mystical stance of the banners and neons (e.g., "The artist is an amazing luminous fountain"), were seen for what they were, namely "being poetical in a beautiful, self-flattering way."

Subsequent criticism seems to have consistently stressed the theme of Nauman's relation to Duchamp and Johns. In a statement by the artist published in the catalogue *American Sculpture of the Sixties* (Los Angeles County Museum, 1967), Nauman also recognized a derivation in Dadaism:

> I suppose some work has to do in part with some of the things that the Dadaists and the Surrealists did. I like to give the pieces elaborate titles the way they did, although I've only been titling them recently. That all came from not trying to figure out why I make those things. It got so I just couldn't do anything. So like making the impressions of knees in a wax block . . . was a way of having a large rectangular solid with marks in it so *I had to make this other kind of reasoning. It also had to do with trying to make a less important thing to look at.* (Italics mine)

After 1966 that "other kind of reasoning" accelerated toward the art object invested with extraformal meaning on the basis of the *title as pun*, for example, *Henry Moore Bound to Fail* (1967). As a literary formula the pun is a loaded area of intellectual experience for, as Duchamp knew, the circularity of the pun appears to provide information without getting you anywhere. Toby Mussman correctly observed in his study of Duchamp's film *Anemic Cinema* (made in conjunction with Man Ray) that "puns, unlike ordinary sentences, do not attempt to make a definite statement but rather they cast ironic doubt on the ability of any written sentence to make ultimate and absolutely conclusive sense."[2]

Reactions to Nauman's punning ranged from the positive ("we all secretly enjoy that hideous sinking sensation engendered by a really bad pun")[3] to the negative ("the most vexing portion of Mr. Nauman's work is related to his ingenuous literary punning").[4] A middle road is possible: "If one accepts the title on the level of poetic commentary, a debate arises as to whether the artist is pure and naive, or a witty and sophisticated literate. My experience favors an amalgam."[5] The works that led to these reactions were a set of color photographs in which the artist was seen performing such elementary activities as *Eating My Words*. In this instance the word "words" had been literally shaped out of bread and was being eaten. Similarly, *Waxing Hot* depicted the artist literally waxing the letters of the word "Hot." The photograph *Feet of Clay* depicts the artist's feet literally covered over with clay pellets. The images, therefore, have been given "meaning" and "recognizability" by fusing them to a cliché. The model for such an activity is obviously Marcel Duchamp. For example, *With My Tongue in My Cheek*, an assemblage relief of 1959 and a self-portrait, combines a drawn profile of the artist with a plaster cast of the artist's jaw. Similarly, Nauman's green wax piece, *From Hand to Mouth* (the color and substance deriving from Johns' early encaustic *Green Target*) is a cast of the right hand, arm, shoulder, throat, jaw, and lips of the artist's former wife (fig. 20).

Another work of 1967 presents the artist's crossed arms cast in green wax, from whose severed biceps there emerges a heavy rope tied into a square knot. Although untitled, the verbal/visual interplay of the work turns on the following equation: as the arms are folded so is the rope knotted, or vice versa. In short, the rope and arms are permutations of the same knotted condition: they are tied in knots. In addition to the obvious relationship to Johns in terms of the cast elements of these works, they are also distinctly Johns-like in terms of the work's insistent proliferation of the *same* thing projected into a *different* state, diagrammatic or otherwise. Johns' celebrated *Ballantine Ale Cans*, 1962, one a cast and the other modeled by hand, is a well-known example of this kind of pairing. Nauman also stated in the catalogue quote from *American Sculpture of the Sixties* that part of his effort was directed toward making "a less important thing to look at." I take this to reflect an active indifference to the issues of reductivist abstraction as they were then being explored and a desire to make works which would *obviously* have no relevance to the solemn earnestness, for example, of Minimalist sculpture then at its apogee.

From 1965 on one sees a hyperbolic attempt on Nauman's part to create forms never before seen, made of substances and colored in ways equally unknown.[6] I do not quarrel with the aspiration; it is the very fiber of art. But the quest, though stated and perhaps even "felt" in these exalted terms, is equally arbitrary notwithstanding the fact that between 1965 and 1967, Nauman came close to realizing such an ambition. The forms which Nauman took to making at the time were spindly affairs, loaflike and split into arching rails. They were of two kinds, soft and hard; the soft group was made of colored rubber latex and the hard cast in fiberglass. The works give off an aura of undernourishment and eccentricity. In many respects these "impoverished" works, supported directly by the wall and floor, anticipate many of the experiments associated with the rise of Postminimalism—particularly the early rubber and neon work of Richard Serra—a history which I have attempted to write in my essays on Richard Serra, Keith Sonnier, and Eva Hesse. I would be hard put not to acknowledge the seminal role played by Nauman's untitled rubber, fiberglass, and neon works in redirecting the nature of artistic aspiration in the late 1960s.

In November 1966, Nauman figured prominently in an exhibition held in New York's Fischbach Gallery called "Eccentric Abstraction," which represented the real surfacing of this counter-Minimalist taste in the gallery context. Works by Keith Sonnier and Eva Hesse were included among others. The exhibition was organized and introduced by the critic Lucy Lippard, who undertook to clarify "an aspect of visceral identification that is hard to escape, an identification that psychologists have called 'body ego'."[7] Lippard was referring to the capacity of the viewer to empathetically respond to unfamiliar forms in visceral terms. Yet the term "body ego" suggests another possibility—that a work may be the means whereby the artist employs his body or sections thereof, his lineaments, his personal possessions, or even his name, and in so doing transforms himself into a self-exploitable tool or the raw material or artistic presentation (fig. 21). He becomes, in a certain sense, his own *objet trouvé*—hence narcissistic. The term "body ego" certainly poses the possibility of this interpretation in Nauman's work after 1967, although Lippard's introduction was written on the basis of the earlier untitled fiberglass pieces, which she regarded as vehicles "unconcerned with conventional manipulation of forms in space and more involved with a perverse, sometimes bizarre expansion of the limits of art."

Such "expansions" obviously posit formlessness as a structural possibility, a condition recorded in Nauman's photographs of patted mounds of flour on the studio floor. Another counterpart would be the *Composite Photo of Two Messes on the Studio Floor* (1967). The affiliation of these works with Marcel Duchamp's *Elevage de Poussière*, a photograph taken in 1920 by Man Ray of *The Large Glass*, which had been lying flat and gathering dust in Duchamp's New York studio, is inescapable. The works are alike in that they refer to insubstantial and amorphous substances. It is of larger critical interest, however, that they exist at several removes from the original, the "real" works having been replaced by photographs, which are, or have become by default, the central document of the experience, hence the central emotional repository of the works. It is obvious that with Nauman the "real" or "original" work had all along been an auxiliary effort. The shift away from an original by whatever means—photography, cinematography, tape recording, private journals, notations, memos, or ultimately merely the unexecuted idea or conception, allied to a valorization of the technological, cognitive, mental, or other processes—is the chief characteristic of Nauman's work. This most clearly identifies him as a founder of the Conceptualist movement, a Postminimalist episode which is, in Nauman's expression of it, Dada in spirit.

The lateral spread of the *Composite Photo of Two Messes on the Studio Floor* is assembled in a manner similar to an aerial reconnaissance map. In this way it resembles a work called *Composite Photo of My Name as Though It Were Written on the Surface of the Moon*, which appears as if a repeatedly beamed electronic signal forming the letters of Nauman's first name had bounced off the moon and returned to earth at constant intervals. The work is predicated on dubbing, on christening, and though the similarity to Duchamp's "Readymades" may appear tenuous the connection is still discernible. Duchamp's investment of artistic identity in a neutral common object (a snow shovel or a bottle rack) was also in part based on a kind of baptism, on arrant say so. As the snow shovel and the bottle rack were Duchamp's "Readymades," so is Nauman's first name his "Readymade." Nauman's name, of course, is subjected to a complex alteration whereas Duchamp's "Readymades" were scarcely adjusted, if at all. Each individual letter of the name Bruce is arbitrarily repeated, similar to the repetitions of the *Six Inches of My Knee Extended to Six Feet,* or any of the duplications of measurements and sections taken from the artist's body. Perhaps the most striking alterations occur in the neon work, which fudges the script of Nauman's *Last Name Exaggerated Fourteen Times Vertically* (fig. 22).[8] In the latter work, the legibility is all but obliterated by the vertical scaling and one reads the name Nauman as a neon gesture. The title serves, in most of his neon pieces, to "explain" or to "justify." In short, it is at this moment, when Nauman comes more and more to rely on technological sources, that Duchamp begins to fade as a central preoccupation. Now, with the overwhelming dependence on technological recording devices, Nauman's art announces its entire reliance on behavioral theory.

No single work is more characteristic of Nauman's use of extraformal, verbal tactics than the two steel wedges of 1968 (see fig. 40); they are inscribed:

$$\frac{\text{LIKE}}{\text{KEIL}} \quad \text{and} \quad \frac{\text{WEDGE}}{\text{KEIL}}$$

The word play is facetious. The German word for wedge is *Keil.* A rearrangement of the letters of this word spell out the English word "like." Therefore the wedge *form* is equated with the German word "wedge," the anagram of the English word "like," or the same word as the first *Like:* punning or palindromic circularity. Moreover, the wedge shape is easily understood to be a phallic symbol into which a lentilshaped chamfer has been grooved, a vaginal symbol. This additional sexual orchestration may derive from the sexual and poetic object of Duchamp's late work, *Coin de Chasteté,*[9] of 1951, in which a wedge has been pressed into dental plastic (see fig. 39). The verbal fixation of such exercises is linked to Duchamp, from the quasi-pornographic caption of *LHOOQ (elle a chaud au cul),* or "Mona Lisa's Moustache" as it is popularly called, to the punning titles such as *Anemic Cinema.* This kind of closed and perfect verbal/visual decoction leads to a chain of equally absurd neutral elements. Such verbal/visual puns are curiously self-referential and hidebound. As experiences they tend toward introversion rather than extroversion. Even after one"gets" them, one is irked by the tightness of their boundaries because of their obviously axiomatic and tautological nature.

From all this one would imagine that Bruce Nauman was a mere Dadaistic *pasticheur* haunted by the specter of Duchamp. But, added to Nauman's verbal/visual juggling, there remains his equal commitment to sheer materiality and physicality which alone would mark him as foreign to Dadaism. Because of this latter aspect Nauman is a bedfellow of Andre, Hesse, Morris, Serra, Sonnier, Smithson, and any of half a dozen artists whose names readily come to mind. Nauman's uniquely private employment of neon would serve to rank him as an important figure.

Nauman's work exhibited at the Castelli Gallery in June of 1969 consisted of a set of holograms (photographs made with laser beams that manneristically exaggerate stereometry) which showed the artist viewed from below in multiple crouched and fetal positions (fig. 23). These holograms alter one's spatial apperceptions in an odd way; they induce a sensation of looking into a stereopticon of a greenish coloration.

In May of 1969 a freestanding passageway that could be walked through was included at the Whitney Museum's "Anti-Illusionism: Procedures/Materials" exhibition. Its oddness was a function of its seeming neutrality, but as passageway it gained meaning on viewing a videotape shown at Nauman's subsequent exhibition held shortly thereafter at the Leo Castelli Gallery. The videotape image revealed Nauman entering and exiting from this narrow corridor. It became evident that the width of the odd corridor was delimited to accommodate the deliberately exaggerated swing of the artist's hips. The passageway itself was virtually without meaning, which it subsequently and suddenly assumed only to the degree that it was revealed to be a visual boundary for the setting of the videotape.

Because of his use of cryptic self-reference, linguistic attachment, resistance to received notions of good taste (and therefore good sense and good behavior), and of experimentation as an end in itself, Nauman, *in the phase of his allegiance to Duchamp,* can be regarded as a significant artist whose work is important because—like much of Johns' later work—he continued to vitally extrapolate on the lessons of Duchamp.

The inferences then of these views are that Nauman's contribution as a critical artist is supported to the degree that he was able to expressively prevaricate on Duchamp. But, with the introduction of laser beam holograms and the greater reliance on technology and behavioral phenomenology, Nauman cut himself off from the experience which centrally formed his art.

It is apparent that two options were open to Nauman: he had either to continue to develop his attachments to Duchamp or he had to exposit purely epistemological information. But the very fact that his Postminimal production was linked to Dadaism obviated an epistemological response and promoted an art of continuing self-exposure in the context of Conceptualism. However, the latter context is unable to support this kind of externalization since it cannot support objectification. And in being unable to support an art of things or of making objects, Nauman's Postminimalism is betrayed by both his beginnings and his conclusions.

Notes

1. Fidel A. Danieli, "The Art of Bruce Nauman," *Artforum*, December, 1967.

2. Toby Mussman, "Marcel Duchamp's Anemic Cinema," 1966. Reprinted in *The New American Cinema*, ed. Gregory Battcock, New York, 1967, p. 151.

3. John Perreault, writing on Nauman's first New York show, *The Village Voice*, February 8, 1968.

4. Robert Pincus-Witten, "New York Review," *Artforum*, April, 1967.

5. Danieli, *op. cit.*

6. David Whitney's picture folder of 44 works by Bruce Nauman, published by Leo Castelli Gallery, is helpful in dating the early shift in the direction of Nauman's work.

7. Lucy Lippard, broadside to an exhibition called "Eccentric Abstraction," Fischbach Gallery, New York, September, 1966.

8. Neon appears in many of Nauman's constructions. Philip Glass, a musician and intimate of both Nauman and Richard Serra, contends that the neon spiral maxim, "The true artist helps the world by revealing mystic truths," is directly related to the optical spiral of Duchamp's *Rotative demisphere* of 1925. (Information supplied by Philip Leider.)

9. *Wedge of Chastity*.

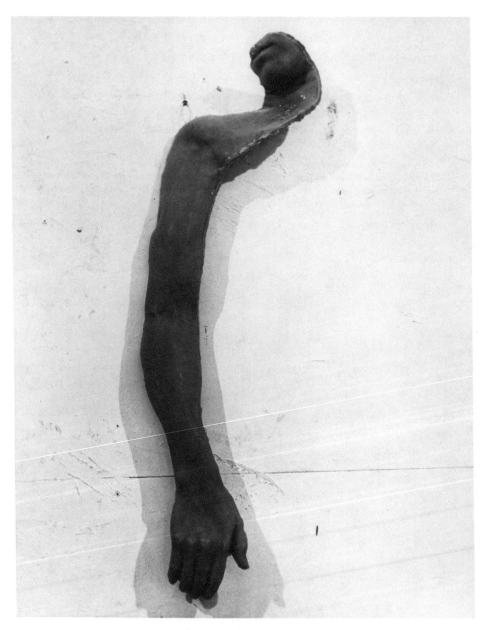

Figure 20. Bruce Nauman, *From Hand to Mouth*, 1967
Wax over cloth, 30″×10″×4″.
(Photo courtesy Leo Castelli Gallery)

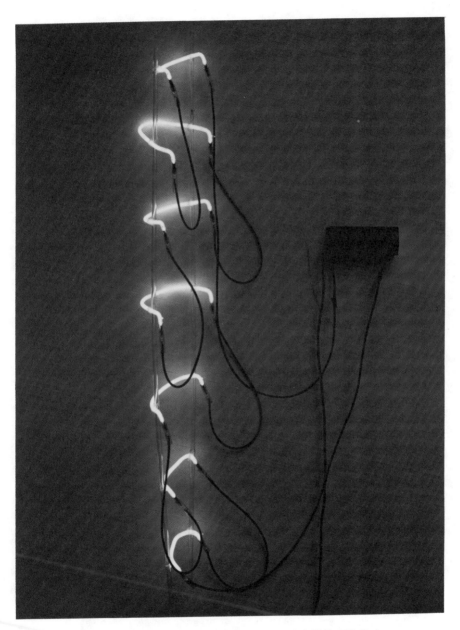

Figure 21.   Bruce Nauman, *Neon Templates of the Left Half of My Body*
Taken at 10 Inch Intervals, 1966
Neon tubing, 70″×9″×6″.
(*Photo courtesy Leo Castelli Gallery*)

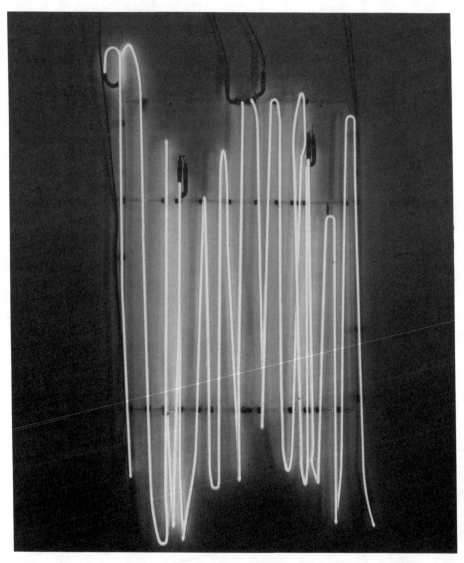

Figure 22.   Bruce Nauman, *My Last Name Exaggerated Fourteen Times Vertically*, 1967
Neon tubing, 63″×33″.
(Photo courtesy Leo Castelli Gallery)

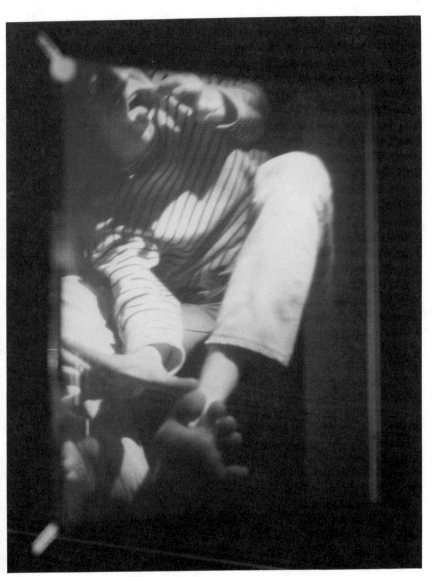

Figure 23.   Bruce Nauman, *Hologram (Full Figure Pose)*, 1969
Hologram image on glass. 8'×10".
(Photo courtesy Leo Castelli Gallery)

Rosenquist and Samaras: The Obsessive Image and Postminimalism

Recently I observed that " . . . an emerging official history . . . places Postminimalism squarely at the conjunction of a meeting between Oldenburg's soft sculpture and the gestural tradition of Abstract Expressionism, discounting thereby the long continuity from late Surrealist theory."[1] I meant that the evolution from Minimalism to Postminimalism had only taken into account a narrow view which regarded Oldenburg and the gestural tradition of Abstract Expressionism positively. Until this point, no connection to late Surrealist theory was drawn because such theory had been relegated to the dustbin by a critical apparatus which placed exclusive emphasis on "formal issues," issues implicit or central only to the executive act of art-making. With the emergence of an art that emphasized the pre-executive or conceptual phase of art-making, a mode of criticism anchored exclusively to art-making activity, as in formalist criticism, became recognizably inadequate. On these grounds some aspects which formalist criticism disqualified as unworthy of examination now elicit consideration.

The intention is not to revalue certain artists or styles across the board. However, the rejection of late Surrealism need not necessarily blind us to the development of a working syntax in this mode. In sum, Postminimalism takes note of numerous options inherent to issues that long precede the mid 1960s, and which derive from the first successful style of the '60s, namely Pop art, as well as numerous late Surrealist antecedents.

An image notorious to the decade, Andy Warhol's *Marilyn* of 1962, is compulsively repeated in mechanistic terms, a repetition that in part announces Minimalist seriality, but which, in fact, is largely related to the artist's obsession with cinematic glamour and media imagery. Marilyn Monroe's suicide in 1962 traumatized the popular consciousness in the period of the pre-Kennedy assassinations. The number of Marilyn-based images derived from this tragedy is in measure a function of ambiguities implicit in the suicide, an event in which a section of the public unconsciously took perverse pleasure. By contrast, James Rosenquist's *Marilyn Monroe* of 1962 in no way cor-

This article originally appeared in *Artforum*, September 1972.

responds to Warhol's repetitive and serialized *Marilyns*. Nor is it especially important in this context to point to a different tradition in the heritage of Rosenquist's *Marilyn* which relates to Cubist collage and even more to Schwitters' *Merzbilder.* Noteworthy in the Rosenquist is a focus on the entirely professional smile of Marilyn, her capped, white teeth derived from cosmetic toothpaste advertisements, a tradition which Rosenquist knew from his apprenticeship as a sign painter.

Advertising smiles suggest interpretive means quite apart from the formal issues of any work implicit to this imagery. An elaborate interpretation of the advertising smile appears in the writing of Thomas B. Hess. On the basis of the Camel cigarette ad "T-Zone" of the 1940s and 1950s, Hess inferred the presence of a sexual archetype, the evil or destructive mother, in de Kooning's first *Women* series of the 1950s.[2] Certainly, the collaged smile of de Kooning's *Women,* instead of putting us at ease, can be viewed as ambiguous if not gruesome and threatening.[3]

In 1962, Rosenquist began to experiment with a loose and arbitrary sculptural arrangement in painting. These "combine" polymorphs relate to concrete biographical events in the artist's life, and enabled Rosenquist to advance aspects of Postminimalism before any recognition of the peculiar pictorial and sculptural issues of the style was noted. One can point to *Nomad* of 1963, with its speckled plastic bag dripping paint on a disordered pile of wood; three versions of pictures caught in the branches of a tree; *Catwalk,* of 1963, which "is merely an idea of walking across a place with lights shining through underneath and it's supposed to be at high altitude but of course, it's only like a little puddle or little thing."[4]

A striking example is *Toaster* of 1963. This Tide-box-like construction is filled with plastic grass, through which emerge two serrated circular saw blades. Rosenquist remarks that they are "like two pieces of toast . . . and trying to put your teeth on two sawblades."[5] The construction is loosely bound with barbed wire, and *Tumbleweed* of 1964 (see fig. 7), like this image, continues to explore aggressive and lacerating possibly mortifying, tactile effects. An open work of enmeshed barbed wire, *Tumbleweed* is intertwined with a gestural neon passage supported by an armature of paint-splattered, crossed wood. The Surrealist implications of Rosenquist's work of this period are clearly recognizable as a function of unanticipated tactile effects, particularly the sharp and spiky. Rosenquist suggests that the introduction of barbed wire as a working material was induced, at least insofar as he can consciously identify, by memories of "animals and grasses hung up on barbed wire fences in North Dakota after floods in the spring."[6]

Remarkably, *Toaster* parallels Lucas Samaras' *Untitled (Face Box)* of 1963 (fig. 24), one of the artist's first important series of pin and yarn boxes of the period through 1964. These self-portrait boxes are characteristically covered with prickly and threatening elements—razor blades, pins, nails of all sorts pierced or pricked through his own photographic image affixed to the surface of the box, or within the trays set in the boxes. Similarly, numerous recent nude photographic variations of the artist in his book, *Samaras Album,* continue to exploit these characteristics. Throughout his work, Samaras deals largely with polymorphic sexual inferences of a generally sadomasochistic ambiguousness. In the early '60s this kind of obsessional material is not only widely found throughout the work of Rosenquist and Samaras, but is also visible in the work of Lee Bontecou, Bruce Conner, and Paul Thek. Bontecou's metal frame constructions painstakingly wired with small canvas elements are typical. In several of the apertures formed by the metal frames, the artist placed— serration to serration—toothed band saws similar to the rows of circular saws in Rosenquist's *Toaster* and the blades, screws, and pins of Samaras' *Boxes*. Bontecou's work occasioned frequent reference to a castration archetype, the *vagina dentata* (the vagina with teeth), though the artist denies so limited a reading.

It is important to emphasize the relationship of this highly varied body of work to the tactile effects of Postminimalism. If we take Eva Hesse as a representative figure of Postminimalism, the models afforded by Samaras and Bontecou cannot be underestimated, since both, unlike Rosenquist, elaborate their art through intricately crafted variations of set obsessional iconography. The prickly wiring of Bontecou's canvas patch to the iron frame is another example of obsessional, craft-based activity. Again, Samaras' affixing of spacedyed yarn in parallel, rhythmic rows undoubtedly influenced Eva Hesse's work, and other artists after 1968 whose work reveals clearly compulsive activity. It could well be conceived that this kind of straightforward and simple craft-based activity rendered dubious the traditional supremacy of easel painting, though some would designate this approach to handcraft as merely surrogate brushwork. Eva Hesse's consciousness of the problem imposed on women as artists would have made her aware of Bontecou's success in the early '60s, but I have not discovered reference to Bontecou in her journals; there is, however, reference to the problem of the woman as artist. To be sure, Hesse was strongly conscious of Lucas Samaras' work and early critics of Postminimalism, such as Lucy Lippard, had bracketed their names.

If Hesse, and now her many followers, picked up on the repetitive, artisanal aspects of Bontecou and Samaras, the anticipatory aspects of Rosenquist's *Tumbleweed* were equally influential on several young Californians who were seeking a more open mode of expression. It should also be remembered that *Toaster* had been reproduced on the cover of the April 1964 issue of *Artforum*, at that time a West-Coast-based magazine, no doubt a contributing factor towards the shift in sensibility. Bruce Nauman used neon early in his spiral maxims and body templates, though his introduction of neon is demonstratively related to an exploration of the thematic materials of Jasper Johns and Marcel Duchamp, rather than of Rosenquist. On the other hand, Richard Serra, associated early in his career with the West Coast and a friend of Nauman's, directly acknowledges his debt to Rosenquist's *Tumbleweed*. Serra's constructions incorporating neon elicited a strong response when exhibited in a group show at the Goldowsky Gallery in 1967. Several of Serra's pieces incorporated gestural neon counterpoints to an eccentric rubber structure pinned by twisted nails. An untitled eleven-unit piece of 1967, the first element of which contains the neon meander, has often been discussed and is now well known (see fig. 1).

Yet another untitled work of 1967, overlooked in the growing literature on the artist, is particularly applicable to the present discussion. Like the eleven-unit piece, it is made of neon and rubber belting fixed in place with nails. Despite the apparently elusive nature of its subject, this work seems to play upon a variation of the initials of the artist's name. In this sense it may be construed to be Nauman-like since Nauman, especially in this period, specifically dealt with neon constructions embodying thematic material derived from measurements of his person or aspects of his persona, such as the letters of his first name *Exaggerated Fourteen Times Vertically* (see fig. 22), and *As If It Were Written on the Surface of the Moon*, both of 1967. Although there are earlier examples, Sonnier's *Triple Lip* of 1969, in which gestural neon loops about two electric light bulbs, can be shown to be partly inspired by this connection. What I am suggesting then is that eccentric and partially unclassified episodes in the art of the early '60s established and inspired a rejection of Minimalism.

Samaras, unlike Rosenquist, is more explicitly related to the Surrealist context. Like Joseph Cornell, who forms an actual American bridge with the French movement, Samaras continued to exploit the conventional vernacular of Surrealism. Surprisingly, this tradition relates to the work of Salvador Dali during the 1930s, when it would have been hard to dismiss this noted artist as captiously as one does today. Although the molten features of the oneiric elements of Dali's "hand-painted dream photographs" of the 1930s are of great importance, his sculpture, such as the *Tray of Objects* of 1936, is equally noteworthy. This work directly exposes objects fetishistically intriguing to the artist and presented with little esthetic arrangement. Within the tray are small erotic sculpture, garments such as gloves and ballet slippers, chalices, puzzles and games—things which later would appeal to the theatrical fantasy of Joseph Cornell, not to mention the fetishistic aspects of Samaras' *Boxes*. Dali's *Tray of Objects* alludes to André Breton's own artistic efforts, the poem-objects, verbal/visual rebuses of significance to the Surrealist group in exile in the late 1930s and early '40s.

Samaras continued in this vein through the '60s. As late as the *Chair Transformations* of 1970 Samaras remains affiliated with Surrealist thinking, which, above all else, strove to inaugurate psychic liberty through the exploitation of familiar objects in unfamiliar contexts, or in terms of disjunctive sensuous properties. The textbook example is Meret Oppenheim's *Poetical Object* of 1936, familiarly called the *Fur-Lined Tea Cup;* the inanimate ceramic object seems to behave as an animate entity, as if it were growing hair. The image violates our sense of function. We shrink from stirring the fur-covered spoon and hesitate to drink from the hair-rimmed cup. Such an elaborate and literary notion is occasional in Rosenquist's work, but in Samaras' work it is a formalized convention. Samaras' *Boxes* are seen as soft and metamorphic. The *Knife Transformations* are equally so. The *Chair Transformations* range from fragile accumulations of artificial flowers to stiff, plaster-dripped drapery. The Surrealist myth of metamorphosis is the central issue animating Samaras' work and it may be because of his rigorous commitment to Surrealism that his work so often appears familiar, despite its recent date.

From the 1930s on, the Surrealists attempted to unify into simple presentations a multiplicity of structural possibilities. These metamorphoses commuted between animal, insect, avian, aquatic, and botanical life. Max Ernst's *Figure* of 1931 is a self-evident example.

The dislocation of tactile effect is still another example of late Surrealist activity which continued to find expression in Postminimalism. Dali's melting watches in the *Persistence of Memory* of 1931 are striking because of the disparity between what we know to be true of the molten state, namely, that its liquefaction is a function of extreme heat, and the cool crepuscular atmosphere in which the watches melt. Thus a sense of cool when there ought to be the experience of heat is similar to the unreasonable association of properties in Meret Oppenheim's work and to a quality of Samaras' work throughout the 1960s. That the metallic and inanimate watches are being eaten by an army of ants in Dali's painting indicates the inorganic become organic. The dislocation between substance and sensuous property is the key to the schizophrenic terror implicit in the work and marks it as a model for Samaras' variations.

On the basis of his work of the '30s, Dali has self-aggrandizingly noted that it was he and not Claes Oldenburg who invented soft sculpture, although it is really the invention of the illusion of soft sculpture that states the case more exactly. "The ideas of Dada and Surrealism are currently in the process of being repeated monstrously; soft watches have produced innumerable soft objects."[7] Dali's sculptures of this period, perhaps with the exception of *Rainy Taxi* of 1937 are in fact primarily hard-surfaced works. However, to develop the relationship between the soft sculpture of Oldenburg and Dali's work of the 1930s would open up an area which this essay need not cover because Oldenburg's work has certainly been acknowledged as establishing a key model for Postminimalism. It is important to note that the retention of aspects of certain Surrealist activities throughout the '60s is responsible for the additional energy necessary to shift the Minimalist style off base. To this dislocating pressure must be added the conceptual nature of Minimalism. On the basis of this factor alone, the style would have evolved in unimaginable ways not evident in a rigidly formal examination of the Minimalist object in isolation.

Notes

1. See present volume, "Eva Hesse: More Light on the Transition from Post-Minimalism to the Sublime."

2. Thomas B. Hess, *Willem de Kooning*, New York, 1968, pp. 76–79.

3. No doubt the model for the smile is the Gorgon pediment of the 6th century B.C. at Corfu; or, if not so specific a model, then classical gorgon imagery generally.

4. Jeanne Siegel, "An Interview with James Rosenquist," *Artforum*, June, 1972, p. 32.

5. Ibid.

6. Ibid.

7. Preface to Pierre Cabanne, *Dialogues with Marcel Duchamp*, New York, 1971, p. 13.

Figure 24. Lucas Samaras, *Untitled (Face Box)* [Self Portrait], 1963
Wood, pins, yarn, 10-1/2″ × 15″ × 8-1/2″.
(Photo courtesy Pace Gallery)

Postminimalism
Epistemology

Bochner at MoMA:
Three Ideas and Seven Procedures

There was a time when art meant painting and sculpture and the acquisition of the techniques necessary to realize these ends required a set of "how-tos": how to mix colors, how to apply pigment to a surface, how to build an armature, etc. In the last three years, at least, it is clear that the techniques of art have been revised to become not so much studies in methodology as of research into what constitutes the elemental features of any particular situation. In my view the methodologies necessary to the artist are now art history and philosophy—the one to know where to begin, the other to know what to do. The methodologies then pose a set of questions, which in a certain sense, have never been raised before, at least not in the sense that the questions themselves constituted both answer and art.

The evolutions of Mel Bochner's work, these past three years particularly, indicate that the problem for him, at least in terms of the Conceptual movement (in which he occupies a seminal place), has become one in which he had to distinguish between ontological and epistemological activity. The first tends, if I understand him rightly, to emphasize the self-referential and the theatrical gesture. It tends to view conceptual activity as a fixed style, a way of doing, of being, of looking as an objective quality. If this is true, then the ontological Conceptualist is the artist who is most readily understood in terms of his art historical connectedness with Dadaism, with the theatrical side of Futurism and with Duchamp. His modern mediating episode became the Pop movement.

By contrast, the epistemological Conceptualist is engaged in the study of knowledge as its own end. He tends to make or do things for the kinds of information, knowledge or data which the things or activities reveal. He tends to be a grammarian, a mathematician, a cartographer. his modern mediating movement is Minimalism. Bochner is, in the latter group, perhaps its best—that is, its clearest—exponent.

Whether or not the distinction is wholly viable between ontological and epistemological Conceptualism is, at this early critical moment, less important perhaps

---

This article originally appeared in *Artforum*, December 1971.

than the fact that its recognition allows one to claim for the Conceptualist movement the very thing it had apparently sought to deny, namely that its "quality" is a distinguishable feature. On the basis of Bochner's dualistic terms, although this was clearly not his intention, the critic now can point to the nominally "good" or "bad" in the movement, at least for the time being.

Bochner's present work is called *Three Ideas and Seven Procedures*. It defines seven methods which give visibility—beginning, adding, repeating, exhausting, reversing, canceling and stopping—to the nonphysical, tripartite expression of number: zero, number, and ultimately line. The work is installed in the MoMA downstairs exhibition space: a room, a corridor, another room, and a vestibule in front of the cafeteria. Having painted these spaces white, Bochner has, at the entrance and at his own eye level, mounted a left-to-right sequence of counting in black felt-tipped pen on masking tape all around the rooms. Conversely, the same action is made in red, on the same tape, starting from the right. The numbers are recorded in arabic figures, one series superimposed upon the other, at approximately inch intervals, some 2000 in all. Oddly, there are more black numbers than red ones.

Bochner finds that his eye level is demarcated at $71\frac{1}{2}$ inches off the ground. However, differences of floors and ramps cause the tape at certain places to end up far above the head of the artist, although the level remains constant to the height established at the entranceway. This idea, as we see in several photographs accompanying the exhibition, was worked out in the white Renaissance rooms of Dr. and Mrs. Lorenzo Bonomo in Spoleto this past summer. (It cannot fail to have moved the artist to learn that these Italian chambers were those, according to legend, in which Michelangelo had once stayed.) Such an association was not dissimilar to the ones I felt in front of Bochner's *Ten Aspects of the Theory of Measurement* installed this past spring in Greene Street (*Artforum*, May 1971) when I spoke of the fact that anyone moved by the experience of empty rooms could find a means of connecting *emotionally* with these bold examinations.

In the Bonomo rooms two pencil lines are marked, one designating true eye level, the other approximating it by hand (fig. 25). The discrepant interstices between these levels is a prefiguration of what we now have at the museum. The museum problem seems that continuous levels can express discontinuous discrete pointing in terms of number. In short, the museum piece enlarges the Bonomo theory of discrepant interstices into one of scan and point. The immediate results of this conception are startling. Above all else a body of several chambers receives a continuous definition and unity. The effect is a kind of discounting of the separateness effected by the concentration imposed by the counter-counting episodes. The wholeness of the space becomes a concomitant of the reversibility of the numerical system which, like a perverse chronometer, marks out a time and place of total arbitrariness.

By extension, then, Bochner relocates the actions of conceptual activity away from reading and the mind, into one of perception and the body. In this way he expresses both a break with the Conceptualist movement as a whole and announces his own evolutionary character. This makes him sound like a phenomenologist—someone like Bruce Nauman. But the difference is in antecedent history. Nauman, working out from his own body, derives his information from the verbal and linguistic activity of Duchamp, transforming his conceptual results into the ontologically quantifiable. Bochner, working from a bank of known and shared information, information which may in this light be regarded as established or objective data, derives his position from the reductivist tradition of the 20th century and therefore his conceptual activities appear epistemological in their effect. Both, however, produce situations which are actively at work upon the body and perceptions of the viewer. Certainly the most important difference between these positions is that the ontologist, by virtue of his history, is obliged to create objects, at their most ambitious cognizant of special environments for which they may especially be created. The epistemologist, extraordinarily enough (considering his history), creates systems free of local situations, the information applicable to any arena of activity.

The associations may even be enlarged. In Malevitch's *White on White* (1918) a white square was tipped upon a white ground, figure and ground distinguished not only by differences of white color but by a still evident pencil line. Malevitch's pencil line is now Bochner's masking tape; line as tape, figure as wall (or wainscoting) and ground as ceiling. Not only then are Malevitch's prophecies regarding the architectural potential of Suprematism realized anew, but another indice of the "inching out" of Minimalism into Postminimalism, while retaining a base within Suprematism, is made evident. In this way Bochner assists us in understanding the work of other Postminimalists, such as Robert Morris and Robert Smithson, while he indicates as well the richness of the problems posed by Minimalism.

Figure 25. Mel Bochner, *Eyelevel Crossection*, 1967–71
Blue and brown pencil on wall around room.
(Photo courtesy Sonnabend Gallery)

Mel Bochner:
The Constant as Variable

I

What has happened in America, and Europe as well, as evidenced in current studio and cooperative practice and in public and private galleries, is that a conventionalized Postminimalism has appeared, a style that damages the Postminimalist achievement simply because it is synthetically spurred. What has been an analytical achievement for Postminimalism has rapidly become for some younger artists an occupation of absorption and synthesis rather than analysis and activism. The nature of the art and the media network has led to a tendentious adoption and dispersal of a novel situation. Obviously, vital new styles promote a high degree of ancillary activity.

A few backward glances are necessary. The central preoccupation of Postminimalism was the rejection of an art embodied in holistic objects—paintings read at a glance, sculptures of unitary presence, or forms that bracket these conditions. The preferred look was geometrical. Structure was simplistic—monadic, binary, tripartite. Color was monochromatic or aerated to sheer luminescence. Complexity was generated through the use of grid or serial structure. But, even as the sacred conventions of base and frame were rejected in Minimalism (sculpture *was* the base and pictures *were* the frame), other conventions were retained: paintings remained functions of canvas borne upon stretcher supports and sculptures were still monolithic, though often hollow. The use of "noble materials" or modern equivalents (steel, glass, acrylics, sheet metals, and plastics) was unquestioned in Minimalism. Paintings, for example, were "made of" paint carried onto canvas surfaces, although an anonymity of touch or other techniques (spray, staining, etc.) may have questioned the role of the brush. So dependent was Minimalism on the convention of colored canvas supported upon stretchers that an entire style was said to find its paradigm in Frank Stella's permutation of this interrelationship, those paintings of his generated by the shape of the support. The principal effect of the stretcher-supported-generated image was the collapse of the figure-ground relationship in to a single entity, into

This article originally appeared in *Artforum*, December 1972.

a class of object that functioned both as picture and sculpture. This encapsulation at length resulted in an early Postminimalism which I termed "pictorial," in that it stressed uncommon substances and colorism (molten lead, neon, rubber, cheesecloth, and latex). Such materials tended to become "signature" substances, particularly identified with single artists: Serra/lead; Nauman/neon; Hesse/latex, cheesecloth; Benglis/polyurethane foam, etc. This "pictorialism," a refreshed use of eccentric substance and unstudied color, led to a counter-Minimalist pictorial-sculptural style.

Postminimalism then began as a style that rejected the stretcher-support and opted for direct wall appendage and the straight hanging of colored substance, whatever its properties. In this choice, the works of Keith Sonnier, Eva Hesse, and Lynda Benglis were exemplary. But an internationally dispersed network of artists attracted by the expressionist premises of the new "pictorialism," often extrapolated into their pictorialism isolated motifs and structures derived from Minimalism. One found the freely dangling stripe cut away from Noland or Stella; maculated cloth reminiscent of Olitski dangled from the wall. The so-called crisis of easel painting, instead of resulting in intellectual retrenchment and reformulation, led to the palliative of technology, provoking the wide use of videotape and film strip. Certain coloristic intonations, easily traced to second generation field painting, began to effect this new technological focus as well.

One aspect of Postminimalism, however, remained faithful to the exploratory nature of the style. The Postminimalist group contains those figures broadly designated as Conceptualist. One part of this group took as its models the lessons of Duchamp, who, in an extraordinary way, first saw that art need not only be a function of tangible or visible form but sought as well to make manifest its existence through linguistic premises. These figures may be designated "ontological Conceptualists," that is, Conceptualists whose art is recognizable as art because they make themselves recognizable as artists. The source of their work comes from their *being*. This art is implicitly pitted against another sort of Conceptualism that may be designated "epistemo-logical," that is, an art which demonstrates through preexecutive analysis a connectedness to the intellectual art of the Russian Revolution. These artists are animated not by their consciousness of *being*, but by their commitment to *doing*. What is already apparent is that those Conceptualists most affiliated with Duchamp have placed too high a burden on the public persona and on self-presentation. The art of the Conceptual theatre has emerged—Gilbert & George, Vito Acconci, etc.

Of interest is the Conceptual activity allied to Suprematism. The esthetics of the Soviet Russian style, which so fundamentally shaped Minimalism, continues to shape the Postminimalism immediately committed to an art beyond the mere visual appurtenances of canvas, color, and material. Instead it seeks an externalization through the employment of principles of language, an expression in language's structure, and demonstrations of the nature of truth. Several artists have pursued such lines of inquiry but none have done so more acutely than Mel Bochner. Bochner is not animated by any notion of "vanguardism." The term itself is anathema to him—

vulgar, meaningful only to a patented sector of the art community and to academic frames of discourse. Bochner does not regard his work as "far out," or "in touch." He simply "does art" from day to day, a doing that in the context of his life is neither disruptive nor extreme.

II

Mel Bochner ought not to have been an artist, unless the cultural neutrality of his Pittsburgh childhood and youth were, in fact, the very requirements for a kind of art seemingly divorced from conventional frames of cultural or pictorial reference. Still, there are hints. His father was a sign painter who had thoughts of becoming an illustrator, an unrealizable ambition given his economic situation. He may have nurtured, however unconsciously on his part, his son's ambition to become an artist, the first stages of which Bochner began as a student at the Carnegie Institute of Technology from 1958 to 1962, after completion of his military service. In this period Carnegie Tech was an uninspiring training ground for illustrators, but word did circulate that one of its graduates, Andy Warhol, was beginning to make a stir in New York when he switched from successful shoe illustration to a harsher painting based on popular advertising imagery. "Warhol made us realize that it was possible to be an artist and to have gone to Carnegie Tech."

The release from Pittsburgh and the *wanderjahre* it inaugurated first drew Bochner to San Francisco, where he supported himself by doing odd jobs in antique restoration. His paintings, he recalls (they have been destroyed) were distantly reminiscent (as befits the locale) of Clyfford Still. Several blunt kinds of pictorial experimentation led him to undertake monochromatic exercises, the most significant of which was a gray 12″ x 12″ panel covered in thick paint and marked with a smeared hand trail. The similarity of this work to Jasper Johns' encaustic number series of the mid-1950s was observed by a friend—a critical connection which drew Bochner to a serious assessment of Johns and one which released him from the onus of painting itself. "When I first came to know Jasper Johns' work I saw that I could stop painting." Bochner was so struck, in fact, by Johns' number series that he began to desultorily jot down a body of notes on the meanings and implications of Johns' work. "Jasper Johns' *O through 9*," he noted, "defines the lateral boundaries of its surface by measure of the stencil typeface used for the successive laying on of numerals. Both the visual and conceptual parameters of what is there to be looked at are present by the procedures necessary for its realization." This worn pocket notebook became the source of a book called *Excerpts and Speculations*, which Bochner produced in single Xerox copy in 1968.[1]

The primacy of Johns in Bochner's work is further testified to in an address that Bochner made at the Institute of Contemporary Art, London, in 1971. Viewing the present situation as one of "post-modernism" he queried his audience if "Anyone ten years ago could have imagined that 'modern art' would become a period style?"

According to Bochner, the inception of the "post-modernist" phase began with Johns, who first rejected sense data and centristic personality as the basis for art, partly replacing these conventions with another more investigative approach. Bochner contended that Johns

> interrogated the phenomenological condition of painting but went further by injecting doubt into the deadening self-belief of art-thinking to that time. Most essentially he raised the question of the relation of language to art. His paintings demonstrated that neither was reducible to the other's terms. It is in vain that we attempt to show by the use of images, what we are saying. After Johns we can never again slide surreptitiously from the space of statements to the space of events . . . in other words, fold one over the other as if they were equivalents. This alone signified the demise of expressionist art.[2]

In 1963 Bochner traveled back east and registered as a philosophy major at Northwestern University on the outskirts of Chicago. At the time Northwestern University was one of the few American seats of learning in which a strong emphasis on Phenomenology and Structuralism was to be found. Bochner began to read Roland Barthes. A reference in Barthes led Bochner to the objectified novels of Alain Robbe-Grillet. Apart from an occasional oblique phenomenological inference in Bochner's larger and later works, the year's tutelage in philosophy was important in that it supported an anti-expressionist drift in Bochner's mode of experience— post-Sartrian, post-existential, resistant to the humanistic glorification of angst, emotion, and romantic idealization. The chief philosophical figure who came to dominate Bochner's thinking is Michel Foucault, who stringently emphasizes preoccupations with exactness, measurability, and definability, issues which Bochner epitomizes for us in terms of his own work. Bochner's preferred reading remains Foucault's *The Order of Things (Les mots et les choses)*.

At this point, in 1964, Bochner arrived in New York City and found cheap quarters in the east 70s. He supported himself as a guard at the Jewish Museum, a job he held until 1965. The first deep friendship he made in New York was Eva Hesse. In my essay on Hesse above, I have indicated the crucial interchange between friends that was taking place in the period of 1966. Notable among the encounters made by Bochner was one with Jasper Johns, to whose number paintings Bochner had attributed a systematized structure foreign to Johns' own view of them, at least in so far as the artist then discussed them with Bochner.

By 1966 the circle of Bochner's friends was formed. The circle ranged from Robert Smithson to Eva Hesse, and included other figures such as Brice Marden, and later Dorothea Rockburne. The catalytic figure in all of this is Sol LeWitt, who exerted a moral influence in terms of the model of his dedication to art and who gave encouragement to artists less well-known than he. Sol LeWitt's contribution to these disparate artists is best understood in terms of the emphasis he placed on preexecutive articulation of any given problem. The complexity of the Postminimalist situation is exemplified by the fact that the exhibition called "Ten," one of the important exposures of Minimalist sensibility then at its apogee, opened on the same day in September, 1966, and in the same building as "Eccentric Abstraction," which was one of the first surveys of counter-Minimalist sensibility. "Ten," with its dignified square catalogue designed by LeWitt, was held at the Dwan Gallery; "Eccentric Abstraction," with its vinyl encased critical broadside by Lucy Lippard, was held at the Fischbach Gallery.

It was in the context of Minimalism that Robert Smithson emerged as well. However, the idiosyncratic view within his work was different from the rational systems favored by LeWitt and Bochner. LeWitt worked from a premise which rejected nothing implicit in a system once the system had been determined. At this time LeWitt was working with examinations of grid structures and all the possible permutations which occur in the facets of triadic groups of cubes one placed atop the other. Smithson, by contrast, in adopting certain systems in his work always inflected this work with elisions, rejections, and increments which were not necessarily schematically inherent, but which came about through a more spontaneous response to geographical environment.

Within this spectrum of shifting Minimalist and Postminimalist possibilities Bochner's earliest consistent work was a set of drawings based on the permuted possibilities of open squares similar to LeWitt's examination of triadic structure (figs. 26, 27). It is not surprising either that all three, LeWitt, Smithson, and Bochner, responding to the heightened consciousness provoked by their social intercourse, pursued brief careers as art critics, writing hardnosed reviews of exhibitions unsympathetic to the larger aspect of the scene, but also writing key articles in the history of Minimalism. A didactic mentor, Don Judd, had also been writing criticism since 1959 when he joined the masthead of *Arts Magazine,* then edited by Hilton Kramer. Judd had sponsored in the context of gallery reviews and the use of sparse description an art of unitary, stripped-down objects. Judd was the only reviewer these artists read with any degree of regularity or approval.

Typical of the connectedness of the critical thinking between these artists was a review written by Bochner and Smithson in a short-lived magazine, *Art Voices.* Quixotically, they "covered" the opening of the still unfinished interior of the Hayden Planetarium annex and wrote an ironic, multi-leveled photo essay called "The Domain of the Great Bear (Fall 1966). These collaborations are especially interesting because they attempt to solve the problem of lack of gallery exposure through the gesture of a review which, before anything else, is its own art manifestation. The most arcane feature of the piece is that several of the authors cited in the work— Piaget and Poe among them—had statements falsely attributed to them or were attributed statements the artists felt such authors were likely to make. Such a conceit crops up again several times in Bochner's career. The grid structure organization of Bochner's review of "Alfaville, Godard's Apocalypse" (*Arts Magazine,* May, 1968), incorporated quotations from disparate sources—some of them again falsely attributed. More recently, in the *"Konzept"-Kunst* catalogue for the Kunstmuseum in Basel (March–April 1972), Bochner's entry thrice reads "Language represents thought, as thought represents itself," a citation attributed first to Hegel, then to Mallarmé, then to Husserl. The work shows that the constant invented by the artist is a variable, whose shifting meaning is affected by our notions of the work of each of the figures to whom the statement is attributed. The statement, if made by Hegel, reads as if it were an epigram of Dialectical Idealism; if made by Mallarmé, an expression of thought as a condition of soul; if made by Husserl, the impression that thought is a phenomenological element, as if something solid. The contribution reiterates a message central to Bochner's premise, namely, that "Language is not transparent," now almost a catchphrase associated with the artist since he chalked it upon a blackened wall of the Dwan Gallery for the "Language IV" exhibition in June 1970.

By 1966, the essential preoccupation of Bochner had become his notebooks in which complete notions and structural premises were worked out in highly finished diagrams. The first of these notebooks dates from 1964 when Bochner was still working at the Jewish Museum. This leatherette journal begins with illusionistic drawings for constructions which, generally speaking, contrast biomorphic forms against assertive geometrical ones. Their relationship to so distant a forbear as the *Abstraction-Création* group is still evident. In the course of elaborating this notebook sketch by sketch, day by day, an important leap took place in 1965. This is evidenced on a page for projected drawings, the shelf pieces, sketches of a work made, but later destroyed.

The drawings' strict measurements and simple structure reveal an appreciation for Don Judd's position. "I saw my first Judd in 1965, after I made the piece, but I read Judd's writing in *Arts Magazine*, as everyone else did, and I was aware that it was an apology for a specific position that artists were already calling primary structures." The shelf drawings occasioned the first verbal descriptions, an attempt to create as sharp an analysis of this object as Bochner had found in Robbe-Grillet's precise descriptions of objects:

> The point of this piece is to concretize one section of 'space'. To objectify, solidify and realize it. The 'form' it takes is a line. A hard, brittle metallic blue core which is also the time that is required to move from point left to point right. The supports take on the characteristics of wall brackets in order to stress their unimportance. They are painted whatever color the wall is.

Impressed by Dan Flavin's fluorescent show at the new defunct Green Gallery in Winter 1965, Bochner began to project small structures contrasting fluorescent tubes with mirrors—materials similar at the time to Robert Smithson's layers of mirror. Bochner's sharing of ideas visible in Judd's and Flavin's work meant that by 1965 his tendencies were clearly articulated and related to the strongest manifestation then open to American art. This becomes self-evident if we study the 1965 drawings which deal with simple numerical systems of triangles and hemispheres. They signal the beginning of a stress on set theory which continues to the present. Equally

It was in 1967 as well that Bochner made his first language experiments such as "Orthogonal Routes for/of Duchamp Re—(Blossoming) ABC," which may be likened to Carl Andre's rebus poems set in grid formations, although Bochner's are more abstractly permutative. Broadly speaking Andre's poems alter actual "sense." There is no search for literary "sense" in Bochner's verbal reformulations, although there is constant structural meaning. In this they may be likened to the artist's interest in serial music, *musique concrète,* the work of Stockhausen and Pierre Boulez, which he first began to listen to when a student at Northwestern. Bochner cites J. S. Bach, Schoenberg, Stockhausen and Boulez as models for works of art "based on the application of rigorous governing logics rather than on personal decision-making," a methodology which Bochner called "solipsistic" in "Serial Art, Systems, Solipsism." "For the solipsist," he wrote, "reality is not enough. He denies the existence of anything outside the self-enclosed confines of his own mind." Among other examples Bochner cites Jasper Johns, Sol LeWitt, Don Judd, Robert Smithson, Dorothea Rockburne and Eva Hesse, that is, "artists who carry out their work to its logical conclusion, which, without adjustments based on taste or chance, is the work." Importantly, he notes that "No stylistic or material qualities unite the artists using this approach because what form the work takes is unimportant (some of these artists had ceased to make 'things')."

As early as 1967, then, Bochner had recognized that art may be, but need no longer be, embodied in some kind of here and now sensuous object, like those things conventionally called paintings or sculptures. The feature that made art of certain activities was the integrity of the thinking that the work entailed. This is not the central focus of Minimalism—though it is implicit in the style—since, whatever else it may be, Minimalism was primarily realized in the fabrication of autonomous objects. At this point Bochner had come to personify what by now is self-evident— that whatever else art may be, it is the best *thinking* of any given moment.

Measurements, Drawings and Projects of 1967 and 1968 freed the artist from making photographs and objects. The primary works of this looseleaf binder were prepared diagrams for work to be executed in brown paper, to be marked with numerical charcoal indications for wall situations. Originally these investigations began with the set of substructures imposed by 36" x 48" elements, a convenient sheet size of industrially cut paper. These working drawings were later edited into a finished leatherette journal, consisting of 28 finished drawings, a one-copy book called *Catalog of Plans 1967–68.*[4]

The *Catalog of Plans 1967–68* may be related to the experiments with set theory and scale relationships that interest Dorothea Rockburne. Bochner and Rockburne were aware of one another's work as early as 1967. During the following two years their preferred choice of material is often the same, paper especially, or simple substances like charcoal. Direct appendage of the work to the wall or laid directly upon the floor, a predilection for mathematics and set theory, "solipsistic" working through of problems, the absence of coloristic interest, and, above all, the intense rigor or intellectual commitment are further aspects of a certain theoretical similarity. The vital difference is one of affect. In Rockburne's work the issues addressed locate themselves within a quite different—seemingly more subjective—sphere of visual argument, particularly in her use of materials.

Bochner's *Catalog of Plans 1967–68* contains numerous experiments of significance, such as the measurements of excised elements of fixed shapes, the cubic measurements of the absent content of empty forms, the comparative relationships of constant paper measurements (one crumpled, one pristine), essays in variable lengths of paper unified through the use of constant widths. Most important was the introduction of the cord compass, a measuring device perhaps traceable to Jasper Johns' use of rulers radially dragged through wet paint. Bochner found the compass to be "the best universal to work with as it does not depend on rectilinear organizations of wall to floor." This idea matured in the period 1968–70 and led to the "Generic Drawings" show at the Galleria Sperone, Turin, 1970, in which the string compass was used to establish the dimensions of the walls through the use of broad charcoal arc-segments self-recording a fundamental circular set.

The use of string compasses—and the concomitant indication of quadrant directions—led to the configuration of the ACE Gallery show, Los Angeles, during the summer of 1969, in which only the circular quadrants remain, not demarcating the rectilinearity of the wall or the floor, but the polarities North, East, South, West, independent of the gallery's actual structure.

Despite the richness of his production in 1968, the artist destroyed a large body of work. A single looseleaf binder remains, *Measurements and Theories: Drawings and Projects, 1968–1970*, a major concern of which is the blunt measurement of space. In May, 1969, the German dealer, Heiner Friedrich, gave Bochner his first one-person show at his Munich gallery. Bochner's installation, *Measurements,* regarded the space as a rigorous compendium of exact measurements such as one finds on the blueprints of architectural specifications. Bochner had originally offered to execute a work called *No Vantage Point,* by which he intended that the gallery be painted white and a line be drawn across the entire enclosure at the artist's eye-level. (This proposal was repeated, but it reappeared in the Museum of Modern At, New York City, "Projects" exhibition of 1971.) *Measurements* led to further German gallery activity. Bochner exhibited at the Konrad Fischer Gallery in Düsseldorf an installation of a longitudinal measurement dividing the entire space vertically in half. This was the theoretical counterpart to *No Vantage Point.* By this time Bochner was considered a pivotal figure of the Conceptualist movement, especially after his inclusion in "When Attitudes Become Form," Kunsthalle, Bern, an influential exhibition held early in 1969. At this international congregation, Bochner was represented by a long row of sheets of graph paper, 8½ inches wide, stapled in horizontal alignment to the wall, one beside the other.

But to conveniently tag Bochner as a "Conceptualist" is too delimiting because it does not take into account the strong sculptural feel of much of his work. I regard

Bochner as an artist conscious of the physical, a kind of sculptor more than just a draftsman, although the setting down of diagrams may more easily be associated with drawing. Diagrams concentrate potentially vast organizations of spatial and surface locations, either in exact terms or in terms of perverse ambiguity—such as when we deal with the compass-drawn circles, or with eye-level lines. The most easily readable sculptural effort is *A Theory of Sculpture,* installed in an abandoned factory in Turin. This work, which tests the possibilities of numerous measuring devices, especially the compass, also incorporates tangible members such as rudimentary plumblines. Moreover, actual physical elements lean and balance, interconnecting wall and floor, and recall Bochner's preoccupation with primary structures as well as the work of Richard Serra. But the issue at hand is not physicality or materiality, but rather the exposure of principles of structure which makes physicality or materiality *seem* tangible.

The preoccupation with *Measurements and Theories* led to the March, 1971, installation at the Greene Street Gallery, New York City. Since Bochner regarded it as the summation of measuring, the exhibition was called *Ten Aspects of the Theory of Measurement.* The computations which engaged Bochner's energies were "derived, compared, reversed, extended, halved, dispersed, partitioned, bent, deflected, non-referred," functions of a working module 11'10", the distance between the centers of two parallel structural columns. However, one "did not end up solely with the measurements, but with a transposition of feeling which, if felt at all, is usually experienced while moving through architecture, particularly of the Italian 15th century."[5]

The full permutation of an idea in the context of deobjectification was realized in the "Projects" installation at the Museum of Modern Art, New York City, November, 1971. The work, *Three Ideas and Seven Procedures,* delineates seven methods—beginning, adding, repeating, exhausting, reversing, canceling, and stopping—employed to give visibility to the nonphysical, tripartite expression of number: zero, number and ultimately line. The exhibition was installed in a sequence of spaces, painted white and interconnected by a length of masking tape applied to the walls running from room to room at a constant height. Upon this tape was recorded a counting sequence left to right in black, and superimposed on this sequence in red, right to left, a countercounting sequence. This exhibition refers back to *No Vantage Point,* but more immediate to our considerations, it developed ideas thought out in Italy during the summer of 1971 when Bochner drew two pencil lines across the face of a Renaissance room, one marking true eye-level, the other approximating it by hand. These kinds of actions indicated that by this point there were indeed two types of conceptual activity—the ontological, and the epistemological. This distinction provides the basis for critical judgment of Conceptualism, a movement which seeks to defeat criticism and art history through the incorporation of the methods of these disciplines.

To some measure the fact that Bochner's work takes place within chambers or upon walls means that a phenomenological thrust, however inadvertent, must be taken into account. Still, whatever the physiological experience implicit in such a situation, such an effect is only an ancillary result rather than a primary ambition. In this way Bochner's work should not be confused with that done recently by Bruce Nauman, Michael Asher, or Keith Sonnier.

Throughout 1969 it was apparent to Bochner that the core of his ambitions had become the discovery of meta-theoretical bases of activity, as well as the exhaustion (diagrammatically or theoretically speaking) of all possibilities implicit in any given informational situation. From this time, he subsumed his work under the generic title of "the theory," or "a theory," such as *A Theory of Objects: Line, Plane, Volume.*

Perhaps the leanest, most perplexingly stripped-down exhibition was *The Seven Properties of Between* (see fig. 28), installed at the Sonnabend Gallery, New York City, February, 1972. Utilizing several small stones, Bochner demonstrated seven axiomatic statements of the kind "If X is between A and B, it is not identical with A or B," or "If nothing is between A and B, they are identical." Among the difficulties of the exhibition was that these statements, inscribed on typewriter-size sheets of paper, were placed on the floor in a seemingly arbitrary fashion, some paralleling the walls, others oblique to them. In fact, these locations were not arbitrary at all, but were part of a system aimed at distinguishing those statements in terms of their verifiability.

With regard to this problem, it is meaningful to view aspects of Bochner's activity in reference to issues brought up by the syntactical structures of Noam Chomsky. One of Chomsky's leading interpreters, John Searle, recognized that

> purely formal constraints placed on the semantic theory are not much help in telling what the readings are. They tell us only that a sentence that is ambiguous in three ways must have three readings, a nonsense sentence no readings, two synonymous sentences must have the same readings, and so on. But so far as these requirements go, the reading need not be composed of words but could be composed of any formally specifiable set of objects. They could be numerals, piles of stone, old cars, strings of symbols, anything whatever. Suppose we decide to interpret the readings as piles of stones. Then for a threeways ambiguous sentence the theory will give us three piles of stones, for a nonsense sentence, no piles of stones, for an analytic sentence the arrangements of stones in the predicate pile will be duplicated in the subject pile, and so on.[6]

In terms of Bochner's work such an analogy indicates that physicality or materiality is not his work's core and indeed it may be only an ancillary consideration of the information projected. Therefore, the stones—and more recently the leaves, the hazelnuts, the architectural fragments, the pieces of chalk, etc.—which constitute the viable tangible elements of Bochner's recent work are not to the point. With Bochner, substance is neutral, its quiddity is beside the point, merely a necessary evil, not used as "signature" material.

The relative insignificance of the physical substance of Bochner's art means that his work is pared down to an almost lean "otherness." In works relating to the Conceptual theater, say, or any of the several examples of Postminimal phenomenology, there is always the tacit assumption of communal exchange between art and viewer. Bochner's work makes the most marginal concessions to even highly attenuated notions of "communication." It remains "out there," beyond the pale of conventional taxonomy.

In a perspicuous review of *The Seven Properties of Between*, Lizzie Borden, taking her cue from a reading of Wittgenstein, understood that "Bochner's literal mapping of these propositions seems to exhibit the relation of abstract logical truths to the structure of reality," concluding that

> The rocks, signifying necessary truths, are abstracted from the contexts we generally use in considering statements. Bochner has attempted to prove that the limits of logical articulation can lead to puzzling and obscurantist statements. The problem lies in an erroneous search for meanings in the objects themselves. By showing what cannot be stated, Bochner demonstrates the importance of ostensive definition, or gesture, in the comprehension of meaning.
>
> (*Artforum*, April 1972)

The artist himself was prompted to write several pages on the subject since the *Seven Properties of Between* represented a "quantum leap" for his thought, one which "led, perhaps hesitantly, to the formulation of a meta-critical art." Since this document, a personal letter, constitutes a key exposition of the artist's thought, in conclusion I must cite from it at length: "Beginning with the premise that art's basis is knowledge, we can rapidly deduce that there is no art imperative for the object," the proof of this being that "there are pre-language operations but no pre-language objects." Still, "The question basic to any endeavor which sets out to examine knowledge is 'How do I know this is true?' . . . the verification problem. . . . Therefore, the *task* of epistemological research . . . is to raise the verification problem to the foreground of esthetic problems." Bochner saw that the verification problem could be reduced to at least four components. "The first is tautological; a principle for determining truth which requires nothing outside itself. This is the truth of mathematics . . . " to which the artist appends the caveat, that to understand the meaning of his art as mathematics is false, since it is not his intention "to replace antiques with textbooks."

> My aim is to apply the same stiff criteria to thought that exists in any other theoretical endeavor, to reclaim the knowledge in art by art . . . The second verification principle involves specificity, a statement which necessitated an appeal to the stones to validate it. If, for example, I said that my pen is black, you would have to see this pen to know if my statement were true.
>
> The third case is more difficult to explain. Here, I was demonstrating propositions which corresponded to the fact of the arrangement, but not solely to that arrangement. The statement was true for this instance, but not for all instances.

This generalizing principle was active in several of the *Seven Properties*, especially the wall.

This all brings me to the fourth principle, namely, the act of faith. In the piece which "stood alone" in the back room I made a statement which was not true [If nothing is between A and B, they are identical] and a demonstration of it. The demonstration *appeared* to verify the sentence, but upon reflection could not possibly. However, given the situation/circumstances it was completely acceptable because of the conditioning inspired by the other six [examples] . . . Finally, all of these remarks are useless if the experience is not congruent with the thought.

My view of Bochner's art is that the experience is congruent with the thought.

Notes

1. It was this material, excepting the observations on Johns, that became "Excerpts from Speculations," *Artforum,* May, 1970. The use of the word "speculations" in the essay's title indicates Bochner's great appreciation of T. E. Hulme's *Speculations,* the general title by which the latter's philosophy and aesthetics came to be known.

2. Unpublished manuscript, "Problematic Aspects of Critical/Mathematic Constructs in My Art," 1971.

3. These photographs may be associated with Jan Dibbets' "perspective corrections," one of which, *Forest Piece* 1969, Bochner used to illustrate "Excerpts from Speculations," *Artforum,* May, 1970.

4. Bochner is strongly attached to didactic ends. He has produced not only books made by hand but also extremely limited edition books—or booklets—dealing with either exhibition material or with working aphorisms. The most influential of the latter is the French/English edition of *11 Excerpts,* put out by the Sonnabend Press in Paris. Its tone and scale are marked by *The Little Red Book of Chairman Mao.*

5. R. Pincus-Witten, *Artforum,* May, 1971. This observation was corroborated by several Italian projects located in architecture of the kind noted, the most recent, installed in the Chiesa San Nicolò, Spoleto, in which the artist laid down in cruciform pattern fragments of Roman moldings, a spare variation of the ACE Gallery polarities.

6. John Searle, "Chomsky's Revolution in Linguistics," *The New York Review of Books,* June 29, 1972, p. 22.

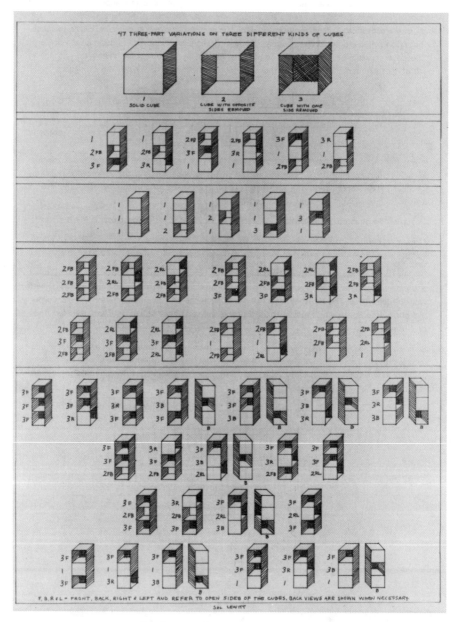

Figure 26. Sol LeWitt, *Drawing for 47 Three-Part Variations on 3 Different Kinds of Cubes*, 1967
Ink on paper, 24″×18″.
(Photo courtesy John Weber Gallery)

Figure 27.   Sol LeWitt, *5 Three-Part Variations in Which a Solid Cube Predominates,* 1967
Painted wood, 44″×12″ (base); 12″×4″×4″ (model).
(Photo courtesy John Weber Gallery)

Figure 28. Mel Bochner, *Seven Properties of Between*, Detail of Installation, 1971–72
Ink, stones, on paper, 8-1/2″ × 11″ each sheet.
(Photo courtesy Sonnabend Gallery)

Sol LeWitt: Word ⟷ Object

Sol LeWitt epitomizes the lean intellectual orientation in current art. His moral and formal example is noteworthy and his influence can be seen in a range of work as diverse as the complex structural innuendos of Eva Hesse to the pared down verifications of Mel Bochner. The ubiquitousness and serviceability of LeWitt's achievement often make him difficult to categorize. There are rare instances of theatrical Conceptual production, for example, *The Buried Cube* of 1968 (a work documented in the catalogue of Sol LeWitt's retrospective held at the Haags Gemeentemuseum in the summer of 1970). That Sol LeWitt's work should seem to touch many bases is problematic—my problem, not his. I believe that there is a more sharply focused vision of LeWitt's contribution than perhaps the artist would be willing to admit.

One especially appreciates LeWitt's seminal position in the evolution of Conceptual activity. LeWitt's singular achievement is that his development of a theoretical posture nominally central to Minimalist structure freed Minimalism from its geometrically quantifiable condition, permitting it in this way to become the foundation of epistemological Conceptualism. In less stylistic jargon this means that LeWitt's attitude toward the simplified geometrical mode of the mid-1960s tended to further reduce such geometric forms to a residue of linguistic equivalence. The value of LeWitt's cube ultimately lay less in the form itself than in the possible and then unexplored use of a simple verbal description denoted by that form. Nor did LeWitt's use of seriality emphasize repeated modules as only a means of inducing visual interest and incident in an otherwise spare reductivism. Instead, the visual importance of seriality in LeWitt's work implied that composition could result from the use of a homogeneous set of forms. These Conceptual sets were offered to the mind for intellectual gratification as earlier hierarchies of shape and color had been offered to the eye for visual delectation. LeWitt's work bracketed these two modes of apprehension and ordonnance. It had the double effect of validating more self-aware experimentation of an art of Conceptual sets (as the epistemological Conceptualists were beginning to explore) while it continued to valorize in a fresh way

---

This article originally appeared in *Artforum*, December 1973.

certain implications of Jasper Johns's more conventionally composed art based on arrangements of heterogeneous Conceptual sets—e.g., the ale can rendered as drawing, painting, sculpture, lithograph, label, and "real thing," or, similarly, heterogeneous thematic accretions derived from flags, targets, and most importantly, numbers. The emergence of an autonomous epistemological Conceptualist group—whose members by now are working in highly disparate areas of research—at this point seems to underplay its once declared affiliation with LeWitt in favor of an ever more credible connection to Johns, one far greater than had at first been suspected.

LeWitt's recognition of a coequality between form and noun tended at the outset to isolate him from what was then considered to be mainstream Minimalism. It was not until the recent consciousness of a distinct Conceptual movement that LeWitt's contribution grew clearer. Precisely because his work is linked so closely to the current usage of language in art LeWitt now appears to be the most stringent Minimalist of all. By contrast, period stylists like Judd or Flavin appear to have explored imagistic, coloristic, or illusionistic issues which seem to have been, in hindsight, additional elaborations within their art. LeWitt's recent exhibition at the Kunsthalle, Bern, however, critically places him again into a paradoxical situation. Having led the transition of Minimal form into a Conceptual presentation, he appears to be reversing priorities in this exhibition.

The main reason for my concern is that apart from the wall drawings which seem to be LeWitt's major achievement, LeWitt is still realizing older projects within the context of tangible, objectified sculpture. Currently, work is being fabricated along theoretical models worked out several years ago, an action which the "nonexistent" or "insubstantial" conditions of the wall drawings, as well as the lessons inherent in the earlier work, ought to have vitiated as an esthetic, ultimately political, choice.

This objection raises an important question, one not only local to LeWitt, but to sculpture in general and to the major figures of Minimalism, painters included. Unlike sculpture of the past, the problem of replication, edition, and later production based on earlier prototype becomes—with contemporary figures—a crucial issue, one tied to the consciousness of the meaning and moral content brought about by a new esthetic.

The problem lends itself to two interpretations. The tendency toward geometrical form and industrial manufacture accounts and allows for replication at any time. The tendency also explains the introduction of teams of assistants who can fabricate the work even in the absence of the artist, who may in turn become the foreman and the conceiver; but the artist's role as executant is phased out, often to virtual nonexistence. The point of art as language is that anybody can do it once the directives are in hand. In this way it is a seemingly democratizing process. By contrast, LeWitt's unique contribution to Minimalism raises the special issue of the verbal model that obviates tangible form itself, and in particular, the manufacture of forms based on earlier schemes, a production that adds nothing to the implications of the original achievement.

In LeWitt's special case, in fact, the manufacture of earlier projects seems a reactionary gesture in a production coexistent with the theoretical rejection of the possessable and the objectified. To wonder what a fresh, cubic configuration will look like, even if such a configuration had not been fabricated in the past, adds, it seems to me, little to LeWitt's art since the principles of such an action have been understood as a result of his work at least since 1967. It is the principle and not the object that is at stake. If it is the execution of an operation or its verbal equivalent that counts in LeWitt's work, then it would seem that my reservations concerning the newly fabricated cube series are well taken. The problem is that LeWitt now seems to reject the implications and the enormous changes in art occasioned by his earlier position. In continuing to produce objects as a function of Minimal sensibility he acts as if it were the object that really mattered all along. If he is right and I am wrong, if it is the object that counts, then I am deprived of an argument. The situation would then be one of object as object distinct from object as idea, his taste versus my taste. My reservations would be trivial. If I am right, however, there has been a serious forfeiture of rank. I reject Sol LeWitt's new work (exclusive of the wall drawings) because I cannot theoretically justify it, not because I do not relate to his sense of human scale (being most put off by the proportions of the *Modular Series*—the 5½' cubic frames fabricated in interlocking, white baked-enamel steel elements). To me, what is vital in current art is not a function of object but a function of idea. It's never "inherent beauty"—whatever that means—that induces a sense of wonder but only the arguments into which that object (and here I am regarding Conceptual art as a kind of object) can be fitted.

Further, to accept LeWitt's art as "object as object" means, as well, that one would be forced to view it as a stylistic affiliate of the 1960s taste derived from the example of Frank Stella: a surprising bracketing since Stella's work is so thoroughly based in a sensibility which, taking its model from the historical evolution of Matisse's painting, is pitted against LeWitt's achievement as it is patently object-oriented. The apparent similarity is caused by the utilization of a generalized sphere of structure—geometry. In this sense LeWitt's straight lines countering curved arcs—the motifs, though hardly the meaning of several wall drawings and graphic pieces—are similar in pattern to Stella's protractor variations. To insist on this similarity, however, denies the areas of discourse which I believe radically differentiate these two productions: color sensibility against theoretical didacticism, feeling and emotionalism against keen rationalism, sensibility against theory, object against concept.

Certain LeWitts are nonetheless Stella-like in effect, particularly the hollow, metal boxes of 1968–72, ornamented in striped pattern sequences. These boxes, virtually unknown in the United States, are the ones which mark the most variant or eccentric application of LeWitt's taste. They divide laterally, vertically, triadically, a sectioning differentiated by strong herringbonelike patterns. Such striped applications suggest that LeWitt can respond to spontaneous impulse, a response that in his case leads to pattern-making. Too many visual properties are at work here for these boxes to read as constituents functioning within a lucid set structure. An ungenerous reading of these boxes would be as a hangover, period ornamentation in the manner of Stella. What has been reopened to question by these boxes is LeWitt's all-important focus, namely that a Conceptual set is a viable organizational factor, equivalent, if not even superior to, visual or pictorial composition. They represent a serious recidivism in LeWitt's career, one perhaps more disquieting than any other.

Not only then does LeWitt himself occasionally veer in the direction of Stella, but so do those who follow LeWitt's operatives as well. it is intriguing that in the presentation of geometric form in terms of verbal correlatives, LeWitt is attracted by the imperative case. His simple language is direct command. There is something about this location in language (as differentiated, say, from Richard Serra's, whose work may be related to the infinitive of the verb, or from Bochner whose work at times parallels sentence structure) which gives LeWitt's achievement an often totalitarian or autocratic intonation.

In "following orders" it is curious to see how many period-taste solutions have already answered LeWitt's verbal postulates. A telling example would be the lithograph executed by the students of the Nova Scotia College of Art and Design in 1972. Surprisingly, an expanding meander pattern—as is found in numerous compositions by Stella in the early 1960s—resulted from the following instruction: "Using a black, hard crayon draw a straight line of any length. From any point"—the executant conceived "any point" as always the point at the end of the line, an extreme but still correct assumption—"on that line draw another line perpendicular to the line. Repeat this procedure." A figure resembling, say, an International Style floor plan could easily if not inevitably result from this directive, rather than the Stella-like fret which in fact evolved.

Perhaps the tautest realization of form as language is *Arcs, From Corners & Sides, Circles & Grids and All Their Combinations,* the working drawings which were prominently displayed in Bern. One hundred ninety-five illustrations—some of them incidentally and misleadingly optical—correspond to such simple postulates as the first, *Arcs from one corner,* to the 195th theorem, *Circles, grids and arcs from four corners and four sides.* LeWitt's attitude means that no indecision exists as to when the art work is complete. The completion of the work is realized in the solution of the number of imperatives.

What is so striking in all of this is the deflation of the actions of art—there is nothing implicitly or explicitly "artistic" in art-making other than making the work of art or doing art itself. Paradoxically, art is execution but it is not in "the touch." So detached from the issue of facture has LeWitt's art become that his work theoretically may be executed by anyone following the artist's set of imperatives. In principle this is acceptable. In actual practice, however, there is a noticeable difference in those works executed by assistants and those executed by the artist himself, a difference both psychological and physical. An unresolved problem. LeWitt appears to have opted for the both extreme and obvious position: the artist is the person who thinks up things to do. Art is over when this chore is done. The art is the thinking.

A loss of confidence in facture (a theoretical loss perhaps more than an actual loss) underscores the wide malaise of painting at this moment. Just as LeWitt's wall drawings dramatize the virtual unimportance of stretcher-borne cloth as support for art, so too does the verbal directive further undermine the belief in personal facture as the cogent embodiment of art.

Not incidentally, the discovery of the wall drawing was an achievement dispersed throughout the Postminimalist phase, one that responded to a variety of dissatisfactions. Several examples come to mind from that moment at which the introduction of seemingly "eccentric" or "signature" substances began to be exploited as a color surrogate for the lost expressionism typical of Minimalism. In the winter of 1969, for example, Bill Bollinger filled the Bykert Gallery with green sweeping compound and powdered graphite, smudging a large disk of the latter substance on the gallery wall. More immediately similar in effect to LeWitt's position were the monochromatic wall drawings of Peter Gourfain shortly thereafter executed in pastel stick on the same gallery's wall. I noted in the fall of 1969 that what Gourfain retained from his past was "registration, enumeration, and rigorous clarity of intention. What has been lost is the intermediary support (and the paint if not the pigment)." Mel Bochner had been working in masking tape applied directly to the wall surface in LeWitt-like grid formations since 1967. These ideological tentatives were corroborated as well by aspects of the work of Robert Ryman. And so on.

It is of importance that the present occasion is not the earliest large overview of LeWitt's work, the first having been organized by the Haags Gemeentemuseum in 1970, for which a more sumptuous catalogue than the present Bern booklet was issued. It remains the basic reference of the artist. Tellingly then, two retrospective exhibitions have been organized in Europe, while none have been arranged in the United States, although of course, the frequency of the artist's exhibitions, first at the Dwan and now at the Weber Gallery, have kept us informed of his evolution.

LeWitt seems to be reaching or arriving at master status in Europe in a way unusual to careers in New York City's. If the artist is opting for a European reputation it may be because of the rawness, the exposed nerve of working in New York City. Still, work by an American artist that is not going to fall into its own mannerism must, I believe, be executed in an atmosphere aware of the implications of any artistic position. It could be said that there is built into the European appreciation of an artist, as distinct from New York City's, the idea that felicity is the touchstone of the artist's mastery. What appears to be happening to LeWitt might be described as a kind of pleasure-principle Conceptualism which occasions a certain hasty or casual execution. The wall drawings at the Kunsthalle, for example, are so diffidently executed (even the one done by LeWitt himself, rather than the group-executed work at the entrance) that they disparage the integrity of this vital contribution.

Divested of an acute sense of the scene means that LeWitt may not have given sufficient heed to the fact that certain pieces, had they been shown in New York City, would have elicited an instantaneous and abrasive result. I think particularly that the recent folded and torn paper exercises should have been edited to include in the Bern exhibition the earliest examples of gridbased, folded and torn paper exercises which, it is claimed, have been part of LeWitt's production for some three years. The artist in this way would have indicated another area of his interest and scotched as well any misgivings as to date and/or directional flow of influence, as so much work of this type has been seen in New York during this past year.

Doubtless there are many persons who regard such an assumption as pointless. One does not quibble about dates when dealing, say, with the color red in conventional easel painting; why then take issue with who first folded and tore paper in the context of an art of idea? The answer to this question is a function of the nature of the Conceptual movement. Since the lesson taught by LeWitt is that the embodiment of an art may grow lean to the point of virtual nonexistence, the only thing then that is left inviolate or identifiable as art in such work is, in fact, the integrity of the idea. The reason that the Conceptual artist is so concerned with dating, *curricula vitae,* bibliographic niceties, and the appreciation of scholarly and art historical methodology is that through such attentions an exact delimitation of boundaries protects a unique achievement. Unlike conventional painting or sculpture, who had what idea first is a real issue, since the only thing that can be appreciated and evaluated as a personal achievement in Conceptual art is the vitality and validity of its idea.

This is not meant to be construed as saying that LeWitt has been influenced by the very community of artists to which he plays so exemplary a role. I only state this reservation to stave off the possibility of misapprehension. As it stands, the Bern retrospective raises as many speculations as it answers. The sheer open-endedness of the result reveals anew the singularity and the importance of LeWitt's catalytic achievement, if only in the degree that it continues to inform and announce its solidarity of purpose with the dry and "deprived" actions of the epistemological Conceptualists.

Strategies Worth Pondering:
Bochner, Shapiro, LeWitt

8 January 1978

Mel Bochner's show opened yesterday—in the front rooms of the gallery there were magnificent wall works (fig. 29), in the rear space, a range of beautiful framed pastels. Despite all this, my first (and, as will be seen, wrong) take: sensibility recidivism. Within the large formats occasioned by Bochner's long concern with 3-, 4-, and 5-sided shape permutations (fig. 30) there was the additional clutter of elaborate "pure feeling" arrangements, Suprematist-like constellations at their most decorative—here and there cropped and near-accidentally placed in the larger formats (or so I thought at first). Hence, the triangle, square, and pentagon-linked master "templates" in Bochner's work were countered by an internal design of the kind that the Suprematists themselves had applied as ornament to classical porcelain shapes codified throughout the 19th century, utopian signifiers pointing up an almost headlong cultural collision. Here too (I thought) the exchanges that took place between Bochner's internal patterns and the external holding "templates" of the master perimeters were very beautiful and very hollow in the same way unless, of course, Bochner's Malevich-like sense of ornament was in fact cropped and copied from specific Suprematist organization; but that would reveal an epistemic irony anathematic to Bochner's high-minded seriousness. Were this even a remote possibility, then it would serve as further testimony to the admitted thralldom within which great epistemic abstraction labors vis-à-vis the Cronus forebears of Suprematism.

15 January 1978

Back at the Bochner show and finally saw that the variations that transpire within the larger 3, 4, 5 figures, for all their seemingly errant play, are generated epistemically. But they function in a scale at one remove down from that of the master edges. There is no intermediate group of shapes; they would have read as too close in size to that of the master shapes. Thus, the internal figures are quite small when com-

This article originally appeared in *Arts Magazine*, April 1978.

pared to the overall figure. The smaller shapes negotiate a tripartite crew of linear kinsmen: oblongs, bars, and lines—the last I construe as slots since they incorporate the ground of the wall inducing an occasional spatial illusion. Bochner's patterns, when scaled down from the initial edges of the master shapes, constitute a concise set of linear figures—oblongs, bars, and lines.

They recall the wooden "lines" that occur on the walls, say, of Le Va's spatial projections—they, too, are epistemically generated—or the lines, tears, and folds of LeWitt or Rockburne for that matter. And for the same reason, epistemic linkage.

But Bochner's use of color is utterly non-epistemic, arbitrary, though to use a word like "arbitrary" sounds negative. I don't think so, at least in Bochner's case, as I consider him a colorist to his very fingertips, though no theoretical premises govern his selection of colors except, of course, that they occur as a result of felt necessities. Such necessities are in the end, only felt, and ultimately justified (perhaps) through the esteem that history may accord the work, but not through the application of any demonstrable system. The same may be said of Rockburne's color in her more recent works—she would have it that the "weight" of a certain shape demands a correspondingly "weighted" color. But to invoke this argument, though it never can be true in the sense that an episteme is true, invokes the specter of the early school of modern abstraction that taught the essential lesson—the congruency of form and content.

Still thorny is a tellingly reasonable comparison with Frank Stella's relief paintings of ca. 1972 and thereafter. Stella's work at the time joined incisively formatted shapes of a clipped and snappy stylishness, internal hierarchic scale comparisons, all manner of tipped plane and substance, and an unworried color. Such good-looking Neo-Deco design would seem to have provided Bochner with the model of work by a celebrated artist at but only a generation's remove—had not Bochner specifically rejected Stella early on, in a review in *Arts Magazine,* May 1966—when Stella was widely taken to be the Compleat Young American Master. Bochner rejected Stella as much for the latter's felicitous sensibility as for a concomitant absence of epistemic base—unless, of course, a season to season shift in strategy may in itself be a kind of formalist episteme.

Still, there is the matter of Stella's early and great "pinstripe" paintings, dating to 1959; they pointed to Malevich as Bochner's continue to do. But Malevich, as we now know him, is largely an art-historical reconstruction that follows hard upon, not precedes, Stella's "pinstripes": or even the stretcher-generated shaped canvases. The reconstruction and wide rehabilitation of Malevich specifically and Suprematism generally coincides to a moment in Stella's career when the latter's avowed commitment to Matisse was inescapably self-evident. What may be interesting in this adjudication is that Matisse, who lurks behind Stella in all his moves—even the earliest (the white lines of the "pinstripes," by the artist's admission, allude to the blank canvas lines of Matisse's *Red Studio* of 1911)—may be said to animate certain of Bochner's recent moves too, as in fact it always has: the "Belief System" part of

Bochner, the part that epistemology doesn't and can't explain. True, Bochner eschewed Stella but Matisse was never off limits—and the Matisse of the Barnes Foundation murals (1931) through the cut-outs of the 1950s provides Bochner with a revered model of sensibility-linked painting, quite in the same way that it equipped and enriched Stella's work.

Thus, if all the preceding is true, despite Bochner's rejection of Stella there remains some narrow sector of overlap between them, some communal patch, since it was Stella, above all the young American masters, who unwaveringly pointed to Matisse from the outset, semaphored the message bright and clear—before Bochner and the affiliates of Epistemic Abstraction's lean and pared-down look took up the signal flags—and indeed of late some have with especial alacrity. In Bochner's case the epistemic enterprise still obtains, but in the work of others now keeping or parting company, *mutatis mutandis*, Bruce Boice, say, or Dorothea Rockburne, they have all but abandoned the claim. Rockburne minces no words: over Christmas eggnog she said, "It was never about the system—it always was about sensibility."

All this preoccupation with Bochner put me in mind of dear dead days—when Bochner, not quite driven from the fold, was nevertheless excluded from the clubby set of godfathers of the larger Conceptual scene. At the top of the heap, the *capo dei capi*, so to speak, were Carl Andre and/or Sol LeWitt, followed by lesser *luogotinente*, Joseph Kosuth, Dennis Oppenheim, and groping somewhere still further below, Robert Barry and Lawrence Weiner—and they in turn condescended to Art & Language types.

Those were tinctured days; somehow Bochner was getting mileage without queuing up in proper pecking order; nor would he signal in proper body language— you know, one's head slightly lower than that of the cluck above. How chafing the derision, and his continuing to garner esteem without ever having worshipped at the altars of LeWitt or Andre (and, mind you, I think them entirely worthy of the tribute) somehow further aggravates the scene. (Not to "worship at the altar" is a far cry from not esteeming. Bochner has always valued LeWitt as an artist.)

1 February 1978

Yesterday, Joel Shapiro—36, teddy-bear-like (fighting weight), black thinning hair about a Claudian Charlie Brown face, white painter's ducks on a cold day. He is always fearful that he is not quite articulating sharply enough—though he talks clearly and securely about art. But he is unpolemical in his views, so that from sheer pleasure of company one neglects to write down what he says and then, pressures of the day being what they are, one forgets his exact phrases.

Shapiro's most conspicuous feature as an artist has been the willful bending of an epistemic art to seemingly aberrant personalistic issues. His timing was funny, albeit deft and light-footed—sort of a sprocket-jumped film strip. At the moments of tight epistemology he drew back in the name of stray obsessions; conversely, as the orgy of self-exposure, the loquacious need to expose one's most telling peculiarity began to cast a fatal appeal throughout the art world, so did Shapiro once more affirm solidarity with the coolest strategies of the epistemologists.

Shapiro's quirky feints were worked out, say, in his obdurate commitment to an obsessionally small scale—though there are models: Duchamp, Johns, and Tuttle— while the declarative public constructivism of Serra and Andre set the sculptural paradigm. Shapiro generously denies nothing to them. His capricious need to expose a privatistic symbology within an art that was, before all, one of stern formalist purpose was perversely captivating—those little Monopoly houses, doll-scale chairs, toy horses (figs. 31 and 32). But a pure investigation of a system—LeWitt's mostly—leads Shapiro to an enervated lassitude largely because for Shapiro, LeWitt is unscarred by the sculptor's brand. Hence, LeWitt's work, for all its manifest significance, is, for Shapiro, in some integral way, not sculpture at all. And I agree with him.

By contrast, LeWitt's great investigation of a whole system really amounted to the imposition of an alternative to formalist abstract values, values that still cling to Shapiro's conception of sculpture. For all his peculiarities of scale, all his tentative anxiety, Shapiro is psychologically fixed as a sculptor. He has made a primordial commitment to the species—yet, ever anguished, he continues to work within a framework of tantalizing ambivalence.

Thinking back, I try to mentally reconstruct his career.

67–68? the eccentric pictorial sculptures, the hairy canvases that form part of the larger concern with the Abstract-Expressionist revival that marks the late Sixties.

69? the shelves—the idiom would later emerge importantly as the eccentric supports for aberrant "houses."

70? the epistemic comparisons of the weights of primary raw materiel—here the allegiance to Serra and Andre is most explicit—so and so much metal compared to a like weight of stone.

In a parallel mode, the 70–71? comparisons between hand work and the machine tooled, an episteme marking a tactile scale between coarse and fine—elegantly floor-bound proposals that assist in recalling what the old Paula Cooper Gallery was then all about, up three stories on grungy Prince Street. Part of the reason that one waxes nostalgic is that one would never have supposed that the present epistemic prophylaxis would have been so complete.

71–72? the little trestle bridge, the whittled balsa boat, the pathetic little bird, the first "Monopoly" house, iconography of high-profile dream analysis presented in the most inaffective way except, of course, for the sheerly profligate drama of presenting tiny pieces on huge floors—an echo of the floor-adhesived masking-tape theorems of Bochner, then being shown in the unexpected emptiness of big gallery space. Brancusi is also a prototype—all those essentially Symbolist disembodied heads presented as the sheer stony weight and compression of unapologetic lithic molecules.

72–73? the little house placed on eccentric spaced shelves, elongated or cut, the toy man strutting in the direction of the cardinal points like some robotic Bauhaus logo and from 1974 on, the house itself studied and restudied, opened up, sectioned and bisected, a studious commitment to grasp ultimately Cubist-connected formal content of this little temple form that would, in time, lead to a greater and greater analytical statement, the most recent works in fact. When seen from above, say, bird's eye, the sculpture is transformed into pure shape relations, the floor playing ground to the sculpture's figure. The imagery now annexes Malevich—and, in this, is again following Bochner's mode—yet when the new work is apprehended from the side, it somehow gets Carl Andre up from the floor again, just as Serra had lifted him up at the end of the Sixties.

Coincidental with the more recent changes was that Shapiro's working drawings began to appear, wonderfully labored drawings—black, smudged, corrected, and recorrected, the kneaded eraser and the razor blade and the pencil worrying the very fiber of the paper—getting down, just right, those hard, elusive abstract-constructivist figures, right down to the very dust of the marking tool—the way Serra had pressed into existence the black paintstick drawings, making sculpture of them somehow, or as Bochner had worked out his gorgeous black and white arrangements of Pythagorean truths (see fig. 30)—the connections between these works are self-evident.

To make these connections pillories no one, least of all Shapiro, for the connections of his work to Bochner's drawings may in turn be taken back to an acknowledged model in Jasper Johns—that's a strategy worth pondering— Johns, to Bochner, to Shapiro—though Bochner might be vexed by the rightness of Shapiro's discoveries, so free are they of any epistemic basis except for their chance "cruciformality," as Masheck called it. Bochner has borne down upon himself; Shapiro, by contrast, is just too unsure to let himself imagine that he really might be allowed to secure so privileged a place in the terms of the equation as I've stated it. But I'm talking about his head, not his art.

"You know, Robert," Shapiro said, "I've been toying with the idea of monumental sculpture." Of course he has—except for a vacillating disbelief in his own strengths, Shapiro had been a closet monumentalist all along.

2 February 1978

By far the great achievement of the past decade was the codification of the epistemic system, the ranging application of the system to the condition of style. The episteme—A–Z, say, or 0–9 or the spectrum sequence, RYB, or the days of the week or the months of the year—all those conceptual figments of truth and dozens more were at last seen as peer to the Realists' representation of nature or the Abstractionists' congruent presentation of form and content. To have imposed the epistemological vision as a stylistic equivalent to the other achievements was a great act of will—one in which LeWitt was accompanied by many other artists, though his retrospective must be viewed as emblematic of the overviews the others await. (And now there is this new odd sensation as well— as the battle has been won, so is the role of the supporting critic strangely egregious, an undesirable witness to the event, *la fée* Carabosse at Aurora's wedding, an embarrassment. At the beginning there is the artist, then the artist and the critic, then once more just the artist. But, in time, art history vindicates the critic too.)

For all its joy, the occasion was muted—since the imposition of an epistemic system as an authentic style in the history of art seems so over and done to me—certainly not for its initiators, but surely for those who came later, those who adopted it precisely because it was fast becoming a style among other styles, one that one might choose, just like that, out of a sales catalogue, as it were. But now that such a choice may be made, not from moral necessity but from taste, that there should now even be the possibility of a "Tenth Street Touch" with regard to epistemological abstraction, staggers me, hurts a bit.

Last night, we toasted the fact that the Museum of Modern Art had awarded credentials, *Lettres patentes,* naturalization papers, what have you—had bestowed on epistemological abstraction the irrevocable prestige that only the Museum of Modern Art can.

With regard to LeWitt specifically, I have always felt his use of the episteme was essentially intimate, best experienced in a scale dictated, say, by that of a textbook format, preferring the small drawings that bear the imprint of his fine draftsman's hand to the kind of work that partakes of a stagy declarative mode—those large reifications, the public metal sculptures, or the imposing wall works. So far as LeWitt is concerned, it is still the hand that carries the day, the little margins of transcending edge that the artist's drawing still mythically preserves—though LeWitt's epistemology expressly argues against my sentimental critical recidivism.

My reservations are linked to a perception that LeWitt is in no essential or fundamental way either painter or sculptor—a cryptomorph, a gynander, as it were, central for all that to the very aesthetic conventions of epistemic abstraction; instead, he is a draftsman whose insights are those of a born designer. That we should have come to accede that drawing is the halfway house between painting and sculpture and their peer, and that drawing is the essential embodiment of epistemic abstraction are the very functions of LeWitt's achievement. Yet when I meet a LeWitt in the guise of an extruded aluminum spray white "jungle jim," so to speak, or as a big Gulley Jimson of an epistemic wall (fig. 33), I feel, well, just indifferent to it. And I know my indifference is a form of risible atavism about what art is, or used to be.

LeWitt has amply and handsomely met head on all of the trying exigencies imposed by the new limits of his vision as to what art might now be. Acknowledging this somewhat tautological outburst, ought I not admire all other kinds of artists who unstintingly answer the imperatives germane to the arts as they conceive of them? I ought to, but don't. Certain ambitions seem so historically petty, so slim, despite the often fearfully difficult, virtuoso-like demands imposed upon the executant—Realism and sensibility abstraction, say. There are certain Realists and abstractionists at work today who generously answer the trying imperatives of their art, yet the boundaries of their Realism or their abstraction—not their art but the world to which their art is annexed—strike me as so petty, so bankrupt, in a word, so known, that for all my recidivist critical admiration for the hand, this admiration seems as nothing compared to the adumbration of a whole new system of visual order—and more, the imposition of the system as a style coeval with the earlier ones. And this triumph we owe largely to LeWitt.

Figure 29. Mel Bochner, *Scissure*, 1978
Casein on wall, installation, 9'×11'.
(Photo courtesy Sonnabend Gallery)

Figure 30. Mel Bochner, *Triangular and Square: Right Angle*, 1973
Charcoal and gouache on paper, 38"×50".
(Photo courtesy Sonnabend Gallery)

Figure 31.   Joel Shapiro, *Untitled (Chair)*, 1974
Cast iron, 7-1/8″ × 3-1/2″ × 3″.
(Photo courtesy Paula Cooper Gallery)

Figure 32. Joel Shapiro, *Untitled*, 1973
Enamel on wood, 6-1/2″×1-1/8″.
(Photo courtesy Paula Cooper Gallery)

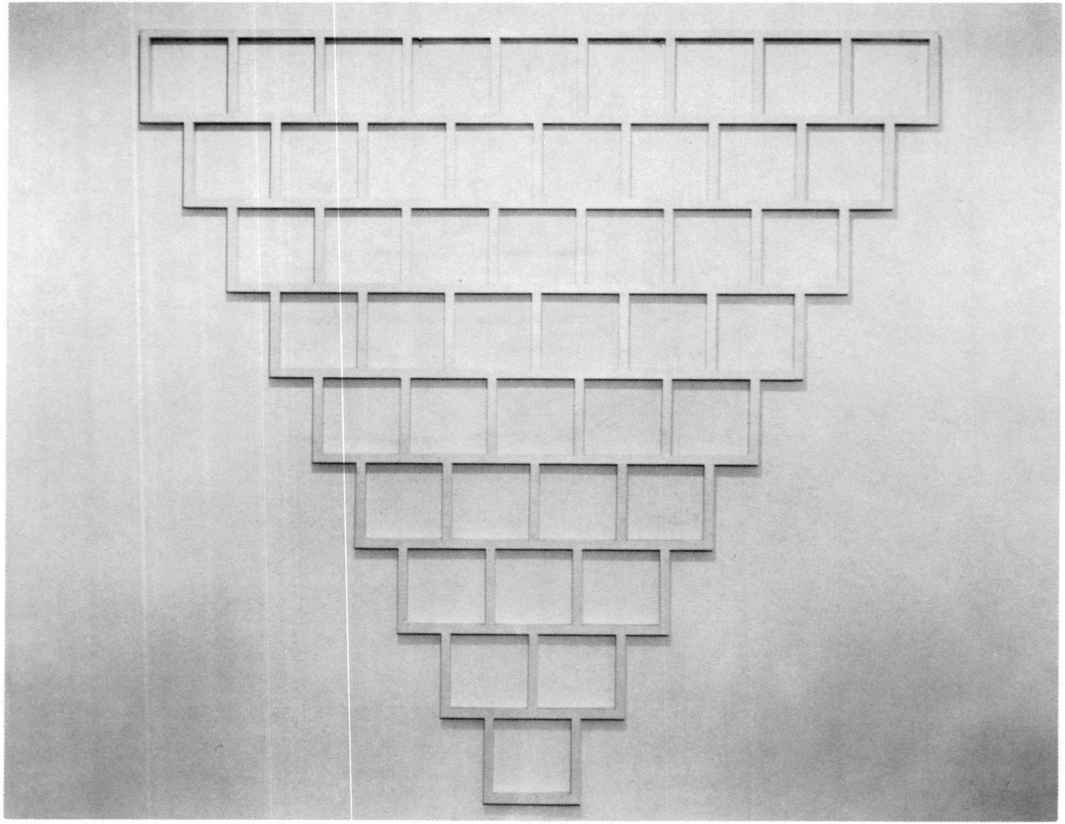

Figure 33. Sol LeWitt, *Wall Structure Flat*, 1977 White painted wood, 87"×87"×1". (Photo courtesy John Weber Gallery)

Barry Le Va:
The Invisibility of Content

A central option of advanced art in the late 1960s was the exploration of a "dealt-out" expressionist pictorial/sculpture. Lynda Benglis' manifestation of the style—linked to ritual issues in Pollock and a cult of media personality derived from Warhol—is typical. In the work of the late Eva Hesse, a vision of the Sublime (endemic to the first Abstract-Expressionist group) was developed alongside of postulates derived from Minimalist seriality. The Abstract-Expressionist quotient of Richard Serra's lead tossings keyed into a concern for process and the quiddity of sheer material implicit in Minimalist sculpture such as that by Don Judd and Carl Andre. Yet perhaps the earliest serious investigations of the pictorial/sculptural phase of Postminimalism—ones that had a wide effect owing to a reproduction on the cover of *Artforum* in November 1968—were the "distribution pieces" made from felt by Barry Le Va.[1] Yet, despite the almost instantaneous (and perhaps transient) awareness of his work of the late 1960s—a celebrity by art school imitation, stylistic rip-offs that in no way acknowledged their source—Le Va's career, of all the figures with whom he can be associated (Serra, Benglis, Keith Sonnier, et al.), remains one neither crowned by financial success nor illuminated by critical discussion.

Like Serra, Le Va comes from California. Born in 1941, he grew up in the Los Angeles suburbs. Protestant ethos stuff; his father's family was originally Alsatian, his mother's Scotch-Irish. High school and the crucial adolescent years in Long Beach. "It's a car culture, so when you get a car, you start finding out things to do." Finding out things to do in the fifties meant two things to Le Va: hard drugs for sure and art school maybe. Although he had always been interested in art and architecture, there seemed no way in. Drugs were a great adventure, but when a number of friends OD'd, Le Va recognized the importance of his original life choice. Art school seemed more attractive.

But art school in Southern California at the time offered little to Le Va; first "the brainless commercial art" of the L.A. Art Center (1964) and then the pro-scriptive expressionist figuration of the Otis Art Institute (1964–67). Still, while at

This article originally appeared in *Arts Magazine*, October 1975.

Otis, Le Va responded to the teaching of Dr. Ralph Cohen, who taught philosophy of aesthetics and provided the artist with an intellectual model whose world was scholarly. "He drew me to metaphysical speculation."

Le Va determined to be a painter, an ambition vaguely informed by images of Pollock and Newman, but as they appeared in *Life* magazine reportages. The "official studio style" in L.A. at the time was that of Rico Lebrun, one derived from Picasso's *Guernica*. By the mid-1960s, fashionable East Coast styles began to inflect this expressionist figuration namely, hard-edge abstraction and Pop. Le Va's student paintings began to take seemingly trivial scenes like cocktail parties as subjects. These were smartened with stripes in the background or bright Pop colors. These "parodies of actions that happened in comic books" led Le Va to think of such organizations as potentially three-dimensional, as a kind of mixture of painting and cutouts. This "objectification of a cartoon action" occupied him until spring of 1966. The soft and funky materials used in this work, as well as its Pop figurative elements, dissipated into a more generally abstract, albeit expressionist, arrangement of shapes situated within a room (fig. 34). Since the studios at the school were too cramped for this development, Le Va got one of his own. At length, "it was the stuff lying around in the making that became interesting, the absence of specific forms. It was the scraps, the stages, the time factors, the stuff around the object that grew more important than the object itself." Oyvind Fahlström, as Le Va acknowledges, informed his work of this time. "By then I knew about L.A. cult figures, but I didn't know any artists. La Cienega [Los Angeles' "gallery row"] just seemed all wrong for good art, and L.A. was too social. When I graduated in 1967, I had plans of coming to New York. By then I knew that all the work that interested me was coming out of New York—especially the artists' writings."

Between 1966 and 1967, Le Va executed ten plexiglass trays filled with felt, "not exactly to get my MFA, but to have something to show at the graduate exhibition as Otis refused to show a floor felt unless it was put on a base." The trays, first to tenth, range in complexity from the simplest to the most intricately folded. The last year of art school coincided with a period of great growth in the off campus studio work. The studio work, for the most part, met with abuse from his professors, fellow students, and the Los Angeles gallery world. "I wanted to reduce art to my terms, then rebuild it—my terms, with nobody else's influence." It was not art, his critics claimed; it was not permanent, it was impossible of ownership. Their unconscious position was that artmaking was determined by a successful art market sensibility; hence it was, in its way, politically conscious (if reactionary) since it was oriented towards gratifying ownership.

Two professional critics on the West Coast were drawn to Le Va's out-of-school work; Arthur Secunda (himself an artist of neo-Dada bent), who sent photographs of the work to Barbara Rose in response to her "The Value of Didactic Art" article, and Fidel Danieli, who wrote the first note on Le Va's distribution pieces.[2] A complicated evolution was taking place in New York at the time. High abstraction was embodied in the architectural/sculptural mode of Minimalism. By 1968, the reaction to this taciturn iconic style was being effected, partly by the very figures who had legitimized Minimalism in the first place (notably Robert Smithson and Robert Morris). This reaction publicly addressed issues that Le Va had been working out since 1966 in his "distributed" studio work.

The first pictorial/sculptural phase of Postminimalism was accomplished in New York in part by Serra (who had started in San Francisco) and Hesse through work that de-emphasized the rigorous solipsisms of Minimalism in favor of an eccentric and expressionistically linked procedure. But it was Morris who, in the public's mind, most embodied this alteration in style. His celebrated essay "Anti Form" appeared in *Artforum* (April, 1968); and in a long analysis of "9 in a Warehouse," the influential exhibition of this new tendency, Max Kozloff stated that it was Morris who assembled the artists represented. Philip Leider's more general account of the exhibition was entitled by the *New York Times* features editor "The Properties of Materials: In the Shadow of Robert Morris," reinforcing the notion that these changes were attributable to the catalytic effect of Robert Morris.[3]

Although Le Va does not figure in Morris' warehouse overview nor in the "Anti Form" position paper, he was a natural for inclusion in the "Anti-Illusion: Procedures and Materials" exhibition held at the Whitney Museum in May–July of 1969. The attitudes behind his California felt pieces parallel the East Coast developments, yet Le Va views the anti-formal phase of Morris' work as "still tied to an object aesthetic, an art still captured in a single glance." He placed this interdiction as well on the artists who participated in the "9 in a Warehouse" show, among them Bollinger, Hesse, Nauman, Saret, Serra, and Sonnier.

Be these connections to Morris as they may, the stronger critical issue to be argued is the relation of Le Va's distribution pieces to Serra's process works which appear at the same moment. At a superficial reading, they occupy a wide overlap. Yet important distinctions must be made between them, the chief being Serra's attachment to distinct axiality and clear directional points of reference. Le Va rejected axiality for wide unclear dispersal in which scale—at times up to eighty feet in one direction—de-emphasizes objecthood. Serra's work of 1967–68 dealt largely with object as weight and constancy, whereas Le Va is interested in the ephemeral. In short, Serra's process pieces reveal his internal psychic condition as a sculptor; Le Va's reveal his fundamental psychological commitment as a painter.

Serra (and Smithson) admitted of entropy—the return of matter through chaos to the state of inert homogeneity—only as it was a function of an entire organic process; it grew and then it came apart. This is very different from Le Va's perpetual chaos. Romantic and expressionist to the core, his work was not entropic; it didn't reveal in a later stage of disintegration indices of earlier phases of integration since, in a certain sense, Le Va's work denied integration from the outset.

Still, definable issues were addressed, even if broadly, in the diffuse nature of the 1967–68 pieces. In highly general ways, tangents were alluded to, overlaps described, and sites, directions, scales, spaces, and memories were all brought into play. Such visual comparisons, as were consonant with the expressionist cast of this moment, were interesting to the artist only in the instant of their being done, but they were visually not to be gathered after their execution. (Today, all of this work is known only through photographs). The irony of this romantic and expressionist position is epitomized in Le Va's comparison between one felt piece arranged by chance through dropping and tossing and another made according to a studious taste-oriented placement. One could not tell one from the other nor say which piece was better owing to a simple paradox: "content is something that can't be seen."

Upon his graduation from Otis in 1967, New York was still two years in the offing. Le Va spent the interim teaching at the Minneapolis School of Art, putting aside money to come East. Perplexed during these years by the invisibility of content, Le Va at his Minneapolis remove reflected deeply on the means to render the elements of his environmental pieces more clear. His reading changed from, say, a cult book of the 1960s like Daniel Spoerri's *An Anecdoted Typography of Chance*[4] to adventures of Sherlock Holmes and Ellery Queen. The point of a mystery story is to render visible the invisible content through a manifest fact, the clue. The artist becomes the criminal, the spectator the detective. Thus, tangent, overlap, site, direction, scale, space, and memory—the concerns of the "distribution pieces"—need not remain in an expressionist limbo of perfect chance if one adduces them as a set of clues which serve as designations that lead to specific contexts and contents. The latter in turn partially determine the original clue. The desire to discover the clue, one that was consistent with and true to the specific work although different from piece to piece, led Le Va to determine a visual syntax consonant with the givens of each new situation. Thus the sources of clues may derive from, say, the counterpoints of attributed circles, the physical obstructions of a specific site, the types of visual elements and their frequency, and most importantly, as it happened, the kinds of physical and mental actions the artist feels are necessary to the investigation of a basic situation.

Granting Le Va's expressionist grounding, the mature results of this quest did not suddenly emerge. One could not guess that the heady aggressivity of the 1968 phase would lead to the spare cleanness of the post-1972 work. This phase—say, 1968 through 1972—while shot through with new poles of attraction, particularly regarding the nature of clues, still retains the inflection of his earlier expressionism just as the spare character of the recent work can be seen with hindsight in the first California felts.

Not that this mid-phase is indecisive or vacillating. Often it is very direct, especially when the work, activities, or procedures are conjoined to unequivocal written assertions (rare though these may be) affixed to photographs of the work. Much of this work may be misapprehended as conceptual documentation since, in the absence of a gallery audience, Le Va's works were executed in the studio and photographed. Thus the photograph has the character of a point of reference, an archival record of the work. The photograph itself is not the issue; it serves as attestation to work done.

Characteristic of the 1968–72 phase are the suite of efforts called *The Layered Pattern Acts* (fig. 35), works that examine explicit cause-and-effect activities. One type is atomized—executed in chalk powder; the other, made from glass sheets, is not. What happens when you toss so much weight of chalk powder over so much distance; or when a glass sheet on the floor is shattered with a hammer blow, and then another sheet is laid upon these fractured shards, and again the hammer blow is struck? This serial fracture is continued through as many layers as the artist finds suitable, suitability, as always, being a function of site.[5] In addition to explicit structural information about physical action *The Layered Pattern Acts* incorporates psychological issues as well, although it is tricky to unravel them. Clearly the works are marked by an aggressive tone—the hammer blows, or the physicality of pitching— but this oblique quality of danger, I think, is still ultimately linked to Le Va's primary psychological painterliness.

By the end of 1972, a characteristic gravity and dignity is manifest in the work, a sober texture which can be accounted for by the artist's prevailing fascination with the role of the clue.

> A clue in the detectival sense may be of an intangible as well as a tangible nature; it may be a state of mind as well as a state of fact; or it may derive from the absence of a relevant object as well as from the presence of an irrelevant one . . . But always, whatever its nature, the clue is the thread which guides the crime investigator through the labyrinth of nonessential data into the light of complete comprehension.[6]

The exploration of a site in terms of clues is mapped out in working drawings that range from the sheerly improvisatory to the highly finished. In this sense, like so much drawing of today's abstract reductivism, Le Va's drawing serves little as a document of manual or visual sensibility (though once its intentions are admitted its "beauty" is manifest), and far more as a halfway house between architecture and sculpture. In this, its Minimalist gerund is maintained. Le Va's drawing is diagrammatic and demonstrative; it illustrates nothing, but instead works out the syntax for the kinds of problems to be solved in each site.

This distancing of drawing away from sensibility takes on larger ramifications in Le Va's work insofar as the problems addressed not only key into scale models, but models of bodily movement, and as such engage kinaesthetic notions. Yet the passing similarity of Le Va's drawing to dance notation (or even to time-motion studies in urban planning), especially from 1973 to 1975, is a source the artist rejects if only because dance notation infers repeatability, mimicry of movement, whereas Le Va's systems of movement within a site, while repeatable, are, more importantly, permutable; one person's movement may be entirely different from another's, although the information constructed from these movements will be the same in the end.[7]

More recently, the artist's visual vocabulary, ascertainable from drawing and scaled up in the actual environment, led him to select lines that on the floor may be registered as lines or as lengths—long or short as the situation demands—of wood lathe. Frequently such lines are marked on the floor by short consistent lengths of wood, small rectangular markers. The organic associations of wood are incidental. Instead, wood is used because it is readily available and easy to work—like paper, chalk, or masking tape. Wood in this context presents no special sculptural problems, nor does it call attention to its gravity or the difficulty of its manipulation. In this sense, no eccentricity attaches to it, that is, none of the idiosyncrasy typical of the use of, say, latex, foam, lead, or felt as these materials have been used as "signature substances" in the pictorial/sculptural phase of Postminimalism.

Le Va's vocabulary of geometric elements, however, remains constant within each piece; and just as the artist's job is to determine a consistent vocabulary within the piece, so the viewer's job is to decipher, decode the vocabulary or syntax. Thus all information within a given piece is "factual"; it can be reconstructed as consistent information in the mind or the movements of the viewer, most probably both. As such it is not wholly based upon artistic taste; but, in the variety of permutations to which these reconstructions are liable, neither can the work be said to be wholly systemic. Artistic volition still plays its role. For example, the circle as an organizing principle, as a device so to speak, is a clue attractive to Le Va insofar as it tends to be "a more ambiguous constant than rectangles." Hence the circle's shape and size may be first determined by variables of choice, just as frequency of tangent and overlap is subject to volition as well. Variables that govern Le Va's decisions may be choice of circle size, original generative placement within the site (on the drawing or in the site itself), and perhaps most importantly, the decisions and movements that the spectator will adopt in apprehending the original organizing processes of the artist.

This description largely relates to the work of 1973–75; insofar as the spectator's apprehension has become more subject to variability than before, it seems fair to assume that Le Va's period of detective mystery clues is drawing to a close. Greater ambiguity in his work may be anticipated, and in this his work is responding to the growing level of ambiguity—in this sense, greater aestheticism, sensible in the larger body of epistemic abstractionists, such as Mel Bochner, Dorothea Rockburne, and Bruce Boice.

Despite many points of agreement with these figures, Le Va is wary of facile couplings. In measure, he disassociates himself from the aspects of their exploration by pointing out their more readily visible "shape orientation." Moreover, "their interest is primarily with content itself. I'm still interested in work that has some content outside of itself; staying with the audience, but still not theater."

Notes

1. For an article by Jane Livingston, "Barry Le Va: Distributional Sculpture."

2. Barbara Rose, "The Value of Didactic Art," *Artforum*, April, 1967; Fidel Danieli, "Some New Los Angeles Artists," *Artforum*, March, 1968. The other artists were James De France, Peter Alexander and Carl Cheng.

3. Max Kozloff, "9 in a Warehouse," *Artforum*, February, 1969; Philip Leider, *New York Times*, December 22, 1968.

4. In this *nouveau realiste* and Fluxus work, Spoerri set up a chance studio still life and then painstakingly, often esoterically, catalogued each element within it. The unfixed nature of chance studio still-life elements were transformed into specific mapping and data retrieval—a kind of research collation.

5. The glass pieces received their most fulsome presentation at Documenta, 1972, where a negligent administration allowed the work to become damaged, first by hostile workmen who tossed beer bottles into the piece, and then by a public who walked upon the layers of glass, thus disordering every contextual reference of the fragments.

6. William O. Green's introduction to *Ars Criminalis* by John Strang, quoted in Ellery Queen, *The French Powder Mystery* (Signet, New American Library, 1969), p. 82.

7. "Visual structures are nothing but an aid to thinking and belong to the psychological apparatus which draws the conclusions, not the content of the thoughts themselves. Thinking does not aim at the pictures but the logical structures which they express." Hans Reichenback, *Space and Time* (Dover, New York, 1957), p. 97. It was this book, Le Va says, which led him to *The Walking Stick Pieces*, 1973. In general, *The Walking Stick Pieces* addressed two possibilities: "The stick can be moved end over end, repeating its own measurement while travelling, or it can be moved laterally across the floor. That's a variable; you can move it with a short or long swing in a zig-zag motion." Representative of the latter type—though in certain works these motions are mixed—is *Equal Wall Base Divisions Crossed: 4 Phases (Walked Zig-Zag; Ends Touch, Ends Cut)*, 1973.

Figure 34. Barry Le Va, #10, Detail, 1967
Felt, wood and ball bearings, 20'×25', scale variable.
(Photo courtesy Sonnabend Gallery)

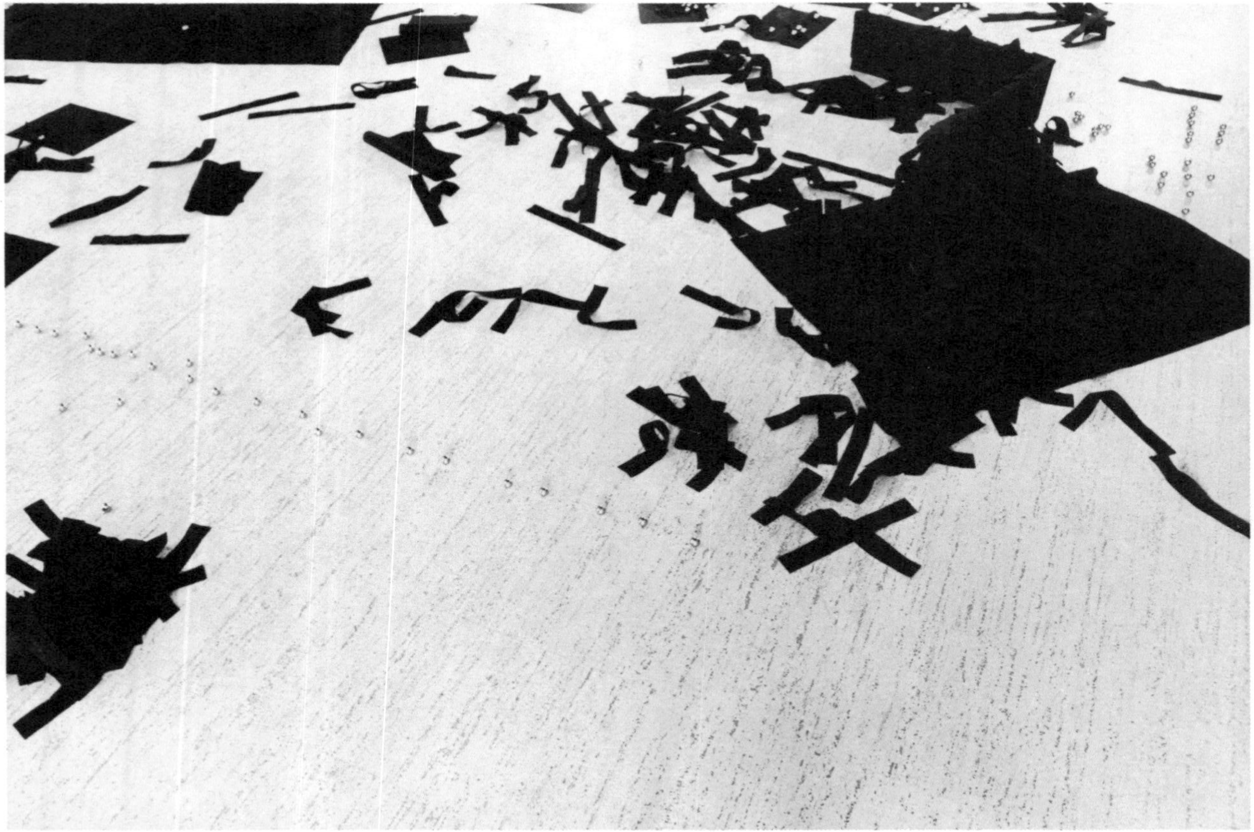

Figure 35. Barry Le Va, *Untitled (Layered Pattern Acts)*, Detail, 1968–72
Glass, 25'×85', scale variable.
(Photo courtesy Sonnabend Gallery)

Postminimalism

Ontology

Jackie Ferrara: The Feathery Elevator

I. The Formalist Dysfunction

Italics. Interior monologue stuff. It's so pretentious. What's wrong? Perhaps what's right? Suddenly I can't write about art as if it existed in a sanitized vacuum. Now it's clear that my fascination with contemporary art has two approaches. One is a sense of excellence before certain experiences—that's it, that's clearly art—sensations which engage the obligation of formal analysis. Well, it's not really that way, since the awareness of excellence is primed by the Knowledge of how objects or activities key into history. It's the unanticipated relationship between art and its externals (history, society, what have you) that provokes the meaningful gut level response (the word "meaningful" is a sellout). My convictions seem so obvious that I speak of this or that artist, this or that work, without prefacing build. The public must surely see it, and yet I know it doesn't.

Until late in the sixties, solemn formalism was assumed to be the only way one talked about art. The mandarin tone obtained as the signal characteristic of distinguished critical and historical discussion. Disinterestedness. I don't get it anymore—well, not exclusively. There's this other side of me, the other avenue—work perceived as significant must be invested with the value deriving from biography, the really lived, the idiosyncratic datum, the human. Biography as form; biography is form. Reluctance to acknowledge this stems from a puritanical abhorrence of gossip, and from a class and guiltridden snobbery against being "in commerce," of being "in trade." The open traffic in biography is seen as promotional, advertising. Perhaps. As always it remains a question of whose voice, who's talking. Another class-conscious exculpation. I scorn the experiential sop, John Dewey's sentimental ploy as a sellout— a balance (bargain?) struck between the analysis of form and the recounting of biography. If it is patently undemocratic (and it is) to draw to oneself the profession of stating that such activities are manifestly art, then surely it is as elitist to stress whatever it is that one does stress, even if it is biography over formal discussion. It all winds down to the mouse's tail (tale?) in Alice—*an infinite spiraling decrescendo.*

This article originally appeared in *Arts Magazine*, November 1976.

II. The Artist's Studio

8 September 1976. To Jackie Ferrara's Prince Street studio: orderly, lovely insofar as Soho's retrieved industrial space can ever be lovely. Her carefully crafted mounds and sloped pyramids neatly rising from the floor, filling out the working space, just missing the heavy-duty buzz saws and electrical equipment needed to make them. The living area is simple and reasonable: books; the occasional trade, work for work, with peer artists; the hangover *bizarrerie* from a much earlier abandoned "figurative weirdo phase." On the shelf there is, for example, a so-called 17th-century merman for some Baroque *wunderkammer*—a South Sea gimcrack, part humanoid, part alluvial. Ferrara tells me that there are two other examples, one in the Musée de l'Homme, the other scarcely perceived in a snapshot of James Ensor's studio. (The merman was a trade with an art dealer who gave it up for a big blowfish, and was bested in the swap). A bedraggled stuffed loon peers down from the bookshelf; a leather lizard perches on the ledge. One more false start; too elliptical. I'm not getting near the problem of Ferrara's sculpture.

Talking to Ferrara is an enormous pleasure. She is not a perfect art star fixated permanently at a sleek and ambiguous Milanese thirty—somewhere between 18 and 43—but a woman fully in mid-life with a rich suite of existences, all whole and fascinating in themselves, and not yet expunged, board-erased so as to insure one story, one myth. Since Ferrara was born in 1929, there are several lives, the most important (to us) coincidental with her move into the Prince Street loft in 1971. Née Jacqueline Hirshhorn in Detroit—"my name had three h's, a j and a q'—she has kept the name of her second husband, Don Ferrara, a jazz musician. Detroit was ordinary background stuff, capped at length by a year at Michigan State. There she met her first husband, Peter Weber, now a hypnotist-phrenologist, then "just a good-looking guy. I wanted to play house. Everybody thought I was wild. I wasn't the least bit wild." The first marriage was brief. Ferrara left with $29 borrowed from her brother Austin. "I always wanted to come to New York. I always looked at pictures of New York, Greenwich Village. I tacked them over my bed. I desperately wanted to come to New York. I worked in a bank, the accounting department."

About 1951—in conversation Ferrara, as everybody else, is a bit wooly about dates—she arrived in New York, at length finding an apartment on the cheap Lower East Side, making her way working for a life insurance company. It's dreadfully banal and very real, the conversation of a fine person (tugged black braids shot with gray) coming to terms with a nostalgia for the past and her sense of shifting interpersonal relationships and the changing art scene.

The discovery of art and the sheer depth of her gift coincide with such ordinary happenstance that I am deeply affected. Certain details key in the most willy-nilly way into movements of my own adolescence; we both, for example, overlapped at the Henry Street Settlement, never meeting. The time is the early fifties. "I was trying to find myself. I was interested in art. I took a couple of classes at the New

School." So far no fallout. "I wasn't allowed to go to art school in Michigan. I couldn't take art classes. I was terribly obedient until I was 18."

Into the early fifties there is little about art; surely a rich field, but scant seedlings. "Then I started to take ceramics. I lived near the Henry Street Settlement House. I started taking these pottery classes and I loved it. After a while I made my dishes. They're all chunky. I couldn't work on the wheel very well." By 1955 Ferrara signs her pottery, and for the next two years there is an intense commitment to crafts: the fifties—strong personalities attracted by strong primitive cultures. Ferrara's pottery, shown to me with bantering reluctance—my snobbishness was to be anticipated—reveals deep bowed forms and animal biomorphism synthesized from a ranging ethnographic lexicon, be it African or Meso-American ritual and domestic utensils. There are additional inferences of a Gottlieb-like pictogram expressed as incised graffiti. It's easy to patronize this work, its folkloric aspirations and integrity, its earthen organicity—there's a lot of grog in Ferrara's ceramics—all that art-as-experience stuff that craftspeople believe in. Perhaps all of that is beginning to have a certain period allure, the campy stylishness of a fictitious folklore invoked by the arty craftswork of the fifties. Twenty years later it becomes "real art" in the way that it never was nor could have been when it was made, despite all of its striving aspiration. I'm not just talking about Ferrara's ceramics, which in this context appears to be given undue stress, but of a broad range of handicrafted objects of which Ferrara's are given a sudden distinction because the mature sculpture, dating to 1972, retrospectively confers distinction upon all early effort. One even recognizes in Ferrara's present sculpture certain hangover enthusiasms traceable to her ceramics. There is, for example, the whole feeling for the Meso-American itself now inferred through pyramidal stacking. This goes back perhaps to the moment of an almost physical enthusiasm but of no structured theory of art, both facets by which the American fifties are characterized.

"While I was taking pottery there was an opening at the Henry Street Playhouse Theater." The Playhouse was then a center for burgeoning dance and theatrical consciousness. Alwin Nikolais, seconded by Murray Louis. Ferrara ran the office, scheduled the theater, classes, that kind of thing. This capacity for neatness and organization must never be forgotten, especially as it counters, as will be seen, so much in Ferrara's work seemingly anathematic to this rage for order, so to speak. "I was still working at the life insurance company. When a promotion came along I didn't get the pay that the man who had the job before me got. I was angry about it, but I didn't see it in sexist terms either. We still weren't thinking that way in the fifties."

Suddenly Ferrara is talking about living in Italy for fifteen months in a village outside of Florence, driving a Topolino, a little Fiat, casting bronzes. I'm brought up short; a synapse takes place, out of synch. I have her go back over the terrain. How did we get to Italy? Another relationship is brought into the conversation; it may be maximized but it can't be minimized. From the late fifties through '67 or '68, say for a decade, Ferrara was living with Robert Beauchamp. "It was my longest relationship." I think for a moment of the artist in question whose work has been regularly shown at galleries of consequence, Graham, Dintenfass, Green. "He opened the Green Gallery. He showed there regularly for years." Two things are going on: a recollection about a man for whom Ferrara feels deep affection, and through whom she had easy access into the changing art climate of the later fifties; and second, another history is being invoked, that of the Green Gallery itself. We tend to think of the latter solely in its final manifestation when Richard Bellamy was showing works that defined Minimalist aspirations. Yet, when it opened, the unstructured and ex-pressionist characteristics traceable to Abstract Expressionism were still sensible in the then underground figures to whom Bellamy was drawn—Beauchamp, Olden-burg, Samaras, Kaprow, Segal—kinds of art informed by the Happening and divergent environmental ambiences. I recall Beauchamp's emergence as a "brilliant comer." Ferrara and I experience the rueful poignancy of years past. I recall my indifference to Beauchamp's painterliness and oneiric sexualized imagery invented in its very painting—animals, women, flight, turbulence. I think of Ferrara's phrase "figurative weirdo" and her early destroyed fetishistic art. It closely keys into the Beauchamp take and makes me uneasy about my facile dismissal.

"I would go to openings, art parties. There was a lot of social activity. Beauchamp didn't like to go so I would take friends. Dorothea [Rockburne] and I were friends. I used to see her every day. We used to talk "girl talk," you know, sex. She was working for Robert Rauschenberg then. It was about people, it was never about theory. I used to see Carl Andre all the time. He was thin and cute. Down from the Cedar Street bar there was Dillon's. It had a kind of shuffleboard game. Andre was the best, but I was the second best." Fragments of transient art life in the late fifties, early sixties, as if from another planet; Andre "cute," "thin"; it's hard to im-agine him free of the Marxist overload that burdens his persona today. Still, much of Ferrara's work is consonant with the vital rehabilitations of contemporary sculpture brought about through Andre's doctrinaire assertions and embodiments. Think, for example, of the exhaustive spiralings, serializations, and layerings themselves. They are locatable to Andre and are germane not only to his work but to Ferrera's or any of a dozen sculptors concerned with the maintenance of the vitality of the abstract reductivist tradition.

I question Ferrara about exhaustive layering, seriality. "I don't see any clear pat-terns," she answers. "The last couple of years on Delancey Street I was doing rope works, very hairy, very biomorphic. I was doing two kinds of work: stuff that hanged and stuff that rose up from the floor." I assimilate the former to the pictorial and eccentric revision of Minimalist sculpture (around 1967–69); the latter I bring into the Andre purview. But to do so perhaps is precipitate, wrongheaded, as will be seen.

When the relationship with Beauchamp faltered in the late sixties and Ferrara entered another with collage-maker Martin Greenbaum, she withdrew from circula-tion. Only in the early seventies, at last divested of human entailments and domestic encumbrances and dedicated fully to sculpture in her own place, her own loft—it's the only way—and beginning to produce work congruent with the major sculptural options of the moment, Ferrara once more ran into the people she knew back then. It was surprising for her to learn, for example, that Rockburne had in the interim become a well-known figure, an artist whose work on some broad ideological level corresponded to issues of her own reductive intentionist constructivism. Similarly Andre. It's hard for me to fully accede to this sense of how styles filter into existence. It seems to me that a certain memory screening has taken place, one that makes complicated episodes seem too easy, but to press the issue would be rude. I revert to Italy.

In 1959, Ferrara and Beauchamp were there. She had been making just awful, now charming, little sculptures, and she knows it. "I lined up bronze figures. The bodies would always be the same, female. The faces I would paint, very African, very primitive. I didn't know how to make hands and feet. I really didn't know how to make bodies. It was very cheap then. Each figure cost about eight dollars to cast. Sometimes they would be in a setting." I asked whether I could see them. You could see that, in a nice way, Ferrara is going to fib, that she doesn't want to, that in the end she won't. She says she sold them recently as bronze scrap to a Canal Street dealer for cost, to be melted down. Maybe they still exist. The dealer still may have them.

All the while we had been talking I assumed that Ferrara's distinguished first one-person show took place in 1973 at the A. M. Sachs Gallery where I saw her work for the first time—serialized platforms and towering pyramids of welted papier-mâché-like cotton batting (fig. 36). Ferrara goes to a little cabinet sideboard and finds an envelope. You know, the memorabilia that remains despite repeated domestic upheaval and the concerted eliminations of the trivia we carry through our lives. She hands me a document about which she has a lot of sweet tension, the invitation (bearing an illustration) to her first "one-man show" held in December of 1961, when people still said "one-man show" no matter what the artist's sex. The Janet Nessler Gallery, 1718 Madison Avenue, the kind of gallery that comes and goes, but not a vanity gallery with which the fifties were rife. The invitation listed the works. Invitations don't anymore. An occasional striving literary title, *Alcestis and Admetus,* that kind of title, but mostly the works were plainly named, say *Watchers,* the work reproduced on the somewhat pinkish paper; gorgeous ephemera— for those of us, anyway, who love the little history of New York art. Were I to check out *Art News* or *Arts* I bet I would find a sentence, a phrase or two, a snatch of a review. *Watchers,* a small group of flat-faced Ernst-like little figures, funny and silly and still a little folkloric (I bet the scrap dealer still has them, didn't melt them down. Who is he?).

III. Tales (Tails?) of the Lower East Side

13 September 1976. The problem is, of course, the time overlap. Ferrara may be unsure as to dates, though not the features of an event itself. Within a general profile she finds no difficulty in verbally detailing the process of making work of art.

Once this process is assimilated to theory, problems arise. Sentences begin, subjects without predicates, ending in frustrated incomplete ideas. Under duress: "I don't ponder problems. I don't ruminate. I don't ponder the past. I am very of the moment. I am unbelievably unassertive about art; yet I have all kinds of opinions on other subjects."

How often have I met this block before! Is it locatable to the sheer anxiety the artist feels about creativity? On one hand, artists know that whatever is coming comes from somewhere; on the other, there is the fear that to locate the source, historically, critically, intentionally, in terms of specific models, whatever—all this may bring down to the ordinary, the mundane, the near religious belief in the creative process and in creation itself; and perhaps it may staunch the flow. Then there is the final blow: to recognize the source is to somehow be open to disdain; the fear that art loses status upon recognition of stylistic contingencies. This is compounded by a constellation of feelings which when pressed will silence the speaker. No more will come for fear of saying too much or too little, of overpraising or badmouthing; feelings of angst, or paranoia.

A big truth blurts out: "My position is very embarrassing. To have begun to make work in 1972 that was more suitable to 1965. I don't feel embarrassed about it now." Not to feel embarrassment is of course the correct tack. What is growing apparent is that the maintenance of abstract reductivism presents its own kind of vitality in the face of the continuing evolution of a highly theatricalized conceptualism. The validity of Ferrara's position is underscored not only by her own sense of rightness and well-being with a continuing examination of pyramid variations, but in the very fallout of that fascination—exquisite, shadowed, dark channeled, complexly stepped, and chambered rises.

True, the critical distinction here is being drawn between a Minimalist logic carried through an exhaustive permutation in the late sixties as compared to similar solipsistic processes executed in the late seventies; the former emerged in a sudden rush, as it were, predicated on an activity located in thinking; the latter derives from direct manual evolutionary practice. Of course I exaggerate the distinction. There can be no practice without ideation, as there can be no ideation without process or activity. But these experiences may allow for different emphases. It is this difference which accounts for a manual, slow-based process and logistics in the present moment. Here, unquestionably, evolution will be slower. But as much may be said not only of Jackie Ferrara, but of Winsor too, whose current cube stackings and variations share several points of reference with those of Ferrara. In this sense, both these artists of merit (and still others who must be drawn into the purview) are responding to aspects of a certain impulse even sensible in the more extenuated and manneristic reaches of conceptual performance qua painting and sculpture. Much in the way that the behavioral conceptualists reject epistemology for content without form, that is, for autiobiography and autobiographical extrapolation, so, too, do the current breed of abstract reductionists eschew epistemology, for pure doing—information or knowledge be hanged. Yet their work is in its final manifestation worlds apart from that of the behavioral conceptualists, and this because they have never relinquished the primordial archetypes of modernist abstraction: circles, spheres, squares, cubes, triangles, pyramids.

If so much of this art stems from a pure evolutionary practice and if, as I appear to be hinting, biography keys into this process, and nourishes it far beyond ways heretofore sanctioned in formalist criticism, then the change in Ferrara's work from the late sixties to the seventies may be examined in terms of her own view of biography, biography recorded as descriptive process. One could say to Ferrara, yes, hanging hairy forms and organic parasexual metaphors adduce an opposing typology— recumbent inert forms free of all metaphorical content whatever. In that sense, one kind of dualistic argument—wholeness based on complementary halves—is the paradigm for this change. One could say something like that but such a cryptic reduction cannot possibly correspond to Ferrara's—or anyone else's for that matter— sense of elaborately lived episode.

"Then I worked in rope too. I lived on the Lower East Side. It was Succoth (the Jewish thanksgiving Feast of Tabernacles). To celebrate the holiday, people came downtown to buy lemons from Israel (*etrog*), I mean big ugly lemons. Some people examined them with a magnifying glass to make sure that they were unblemished. A perfect fruit sold for up to thirty dollars apiece. It was unbelievable. Bad ones, I mean where the point of contact with the tree had fallen off the fruit, were dumped for ten dollars. It's all about this Lower East Side lore. Anyway, they were packed in a packing material, hairy raw flax, laid out in skeins. I started using this hary stuff, joining it to tiny heads of dripped wax. I ended up liking the material more than the heads and the chicken nails and the fur-covered boxes. The boxes got to be very small, and long flax tails hung down. I started making these 'tails,' I guess that's what you'd call them. The 'tails' went into the rope pieces. At the end of 1969 I absolutely never made heads or figures anymore. At the same time I started to use birds" (fig. 37).

The use of organic substances invokes a talismanic, even ritualized function. Organic substance as material is intriguing because it may receive magical status for its having been originally totemic in some sense. The use of blood, for example, and most particularly in women's art (which might use it reasonably to celebrate the blood mysteries) is a case in point. Add to such substance the poetical stress of minute human referents such as doll-like heads and the point will be clearer.

The sixties especially experienced a lockstep synchronism between an abstract reductivist art and a formalist criticism. One of the salutary effects of Postminimalism was to rupture the symbiosis of art making and critical writing. This was effected in part by the creation of an art for which criticism, by which (at the time) was meant formalist criticism, had not developed a vocabulary. Keying into this widely felt therapeutic was the need to externalize an extremely personal statement, especially on the part of women artists who, long disenfranchised (except for a few token individuals), were locked out of the success of abstract painting and sculpture at the time.

The advent of feminist activism (and I don't mean by this that Ferrara was an activist) gave a political value to the private history and mythology of women, a mythology capable of being exteriorized in a talismanic fetishistic art; surely never before in modern art had this kind of elaborately eccentric, magically-endowed, autobiographically transmuted, talismanic art appeared. The point of this was not only to endow the female status with a power nigglingly accorded it if not entirely denied, but also to circumvent history and criticism since talismanic arts generally fall outside the province of history and criticism. Such art, like naive art, like ritual/primitive art, answers not the sequence of styles built into the modernist European calendar, but of a magical chronometer the solstices of which, its months and days, cannot be measured. This occurs because, on the one hand, this kind of art is always out there somewhere, impervious to normative stylistic history (if such a flow can ever be said to have a normal context), answering only psychic inner necessity; and, on the other, because it is occasionally suddenly there—in this sense, art atavistically responding to sudden new pressures occasioned by the changing flow of social economic force of Western culture; the advent of the women's movement would be the most dramatic modern eruption of the latter type.

A last story. In 1969, ironically grown allergic to flax and rope, Ferrara abandoned the "tails," and more humanoid fetishistic character of the work. "At the same time I started to use birds. The first bird I got was a crow . . . [remember the musty loon on the bookcase?]. I found it in an antique shop near Tompkins Square. Then I went to this feather factory on East 4th and Avenue D, a terrible junkie street. I asked whether they had any crows. A guy remembered that somewhere upstairs there were boxes filled with pigeons. We took this old grimy elevator. Feathers had stuck to it everywhere. We were in a feathery elevator. We found box after box of pigeons, 440 in all. If I took the lot I could have them at ten cents apiece. I took them. It cost $44. I brought them home, sorting them out by color. I used them in my work. Eventually I used up all the birds."

In a corner of the studio there is still one left. Practically all of Ferrara's early work has been destroyed. I climb a ladder to examine a work high on a wall, covered with plastic sheeting to protect it from dust. The birds have been arranged in softly interlocking paths across the surface. Monkey fur surrounds the stretcher supports and an array of pigeons dangles on threads from the bottom.

The totemic magical characteristics are apparent. I wondered about so elaborate a switch between this talismanic art and the taciturn monumental abstraction by which Ferrara's reputation has gained ground. Had I failed to mention that needing a pencil, Ferrara fetched one for me from the sideboard, originally a dental technician's cabinet? Pencils, pens, nylon-tipped markers, art supplies within had been neatly arranged according to particular function and grade. "I took them home sorting them out by color." She was talking about the birds. Of nails (chicken nails?) used to construct the wooden pyramids: "I took them home and arranged them by grade, by scale, by color." Such an occasion is not the place to trace, were it even possible, the filigrained network connecting fetish and compulsivity. Surely, though, both the lost early Ferraras and the present neat, complex, quasi-impersonal pyramids are functions of the same initial impulse to constructivist compulsivity.

Figure 36. Jackie Ferrara, *Cotton Batting Works, Studio View,* ca. 1970–72 *(Photo courtesy Max Protetch Gallery)*

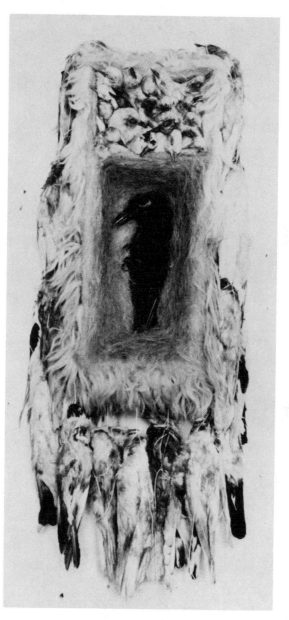

Figure 37. Jackie Ferrara, *Untitled,* 1968
Wood, crow, fur, string, pigeons.
*(Collection of Allen Stone; photo courtesy
Max Protetch Gallery)*

Vito Acconci and the Conceptual Performance

... there is mention of an Italian artist who painted with feces; during the French Revolution blood served as paint for someone ...

—Guillaume Apollinaire, *The Cubist Painters*, 1913

Vito Acconci, perhaps more than any other figure working in that aspect of Postminimalism associated with the Conceptual performance, is the one who in a puzzling and constricted way allies those open and anarchic stances with the abstract reductivist enterprise known as Minimalism. In so doing he demonstrates a point that I have been at pains to make—that it is possible to recognize in Minimalism itself many of the clues which in fact led to its own stylistic dissolution. In Acconci's work this was achieved by conjoining Minimalist form with Duchamp-like thought and behavior, a fusion which may only be short-lived because of the virtually antithetical nature of these two positions. Instead of forming autonomous objects this fusion has led, bizarrely enough, to the Conceptual performance—one which heretofore had been thought to derive exclusively from the Futurist and Dadaist theaters of the First World War.

The general response these past two years to Acconci's "presentations," or "performances"—there seems to be no precise term to cover what he does, although in the past it has often been referred to as "body art"—has been, I suppose, to scoff ever since Acconci's activities, in certain measure, have become familiar. In this respect, as well as in others, one cannot fail to make connections between Acconci's performances (if they are that) and those earlier manifestations of behavioral phenomenology occasioned by Bruce Nauman's absorption of technological apparatus into a sensibility which had drawn upon a source in Duchamp. Instead of continuing to work in a diffuse no-man's-land of Conceptual pretensions, Acconci now seems to concentrate his actions with such acuity that initial scepticism is replaced by the possibility that perhaps what he is doing may be akin to art, at least that side of art which has its affiliations in an obsessional focus. As Acconci himself has remarked:

This article originally appeared in *Artforum*, April 1972.

My work seems mainly concerned with what I guess could be called "attention" or "concentration"; like if I'm going to concentrate on my own body or a part of my own body, this intense focus on it, this intense channeling toward it is going to lead to a kind of turning in on myself which is a kind of masochism. But these elements are just sidelines, or by-products of this kind of attention or concentration. In the same way, if I'm concentrating on this other person or on my action with this other person, an exaggerated version of this is going to be what people can call sadism.[1]

In short, the earlier Acconci which was fashioned of a synthesis of Conceptual aspirations, has become more convincing as art because he is now able to manipulate and relocate inherited attitudes which need not only be understood as behavioral phenomenology.

"I used to think that art was not about therapy, I mean I learned to believe that art was not about therapy. But now I think that it is." Acconci was talking in a stuffy, makeshift booth, surrounded by the photographs of six persons close to him and about whom he had been meditating. The closet was airless and muggy as a result of the heat given off, I believe, from a tape recorder and amplifier. The light source was a hand-held flashlight. Acconci was speaking about *Seedbed*, a work which takes the form of a wedge-shaped ramp which slopes up from the floor to cover an entire gallery (fig. 38). Within this wedge, Acconci passed two afternoons a week in a "private sexual activity," stated bluntly, in masturbation. Acconci's written and posted description of the piece touches on the following issues:

1. The room is activated by my presence underground, underfoot—by my movement from point to point under the ramp.

2. The goal of my activity is the production of seed—scattering the seed throughout the underground area. (My aim is to concentrate on my goal, to be totally enclosed within my goal.)

3. The means to this goal is private sexual activity. (My attempt is to maintain the activity throughout the day, so that a maximum of seed is produced; my aim is to have constant contact with my body so that a maximum of seed is produced; my aim is to have constant contact with my body so that an effect from my body is carried outside.)

4. My aids are the visitors to the gallery—in my seclusion, I can have private images of them, talk to myself about them: my fantasies about them can excite me, enthuse me to sustain—to resume—my private sexual activity. (The seed "planted" on the floor, then is a joint result of my performance and theirs.)

The poetical ellipses in points 2 and 4 play between the idea of Acconci's sperm spurted onto the floor but understood in its agricultural metaphor: as seed. Duchamp's parallel is *Elevage de Poussière*, or *Dust Breeding*. Not incidentally, Duchamp's subtitle for *The Bride Stripped Bare by Her Bachelors, Even* is "agricultural machine."

Superficially the piece might correspond to a sadomasochistic submission fantasy in which the spectator—unwittingly or wittingly—may literally walk over the prone figure of a masturbating "servant." Such an interpretation is too facile as it does not take into account what is finally interesting, namely that the Conceptual performance, at least in Vito Acconci's case, may be a fusion of the Minimalist position in sculpture with a refreshed comprehension of the erotic implications in Duchamp's late sexual works, most particularly *The Wedge of Chastity* (1951, fig. 39). What is perhaps the least interesting aspect of the work is its seemingly outrageous or so-called shocking subject matter.

To adopt an extreme taboo in the context of a gallery situation in fact neutralizes its sexual emphasis, as it neutralizes the very notion of taboo. Since the spectator is a *voyeur* only in the sense that he is an auditor of the events[2]—Acconci's mumbled fantasies are amplified and broadcast into the gallery—the spectator may not comprehend the activity which is taking place literally beneath his feet. It seems more likely that work does not attempt, as part of any programmatic intention, to neutralize sexual taboos, although this is its practical effect. Sufficient stylistic information suggests that Acconci, like Nauman—and I think the primary model was Nauman at his most Duchamp-like, ca. 1966–69—is dealing with an exaggerated, nonobjectified relationship to the erotic legacy of Duchamp.

An interpretation of Duchamp's evolution that is especially appealing at the present moment is that the elaboration of the adventures of the Nude to the Virgin to the Bride Stripped Bare by Her Bachelors is an extrapolation on the possibility of Duchamp's first name understood as a "Readymade": Marcel = MAR + CEL = *Mariée* + *Céli*bataire = Bride + Bachelor = Female + Male = Androgyne = Rose Sélavy + Marcel Duchamp. In this context, Acconci's sexualization may be viewed as an extrapolation upon the androgyne of Duchamp. For example, the wedge-shaped floor seems apposite to the meaning of wedge as a fusion of male and female in Duchamp's third sexual object of 1951, *The Wedge of Chastity*. I have already attempted to demonstrate that the verbal-visual objectification of Nauman's two wedges *(Wedge Piece)* of 1968 (fig. 40) are developments of the possibilities inherent in Duchamp's *Wedge*. In this connection Acconci's theatrical *Seedbed* and Nauman might be regarded as cousinly efforts.

However, the ramp floor of the Acconci speaks for a source in Minimalist sculpture, Robert Morris' several untitled wedge-like works from 1965–68 particularly (fig. 41). I do not think that Nauman derives in the slightest from Morris. Nor do I claim that Morris' Minimalist "wedges" even remotely correspond to Duchamp despite Morris' early production which seems so closely allied to Jasper Johns. One might have imagined that through the mediation of Johns, Morris' "wedges" might derive from Duchamp.

"Are you aware of Duchamp's three sexual objects," I asked Acconci, "and do you recognize the relationship of *Seedbed* to these objects?" "Yes."

In the 1971 film *Conversions*,[3] Acconci is seen tugging at his breasts, burning hair from his chest, and hiding his penis between his legs, that is, attempting to transform himself into a female, or, at least, into an androgyne. "Did this film record a process parallel to the sexual multivalence between Marcel Duchamp and Rose Sélavy?" "Yes."

Despite their fearful sexual obsessiveness, Acconci's activities raise a number of questions that are difficult to answer particularly as regards the cathartic relationship of the mental and physical dislocations of his work. Still, what is intriguing in Acconci's latest performance is not its increment of the "polymorphous perverse" or the virtual denial of taboo through exteriorization, but that Acconci is able to handle the Conceptual performance in a way which expresses a closeness to the processes of the mind as opposed to the experiences of the senses. By contrast, we have the puzzling performances of Gilbert and George. In comparison with Acconci the Britons have an "act," something which is playable in a cabaret as it is in a studio or a gallery. In that sense their Conceptual performance refers back to the European Dadaistic experience, to the Cabaret Voltaire, to a Dadaism which mixed together sociological, political, and economic commentary realized in Futurist and Cubist modes. Their Conceptual performance, therefore, is social in its ramifications and implicitly sensory in its appeals. It is a presentation of deliberate theatricality and campiness. On the other hand, Acconci, beginning with the apparently sensual theme of externalized taboo and sexuality, conducts the Conceptual performance in a virtually autistic vacuum. In this sense he approaches social indifference—despite the enormity of the social implications of his work—and remains as elitist and infrareferential as Duchamp always was and as the general tenor of New York Dadaism in its heroic period was as well.

Notes

1. Vito Acconci, from an unpublished interview with Barbara Fishman, November 23, 1971.

2. *Voyeur* and *auditor* probably correspond to the alter-egos of Jasper Johns' paintings of the mid-1960s, *Watchman* and *Spy*. See Jasper Johns, "Sketchbook Notes," *Art and Literature*, Spring, 1965, especially p. 192.

3. Based on the photo-essay by Acconci/Shunk-Kender, "Conversions," *Avalanche*, Winter, 1971, pp. 90–95.

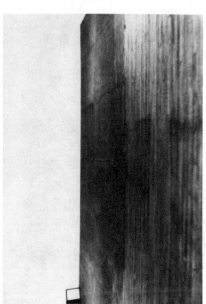

Figure 38. Vito Acconci, *Seedbed*, Installation, 1972
(*Photo courtesy Sonnabend Gallery*)

Figure 39. Marcel Duchamp, *Wedge of Chastity*, 1951
Original plaster from which metal and dental wax work was fashioned,
2-3/4" x 3-7/8" x 2-1/2".
(Photo courtesy Yves Arman)

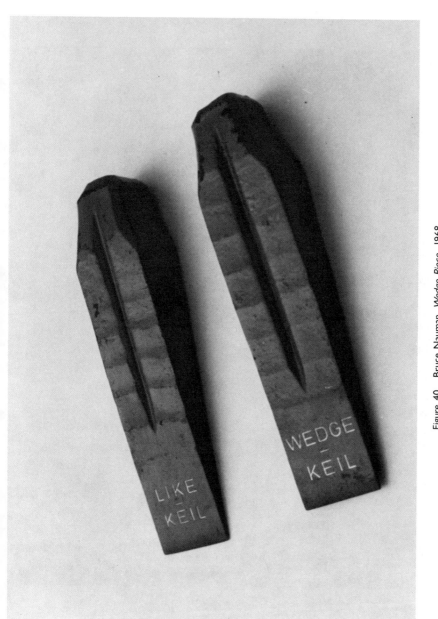

Figure 40. Bruce Nauman, *Wedge Piece*, 1968
Engraved painted steel.
(Photo courtesy Leo Castelli Gallery)

Figure 41. Robert Morris, *Untitled Sculpture*, 1965
Gray fiberglass, 2′×1′×16′.
(Photo courtesy Leo Castelli Gallery)

Lynda Benglis: The Frozen Gesture

Lynda Benglis contributes to new options in American art—my reluctance to admit this is tied to her extravagance. Few talents today are so alert to the weights and balances of the actual moment and no artist seems more capricious, more casual. She appears to toss aside important realizations at the instant of their discovery. Rarely has the observation that art is about beginnings been more apt than in her case. In this sequence of feints and probes, Benglis stands in striking contrast to many of the major minimalists of the '60s, who built their careers on one idea as an intense and committed demonstration of the continuing validity of a single option. In Benglis' apparent reluctance to remain with a problem taken to its most extenuated circumstances lies the notion that the artist evolves in disjunctive, not conjunctive, terms. Her formal volatility is her primary message and strength.[1]

Lynda Benglis left Louisiana in 1964 to continue her art studies at the Brooklyn Museum Art School. In 1969 she participated in a group exhibition at the Bykert Gallery with, among others, Richard Van Buren and Chuck Close. From May of that year to the present is hardly a long period. In terms of art, however, virtual generations have come and gone. The major shift of sensibility has been the emergence of a Postminimalist stance, first realized in the pictorial sculptures so well exemplified by Benglis' latex and foam works. Conceptual work and performances succeeded this pictorializing phase of sculpture, developments reflected in Benglis' use of video and her current mannered erotic art.

In the Bykert show, Benglis exhibited a latex floor piece called *Bounce*. As Emily Wasserman described it:

> Miss Benglis spilled stains of liquid rubber in a freely flowing, twining mass directly onto the floor of the exhibition space, mixing fluorescent oranges, chartreuses, day-glo pinks, greens, and blues, allowing the accidents and puddlings of the material to harden into a viscous mass. The outer contours trace the natural flow of the latex and define the amoeba-like but self-contained field of this strange and startlingly *colored* spread. The method by which the piece was (non) formed is thus actually objectivied while the events and timing of its process are congealed.[2]

This article originally appeared in *Artforum*, November 1974.

Calling *Bounce* a "protoplasmic mat," Wasserman recognized that the work was "a kind of painting entirely freed from an auxiliary ground or armature"—a free gesture gelled in space.

By now, it is clear that Benglis was answering the fusion of painting and sculpture that had taken place in the mid-1960s. The pictorial sculpture I refer to generally, and Benglis' particularly, furthered this fusion by making a new object which is the result of an Expressionist episode enacted directly upon the floor. Choosing this option, Benglis, like Van Buren, Hesse, Saret, Serra, and Sonnier, transposed the easel tradition questioned in Abstract Expressionism into actual environmental enterprise.

Agreed: Pollock's career, from the 1940s on, drifted in the direction of muralizing and wall-oriented ambitions. In addition to adumbrating the changed scale of American art, Pollock had keyed into an interest in eccentric process and substance as well. The most famous photograph of the artist, taken by Hans Namuth, shows him stepping into a canvas spread upon the floor. "Pollock pioneered the movement of dealing with materials used by the artist as the prime manifestation of imagery," said Benglis. "He drew with paint by dipping sticks into cans of liquid color and making an image on canvas placed on the floor, which was subsequently framed and hung. This was a new way of thinking."[3]

In Pollock's work, literary content was clued to ritual myth and Jungian archetype, the figure of constant human meaning revealed in psychoanalysis. By contrast, such content in Benglis' work is inherent to substance. As Pollock's paintings grew larger, ultimately to wall scale, he was able to step into them during their execution as he might have entered a great hall of prehistoric painting. I believe the register of handprints in the upper right corner of *Number One*, 1948 (The Museum of Modern Art), reenacts for the Jungian a major gesture of Paleolithic painting—the negative or positive handprints found, for example, throughout the caves of Pech-Merle, Altamira, Lascaux or Santander.[4] It was important for Benglis to be in her latex and foam "pours" of 1968 during their execution as it was for Pollock to step into the paintings of his 1945–51 Jungian phase. And, once Benglis' works are exhibited, the spectator enjoys a similar access.

Simultaneous with the pours, Benglis was producing eccentric and narrow wax paintings. Klaus Kertess observed of these capsule-shaped works that, "pigmented wax was put on layer over layer with a brush of the same width as the support, creating an image of two brushstrokes coming together and splitting apart at the center." *Tulip* (1968) "evokes the waxy beauty of tulips or of lips (two lips, my lips)." Benglis said to me, "The wax painting were like masturbating in my studio, nutshell paintings dealing with male/female symbols, the split and the coming together. They are both oral and genital. But I don't want to get Freudian: they're also Jungian, Yin-Yang." Benglis produced these covert wax paintings for some time, although after 1970, the cracked and fractured wax encrustations move toward high relief.

Benglis' identification with Pollock in terms of substance, procedure, and secret imagery came during a period when the nongestural side of Abstract Expressionism— the Rothko rather than the Pollock—was viewed as the paramount issue of progressive painting. Benglis sought a painterly episode derived from Abstract Expressionism and informed by the "collapsed" objects of Minimalism. Both these sources are important for her since they tend, in divergent ways, to isolate or excise the autonomous gesture from the ground.

The free gesture is the central notion of Benglis' art. Since the early 70s, she has understood "the frozen gesture," as she calls it, to mean something both physical and psychological—psychological in the sense of a phrase like "it was a lovely gesture," or the term *beau geste*.

By 1970, Benglis was aware of new artistic models. After her latex throws, she turned to brightly colored polyurethane foam forms prefigured in Claes Oldenburg's more borborygmic soft sculptures of the early 60s. Benglis' floorbound puffy works only appear soft, however; actually they are hard crusted aerated bodies of plastic. "Oldenburg turned material and subject matter inside out," she said. "I don't like the recent Mickey Mouse stuff. Too Cubist. I like all his earlier work around '58 to '62." In addition, in 1970 Benglis became interested in day-glo pigment, pure color without black admixtures, and stabilized by ultraviolet resisters. Because of its high chromatic vibration and retinal irritation, day-glo sidesteps the usual issues of color, even though it is clearly hue. It tends to defy conventional color exploitation and the search for the subjective or personal palette of sensibility painting. Day-glo, tawdry and neonlike, tends to celebrate the commercial and the commonplace, and this seeming vulgarity fascinates Benglis. She wishes to "question what vulgarity is. Taste is context." Benglis, then, worked out of Pop sensibility, but freed of that movement's specific imagery. "I do not want my work to be iconographically Pop. I am still involved with abstraction. The first abstract paintings I ever thought about were some Klines shown at the Delgado Museum [in New Orleans]. Content grows out of form. Having an iconographic content can give me a form—say feminism, say Pop."

Day-glo offered the intensity most resistant to the floor—as Benglis remarked, the pigment "was down on the floor, but the color was up." Despite its low-class associations, day-glo has been used even in the rarified high art ranges of formalist abstraction. After his metallic series—itself reflective, therefore "uncolored"—Frank Stella, for example, undertook a day-glo series of works. The color in Morris Louis' *Unfurled* series (although of a different chemical structure than day-glo), also provided Benglis with a formalist model of high key color. Moreover, Louis' gestures in the *Unfurled* paintings are similar to the spectrum-like arrangements of lambent stripes in Benglis' latex and foam pours.

Do not be misled. All this connection to other work (and to formalist art which, after all, was "the enemy"), is outside the essential interest of Benglis' works themselves. As glamour is Warhol's message and the star his icon, and the square, circle and triangle are the existential characters in the dramas of Minimalism, so is the frozen gesture—the excised, congealed, colored stroke—Benglis' prime fascination and essential icon.

Instead of figure/ground Gestalts functioning within a conventional rectangular field, the environment becomes the ground for the figure. By 1970, Benglis' pictorial sculptures no longer ratify the horizontal of the earth, but begin to engage the entire environment. With the endless environment as the ground for the frozen gesture, she embraced the notion of theatricality and all that it implies—temporality, performance, personality, media exploitation. She transformed the place of exhibition into an environment, a site awaiting a Happening. The excitement of these works is a function of the unconscious anticipation of such an even; they signaled a return to issues which had been carefully pruned from American art for a generation.

This anticipation of a temporal episode in her work, combined with her emerging conception of the frozen gesture as a free act, tipped Benglis to the use of video, though video was then being widely explored in terms of technological appeal. A kinetic result from a static impulse should not be surprising. Warhol, of course, preceded Benglis in this understanding when he moved from the seriality of, say, the Marilyns or the Brillo boxes to the sequential frame of filmstrip.

Benglis first used video equipment while teaching at the University of Rochester in 1970. She rejected the utopian ambitions of a generation of artists absorbed by the creation of the video synthesizers. Instead, she was drawn to the unselective recording of the actual as it happens, free of aesthetics or ideology, a kind of mindless one-to-one. Spatial superimpositions—piling image on image—interest her. These blurry overlaps deal with transposed seriality—not the lateral seriality or modularity of the Minimalist grid, though surely this is a source, but an in-depth seriality which takes time, blur, static, and transient environmental interferences into account—an imagery with memory built in. Benglis' video piles up imagery in Expressionist terms similar to the way she throws paint or mounds foam. For Benglis, video is ubiquitous and expendable, like magnetic sound tape that, when it is recycled to record new information, effaces the old. Thus it renders expendable the very notion of the artwork.

"I got involved with video. I saw it was a big macho game, a big, heroic, Abstract Expressionist, macho sexist game. It's all about territory. How big?" Video offered Benglis a perfect medium of gesture freed from materiality; thus gesture could be as large as possible. This contradicts the prevailing view of the artist as singlemindedly devoted to eccentric substances and physical processes.

At the same time that Benglis grasped the implicit scalelessness of Postminimalism (and found in video a medium devoid of issues of scale since it was immaterial), she abandoned the comparatively small latex or foam work for the cavernlike environment. The environments *(For Darkness, Totem, Phantom, Pinto)*, constructed at numerous galleries and museums, actualize the cave, spilling grottolike forms well out into real space, often enclosing the visitor (fig. 42). Benglis poured and tossed polyurethane foam across inflated scaffolds which were subsequently removed. Since the foam sets quickly, the material needs no internal armature; the works are supported by the real walls of the exhibition space. Some pieces employ a neutral color range. Others are hyped up with day-glo. Benglis sought theatrical special effects, adding phosphorescent salts to her pigments like those in rotting woods, lichens, and certain minerals. Under various lights or at special times, these grotto-like formations glow "like relics from the natural history of some imaginary planet."[5] Again, the model for this rediscovery of the ritual site is Pollock. Nancy Graves, whose early work particularly is marked by a fascination with shamanism and the archeological site, made a similar rediscovery. Their position reintegrates the present with a precultural past.

Certain issues then stand clear in Benglis' work: she is fascinated with substance and eccentric materials as a function of Expressionist sensibility, and she takes pleasure in vulgarity, an attitude central to Pop. At Benglis' exhibition of metallized knots at the Clocktower last winter, for example, the artist, mindful of the holiday season, draped the balustrades with flashing Christmas lights. This colorism was specific to the occasion, but it also continues the eccentric coloration in Benglis' other work. The Christmas lights, the spangle and sparkle, the powdered metallic dusts, are a kind of infantile and magical coloration that violates "adult" notions of taste and artistic decorum.

Although Benglis is a southerner by birth, these tawdry cosmetic colors evidence the unapologetic, unrepentant range of California taste. She chooses glinting metallic flecks and plastic substances like the automotive sheens of art in Southern California, where she spends a good part of the year.

The announcements for Benglis' exhibitions, like her choice of colors, function as infra-information. Rather than reproducing a work on the announcement of her 1974 exhibition of knots at Paula Cooper Gallery, she sent out a Hollywood style chromo of herself—a cheesecake shot from the rear, blue jeans dropped below her knee (fig. 43). (An earlier exhibition invitation pictured the artist as a child dressed for a party in Greek *evzon* costume.) The cheesecake shot—in part homage to Betty Grable pinups—recalls for me a late version of Odilon Redon's *Birth of Venus*. Though this work can hardly have been in her mind, Benglis is strongly interested in Classical myth. Among her most recent works are pornographic Polaroids rendered ambiguous by their cultural context—they are parodies of Mannerist and Hellenistic postures, il Rosso Fiorentino and ithyphallic kraters, a Leda without a swan. Robert Morris is her companion in several of these photographs, and in fact her cheesecake invitation is the pendant to his recent S-M fantasy poster announcement (fig. 44), which in turn references recent videotapes done conjointly. Morris exemplifies in stringent terms another intellectual artist attracted and repelled by instances of brute irrationality; something of Benglis' free-floating openness seems sympathetic to his conflicted outlook. In the work of both artists, overt sexuality points to a covert content—an ironic self-parody of sexuality, and not the exteriorization of a root eroticism. Benglis' sexual photographs are not be to confused with Vito Acconci's performances on erotic themes, although from the early 1970s on, Acconci had provided a sensational model of this kind of disclosure. Superficially, Benglis' work reveals the tasteful, the glossy, and the narcissistic, while Acconci's secret sexual systems are more populist, and tend toward the squalid, the exorcistic, and the puritanical.

The distanced experience of instinct lends Benglis' and Morris' sexual work its Mannerist edge. Writing of Morris' S-M poster, Gilbert-Rolfe observed that it was "an ironic encapsulation" of the artist's position, and noted that the poster "concentrates on the artist's identity as a performer within an institution of a certain sort." The critic observes that this "implicitly heroic identity . . . can only be credibly maintained or it's capable of self-parody. Without that capacity, one is left with a rhetoric that doesn't possess the ability to question itself."[6]

Both the explicit and disguised sexual orientation of Benglis' media exploitation remain a function of the frozen gesture. It has become the big risk. In Benglis' work, the new medium is now "the media." What is fascinating is the degree to which the artist, so sharply conscious of risk and stakes, perhaps remains unsure of the jackpot. I suspect she sees it as part of the mythical payoff that was Andy Warhol's by the end of the 1960s. But to insist on this interpretation alone is to render base an equivocal activity which, though hardly neutral, is nonetheless disinterested in the way that all art is—however hard that may be to believe of the new erotic work. The problem with Benglis is not one of her creative blockage, but rather of the inadequacies of criticism to keep perspective without falling into mere reportage.

Notes

1. There are nevertheless traceable groups of work in Benglis' career—the wax lozenges, the knots, and the environments of tossed polyurethane foam, for example—these are types to which she will intermittently return. There is also the persistent Warholianism which lurks behind her formal choices. That too is a constant. The iconographic sets were examined at some length in Klaus Kertess, "Foam Structures," Art and Artist, May, 1972, pp. 32–37. This sensitive article addressed the link between formal choice and female consciousness in Benglis' work.

2. Emily Waserman, "New York: Group Show, Bykert Gallery," Artforum, September 1969, pp. 60–61. In an exhibition catalogue for "Materials and Methods: A New View," held at the Katonah Gallery in the Spring of 1971, I maintained that "the disintegration of Minimalism" was the central operation of the period circa 1967–70. This supplanting of a key '60s style was achieved through "a need for identifying sculpture in pictorial terms—particularly with regard to color and unusual substance." This exhibition included the work of Keith Sonnier, Eva Hesse, Richard Van Buren, Alan Saret, and Dorothea Rockburne, although it could have as easily included works by Benglis.

3. Quoted in S. R. Dubrowin, "Latex—One Artist's Raw Material," Rubber Developments, Volume 24, No. 1, 1971, pp. 10–12. Post-Minimalism's connections to Jackson Pollock are widely acknowledged. A popular piece of reportage on Lynda Benglis, Van Buren, Serra, and Hesse, "Fling, Dribble and Drip," Life, February 27, 1970, stressed this affiliation.

4. How access would be facilitated through Jungian psychoanalysis is explained by Judith Wolfe, "Jungian Aspects of Jackson Pollock's Imagery," Artforum, November, 1972.

5. Hilton Kramer, *New York Times*, May 30, 1971. Kramer was covering the opening of the Walker Art Center in Minneapolis, where he found "the most arresting [work] was Lynda Benglis' enormous and altogether macabre sculptural environment consisting of 10 bizarre black shapes that append from the wall . . . this is the most impressive work of its kind I have seen since Louise Nevelson first exhibited her black walls in the nineteen-fifties. . . . " A black-and-white videotape was made of the process of such an installation, "Totem (Lynda Benglis Paints with Foam)," by Annie McIntosh, taped at the Hayden Gallery, Massachusetts Institute of Technology, November, 1972.

6. "The Complication of Exhaustion," *Artforum*, September, 1974.

Figure 42. Lynda Benglis, *For Darkness (Situation and Circumstance)*, July 1981 Phosphorous pigmented polyurethane, 10'2″×34′×25′ (longest ext.: 12'5″). *(Photo courtesy Paula Cooper Gallery)*

Figure 43.   Lynda Benglis, Exhibition Announcement, 1974
10″ ×6-5/8″.

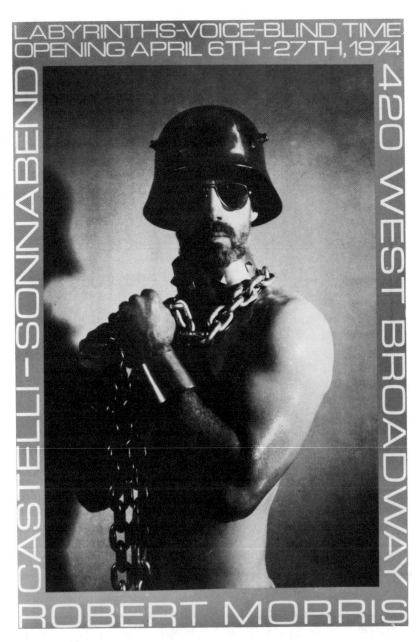

Figure 44. Robert Morris, Exhibition Announcement, 1974
36-7/8″ ×23-3/4″.
(Photo courtesy Leo Castelli Gallery)

Benglis' Video: Medium to Media

Although Lynda Benglis' work is difficult of access, certain of its elements stand clear: (1) an Expressionist bias; (2) a fascination with vulgarity as a willed act of style; (3) a mannerist distancing; (4) diffidently applied abstract structural systems; and (5) an elaborate crypto-autobiographical or infra-information system, referencing biographical detail as well as other primarily contemporaneous art. (This network of referrals stands in relation to Benglis' work as iconography stands in relation to earlier art.)

Postminimal art of the late 1960s is marked by a resurgence of Abstract Expressionist methodology transposed to a fully environmental scale. Benglis' work epitomizes the automatic gesture congealed into an object both painting and sculpture at the same time. Benglis grasped the idea that gesture may be understood as either manual activity or as linguistic metaphor, as, for example, when we say "beau geste." Similarly, she recognized that the notion of an artistic medium—a substance that the artist works with—is linked to the notion of media. In this sense, personal or private manipulation of substance is, at its most public expression, preempted by "mass media." Such an insight allowed Benglis to "manneristically" distance herself from subject matter. "Media," as the term is used today, denotes the movies, T.V., newspapers, magazines, popular organs of information dispersal. It connotes "issues," topical politics—for example, feminism or pornography. A conventional artist, man or woman, addressing such issues would see them wholly in terms of subject, as "subject matter." Benglis, playing the hunch, medium to media, sees in feminism or pornography not just their possibilities as illustrative content, but more, their manipulative potential as form. Her work may be about these issues, but only insofar as feminism and pornography may be abstractly incarnated as form, as "frozen gesture."

A leap from tangible methodology to a freer play of language keyed Benglis into the use of video in 1970, while teaching at the University of Rochester. What Benglis had grasped, however intuitively, was video's implicit scalelessness. In some

This article originally appeared in conjunction with a Lynda Benglis exhibition (Fine Arts Center, State University of New York at Oneonta, January–February 1975).

radical sense, what or where video is, is unknown; is it in the tape, on the monitor, in the electrical impulses, in ambient configurations of light or dark, in the audio? Is it in what we are looking at, or what the artist does or has done? Unlike earlier technologies, say oil painting or woodcarving, video engages intangible colored or black-and-white atmospheres. Benglis' video gestures further freed her from the impacted molecules of paint and brush methodologies. Earlier, her intense Expressionist urge had been gratified in luminously colored latex pours and aerated plastic foam moundings dating to the late 1960s. (These vulgarly colored "pictorial" sculptures responded in part to developments within Claes Oldenburg's soft sculptures of the early '60s.) The strong loping gestures used to make the latex and foam works are often retained in Benglis' broad video camera movements.

The view that Benglis' art is merely another Expressionism—unsystematic, inexplicable crystallizations of perfect happenstance—ignores much of the "rational" aspect of her work. I prefer to point to certain "logical" systems employed in making these tapes rather than stress their Expressionism, which after all, is their most self-evident feature. (This "analytical" approach was cued by Lizzie Borden's exemplary entries for the Castelli-Sonnabend videotape catalogue, Volume I, No. I, 1974.)

Among the "rational" devices Benglis frequently employs is tape successiveness. Here, completed signatures of video are re-recorded while being played, so that the second tape reveals the artist newly relating to the earlier image. This sequential aspect, time and image cycled and recycled into third and fourth signatures, seems more common in tapes made before 1973.

Such "informal seriality" still demonstrates Benglis' commitment to an abstract structure that had been codified in Minimalism. The Postminimalists retain as well as alter their abstract origins; often their temporal sequences parallel the checkerboard and grid structures central to the Minimal style which had reached its apogee in 1964–66. Many of the audio and kinetic effects sought by contemporary "story artists" or "dancer artists," in terms of sound or movement—linguistic and theatrical means—reveal that these artists also seek to demonstrate a rootedness in the purely abstract concerns of Minimalism.

At the first public screening of Benglis' earlier tapes in the Spring of 1973, Bruce Boice, the painter and alert critic, pointed to several abstract underpinnings in the larger matter of Benglis' Expressionist video work. These tapes particularly are marked by a heady recording, and a technical rudeness central to Expressionist immediacy and to Benglis' very delight in new technology. Finding Benglis' video simultaneously "boring, interesting, and funny," Boice noted that "the content of Benglis' videotapes is another monitor screen, which sometimes shows still another monitor screen . . . Usually the visual static is at one remove or more from the machine we're watching, it is on the monitor pictured in the tape."[1] Boice might have as easily pointed to the disparate relationships between what is said and what is seen on the tapes. These "synch/out-of-synch" relationships function often as not as an abstract holding pattern as well as an intuitive expressive device. In *Mumble,* particularly, the divergency between statement and image, between what one sees and what one is told one is seeing—a kind of reality testing—reaches elliptical heights. "The figure that is not on the screen right now is my brother. He plays football." Thus Magritte's famous legend "Ceci n'est pas une pipe" ("This is not a pipe") beneath the image of a pipe, has been transposed to our idiom.

Mumble was originally shown with *Home Tape Revised.* Both tapes are important for the number of autogiographical clues they reveal. *Home* records a voyage backward to another time and place, from one kind of contemporary love to an earlier and, in its way, more protective love of family. An aged grandmother repeatedly says, "I love you Lynda," during the shambling middle sequence that documents the artist's visit to her Mississippi-Louisiana homeland. The beginning and end of the tape reveals her friend Klaus Kertess, the art dealer and writer, typing in his New York studio. From *Home* one learns that Benglis is of Greek American and Southern Presbyterian descent. Her Greek origins provide a key to many Greek and "Hellenistic" clues throughout Benglis' work. This infra-information aids in transforming autobiography into formal and abstract issues. For example, several exhibition announcements reproduce a photograph of the artist as a little girl dressed in Greek *evzon* costume, the traditional Greek male garb. Such a man-girl fusion is perhaps linked to ethnicity, one that may feed as well the current image of the artist as a contemporary California Venus, or as the object of extensive mannered erotic studies executed jointly with the artist Robert Morris.

Mumble is the earliest public disclosure of their key collaboration. I don't mean by this that together they made a single work, but rather that they fed each other's consciousness about the potential of video in a way that was mutually useful and interreactive. In a certain sense, Benglis' *Mumble* cannot be understood without reference to Robert Morris' tape *Exchange* and vice-versa. As *Home* reveals Benglis seeking solace in the bosom of the family, in deep America, in the present, *Exchange* reveals Morris seeking solace in art, in Europe, with its visual and verbal clues to past art—to Manet's *Olympia,* and Donatello's *Gattamelata,* among other examples. Both tapes deal with the frustration and confusion of physical desire with artistic creation. Morris' long text, which refers to "his" and "her" effects on one another (and therefore to earlier films and dances by Yvonne Rainer, with whom Morris has long been associated, that also focus on these archetypal male/female characters) is purportedly fictitious.[2] Yet the text's autobiographical tone—a pendant to Benglis' *Home*—suggests that there's more truth to it than the artist perhaps cares to acknowledge. For example, he speaks of "a tape he made of a tape she made" as Benglis has included "his" image in "her" work. At one point Morris speaks of a seventh tape made together, and then later the accounting comes to 21 tapes in all, although I doubt there were ever this many. In one particularly naked moment, after all, this may only be literature he says, "the maniacal pursuit of art has led me to hurt women." This gets awfully tangled. At its simplest—yet most artistically complex—let's say that Morris is both grist and image for Benglis as she is for him. While the blurrings of truth are intentional one can't lay out all the relationships (so complex are they), not the least reason being a concern for propriety.

Erotic subjects figure largely in Benglis' internalized system of content as form. Like many other contemporary artists, notably Bruce Nauman and Vito Acconci, Benglis—cued by Duchamp as were the others—turns to her body as Readymade. "My video is personal to me, and I hope it might be personal to someone else. Video is one way in which I began to study an image, my image, and often those closest to me."[3]

The sequence of videotapes On Screen, Document (both of 1972), Now (1973), and finally Female Sensibility of 1973–74 (fig. 45) demonstrate an increasing refinement of sexual or erotic Mannerism. In the first, the manual attack upon the body, say the drawing of the mouth apart in the manner of a Gorgon mask, while referring to Nauman's pioneering films such as Pulling Mouth (1969), indicates formal properties central to the early Postminimalist style around 1968. Benglis' Expressionist focus on regressive activities and sounds, long passages of visual static—an early tape is called Noise—as well as the more abstract content of screen seriality, alienates the viewer from conventional notions of female beauty. If this process does not exactly evoke "art" to the viewer, it is at least suggestive of "not nature."

In Document, while again acknowledging the paradoxical level upon which seriality is structured into the work, Benglis alludes specifically to a source in Duchamp when, in a clasic gesture of irony towards art, she concludes the tape by drawing a moustache across the image of her own face. The source is Duchamp's LHOOQ, and like this celebrated work of 1919, Document infers the binary relationship between male and female, as do for that matter Gorgon-like grimaces. As Freud pointed out in a short but essential paper, "The Medusa's Head" (1922), Perseus, when beheading the Gorgon Medusa, enacted a culturally valuable surrogate castration. He points to the serpent locks of Medusa as a way of psychically overcoming castration anxiety—a fear central to the Oedipus Complex—through a multiplication of the analogue of the very organ which has been lost, the sight of a Gorgon induced petrification. This, Freud concluded, indicated that the vanquisher had totemically absorbed the central power of the vanquished and if decapitation here equalled castration, then petrification equalled phallic tumescence.[4]

Now, Benglis' first color video, engages a narcissistic dialogue with the artist's own image. The videotape's most acute passages suggest a transformation of the image of the artist's tongue into that of a surrogate clitoris or penis. The autoerotic is perhaps the essential source of Mannerist sexual feeling. For the 20th century, this erotic myth was codified in the functioning of Duchamp's central work, The Bride Stripped Bare by Her Bachelors, Even. The relationship between Bride and Bachelors is auto-copulative, since both emerge (as does Benglis' sexual personality) from the same person—MAR (mariée, the Bride), and CEL (célibataires, the Bachelors)—that is, MARCEL (Duchamp).[5]

The notion of "infinite regression" that Borden points to in her catalogue essay for this videotape is further toned by the verbal directives of Now, since the query

"Do you wish to direct me?" is always self-addressed. As Benglis' eroticism is metaphorically male and female at the same instant, so too is it slave and master. (This may be the source for Robert Morris' S&M exhibition announcement of April 1974, which, like much of his more recent activity has been spurred by, as it in turn inspires, Benglis' work. Benglis' riposte to this announcement was a cheesecake, rear view shot, used as the exhibition flyer for a May 1974 exhibition of her work (figs. 43 and 44).)

The acuteness of sensibility revealed in *Now* culminates in Benglis' most startling and beautiful tape to date, *Female Sensibility.* This accomplished tape also exploits Benglis' most explicitly Mannerist color sense. The color of *Now* has a day-glo brilliance akin to the kinds of color Benglis used earlier in the execution of her latex and foam sculptures. *Collage* (1973) has a primary range of colors paralleling the rudimentary counting procedures and mechanistic Serra-related gestures (the mechanical chewing of the orange rind is like the repetitive catching gesture in Richard Serra's *Hand Catching Lead* of 1968). By contrast, *Female Sensibility* opts for a Bronzino-like range of color: blue-green lips for one female participant (Benglis herself), and red-black lips for the other. This tape partly infers a mocking stance towards what certain commentators have viewed as the *de rigueur* lesbian phase of an emerging feminist politicization.

The slow, stylized caresses of *Female Sensibility* of course connote masturbation. In none of this however is there any gross fiber; nor is there any I believe in the now "infamous" advertisement published in the November 1974 issue of *Artforum*, which certain critics took to be "an object of extreme vulgarity" that "represents a qualitative leap in that genre."[6]

This sanctimonious puritanism did not recognize that Benglis, in presenting herself as a nude-with-dildo, abrogates distinctions between male and female, as does so much else in her work by subsuming these polarities within a single entity, echoing thereby the male-female subsumption in *The Bride Stripped Bare by Her Bachelors, Even.* In exploiting "the media" through pornography, and in so doing, transforming pornography into art, Benglis also pointed up the virtual loss of content—an absence fostered by academic repetition—into which female nude imagery had fallen in 20th century art.

Notes

1. *Artforum*, May, 1973, p. 83.

2. Some of the confessional tone of this text was struck in a nearly complete version that was published in *Avalanche*, Summer/Fall, 1973, pp. 22–25.

3. *Art-Rite*, special issue on Video, Autumn, 1974, p. 12.

4. First published in *Imago*, vol. 25, 1940. Reprinted in *The Collected Papers of Sigmund Freud*, ed. James Strachey, vol. V., Hogarth Press, London, 1950, pp. 105–106.

5. I have pointed to this interpretation of the functioning of *The Large Glass* (as *The Bride Stripped Bare by Her Bachelors, Even* is more simply called) as a mythical model for the "Body-Art" of

Figure 45. Lynda Benglis, *Female Sensibility*, 1974
Color videotape, 14 minutes, sound.
(Photo courtesy Paula Cooper Gallery)

Bourgeois Truth

Murder or suicide. It is shocking to meet an artist who can so succinctly state what her art means. To note this is not to say that this terse statement proposes what her forms signify as art; or how that meaning, intention or signification is perceived by the viewer. These are different matters. Still, Louise Bourgeois can be chillingly exact as to meaning, meaning at the level of "essential motivation." Then, again, often at the moment of commitment Bourgeois may sabotage interpretation with a tantalizing pantomime of gallic outrage: *"Mais voyons . . . "* Now see here . . .

The meaning is simply this: the murder by the artist of the father's mistress. No hasty conclusions. This is no revenge fancied upon the father out of Oedipal yearning, the Electra complex (though it may partly be that even if Bourgeois is in her seventies). Nor is it justice done in the name of a wronged mother. Empathy is not wholly Bourgeois' game; nor is it even clear that she hates her victim. Ambivalence is the key. It's all so French.

The object of this murder is only superseded in importance, for sculpture that is, by the method of the crime—the wringing of the neck. For Bourgeois this signifies more than strangling, more than garroting. It is *"la torse."* Think of what this means for sculpture. While *"la torse"* may mean the wringing of the neck, the twist, it also means, on an etymological level, the torso (that grand discovery of Rodin for whom the fragment possessed a greater artistic integrity that the lost totality); and the notion of torsion (upon which, say, the Baroque was invented—you remember Bernini's David rather than Michelangelo's or Donatello's?); let alone modernist forays into stereometry and circumvention. So this linguistic pivot allows for a sliding field of meaning from the most general stylistic areas of artistic enterprise to the most specific biographical event germane only to this sculptor (fig. 46).

"La torse" twists on a fulcrum at certain instants, pointing to form possessed of no other meaning than sheer quiddity (I suppose what we mean when we say "pure art meaning"); and at others veering towards impulsive intuitive processes of

This article originally appeared in the catalogue for the Louise Bourgeois exhibition (New York City, Robert Miller Gallery, December 1982).

creation Bourgeois perceives as essentially erotic. She wrings the neck of the father's mistress as a peasant woman might wring the neck of fattened geese in a barnyard—and sever them, tear out entrails, cleave and quarter, perhaps even further dress them, cutting away wing tips, separating neck and spinal column, even deboning the poor things. A good body of Bourgeois' sculpture conflates processes of making with kitchen butchery, a kind of domestic slaughter. Her most ambitious environmental work, in latex as it happens, *The Destruction of the Father,* presents us with the limbs and flanks of butchered sires easily read as total annihilation. "It is basically a table, the awful, terrifying family dinner table headed by the father who sits and gloats. And the others, the wife, the children, what can they do? They sit there, in silence. The mother of course tries to satisfy the tyrant, her husband. The children are full of exasperation. We were three children; my brother, my sister and myself. There were also two extra children my parents adopted because their father had been killed in the war. So we were five. My father would get nervous looking at us, and he would explain to all of us what a great man he was. So, in exasperation, we grabbed the man, threw him on the table, dismembered him, and proceeded to devour him."[1] It is as direct and potent as the conclusion of a children's fairy tale.

Who was the victim of Bourgeois' imaginary murders? Who was the object of her ritual slaughters, ritual insofar as we are still able to view art as a sacerdotal enterprise in our secular culture? Her name was Sadie, introduced into the house as a governess who would teach the children English. Bourgeois' mother did not simply capitulate. As a conscious, strategic act she allowed Sadie to remain in the house for almost ten years. "After all," Bourgeois now sees, "she decided that she would rather know the mistress than be ignorant of what her husband did outside the house."

On one level, the victim was Sadie—but on another more intimate plane, it was Bourgeois herself internalizing this desire so that it became a suicide. Bourgeois employs the spiral to signify self-murder, taking "the turn-in-on-itself" as cue.

So Sadie came to the house where a first daughter had died, where the second, Henriette, survived, was lame and six years older than Louise. Louise turned for companionship to her little brother Pierre, fourteen months her junior—silent Pierre with his fearful effaced mouth. One sees it still in the beautiful sculpture of her brother, a head lying there like some ancient stone unearthed. You see, of course, that his name means "stone," which is what his father wished him to resemble—the simple granite of the Creuze.

Louise Bourgeois was born to an old family of weavers with ties to the stony ground of the Creuze. In generations past the women had been lace and tapestry makers, the men stone carvers. She lovingly remembers her grandfather, the carver of stone lintels and a gambler. She adds summarily: "Gamblers and womanizers, that's how they were." So barren was this earth that of its "bounty," her mother would say "the milk of the cow is blue."

With the patronage of expatriate Americans who flooded France during the period between the wars, Louise's family prospered and, at length, moved the atelier to the banks of the Bièvre to Antony, a town near Paris upstream from the Gobelins tapestry works. This river, this town—then more rural than suburban—is the town of imagination seen in Bourgeois' work from the late 1930s on—houses of timber and staff rooted in the ancient architectural forms evolving out of Viking types and medieval carpenter traditions. Imagine then the sense of dislocation, *"dépaysement,"* occasioned by Bourgeois' arrival in New York. The city's skyscrapers become, as the artist says, "the symbol of loneliness."

The family trade was in tapestry, both dealing and restoration. *Haute Epoque, Gobelins, Aubusson, Mille-Fleurs*—all were part of the ordinary conversation of a household that would restore no tapestry made later than the Empire.

The tapestry workshop was, at the time, still run as a closed studio system, the workers and apprentices playing a strong role in family life. Furthermore the workers were bound to the enterprise by their almost exaggerated pride in craft and they shared, if not all the material rewards of the atelier's success, at least some of the status accorded Bourgeois' family as it occupied a position of privileged artisans.

Here the homonym, bourgeois and Bourgeois, class and name, comes into play. And so appearances counted. This was well before the period of class confrontation that marked the developing *Front Populaire* and the attendant lowering in expectations regarding artisanal qualities to conform to industrialization and syndicalist values in the ascendant.

The family designed no original work of the kind we associate with tapestries made in France since the Second World War (upon designs, say, of Lurçat or Gromaire), though little Louise's skills in drawing were perceived early. From about the age of twelve she prepared the cartoons for missing sections of tapestry. Her first experiences as an artist then were as a designer, an orientation reinforced during studies in the 1920s with Paul Colin, the leading exponent of the jazzy *"Style Nègre,"* as the poster designer for the Black American music hall reviews of the period. Attachments to Art Deco are manifold in Bourgeois' career and remain easily legible in such efforts as her *ferronnerie*, the ironwork gates of her studios in the Chelsea historical district and Brooklyn.

At the time it was thought that the best tapestry craftsmanship was that which would go undetected, in which restored passages were continuous with the original—unlike today, when distinction is favored in the name of archeological truth. Louise remembers that the new colors—natural ones, earth and plant derivatives, fixed in the cold and sympathetic waters of the Bièvre out back of the house—would never fade and mark themselves as different.

Louise watched as women took the hanks and skeins of dyed wool to the Bièvre to be set; she watched when the tapestry had been lifted from the frame and placed in the Bièvre; she saw that these procedures were both concluded by twisting and wringing away the water—*la torse*. The motif is pervasive.

The confessional, however distant, is a key to Bourgeois' art; this is to be seen from the first copper-plate burin engravings with their many references to life in the house executed here around 1940. The series *He Disappeared into Complete*

Silence, is made up of nine plates published in 1947 with a commentary by the poet/critic Marius Bewley, who warns us, even then, of the dangers of "the psycho-inquisitorial session." Here an atmosphere of shy psychology prevails. The fusion of the spindly and the tenuous to structures of purely abstract appeal mark the evocative towers and turrets of these illustrations.

Then appears the first body of sculpture made in this country which Bourgeois calls *"Personnages Autobiographiques,"* "Autobiographical Characters." These great works are wooden "totems." "No," Bourgeois asserts—confirmed in her view across friendships with Claude Lévi-Strauss, the dialectical anthropologist, and the structuralist psychoanalyst Jacques Lacan.—"No. A totem is just a decorated tree! It is not a sculpture! It never intended to be!"

Bourgeois is more direct. "This is my brother" she says with almost shamanistic certitude; or "This is my sister." "This is *A Tomb and a Child,*" referring to a figure of her architectural historian son Jean-Louis, one of her three children.

The *"Personnages Autobiographiques"* is perhaps Louise Bourgeois' best-known body of work insofar as the widely reproduced *The Blind Leading the Blind* (of which there are five variants) (fig. 47), dates to the early fifties.

These major works sardonically comment on the provocations of The Cold War. Despite all ambiguity, Bourgeois is a hard-headed realist. From the 1920s on she was drawn to the pragmatic, which to a degree explains her affinity for Purism and Constructivism. By the 1930s, like all fair-minded persons, she was attracted by the political Left, making two trips to Moscow. In this curiosity to verify the claims of the communist state she is no more culprit than, say, pure aesthetes (Isadora) or pure historians (Alfred Barr). But the House Un-American Activities Committee [HUAC], headed by Senator McCarthy, saw matters differently. Among other considerations, Bourgeois' citizenship was at stake. However conflicted her relations with her father, his approval remained central and it was unthinkable that she apply for naturalization prior to his death in 1950, a moment coincidental with the red scare. Need I add that Bourgeois, ever practical, had always been wary of the party myth and never enrolled in their lists. Others, of course, did.

New York City during the Second World War was again what it had been during the First, Parnassus in Exile. Bourgeois was especially close to a circle of French intellectuals and artists who shared common history, ideals and, as it happened, cheek-by-jowl addresses. The closest included Marcel Duchamp, Le Corbusier and Ozenfant.

My point is not to reopen the embarrassments of the day alluded to in the work's title but to stress Bourgeois' Purist and Constructivist formation. Her commitment to theory (preeminent, say, in the writing of Ozenfant and Le Corbusier), continues to the present.

Her family's work answered the needs of a patronage we associate with the Art Nouveau. Today we see Art Deco designers as nourished by the same roots though they were first perceived in terms of their rejection of Third Republic class privilege. Le Corbusier, Ozenfant, Léger (with whom Bourgeois studied during his

Purist phase), André Lhote (whose texts Bourgeois ardently read), all were understood to be utopians who had, at least temporarily, rerouted art to serve a higher good than the mere gratification of upper-middle-class perquisites.

The Salon des Arts Décoratifs et Industriels Modernes—whence the sobriquet Art Deco—held in 1925 proved a revelation. The Purist *Pavillon de l'esprit nouveau* dominated this epochal exhibition. It was this "new spirit," so marked by rationalist Platonism, that drew Bourgeois to it—partly because it seemed so defiant of paternal values. Beyond this, her attachments to the rationalist tradition continue to be compelling no matter how much we are tempted by the metaphorical or poetical reaches of her work. This pragmatism marks, say, Bourgeois' utter openness with regard to raw material and her ability to exploit these substances in ways that allow for unanticipated, unexpected usages. An Apollonian light must be stressed since we critics are rather more drawn by a Cthonic darkness that Bourgeois scarcely values. She sculpts; we write.

As noted, she was a friend of "Corbu" and Ozenfant. The latter's *Foundations of Modern Art* was an influential text that devalued classical Eurocentricity, often using folk and non-western achievements to exemplify his theories. André Lhote codified the primacy of *la petite sensation* (deriving from Cézanne) into a pedagogy marked by Albert Gleizes' Catholic appropriations. Lhote's teaching with its dose of Delaunay's color theory forms a textual bridge to the teaching of Hans Hofmann in this country and as such may be viewed as a French equivalent to a parallel pedagogy of Klee and Kandinsky when they were masters at the Bauhaus. Ironically, because they were teaching in Germany the latter were prohibited—out of lingering nationalism—from exhibiting at that great 1925 exhibition though the one was Swiss, the other Russian. The Soviet Constructivists, by contrast, were shown in Melnikov's plywood Red Pavillion.

All this broad-ranging experience lies behind The Blind Leading the Blind. In terms of simple facts, Bourgeois and Duchamp were cleared—Ozenfant not—by a court whose moral credentials made it unfit to judge from the outset.

There is more that might be said of this key work. One of the five versions bears the subtitle *C.O.Y.O.T.E.* —"come off your old tired ethics"—a cognomen more immediate to its form. This wooden comb-like structure rests unsteadily on legs of extremely slender triangles some of which don't even reach the floor, adding to the tenuous posture of the work. The latter are the "short legs" of short-sighted prostitutes who failed to respond to Margot Saint James, the American social reformer and friend of the artist, who in a tract called *C.O.Y.O.T.E.* attempted to impose upon prostitution a reasonable worker-like organization.

The sense of a makeshift, diffident carpentry—tentative Constructivism—sensible here as throughout her career, is especially dominant in the next group of works, largely vertical organizations of free-turning horizontal wooden elements joined on a vertical spindle. The succession of "lintels" in this structure may be turned at will, thus again encoding the notion of the twist. In their appeal to touch and turn these variable columns, at times erected in units of four, embody for the artist *"l'extérior-isation du désir de tordre,"* the externalization of the desire to twist. When negative passion erupts, passion Bourgeois perceives as fundamental to the erotic, say, keen sexual jealousy, the freely turning elements may be blocked, forced into sudden rigidity. This blockage is effected through simple carpenter joinery, the use of slotted elements or the mortise, for example. It is noteworthy that floor-standing structures of this type were used as practical stage settings by the dancer Eric Hawkins in the way, say, that Martha Graham (with whom Hawkins first danced), employed the bone constructions of Noguchi.

This extremely rich period is capped by great sculptures of phallic intonation, though Bourgeois is leery of admitting this metaphor into discussion. There comes to mind, for example, the carved and crenelated lingam, *Labyrinth Tower* (fig. 48). Bourgeois would have us be responsive to the shy embarrassment of the organ, its gentility and almost larval vulnerability. The word *"tordu"* as a psychological term applies here, the way the French use it. She points for example to the area just beneath the head as a kind of digital, feeler-like mouth where, were the phallic metaphor admitted, the frenulum of the prepuce would be found. This latter fold of skin covers both the glans of the penis and the clitoris. Thus the multivalent genital metaphor central to all religious iconography is maintained. But as one writes these sentences of caution and abstruse words, in the desire to turn them exactly, there is also something a trifle pompous. After all, this work may also recall a simple childhood reading of *Alice au pays des merveilles,* with its genial illustrations by Sir John Tenniel. Cannot these forms have derived from a memory of the hookah-smoking caterpillar?

Labyrinth Tower is immediately preceded by the Lair series first shown at the Stable Gallery in 1960. This corpus is crucial. While presenting variant spirals it establishes the prototype for the new nest-like portraits. With the Lair group in mind one can more clearly measure the abstract principles behind Bourgeois' work, even as these principles are thrown into doubt through the inclusion of figurative elements. Indeed, this contrast is so obvious in the sculpture as to suggest that the abstract-figurative dichotomy is probably irrelevant to the sculptor.

Such notions continue into the complex serpent portraits which begin in the early 1960s when a privileged hint concerning *Male Portrait* may reveal the conflict between Robert Goldwater (the art historian and the artist's husband) and, Bourgeois and her background. Goldwater's maternal formation was emphatic over the liberal pieties of Ethical Culture. This at length transformed into a hyper-puritanism, modelled after that of Goldwater's mentor-colleague, Alfred Barr (the curator of painting and sculpture of the early Museum of Modern Art), who came to it through birthright.

From the instant of their meeting in the 1930s Goldwater's austerity drew him to Louise as much as it alienated her father, an alienation that invested the new hero with even greater attraction. Goldwater's analytic irony was perceived as only an impertinence that went far to set the father on edge. How could it be otherwise with he who was one with the visceral?

But the religious metaphor of the phallic work is equally sensible. Hindu and Buddhist sculpture, for example, often presents prototypes of hooded gods. Still one need not look far beyond the conflicts of Bourgeois' life to suggest that Goldwater's portrait, set upon a mass of serpentine knots, may signify his triumph over the artist's father. The hooded nests suggest a perverse connotation to the artist, measurable in the twenty-year wait, both hiatus and gestation, until the reappearance of this configuration in the present moment. Bourgeois now sees the serpentine masses crowned with a head as "monstrous" and all are female. The most crude monster she sees not only as female but as Rabelaisian, a creature of mythically disproportionate and gross viscerality.

One may dwell on such details at any moment of Bourgeois' rich career because they are essential to understanding an art of which one can say, even after fifty years, that the sum is greater than any of its parts, as the cliché puts it. Indeed, there are few works that provoke pleasant or agreeable experiences. Rather a disagreeable even perverse character seems more marked.

That it may be these things is of course still a measure of their extreme formal unfamiliarity. Despite her prestige, Bourgeois is in no sense an emblematic figure of any general period since the 1940s, the way David Smith is of the '40s and '50s or Tony Smith is of the '60s and '70s. That kind of common consent, fixing of image, academized logo, still has not come to Bourgeois. All to the good. This has permitted her work to be as representative of the present as it is of any moment from the late 1930s on.

What is more, the artist speaks of no sense of generational camaraderie with any of the sculptors who mark the Abstract or Minimalist position, Formalist or Constructivist ones. Quite the opposite. She feels a sense of community with young artists some of them almost a half century her junior. And in her peculiar sense of form, its almost programmatic inability to copy itself, its denial of felicity, so too is she perceived by them to be a member of their generation, a colleague.

If, however, Bourgeois may be said to embody a Modernist position one must perceive it in non-Formalist, non-Constructivist modes, by and large in the Surrealist Tradition—a consciousness that surfaced with the Anti-Formalist Postminimalist subversions of the late '60s.

While the character of Bourgeois' sculpture seems perverse, at least to me, to attribute this to the mere lack of familiarity of her forms, though true, goes nowhere far enough. I can think of no other artist, certainly not the rare one of her rank, who exteriorizes so peculiar and personal a sense of form. Whether or not she thinks them beautiful is quite beside the point. Bourgeois' forms are located at the verge of acceptability, never entering the domain of the familiar, hence, on a public level, "the beautiful."

In her imaginative search for an internal symbolism, her work may be likened to certain efforts of Feminist Consciousness though here again Bourgeois may bridle.

Still specifically Feminist images, such as the serpentine, put aside, the question of eccentricity of mass and weird part-to-part relationship still remains. In such more abstract considerations Bourgeois' work is prototypic of much Postminimalist sculpture especially in its early eccentric phase.

(There is also in the present a variant of Bourgeois' truths, the recently cast tables by Lucas Samaras, works which must be seen as this late Surrealist's most sincere form of flattery, if you take my drift.)

These modes are reified in Modernist consciousness through an appeal to credentials, the legitimization conferred by authority. In this, the *Transparencies* and the *Fantasies upon a Chisel* made by Jacques Lipschitz in the 1920s are progenitive, as are certain "disagreeable" forms, as he called them, made by Alberto Giacometti. By virtue of the desire to examine the unstaunched flow of impulse from the unconscious that these works reveal, we call this work Surrealist. Its acceptability to a Feminist agenda becomes clearer when one rehearses the telling phase, "unstaunched flow," with its fusion of a menstrual metaphor to the plumbing of the unconscious.

Of course Surrealism has always been difficult for modern sculpture because of the unexamined axiom that sculpture encodes heroic and figurative aspirations whether the work is figurative or abstract. But if we pretend that we participate in the modern, accept the Modernist condition, then difficulty is no stranger to us. Modernism's essential feature is difficulty itself and its greatest monuments are all marked by perverse indigestibility, at least at first. In that sense there can be no more representative figure than Louise Bourgeois. Hers is a great body of work, canonic even, and extended over decades, that has never been trapped into mere repetitive signals.

Note

1. *Centerpoint, A Journal of Interdisciplinary Studies,* Vol. 3, no. 3/4, Fall/Spring 1980, p. 16. All other quotations of the artist's conversation were transcribed by the author on August 16 and 26, 1982.

Figure 46.   Louise Bourgeois, *Nature Study*, 1986
Pink marble, 33″×28″×21-1/2″.
(Photo courtesy Robert Miller Gallery)

Figure 47. Louise Bourgeois, *The Blind Leading the Blind*, ca. 1947–48
Painted wood, 67-1/8″×64-3/8″×16-1/4″.
(Photo courtesy Robert Miller Gallery)

Figure 48. Louise Bourgeois, *Labyrinth Tower*, ca. 1962–82
Black marble, ca. 29-3/4″×17-1/2″×14″.
(Photo courtesy Robert Miller Gallery)

Winsor Knots:
The Sculpture of Jackie Winsor

I remember asking Paula Cooper, Jackie Winsor's dealer, just what, after all, was the meaning of Winsor's sculpture, that is, what meaning did her work have beyond a merely functional description of the individual pieces. Cooper supplied the following précis: "They are well considered entities that take up there own space." This seemingly scanted reply capped a long discussion of the artist's work, and is exactly what Winsor's sculptures are about. Cooper was not being flip. Her reply, based on an appreciative familiarity with Winsor's work, is very much in keeping with the way the artist herself talks about the work: the desire to shape the exactly right reply, to find a nicety of meaning, often forces the response to take on the coloration of an evasion.

Winsor's background goes far in allowing us to gauge some of the sources of this reluctance to translate formal experience and sculptural practice into the possible misrepresentation of words.

Winsor was born in Newfoundland in 1941, to a family of some three hundred years' worth of Newfoundlanders. Thus, she was born, so to speak, in the North American eighteenth century, in a place marked by separatist leanings and a quite literal insularity. Only during Winsor's childhood, in 1949, was Newfoundland made a province of Canada. Agnes Martin, Dorothea Rockburne, Ronald Bladen, George Trakas, and Michael Snow, among others, are also Canadians by birth. This circumstantial detail provides Winsor with a natural curiosity about their work in ways having little to do with formal similarities or programmatic affinities. Winsor's attitude towards her colleagues, whatever their national origin, is largely one of indifference: they are there, taken for granted, a communal bedrock.

Winsor's father's people had been constables and ship captains; her mother's, farmers—comparative newcomers to Newfoundland, there but some two hundred years. In 1951, Winsor's father, a factory foreman with a natural bent for engineering, emigrated south to Boston—Cambridge, really—hoping to find greater opportunities for his three daughters. Boston represented a radical contrast to Winsor's New-

This article originally appeared in *Arts Magazine*, June 1977.

foundland home at an age when such distinctions were most sharply experienced. The country suddenly became the city. Though not farmers, the Winsors were countrified. Indoor plumbing was a novelty. Jackie had never seen a black. The onset of puberty had begun. In Canada, Jackie had been a tomboy. Despite her family's liberal Protestantism, no notion that one might want to be an artist prevailed. As a possibility it simply never had manifested itself. "Professional woman means being a nurse, at best a teacher. Women had broods. There was just nothing for women professionally."

So the family came south. Jackie was taunted for her Queen's English by Boston schoolchildren whose regional accent is among the most pronounced in America. "I couldn't stand it here. I thought it vulgar. Until I was eighteen I returned to Newfoundland every summer, staying with first one aunt, then another. Boston was such a shock. I reconciled myself to puberty when I was twenty. Canada was my childhood. My adolescence was here."

Winsor's high school years were spent at Cambridge High and Latin School. That Cambridge was the seat of Harvard University seemed not especially important. "I started taking advantage of Harvard in my senior year in high school. I had no intention of going to college. It had never happened in my family. I even spent an extra year in high school. As a junior I started going to art lessons at two art colleges. I had always taken art as an elective in high school. My art teachers, Mrs. Ritterbush and Mr. Santoro, sent me off to the Saturday morning art school programs designed for high school students in the Boston area, at the Massachusetts College of Art and at the Museum Art School." Winsor graduated high school in 1960 and took odd jobs—in order to put aside funds to go to the Massachusetts College of Art. Her last year in high school—tutored, working hard—was marked by a drive just to be accepted in art school.

Between 1961 and 1965, she generated her Bachelor of Fine Arts credits. "The ambience at M.C.A. was very regimented. I did a little bit of everything."

All of this presents a conventional unrelieved consistency. The art produced at this time was "kind of representational and expressionistic." Winsor as yet had no real sense of herself as an artist, although it was "all very exciting and I loved it. It was a whole new experience for me." Still, there was a teacher of color theory, Emma Lennon. Winsor doesn't know what her work was like, indeed if she made any, but "she was a woman, and she was doing something. She was peculiar. Her persona was very exciting even though she was older. She was a woman who was doing something and she was professional."

In 1964, Winsor went to the Yale Norfolk Summer School. "For the first time I met artists rather than art teachers. They argued a lot about art." Winsor never entered the lists. Al Held, Louis Finkelstein, Bernard Chaet, among others, passed through that summer. That they may have given Winsor a "crit" was far less important to the artist than an exposure to people who were "artists before anything else. From nine in the morning until ten at night people were painting, taking themselves very seriously" even if the paintings produced were sensibility-based landscapes. Winsor effected a transition out of figuration while taking up photography; photography would continue to engross her through graduate school. "It was a way of making form important—photography had a more refined grain than the very heavily manipulated, stroked surface of painting."

The critical, verbal side of the teachers and students at the Yale Norfolk Summer School failed to impress. "I couldn't identify with verbalizations. The arguing was not about intelligence but about who won. There's no reason to be right about art."

In 1965 she began her Master of Fine Arts degree at Douglass College, Rutgers University, New Jersey, working primarily with the painters Ulfert Wilke and Reggie Neil. Tellingly, Winsor, despite long years in various art schools, never studied sculpture in any formal sense.

During the run of her college years, B.F.A. through M.F.A., there had been occasional trips to New York. The choice of Douglass College was made primarily because of its proximity to New York. Winsor, at some length aware of politics, factions, stratagems, and worlds within worlds that make up the New York art scene, has always chosen to back off from these aspects. "I'm just not political that way. My interest is in making things that are important to me because they are real, experienced, because they are tangible. I am interested in transforming an idea into something physical."

"Is there any quality in your work today that is traceable to your college times?" I asked. She replied, "Energy going into itself. Solidity. Overallness. Those are qualities that come to me from those days." Perhaps it can be seen a bit like this.

Her student work was figurative and revealed a proscriptive interest in anatomy. This led to drawings in which muscularity was exaggerated to a point where later in sculpture it was seen mainly as a sequence of bumps and repetitive ridges. The overallness, the uniformity of surface, attracted the artist to rope and the process of coiling. This in turn led to work embodying a certain sense of the monumental, the recognition that a psychological state may be greater than the literal space it occupies.

Since the rope pieces grow out of the immediate environment of New York, Winsor's art recognitions traceable to that time, many of them negative, require some note. Between 1965 and 1967, when she was awarded her M.F.A., she grew aware that "not much was available to women. When I came to New York in December of 1967, my first impression held: women were transparent." Between 1967 and 1969, "I had a clear idea of my invisibility." Perhaps all this is so. It certainly corresponds to tractarian feminist history.

I visited Jackie Winsor in her studio in 1969, an odd triangular space overlooking the Manhattan Bridge access and the old diamond market at Canal Street and Bowery. Soho was as yet *terra incognita;* space was still cheap. Her studio was filled with the early monumental coiled rope pieces. I saw them in terms of the analogy of materials—which they presented with the work in cord by Keith Sonnier, her husband, who led me to her studio in the first place. When questioned about these contingencies, the artist bridles; it misapprehends her sense of artistic autonomy. The building of a career, of a separate identity, was so difficult for a woman artist at that time that Winsor is still reluctant to enter my sense of historical and critical affiliations, preferring instead to allow each artist the integrity of an individual achievement. In Winsor, this attitude amounts almost to a professional credo.

What of the connections to the work of Eva Hesse? The substances that Winsor worked with 1968—say, latex and rope—engage substances and procedures much associated with Hesse's work. Winsor reflects: "The way she would finish something was exactly the way I wouldn't have finished it. I would be clearer about the form, how the surface got to be there in the first place. How it reveals itself in the process of its making. She seemed more interested in the material itself. And now since her death she's been blown out of scale by the women's movement—deified."

While Winsor was at Douglass College, the earliest independently minded pieces appeared. That they are synthetic—amalgams of sculptural work that the artist knew—in no way denies their interest. They amalgamate issues and substances in a way that expresses an awareness of an alternative to the conventional constructivism—too often fobbed off as the only option open to modernist sculpture—epitomized in the suite of David Smith to Anthony Caro to the Bennington School of sculptors. By contrast to that academy of constructivism, Winsor's interests in 1966 address a colorism, a pictorialism, and an imagery roughly traceable to Surrealism—not Cubism—especially Surrealist sculpture of the 1930s, a source that marks the broad range of early counter-minimalist sensibility in terms of a focus on compulsive procedures and eccentric substances.

At that time Winsor was contrasting highly polished and finished abstract elements—sphere sections or rectangular solids—against organically inferential passages, so that cubes, say, seemingly sprouted hair or tails, not to mention even more anatomically specific forms, testes-like or phallus-like in character, though as always, Winsor plays down this latter aspect. "I was doing what interested me. I'm not theoretical in orientation. The forms arose out of studio practice. I came at it as a painter. You never lose that."

These sculptures were made in hand buffed clay or casts in resins and plasters. The surface results literally from the casting process; there is no subsequent polishing, although refined pigment and resin combinations can result in works of extremely delicate coloration and/or subtle sheens. [An exaggerated sense of editing has prevented Winsor from exhibiting these works.]

These student sculptures of melon-like sections have a prototype in the Giacomettis of the 1930s. In perhaps his most characteristic work of that early style, *The Suspended Ball*, a ball depends upon the ridge of a crescent shape, even to the point that a slight indentation is marked upon the sphere itself, inferring sexual roles— the crescent male, the sphere female. This tradition, maintained in Surrealist sensibility, finds a parallel in more recent work, say by Eva Hesse, such as the *Vertiginous*

Detour in which a sphere is caught up in a net from which strings dangle, or in the *Ball and Saucer* of Jackie Ferrara, made out of paper and rag pulp or in Jackie Winsor's own *Solid Cement Sphere* (1971). I don't mean by this observation that Hesse influenced Winsor or that Winsor influenced Ferrara; but rather they all maintain an anti-constructivist, anti-formalist stance in their sculpture—at least in their early work—one that invokes sexual nuances through substance and methodology whether or not the artists were even aware of a specific model in Giacometti. This is more a question of the kinds of imaginative acts that an anti-formalist ideological stream. Winsor says, "These works were not intended as sexual shapes, though the sexuality may be there."

Last, the range of substance which Winsor explored that time included sensitive rubbers, latexes, and polyester resins. These extremely pictorial and painterly substances, typical of the early phase of Postminimalism, have been abandoned in her work since 1968, though the fibrous or hairy textures of rope as well as its surrogate linearity continues to refer to the equally pictorial and painterly predispositions that she brings to sculpture, ones that first received definition in the mid-sixties. It is surely not circumstantial that the more pictorial and eccentric range of substances she exploited at that time found echo in the latex, string, and rag pieces of Keith Sonnier's earliest phase. But always, Winsor's work must be differentiated as it emphasizes ritual and duration, radically at odds with Sonnier's extroverted expressionism.

While the methodologies she employs—hand based, repetitive, exhaustive—may have been traceable to non-constructivist sculpture, that is, Surrealist sculpture of the 1930s, and although her substances and methods may reveal a crypto-sexual tagging, Winsor's essential forms nevertheless derive from the icons of Minimalism. The square, circle, and triangle, the last being more rare in her work, are the essential figures of a prevailing contemporary sculptural/architectonic style. In part, the very abstract reductivism of Minimalism (c. 1962–66) triggered, by its sheer austerity, a widespread pictorial and expressionist response in sculpture of the later 1960s, notably, though hardly exclusively, in the work of women.

Of course these circles and squares had been given ideological preeminence for the American Minimalists—Judd, Tony Smith, early Stella, early Morris—in their having been sanctioned by Malevich for whom they formed the basic Suprematist elements (c. 1915), and more surprisingly by Kandinsky. In *Concerning the Spiritual in Art* (1912), Kandinsky had first codified this chart of primary shapes. At length the near-mystical belief in the inviolability of these forms can be understood as extenuated Neoplatonism, for throughout the *Discourses* and the *Epistles* Plato identified the perfection of the sphere and cube as beautiful in themselves, but in no sense in any relative way: "What I mean . . . is something straight, or round, and the surfaces and solids which a lathe, or a carpenter's rule or square, produces from the straight and round . . . Things like that, I maintain, are beautiful not, like most things, in a relative sense; they are always beautiful in their very nature . . . " *(Philebus).* Not that such shapes are free of an absolute meaning for Winsor; rather the exact nature of their specialness is hard to pinpoint. It appears that such figures and forms in Winsor's mind "mark off a private space." It's an odd idea since a certain sense, squares and circles are, by the very success of abstraction in modern art, perhaps our most public artistic designations: "It ends up not being the shape per se, but what activity the shape is involved in."

From 1969 on, it became clear that with rare exception Winsor's sculpture would be based on these Neoplatonic referents. Thus, the covert content of Winsor's sculpture is located in method and process as compared to the outer form of the work—which is overt, a cube or a sphere, a kind of known and received fact. Variations in scale as they occur do so from Winsor's need to negotiate generalized forms that duplicate themselves easily in the mind with a methodology in which the hand, the body, and rudimentary carpenter's tools—hammers, chisels, clamps— play a primary role. Thus, the work takes on a warm, affective character. Its scale neither exceeds nor shrinks from a basic human module—the arms outstretched, the arc of the descending forearm, a kind of handlebar length of rope. This description of the general intention of Winsor's work emphasizes the separation between form, substance, and process. By contrast, it is Winsor's contention that work identifies the congruency of process, hand and shape. "My intent is to make them seem together, integrated."

The first wholly mature works were the rope pieces—the *Untitled Rope Cylinder,* the *Double Rope Column,* at length the *Rope Circles* (fig. 49) and *Double Circles.* These appeared in 1969–71. The method explored processes of rope twisting and invented ripe technologies, so that the diameters and heights of the sculpture were based on trial and error. "Real knots never worked. There seemed no reason for them and they didn't work out very well." The slow trance-like process of exhaustive coiling or binding or winding (then as now) is a kind of physical gratification. "I just never feel comfortable unless it takes some time to do. My interest is in slowing everything down, as slow as it can be, so it's imperceivable. To create a one-to-one relationship between 'making time' and 'perceiving time' so that form grows out of process. Process with alternations leads to different forms. There's a lot of choice."

Of course the circle's associative power, particularly at that moment of acute feminist activism, cannot be overvalued as it invokes an imagery of breast and orifice, of mouth, the navel, the vagina. For example, in the sanctuary of Delphi, the ancient Greeks marked the navel of the world, the place where the world physically connected to the universe, with their celebrated monument, the *omphalos.* The agrarian cycle of the world—guaranteeing the sequence of seasons—is assured by dancing around the maypole, a circle dance enacting the vagina, the maypole, its fecundating penetration by the phallus.

These symbologies and associations are almost infinite. However, a new emphasis on this kind of imagistic consciousness—contemporary with the provocations of the women's movement—recharacterized the intentions of artistic methodology pertinent to that moment. For example, painting and sculpture till then had been conventionally viewed as "male" activities. Sewing, skeining (a preliminary step to knitting), knitting itself, dyeing, work in soft thread-like materials were crypto-sexistically tagged as "female." This awareness—right or wrong—provoked two schools, one which held that a feminist art must emphasize such methodologies and imageries historically or conventionally thought to be female—the so-called school of "vaginal imagery"; the other faction adopted an adversary stance—it was precisely such activities and imageries as had been identified as "womanly" that must be avoided if only to break down the artificial stigma attached to the term "woman artist" and at length to claim the turf of painting and sculpture for women as well. Both views, incidentally, are perhaps by now no longer the burning issues they once were— the arguments seem dated in their very writing.

Though Winsor emerged at a moment of great feminist pressure in the art world—a pressure annexing such methodological and imagistic inferences as her work invokes—she has never felt herself to be in any exclusive sense a feminist; rather her concerns are for a recognition of the status of the artist as the embodiment of something special and of merit compared to the unconscious contempt in which artists are held by bourgeois society. Thus, often at considerable sacrifice, Winsor insists upon using the Art Transfer Agreement, at the time of a sale, in which the right of artists to value accruing to their work after it has been acquired by collectors or institutions is maintained.

In Winsor's early phase, certain variations growing out of her making process appeared. In the *Chunk Piece* (1970), yard-long pieces of hemp rope have been cut and bound at the edge, frayed ends doubling back over the binding. This cylindrical formula in certain ways corresponds to the *Solid Lattice* (1970), in which lath-like lengths of wood have been nailed in consecutive sequence like a fasces around a core. This hammering sequence by which the form reveals the process—an attitude contemporaneously explored in Richard Serra's lead tossings (though his process emphasized Abstract-Expressionist speed and asymmetry), is most explicit in the *Nail Piece* (fig. 50). Here a sequence of boards is nailed one upon the other so that each layer is understood in terms of its lamination to the previous one. At length, nine layers later, the floorbound oblong (a late sixties archetype) has gained an enormous weight of nails—"the energy going into the piece is amplified the previous energy." This may be one of the few works allowable to a specific autobiographical referent. When interviewed by Lucy Lippard, Winsor recalled the moment when as a girl her father let her partake in a building chore. Although requiring no more than a few nails, Winsor, aged nine, hammered twelve pounds worth of nails into the project. (*Artforum*, Feb. 1974, p. 56.)

By 1971, the focus on exhaustive solipsistic process—though never to be given up and in the most recent work intensely restressed—was deflected by alternative issues. In this shift Winsor was keeping pace with the general de-emphasis of process which marked progressive sculpture at that time. By 1971, for example, Serra also abandoned the painterly expressionism of his serialized lead tossings for a scale-oriented constructivism informed by Barnett Newman's late paintings. Similarly, in 1970, the last year of her life, Eva Hesse had abandoned the crafts-related altera- tions of open cubes and grids for a sense of monumentality derived from the gestural side of Abstract Expressionism.

By the early seventies, then, a certain dissatisfaction with an emphatic process fixation in Winsor's work led to the introduction of new organic elements—saplings, tree branches, logs—fastened together by notches disguised by bound rope knots—the "Trees." The sequence moved from an organic grid—the *Bound Grid* (fig. 51) in which at one symptomatic point the crotch of a sapling forks the grid—to the in- dividual square of the grid (*Bound Square,* 1972); and from there to the more ec- centric compressed side-by-side format of *Bound Logs* that recalls the earlier rope *Double Column.* In part, the use of the grid still relates to the Minimalist icons of pure information. No less than a circle, square or triangle, the grid is an index of rationalist structure, one that additionally implicates a temporal increment occasioned by the side-to-side or up-and-down movements necessary to read a grid. Similarly, much painting at this time—and Winsor's sculpture never revoked its painterly bias—sought to evince its expressive status by contrasting a free gesture and sensibility-based color against the stable configuration of the grid. In short, Winsor's work employing tree elements may be said to bind up sensibility and stability while reflecting, however unintentionally, a disabused society's new fascination with ecology, however short-lived this social awareness may have been. The "Trees" emerge out of Winsor's search for other materials that invoke the homey and secure affectivity of rope and twine—materials such as wood, worn brick, and certain kinds of trees, branches, twigs, and barks.

Caught up in this ambiguous associative conception of naturalness, the exag- geration of the knot in the "Trees" took on a double role, one actually constructivist—it literally held the logs together—while it equalized or balanced the extremely powerful effects of the wood texture and substance itself.

The twining, skeining experience, as before, continued to gratify. The endless repetitive character provoked in the artist a constant attention and fresh decision making: add more rope here, make sure the rope hasn't slipped there, fill in and negotiate the general profile, etc. So compelling did this carding become (certain of these pieces required the use of 600 pounds of twine) that one could say that *Four Corners* (1972)—a square frame each corner of which was so exaggerated bound as to create four enormous lentil shapes virtually hiding the frame—is its paradigm.

With the completion of the "Trees," my sense of Winsor's work having keyed into the scheme of events diverges from her sense of keying into them. This re- quires some explanation. From 1973 on, it seems to me that Winsor has been engaged in a kind of revival paralleled in the work of contemporary sculptors of considerable reputation.

From my point of view, the artists who resist acknowledging that their work embodies issues, or ideas, or arguments, whatever else it surely does embody, these artists commit themselves to slower developments. Mind you, I have often noted that today's artistic consciousness at the moment of making an art that is deeply felt rejects the primacy of theory typical of high formalist abstraction. By contrast, artistic ratification is secured by the experimental piece, the work that bespeaks trial and error. Today, theory, if honored, is done so in the breach; but honor in the breach is also a theory of art.

It strikes me that something like this is presently affecting Winsor's work. The laminated and gouged plywoods of 1973 invoke the layerings and hammering processes of 1970. *Paul Walter's Piece* (1974), skeining copper wire around bundles of creosoted wood, recalls the *Solid Lattice* of 1970, as much as the hemp *Chunk Piece* of the same year. Just as Brancusi might be said to have tested acuity of sensibility in transferring a work from wood to stone to bronze, so too does it seem that Winsor's twining of *#2 Copper* (1976) deal with such a parallel when compared to the *#2 Rope* (1976).

Similarly, the elegant wooden cubes of 1976 neatly invoke the incremental procedures and exhaustive additive processes of Winsor's early more expressively extroverted phrase. In each of the recent cubes, the serialized processes are self-evident, forming either solids and internal layers or regular interchanges layer to layer in their inevitably, somewhat dogmatic scholarly presentations.

In a certain sense this regularization of nice method is echoed in the recent layered steppings of Jackie Ferrara's curved pyramidal mounds. Only she, as Winsor notes, is involved in a "scale model sensibility." Ferrara's work assumes the character of architecture, whereas hers are literally *there* in the one, actual human scale.

Winsor's procedure is equally traceable to the organic character of any real artist's career: themes thread in and out to be revived and discarded as need be, or to exist in a multiple range of possibilities whereby a work in metal, say, alters our awareness of what is important in, say, one made of hemp. This conjures a method of shuttling comparison within a long-term thematic evolution.

What troubles me in the "organic argument," today especially, is the tacit assumption that artistic production is coeval with or built into a career, a long-term evolution. This may be so, but to me it is not necessarily so, at least not at this moment. Contrary to the "long career" premise—and Winsor is only in her mid-thirties, just entering mid-career—can we not at least entertain the notion that art may be as well in a "one-shot" event from which there is no "'fallout," no sequence, no suite of things, no "career"?

The advent of the conceptual movement as the basis for urgent arts activity and its subsequent rapid dissolution into ever more theatrical and body referential modes of expression from which there is scant tangible "fallout'—no paintings, no sculpture—sufficiently justifies my perhaps passing attraction to the above possibility while indicating the continuous pressing intensity of our changing ideological climate.

Actually, in fairness it should be noted that Winsor had paid heed quite early on to non-objectified performance work in her *Up and/or Down Piece* (1971), a piece invoking "the deadweight of rope and the personality that rope takes on." (Liza Bear, *Avalanche*, 4, Spring 1972, p. 11) In this theatrical work a male performer slowly pulled a vast amount of rope provided him by a female performer through an aperture in the floor, one story to another. This task completed, he lowered the rope through the aperture onto the body of then now recumbent female, at length burying her in its coils. The sexual nature of the piece, however ambiguous, was inescapable.

Thus, our moment is marked by an essential divergence of attitude: one answering an artist's need to carry on the transcending logic of processes and substances leading to a continued production of objectified art; the other, perhaps primarily a critical attitude, being drawn by an alternative ironic range of expression.

Figure 49. Jackie Winsor, *Double Bound Circle*, 1971
Hemp, 16"×61".
(Photo courtesy Paula Cooper Gallery)

Figure 50. Jackie Winsor, *Nail Piece*, 1970
Wood, nails, 7"×82"×8".
(Photo courtesy Paula Cooper Gallery)

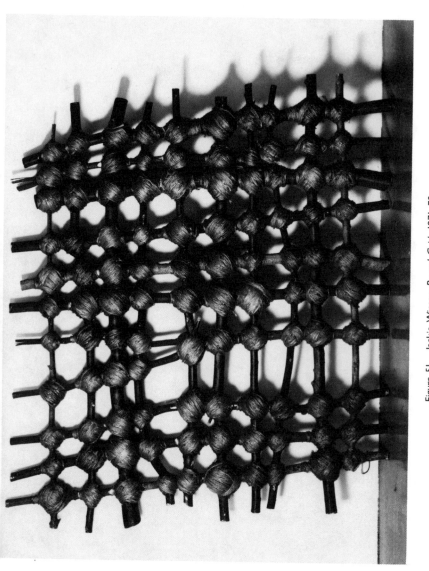

Figure 51. Jackie Winsor, *Bound Grid*, 1971–72
Wood and twine, 84″×84″×8″.
(Photo courtesy Paula Cooper Gallery)

Scott Burton:
Conceptual Performance as Sculpture

A perfect cube looks stable in comparison with the flux of appearance, but one might be pardoned if one felt no particular interest in the eternity of a cube.

—T. E. Hulme

With the relaxation of Minimalist principles in the late sixties, the practice of sculpture was able to enter a highly pictorial and coloristic phase in which many tangible embodiments were incarnated through an expressionist painterliness. This was succeeded by a theoretical and absolutist intention, a systemic rigor of thought still embodied, however, in objects conventionally conceived of as paintings or sculpture—the squares and cubes of Minimalism. Another strain of conceptual activity rejected the external embodiments of painting and sculpture for an internalizing, self-referential urge that sought sculptural incarnation through the artist's use of the body itself. This led to a resurgence of "theatrical performance" and a concomitant reliance on documentation: photographs, videotapes, films, etc.

Of all the figures in this by-now classic vanguard activity—e.g., Acconci, Benglis, Morris, Oppenheim—Scott Burton, by his modesty, poverty, and ambient association with the more unstructured and unpowerful elements of this tendency, managed to get lost. Yet if one thinks of his valuable *Pair Behavior Tableaux* revealed at the Guggenheim Museum early this year, or his freakishly personal and exquisite furniture pieces shown at the Whitney Museum Annual (1975) and at Artists Space (1975), or his sociologically manipulative erotics at the "Lives" show at the Fine Arts Building in September 1975, one realizes with what a sharp aesthetic and critical intelligence one is dealing.

Some background is necessary. Burton, born in June 1939 in Alabama—"that's not important; I don't feel like a Southerner"—was raised within a genteel Presbyterian ethos, a boyhood salvaged by a mother who made him feel extraordinary. When his parents divorced, he was relocated to Washington, D.C.

Power came from reading, through aesthetic commitments, through scrutiny of the National Gallery and the Phillips Collection, and through adolescent bohe-

---

This article originally appeared in *Arts Magazine*, September 1976.

mianism. At public schools during the fifties he was sharply aware of distinctions of all kinds, not the least of them his dissembling vicarious life at the fringe of economically privileged Georgetown kids.

At fourteen Burton decided to become a *New Yorker* cartoonist: "Steinberg led me to Picasso." He began to attend the Saturday art classes at the Corcoran— went to one but never returned. Instead he chanced on the Washington Workshop for the Arts. The painting instructor was Morris Louis. Burton stayed only for a session because everybody around him was staining bed sheets: "I was only up to Picasso." At Western High his art teacher was Leon Berkowitz, through whom he met de Kooning. Across such happenstance he at length grew aware of the importance of the emerging Washington Color School, of Greenberg, and the mythology of who was introduced to whom by whom. Through these interchanges, he learned the pecking order of the heroic generation of New York painters and its suite into second and third schools. In 1957–59, Burton summered at Provincetown to study painting with Hans Hofmann; in 1959 he came to New York to study literature at Columbia University.

The Washington Workshop side of things made up his emergent public adolescent identity as artist. Its covert aspects are more compelling. Burton came to take an obsessive fascination in architecture and decoration, fixated by, among other things, the classic furniture advertisements of Wormley/Dunbar in the fifties which repeatedly locate pieces of furniture in landscapes, on beaches, and in forests. Burton now understands this fascination to be an evocation of his "longing for an ideal family life." He construed the reordering of the furniture in his room as "the re-living of one's childhood in an ideal way." Even then he began to see how furniture transforms one: "A table is not anthropomorphic. It's just a vertical against a horizontal. But a chair is anthropomorphic." These ideas were then inchoate notions, just barely liminal art fodder. Day-to-day life was played out as "a teenaged Tenth Streeter."

Visiting Scott Burton in his Thompson Street tenement walkup, third-floor corner apartment: life is an accumulation of things crowded in the suite of kitchen-cum-studio, sleeping room-cum-studio, livingroom-cum-studio. Work is everywhere. The exquisitely finished furniture sculptures are protected from dust under sheets of plastic. Burton, a small tight man in small room, cocked and peppery, a bit like a caged animal. Bookshelves tower and piles of books lean crazily. The Mario Praz *Illustrated History of Furnishings* and his study of *European and American Conversation Pieces* accessible for fast reference. Picture postcards dot the cracking walls: images of furniture from Tut's tomb, Shaker chairs hung on pegs, Louis XVI fauteuils, American functionalist dinette furniture of the thirties and forties.

We talk of the first furniture pieces, the Iowa *Furniture Landscape* reproduced in *Triquarterly* 32 (Winter 1975): temporary installations of furniture in smallish clear-ings of forest. He had made an intense search for the right pieces all over town. Floor movements in the forest were determined by a house-scaled clearing that honored a rationalist ground plan. The intention was not a new picturesque; and it certainly was unintentionally surrealist though its poetical affiliations were inescapable. "The *Dream* of Rousseau, how could that not be an influence?" he replied to an obvious question.

If one could trace the role of furniture in Burton's thinking it might run something like this: The objects in the landscape of the Iowa piece yield up the notion of furniture as psyche; this in turn leads to furniture as surrogate people, which reverses itself into people-equal-furniture, a prefiguration of the behavioral tableaux (fig. 52); last, if this system is correct, it recreates an entire process of psychic reintegration. Burton will be "made well" (assuming for argument's sake that he is "unwell") at the moment when the last equivalence is reached, when people equal people. I am describing a kind of therapeutic history, not a consecutive series, but one in which events happen all at once.

The furniture pieces splay into three sectors: first, performance; second, furniture (as tangible and objective sculpture); third, photography—not for photography's sake, but as an ancillary creation invoking a complex, private, frequently sexual iconography. Often of necessity these three threads meet and interlace. All of the elements of Burton's work—be they furniture pieces or furniture as psyche—can be shown to have first emerged in the late sixties. Like most significant figures in Postminimalism, consciousness came around 1968—"Something in it allowed me to orbit. After conceptual art I could see how to do work."

The performances are traceable to street works and activities animated by John Perreault, Vito Acconci, and Marjorie Strider, among others, in the late sixties, in which the events are so similar to daily street life or created seemingly with the stuff of street life as to be near indecipherable from the very fabric of street life itself. Among the activities: "Appears in public as a woman, drugs self to sleep at public art-opening, runs naked in street."[1] The intention of course was to create an art of little aesthetic profile, a raggedness given moral consequence through a conscious rejection of high abstract principles as they continued to be articulated by Greenberg and neo-formalist critics. For these critics "enemy art" was one that relinquished a vis-à-vis confrontation, an inert separateness from the viewer. To undermine this inhuman parity meant that this fringe group transformed painting and sculpture into a kind of psychological behaviorism and para-performance activity—inconceivable as art (then as now) to the formalists.

High formalist art was at the time inculpated by its assimilation to corporate identity, its shimmering veneer aestheticizing the American adventure in Vietnam, and anesthetizing the odious Nixon years. Gut level conceptual street performance at least had to its credit the fact that whatever kind of art it was, it was not formalist art. This transformation in urban aesthetics around 1969 often forced the artist to turn back upon himself as the primary raw material of his art. It was accorded a final prestige à *rebours* in that not only the formalists, but the whole art world tended to find its psychological and autobiographical content suspect, not quite respectable. Mind you, Burton rightly views the use of autobiography—content without form—as only a bridge, a transition out of conceptualism. His major concerns today, traceable to aspects of the earlier experience, engage the complex semiotics of behavior and reintegration or reassimilation of decoration to art.

The early conceptual activities at length led Burton to characterize the artist as a prancing ithyphallic satyr—a "tragic priapic artist,"[2] the classical *cothurnus* burlesquing the archetypal macho expressionist. Burton brilliantly costumed this startling sexual image in the manner of grotesque obscene buffoons in the classical theater by affixing a black dildo to specially maculated overalls. The costuming of this personage was worked on through 1973–74 to take into account the subtle changes in overall cut and heel size—say, the emergence of the platform heel (an imaginative metaphor for the satyr's cloven hoof)—that have taken place in men's apparel during these years. It may be that the finessing of such details grows out of Burton's frankly anti-technological conceptual bent—anti-"tech art," video, films. Instead of being composed of a lot of electronic equipment and hardware, Burton's art is built out of bits and pieces, clothing, second-hand furniture, aesthetic detritus and hand-me-downs of all kinds, and, as such, is close in spirit—however extenuated—to early collage tradition as maintained across the combines of Rauschenberg. I suspect that Burton's revulsion for high technology is sustained by an association of technology with "the Father" and/or other conventionalized notions of the male.

In a May 1973 lecture at Oberlin, the artist dissembled as a clean-cut American, wearing a short-haired wig and suit and tie, presenting a slide lecture on his own work in the third person, as if he were a young instructor talking about someone else's work. A blackout followed, and wig, jacket, shirt, and tie removed, the artist was suddenly revealed in overalls and white face, a conscious parody of the modern American male artist with the phallus sharing importance with the overalls. Oddly, such laborer's garb forms a sartorial continuum from Regionalist conservatives to urban modernists, from John Steuart Curry through de Kooning to Carl Andre. Despite the failings of this performance, Burton saw the power of work in terms of its photographic documentation, and the photograph then became something to be re-exploited in ways both intrinsically and extrinsically artistic. Its intrinsic value functions as a self-referential and autonomous art about which commentary is speculative; its extrinsic material is involved with an elaborate dialogue on certain evolutions in current art.

To understand a bit of this one has to go back to the Lynda Benglis ad published in the November 1974 issue of *Artforum.* In this advertisement, the artist appears with short-cropped hair, "shades," sporting a dildo. Here Benglis is, on a public level, commenting on issues of pornography and feminism. "Benglis, in presenting herself as a nude-with-dildo," I noted, "abrogates distinctions between male and female—as does so much else in her work—by subsuming these polarities within a single entity, echoing thereby the male-female subsumption in *The Bride Stripped Bare by Her Bachelors, Even.*"[3]

Benglis is additionally engaging in a private interchange with Robert Morris, memorialized particularly in Benglis' videotape *Mumble* (1972) and Robert Morris' *Exchange*. "I don't mean by this that together they made a single work," I said of these videotapes, "but rather that they fed each other's consciousness about the potential of video in a way that was mutually useful and interreactive."[4]

The shocking advertisement was part of still another retort to Robert Morris' advertisement for his exhibition of April 1974 at Leo Castelli and Sonnabend Galleries (see fig. 44).[5] In the S&M poster, the male-female ambiguities of the Benglis ad are expressed at the same instant in the artist's appearance as a master (the Nazi helmet) and a slave (the studded collar and manacled hands). On one hand there is the extroverted oiled beefcake shot of Morris contrasted against the dainty modesty of the barely visible elastic of his jockey briefs. In turn this exhibition poster inspired Benglis' rear-view jeans dropped cheesecake announcement for her May 1974 exhibition (see fig. 43). There was also in this Benglis material a reply to Vito Acconci's performance *Conversions* (1971), the most startling moment of which is when Acconci tucks his penis between his legs to express himself as a female. Benglis with a dildo reverses this process, expressing herself as a male. Acconci, Benglis, Morris, and Burton maintain the preeminent status of the androgyne whose myth is codified throughout the oeuvre of Duchamp. Despite in inescapable sensationalism inherent to such imagery, its real interest reflects a maintenance of the Duchampian tradition.

What we are dealing with, of course, is the much higher visibility of erstwhile secret sexual life coincidental with the early seventies, an awareness that owes much to the liberating forces generated by the women's movement and its attendant male consciousness including gay lib. For consumers this was reflected in the proliferation of sex shops, "toys" like dildos and vibrators, sex movies, etc. Susan Sontag could take the Nazi imagery of homosexual masochism to task in the *New York Review of Books* (February 6, 1975),[5] while on a more public level the *Village Voice* featured articles about S&M homosexuality (e.g., Richard Goldstein, "S&M: The Dark Side of Gay Liberation," *Village Voice*, July 7, 1975), elements of which had been circulating in gay pornographic movies such as *L.A. Plays Itself* (Fred Halstead, 1973).

The volatile issues of pornography, feminism, homosexualism, and manipulation of the media generated by Acconci, Benglis, Morris, and Burton are surely traceable to certain assumptions about what we consider the materials of art to be. One says that a sculptor uses wood or plastic or bronze; saying that means that sculptors employ various mediums in their work. The plural of medium is media. Only media doesn't mean mediums in American usage, but rather it means radio, television, magazines, movies and advertising. In short, it means Warholianism, the manipulation of advertising and promotion as a central message of one's art. As such, Warholianism—the introduction of media to the possibilities of artistic materials—is the most recent "ignoble material" admissible since the Cubist collage definitively established the parity between what academics had earlier viewed as a conflict between "noble" and "ignoble" substances. In this sense, Warholianism—the media as medium—admitted to the sculptors range of investigation an intangible substance hitherto unrecognizable as even open to manipulation. Such an idea ends in clarifying the distinctions inferred in the English language usage of the verb "to manipulate," a meaning which engages not only the physical working of a real material, but the psychological or ideological alteration of minds and bodies. A last word: Warhol as an artist of immediately contemporary interest is a dormant issue, while Warholianism exerts its emphatic interest.

Of course, I stress beyond Burton's own view of his activities his role in the Acconci-Benglis-Morris-Burton sequence because, of the four, Burton has had the least mileage. Thus, it was with a certain feeling of having been overlooked that Burton read my associations with ithyphallic kraters to describe the manneristic and Hellenistic intentions of Benglis' shocking imagery. In his piece in the "Lives" show, Burton proclaimed his dominance over Morris and Benglis by a public recitation of a jealous sexual fantasy, a group of dream fragments. This is distilled in the catalogue to the laconic "1975: Relates Wet Dream." It is not the provocative sexual matter of the work which is impressive—that kind of material has already entered the middle-brow media—but an irony stimulated by and, in turn, entering the deeply covert interchanges of artists who are successfully "making it" in the larger sense of the art scene and market by an artist working at the margin. It's obvious that this fantasy exists only as a fantasy. Yet, within Burton's work, it is the most explicit and aggressive sexual content in an art that is otherwise marked by extreme reticence and allusiveness. In fact, according to Burton's reading on his work—insofar as any artist can dissociate—the "Lives" piece serves only as a modest footnote to the behavioral studies and furniture pieces. I attribute to it an importance that its very modest incarnation can barely sustain, an importance indicative of the often involuted, almost incestuous commentaries carried on in more recent antiformalist art.

By contrast, the most extreme contraction of experience, obsessive understatement, and exquisiteness of craft is realized in Burton's *Pair Behavior Tableaux*. Here the *mise-en-scène* is two ordinary wood chairs, set at either end of the stage, that are in every proportion either too high or too awkward or too uncomfortable, owing to the platforms on which they are placed. Between the chairs two lean men anomically interrelate. The viewers seated on folding chairs, are forced to view the stage from a distance of fifty feet across a closed auditorium pit. The actors—one can say "sculptures"—wear chinos, white t-shirts, and high platform shoes—a further derivation from the artist-as-satyr image. They go through a set of forty-seven fixed tableaux based on attraction/repulsion motions recalling, if you will, Léger's *Ballet Mécanique*, or more immediately, the presentations of Gilbert and George. But, importantly, Burton does not appear—he is offstage—unlike the English sculptors who are their own sculptures. Burton makes no such confusion, one perhaps necessary to an early stage of body art, viz. Acconci, Bruce Nauman, et al. In Burton's case, the *metteur-en-scène* is the sculptor, his "actors," his "sculptures." The positions chosen in this suite of poses are static and tense, chilling, inhibited, tight.

The movements are rudimentary: get up, sit down, step forward, step back, sidle, with a sharp attention to mannered glossy poses or positions. A close parallel is found in the ambiguous hieratic gestures of Ferdinand Hodler's Symbolist paintings. Thirty-five minutes into a long hour, a performer at last touches the other's shoulder. It is a kind of performance devoid of dramatic climax—a suite of archly mirrored interchanges. The mechanistic actions are those of the performer; the human, those of a dissociated and straining audience that fidgets, coughs, checks watches, and the like.[6]

This muteness in part stems from the seemingly inert forms of Minimalism, forms which an early generation of modernists might have though incapable of eliciting empathetic responses. (T. E. Hulme's aphorism is a pithy example of this attitude.) Here characters are reduced to the inanimation of Minimalist sculpture. I have noted the stark formal character of Minimalist sculpture. While rejecting the isolated vertical monolith as the *sine qua non* of the species, it replaced it with a new metaphor—that of furniture—floorbound, horizontally sprawled, industrially prefabricated (rather than handicrafted)—the "rugs, " so to speak, of Carl Andre, or Richard Artschwager's early still-Pop formica boxes, one part Judd or Tony Smith, the other simplified images of table cloth, chair leg, or chair back. Thus sculpture became a kind of non-utilitarian furniture, the radical art quotient of which was expressed in a quirky absence of usefulness and in terms of its horizontality.[7]

If a modernist option in sculpture engages or incorporates an awareness of sculpture in terms of furniture-like affiliations, and if the artist is in fact not a mute generalist abstractionist but indeed a highly specific mannerist dealing with an ambiguous but still decipherable iconography, then sculpture may be expressed either as a conceptual performance or as painstaking reconstruction of pieces of furniture of specific stylistic character. Burton's case is exemplary. His sense of furniture moves from the found to an invented design based on an exact knowledge of period style. To date, several reconstitutions—the tables at the Whitney Biennial—for example, have been finished, though a dozen have been projected, some already in fabrication. Fascinated by rationalist design and vernacular art deco, Burton's taste leads him to variant forms of Bauhaus and de Stijl and the Arts and Crafts tradition. These pieces of furniture are counterparts to the human in his work: in a more extensive installation of chairs at Artists Space, chairs had been set up within a shallow state-like space and exquisitely illuminated in the manner of Jean Rosenthal or Jo Mielziner, celebrated masters of stage lighting.

The most startling of the works is a huge bronze armchair cast from a kind of Grand Rapids version of Queen Anne—a baluster-back slat and muffin legs (fig. 53). This real-life chair evokes less the shadow of Pompeiian bronze furniture than that of Johns' *Paintbrushes* cast in bronze in the Savarin coffee can, or the ale can pair, one of which was cast, one modeled. In Burton one witnesses the force of convictions embodied within a finessing, ironic parody.

Notes

1. From Burton's xerox catalogue piece ironically titled "Odd Years"—odd numerically, not even, bizarre. These activities date to 1969. See *Lives (Artists who deal with People's Lives [Including their Own] as the subject and/or the Meaning of their Works)*, Fine Arts Building, November-December, 1975, n.p.

2. Ibid., 1973.

3. "Benglis' Video: Medium to Media" for "Physical and Psychological Moments in Time," a first retrospective of the video work of Lynda Benglis (Fine Arts Center, SUNY, Oneonta, January-February 1975), n.p.

4. Ibid.

5. Susan Sontag, "Fascinating Fascism" (a prime study debunking the post-War whitewashing of Leni Riefenstahl, prompted by the publication of Riefenstahl's *The Last of the Nuba* and Jack Pia's *S. S. Regalia*), *The New York Review of Books*, XXII, 1, February 6, 1975, pp. 23–30. "If the message of fascism has been neutralized by an aesthetic view of life, its trappings have been sexualized . . . The solemn eroticism of fascism must be distinguished from a sophisticated playing with cultural horror where there is an element of the put-on. The poster Robert Morris made for his recent show at the Castelli Gallery in April 1974 is a photograph of the artist, naked to the waist, wearing dark glasses, what appears to be a Nazi helmet, a spiked steel collar, attached to which is a large chain which he holds in his manacled, uplifted hands. Morris is said to have considered this to be the only image that still has any power to shock: a singular virtue to those who take for granted that art is a sequence of ever-fresh gestures of provocation. But the point of the poster is its own negation. Shocking people in this context means inuring them, as Nazi material enters the vast repertory of popular iconography usable for the ironic commentaries of Pop art." p. 28.

6. Linda Shearer, commenting on the *Behavior Tableaux*, notes in the Guggenheim flyer for them (February-April 1976) that "they're not like Happenings insofar as the spectator is not allowed to become a participant in the proceedings. He [Burton] also refuses us the theater's traditional distractions by imposing both physical and psychological distance. In so doing, he forces us to concentrate on specific gestures with an intensity parallel to the intensity of his manipulations of these gestures."

7. For example, "We have seen, in the past two years particularly, an almost concerted assault on the axiomatic verticality of sculpture in favor of horizontality. There is, of course, a kind of familiar horizontal form which, although not called by the name of sculpture, has always insisted on certain sculptural qualities—furniture. When Brancusi made horizontal sculpture, he justified himself by regarding the results not as 'sculpture' but as 'furniture,' calling such sculptural artifacts 'Bench,' or 'Table,' stressing in such appellation a functional rather than horizontal connotation.

   "In this respect, that Carl Andre's floor-bound square modules should be called 'Rugs' seems less fortuitous than may appear at first hearing . . . " see "Richard Serra: Slow Information."

Figure 52.   Scott Burton, *Individual Behavior Tableau*, 1980
Performed by Kent Hines, University Art Museum, Berkeley.
(Photo courtesy Max Protetch Gallery)

Figure 53. Scott Burton, *Bronze Chair*, 1972–75
Bronze, 48″×18″×20″.
(Photo courtesy Max Protetch Gallery)

Camp Meetin':
The Furniture Pieces of Scott Burton

"In Burton one witnesses the force of convictions embodied within a finessing ironic parody." Lapidary, but too soon abandoned, this ending to a first essay on the artist. Something more should have been said about the furniture pieces, but the works were not finished, or too few of them were—just the *Bronze Chair* and two tables shown at the Whitney Biennial of 1975. But now that, in the last season, nine new furniture pieces were shown—four at the Droll/Kolbert Gallery, four at the Brooks Jackson Iolas Gallery, and one at the Guggenheim Museum (and each of these exhibitions filled with other already fabricated works)—there is now a body of work on which to build a surer assessment as well as to spur a broad range of speculation.

Only it is thorny. So many skittish issues are brought up by Burton's work, hard to straighten issues—especially since Burton's work, on its most obvious level, aspires to wedge between issues, all the while seeming very frank, very straight-out, very Square John.

From the outset, there is a certain casuistry in speaking of Burton's sculpture as either "furniture" or as "pieces." Their generic grouping, as a broad consideration, suggests something of the theatricality by which Burton is drawn. Keep in mind that, in quite another light, he is an important force for a new style of theater and performance. An osmotic interface both separates and connects Burton's furniture pieces from and to his theater pieces.

Burton's furniture pieces shuttle between a double-edged postulate. While viewed and experienced as furniture and presented as functions of conventional ideas about furniture, Burton's furniture pieces, for all that, leap the very boundaries of those preconceptions, transforming them at the same instant into a meditation on furniture, on theatricality, on art, and on style. His work is both object and commentary at one go: sheer schizzy aesthetic autistic—he would have it—altruism.

Some descriptions of certain pieces: a Moderne-style table à la Milanese—blue granite exquisitely crafted, trifoliate corners, resting upon sledlike runners; or, a Constructivist/Suprematist table of Neo-Deco bent—square for the top, triangle as mid-

---

This article originally appeared in *Arts Magazine*, September 1978.

support, and circle for the base. (The triangle edge extends one inch beyond the square's width—a dimension equal to the depth that the point of the triangle punctures the circular base—an intrusion equal to the thickness of the base itself. The measurements and surfaces and styles that are guyed [if, in fact, they are "guyed"] reveal Burton's exquisite sense of proportion, elegance, and decorum—qualities that would more likely unnerve a Malevich through sheer hyperaesthesia than please him—quite despite the fact that the table is composed of the shapes in which Malevich discerned the presence of "pure feelings," the Suprematist triad, circle, square, triangle.)

At the other end of the style spectrum is a cast bronze outdoor table in the rustic Adirondack "camp meetin'" mode—a table associated, say, with the designs of Davis and Jackson, Downing and Walter—though, perhaps, it is met most frequently in its carpenter vernacular (fig. 54). Burton's version is single cast, unique; the wood prototype was lost in the casting. These objects—and the Guggenheim's *Children's Furniture Set*—continue to mark Burton's central place in the vanguard while demonstrating anew the degree to which the vanguard is concerned with and informed by past art—quite in opposition to the way conservatives behave, even conservatives of "modernist" stamp. Since the latter group "knows" just what art is, they haven't a care for vanguardism. How alone Burton seems then when compared to the prevailing abstraction, though his work is much influenced by its taciturn reductivism—one that is faltering, at any rate, even the best of it. Style gets used up—and, in time, Burton will also have to deal with that depletion.

All the time that Burton's furniture pieces are seen as furniture they are presented in a way that forces the contextual interpenetration of "art"—they are shown in a gallery, a special kind of signifier of sacramental or aestheticized space. Of course, the converse is also true—the furniture has the effect of reinforcing the initial profane identity of a gallery—that of a shop or store. Sure, that's difficult—since Burton's pieces retain their functional premise, a usefulness not eschewed even though shown within an art gallery or museum. His work refuses to take sides. It strikes a bargain between an accepted notion—the uselessness of art—while it argues against so received and unexamined a prejudice.

Beyond this, Burton's furniture exists as an amalgam of abstract considerations—surface, form, material, color—pure abstract information. This, plus a sense of learned historical style and paraphrase. (Before the square-banded legs of is black lacquer table, Burton suddenly grasped that what was coming through a lifetime of regional denial—a protest against feeling in any way Southern despite his Alabama Presbyterian birth—were the Greek Revival columns of the ante-bellum manse, church, and court house. Incredibly learned.)

Burton repeatedly worries at the hollow core at the center of art, teases the question of how art is a function of context as well as being its own formal self-realization (if it is really these things); how mannerism ricochets off a high normative mainstream, no matter how disdainful and unsanctioning that same tendency might be with regard to the reaches of irony that it feeds—and of which Burton is so arch an exemplar.

Still, Burton's art is not in the object, no matter how fetishistically, how perfectly fashioned his objects. If the art is in the argument, one wonders, why even bother to bring its embodiment to so keen a pitch of finish—unless the work was all along meant to be a perfect object whose projection of beauty is a function of an indefatigable hand—Brancusi's ceaselessly smoothing way. In short, no one knows where the art of art is.

For all these "beyond," these "yes, but" contradictions, Burton's furniture is meant to be used. There is the key. Burton has thought the matter through so much farther than the simple antagonisms I have pointed to; his speculations postulate a vacuum-creating third phase and, further than that, a democratic/populist "fourth dimension." It is these latter aspects and considerations, so marked by social mission, that transform for Burton the mere making process into a far more gratifying art-making one.

At the third level, simple erasure occurs—one occasioned by the incessant shuttling and blurring of context and content, in the playing of one side off against the other. On a certain level these contradictions are not even interesting any longer because they are so self-evident—to the artist at least. For the most part, the public may have difficulty even grasping this much. Burton thinks that the process of self-erasure postulated by a theoretical effacement of object by argument and back again conjures the far more important fourth phase—one that emerges to fill the void created by the preceding powerful frictions and, for him, obvious oscillations.

All this invokes a perhaps unexpected Whitmanesque streak in the artist, the idealistic belief in the democratic mind at its best, least sectarian application. For him, the furniture pieces, by a range of confluent processes still too fine to clearly analyze, aspire to some larger social and communal democratic content. Thus, the furniture pieces may be said to have their roots in his *Iowa Furniture Landscape* (1970). Here Midwestern storebought furniture was photographed in woodsy Iowa landscape sites.

Prompted by that seminal work—Burton says, "it just came out of nowhere"—I noted that:

> If one could trace the role of furniture in Burton's thinking it might run something like this: the objects of the landscape of the Iowa Piece Yield up the notion of furniture as psyche; this in turn leads to furniture as surrogate people-equal-furniture, a prefiguration of the *Behavioral Tableaux*. Last, if this system is correct, it recreates an entire system of psychic integration. Burton will be "made well" (assuming for arguments's sake that he is "unwell") at the moment when the last equivalence is reached, when people equal people. I suppose I am describing a kind of therapeutic history, not a consecutive series, but one in which events happen all at once.

The elements of those analogies have been roiling now for over a decade in Burton's work: the object in the landscape, the furniture as psyche, the furniture as surrogate people, the people as furniture, the people as people. Such a graduated list informs the argument that inheres—for the artist at least—to the furniture pieces: furniture as furniture (use, style), furniture as art (the gallery context); the sheer obviousness and self-cancelling nature of a dialectical ploy in which neither primary term assumes control but which instead occasions phase three, a sense of "presence," that is, of objects of "persuasion."

This brings Burton to the most romantic belief of all: the vacuum that may be said to have been generated by an awareness of the intermeshed workings up to the third phase imbues his furniture pieces with qualities and values that as yet are but only hinted at, a sporadic description in the vast shifts in the sociology of art going on about him and to which he adds his special inflection, phase four. Through all of this Burton rejects all rhetoric or polemics. Such stances are, for him, a debasement, born of a confusion of rhetoric with "tone." Tone equals "presence" for him. "It is not what you start from," he says, "but what conclusions are drawn that marks the important critical act—for both the artist and the critic." The "fourth phase"—as if things could ever be so easily structured—equals a personal vitalization (how trite these phrases seem), the destruction, that is, of the fine-arts notion of art-objects in isolation. In short, Burton aspires to the relinking of the so-called "decorative" with the "fine arts," or as I noted, " . . . the reintegration or re-assimilation of the decorative to art." Burton believes that, perhaps, through the making of tables and chairs, at least the beginning of what he views as a "true populism" may occur.

The task is two-fold: for the artist the formal task will ultimately work for the creation of objects in isolation to the formal task of the entire space—of wall, floor, environment, the whole decorative ensemble; for, as Burton rightly sees, "the whole space equals the real unit of social history."

But, on the other hand, perhaps an even weightier question concerns the nature of the spaces being or to be provided; what spaces are given to be serviced—are they ceremonial or sacramental, domestic or commercial, virgin nature or reclaimed territory? Perhaps here is the most critical consideration of all—though first steps have been made in the tables and chairs: what he is really dealing with has yet to be given to get done.

Burton is no woolly democratic zealot. He is far too canny and hard-headed to succumb to the contemporary delusion that artist legislate change—viz. Joseph Beuys, Joseph Kosuth. Still, the wild thing about the furniture pieces is that they—certainly for the artist—approach his fourth phase of consciousness, one which taps a broad range of artistic and social connections that are as similar in spirit to, as they are dedicatedly different in appearance from, say, an earthwork by Robert Smithson—to take the example of a sculptor totally animated by an Olmstead-like and Whitman-like vision of what American art ought to be. What Burton's furniture pieces abolish, obviate, or, at the very least, momentarily staunch, is the powerful and determining grip of shabby etiquettes, labels like "mannerism" or "realism." I suppose what Burton's furniture pieces make me see—having come this far with him—is that the issues he hopes to address are issues beyond style, styles, or even stylishness.

Figure 54.   Scott Burton, *Table from Four Table*, 1978
Bronze, 42″×27″.
(Photo courtesy Max Protetch Gallery)

Siah Armajani: Populist Mechanics

Siah Armajani is a wiry, gracious man pushing forty, small of frame but not slight—dark hair shot with gray, a nose flattened and askew, but, for all that, a handsome Persian. His conversation is animated and generous. He wants to tell you everything and not leave anything out. For all its learned points of reference his conversation is never pedantic or idly name-dropping; it never calls up inappropriate sanctions. Each of Armajani's references—and there are many—have been assimilated in an experienced, authentic way.

His people are Moslem Iranians with admixtures of Christian and Jew, an important detail suggesting the tolerant atmosphere in which he was raised. His father and uncle were both mission-educated—discreetly. It was (and, in even greater measure today, still is) of dubious form to be western-educated. Current Arabist chauvinism is especially marked by the activist, expansionist nature of Sunnite Islam, so different from that of the less-worldly, bookish Shiite sect from which Armajani stems.

Armajani's uncle Yahaya emigrated to the United States, becoming a professor of history at Macalester College in St. Paul. Through the avuncular good offices, Armajani was in turn able to come to this country. He recognizes that his humane populism—he believes in the natural and evolving goodness of humankind in a way I find difficult to accept—as an artist and thinker marks him as alien to present-day political repression in Iran and he entertains no thought of returning there. In 1967 he became a citizen of the United States.

Partly the result of his work, partly that of his sheer disarming force of manner—Americans are more apt to countenance Jeffersonian ethics when uttered by outlanders—Armajani has been party to a wide change throughout American sculpture where its most progressive expression leans toward an unapologetic construction, not an aestheticized Constructivism. Armajani lurks at the edge of this development, perhaps without receiving the full share of praise he deserves for the extraordinary effect he has had—although Linda Shearer's inclusion of the sculptor in her exhibition *Young American Artist 1978* (The Guggenheim Museum, May-June

This article originally appeared in *Arts Magazine*, October 1978.

1978) and the early supportive writing of Michael Klein, notably the essay for *Scale and Environment: 10 Sculptors* (Walker Art Center, 1977), made inroads in dispelling Armajani's neglect on the East Coast. But to suffer from neglect—is equally the lot of the very sculptors with whom Armajani is reasonably associated—say, Michael Hall at Cranbrook or Edward Levine latterly of Wright State, now Dean at the Minneapolis College of Art and Design, where Armajani has taught for years. And behind these names, Armajani's included—though in varying degrees of absorption—stands the moral, if not always formal, example of Robert Irwin, as stirring for Armajani, quick to acknowledge his admiration, as was the impact made by the American Patrimonial texts Armajani so ardently committed himself to on arriving here.

Doubtless one thinks that I overstress the political content of Armajani's work, especially since—on a certain level—one really can't see it. But any claim for form—from the most empirical to the most transcendent—is invisible. Still, Armajani's work is virtually ununderstandable without reference to his political awareness, one that leads him to make an abstract sculpture embodying, according to the artist's view of the matter, a special take on the long suite of Enlightenment philosophy from the Rationalist ethics of the eighteenth century to the structuralism and epistemology of the present day. On its simplest level, form for Armajani is iconographically predetermined and embodies a populist democratic ideology and frame of reference. Yet his forms are never explicitly illustrative; or even if in some sense they are "illustrative," they are never "narrative," this despite the enormous number of philosophical and literary references his sculptures make, at least in terms of their titles *Thomas Jefferson's House . . . , El Lissitsky's Neighborhood . . . , The Red School House for Thomas Paine* (red school house, a nostalgic symbol for a lost pre-industrial America; red for the "radical" views of the revolutionary pamphleteer) (fig. 55), and so on.

What is most immediately visible in Armajani's work is its absence of conciliatory sweetness or tactile appeal—it ain't smooth—physically or conceptually. This indifference to—even rejection of —the merely pleasing is realized through disruptive passages, bumpy elements, frank abutments, blocked approaches, "wrong" heights, makeshift executions, obvious colors—all sorts of diffident discrepancies that force a mythically desired aesthetic "whole" to fracture into a valuable particulateness; and his work is large, always as big as a house or a barn or a bridge—or even larger. Klein describes, for example, *A Fairly Tall Tower: 48,000 Miles High* and *The Ghost Tower:* "The former is envisaged as a self-supporting tower suspended in space, anchored to, but not supported by the earth. The latter was a holographic image floating above the First National Bank of Minneapolis. An inverted mirror image of the bank, the hologram would appear and disappear, depending upon cloud conditions and would seem to extend 382 feet into the air." Klein goes on to describe still a third project of 1969, *The Tower: North Dakota:* "For this project Armajani calculated—again with the aid of a computer—the dimensions and shape of a giant tower and would cast a shadow across the state of North Dakota" (*Scale and Environment*, pp. 16–17). That Armajani recognizes that these conceptual projects paraphrase, say, the Eiffel

Tower, Tatlin's *Monument to the Third Internationale,* and Frank Lloyd Wright's *Mile High Skyscraper,* goes without saying. But in what way such paraphrase is stylistically linked to these models is unclear. Formally? Sure—and yet there is that oblique, literary nerve center, that punning verbal/formal side of things in Armajani. One can't help, say, chuckling over Armajani's *Boat/Bridge* (1969): two feet short of the width of the river it must cross, the traveler enters one end of the *Boat/Bridge.* Having sailed but two feet, the traveler disembarks on the opposite shore.

To be in an Armajani (or to look at an Armajani) is to be inside a big structure that isolates and atomizes rather than harmonizes or aestheticizes. Armajani's part-to-part legibility marks a difference from the smooth sailing, the even flow of part to part, or part to whole, provided by some of the very sculptors upon whom he has exercised, at least in part or in passing, a certain appeal, let alone of the entire Constructivist tradition. And for all the scale of his work, there is nothing engineered in an Armajani, despite an often engineered look—nothing that smacks of high technology. Though Armajani may have had recourse to complex machinery—indeed had—it all looks as if it had been made with simple technology and tools, not complex ones.

For Armajani, sculpture is big, built and experienced in separate episodes—and, unlike David Smith and his suite, it is never cryptically anthropomorphic. Each of Armajani's forms is unrepentantly clichéd—clichéd colors (The red, black, white of Suprematist graphics, a favorite reference); clichéd building material (schlocky two-by-fours, corrugated tin, shabby transparent plastic, all chosen for populist associations); clichéd space (room, corridor, window, pen). Ironically, his sculptures revoke the very American notion that form follows function—taken for a Bauhaus adage but one initially drawn by Horatio Greenough in his *Observations and Experience of a Yankee Stonecutter, 1852:* "When I define Beauty as the promise of Function; Action as the presence of Function; Character as the record of Function, I arbitrarily divide that which is essentially one." By contrast, in Armajani's work, forms connect to specific pieces of information, specific spaces, specific materials—but as to function, there simply is none. Room-like spaces are not passageways meant to lead you somewhere else. Forms and functions accrue not from spatial necessity or any kind of felt urgency (the doctrine of early abstraction), but because there exists a kind of guide, some builder's manual, some popular-mechanical point of reference of which this space is merely a sample. His is a kind of flatfooted, Benjamin Franklin, Show-Me-I'm-From-Missouri, literalist empiricism—literal matter, literal/verbal. Indeed, Armajani's most intensive literal/verbal work may have been the creation of a kind of builder's reference guide in which all possible combinations of space are indexed—a "room," say, with a "window" on the "wall," in the "ceiling," or on the "floor"—similarly one with "doors," flat on the floor, standing up, the wall open, closed, inside-out, top and bottom. In such a sense, aesthetics doesn't even come into consideration. It is a kind of architectural sculpture by rote. He calls this encyclopedic manual, and he has made it, his *Dictionary for Building* (ca. 1973–78).

Armajani ardently rejects any type of Palladian centricity, even in the Thomas

Jefferson houses where it would be natural, as too patent an aristocratic class signifier, one often superficially elaborated in middle-class architectural spinoffs—chintzy, plastic symbols of upward mobility. Armajani understands this as well as Robert Venturi, without projecting the latter's enthusiastic, slumming condescension. He rejects time-honored aesthetic considerations—more interesting perhaps in the degree that they are ironically imitated—for the blunt proposition that structure merely encloses or discloses, but not necessarily in any hierarchical or aesthetic way locatable to taste decisions—though, in the end, this too becomes another taste.

Armajani postulates a sculptural transition from inside to outside, resulting from an ironic commentary on philosophy, one realized in the simple forms and actions of a carpenter vernacular. The reason that this vernacular is so important to the artist is that it itself has come to signify pragmatic, democratic self-reliance. Additionally it provides a way of typing the American expansionist building types of our Manifest Destiny—carpenter Gothic, shingle style, pseudo-Queen Anne beach cottage, boom-town balloon frame and Main Street facade, etc., to a populist-derived architectural theory. This theory, really a "post-modernism" as architectural historians are coming to say (Robert Venturi, Vincent Scully, et al.), is coterminate with the abstract formalism of the Suprematist/Constructivist ethos. There you have it. The balloon frame of the Midwestern town transformed into Tatlin's *Monument to the Third Internationale*. Only in America. For Armajani, the question whether such principles can lead to beautiful sculpture simply never arises—and in not having arisen, leads to beautiful sculpture.

Armajani's focus on experience, sifted from the texts of the Founding Fathers through the Transcendentalists, thrusts him headlong into a form of pure Phenomenology from Husserl into Merleau-Ponty. The isolation of the physical fact is the real intent of his sculpture, and to explain this Armajani tells the parable of the hammer taken from Heidegger's *Being and Time:* in hammering away at a nail there is but one consciousness, one psycho-physical experience—one's focus on the hammer driving the nail through the board. In this way, experience becomes whole and continuous; as such it is in touch not with the present but with the future. Thus, through wholeness and continuity, the experience is transformed into an aesthetic and kinesthetic episode. But what happens when the hammer breaks, asks Heidegger. Armajani happens. Instead of continuousness of movement, one is faced with an experience composed of isolated parts devoid of a sense of futurity: to wit, the hammer, the nail, the board—alone, in and of themselves. The continuous drive to a future—seamless and unawares—that renders such a building experience aesthetic is rescinded in Armajani's way of building. To regain the sense of each instant, each part, but *not* to bring one to an aestheticized future, but rather to the consciousness of the intensity of an ongoing present—such is Armajani's ambition. And achievement. Only the present is real for him. So he is drawn to the quotidian banal, the simple, prosaic, and the over-familiar; through the ad hoc working of grungy physical matter, he keeps one honed against a keen present. The truest dichotomy of Armajani's work is not that of the disassociation of art from nature, but between doing/being and the sense of aesthetic futurity. In achieving this he replaces a shopworn sense of sculpture with a fresh and, dare one say it, American one.

Figure 55. Siah Armajani, *Red Schoolhouse for Thomas Paine*, 1978
Corrugated steel, painted wood, plexiglass, 10'×34'×22'.
(Photo courtesy Max Protetch Gallery)

Theater of the Conceptual: Autobiography and Myth

The posthumous revelation of the diorama *Etant Donnés* gave lie to the canard that Marcel Duchamp abandoned art for chess in 1923, when he left the *Large Glass* unfinished. For twenty years at least (c. 1946–66), Duchamp had been intensely engaged by the continued elaboration of the mythology that had occupied him between 1912 and 1923—the arcana of the *Large Glass*. Duchamp scholars now realize that the imagery of *Etant Donnés* represents a working toward nature from the mechanomorphic elements of the *Large Glass*—empirical representationalism deduced from diagrammatic terms instead of the reverse.

The title *Etant Donnés* as an expression indicates those syllogistic premises that are "given" or "granted" in a logical argument. When we say so and so is "granted," in French we say "etant donné." In *Etant Donnés*, the granted elements are identical to those of the *Large Glass*—the waterfall and the illuminating gas—physical and metaphorical sources of energy.

Significant to the development of *Etant Donnés* are three small erotic objects of 1951, the *Objet-Dard*, the *Female Fig Leaf*, and the *Wedge of Chastity*. All the titles of these familiar and curiously ambiguous talismans play with literary conceits and/or outright puns. The pun is the touchstone of Duchamp's thought—a circular process of reasoning that thriftily returns to the same place while releasing fresh insights.

These three sexual objects account for certain inferences that clarify the mode of Conceptual art that deals with autobiography and/or myth. The three objects respectively are male, female, and a binary image—a male-female form. The male object is *Objet-Dard*—in appearance flaccid and vaguely detumescent despite a raised veinlike element running along a curved ridge. This metal object, it seems, was a brace from the mold in which the breast of the violated female nude of *Etant Donnés* had been shaped. *Objet-Dard* is marked by an oval plane at one extremity upon which are incised the words "objet dard." This pun bridges the notion of "art object" and "dart object," the word "dard" in French meaning dart. The dart aspect of

---

This article originally appeared in *Artforum*, October 1973.

the work, as Duchamp acknowledged, intensifies the phallic implications of this conundrum.

In my view, the implications inherent to *Objet-Dard* clarify a source of the iconography of early Jasper Johns dating from about 1955, when he first met Duchamp. The appearance of *Objet-Dard*, a work that on Johns's first encounter did not remotely look like an "object of art," led Johns to ask how such an object could have been imagined in the first place? Duchamp's reply, according to Johns, explained the derivation of the object from the mold referred to above.

The secondary meanings of *Objet-Dard* are even more elusive. What is the object of a dart? Clearly the answer is a Target, a central icon associated with Johns's painting from 1955 on. Thus, from the implicitly ironical attitude toward the pun and language in Duchamp's work, Johns made an imaginative leap which further transposed these implications into an oblique, conceptually multivalent iconography wholly different in type from the character of much American abstraction between 1950 and 1955. Johns's insinuating imagery displaced such glyphs as were then based on the prevailing fusion of Willem de Kooning and Franz Kline. Taking Duchamp's pun literally, at face value, Johns inaugurated an imagery of conceptual ambiguity, one that continues. The Pop artists, working in ah ambient situation fed my many sources, were far less hyperbolic than Johns in their approach. To the degree that any were influenced by Johns they took his work—and Rauschenberg's also—to emphasize primarily an iconography of conceptual sets that only incidentally engages the commonplace. But another generation of artists sees that it was the conceptual set that was as crucial as the imagery itself—target, American flag, map, numbers, measuring devices, and orthographic signs that identify primary colors.

The sheer perversity of Duchamp's *Objet-Dard*, shockingly unclassifiable as art to an Abstract Expressionist taste, is even more paradoxical when the question "what is the object of a dart?" is answered by Johns' Target—an oddly specific response to a hypothetical query.

Johns rejects this iconographic connection. He claims he knew no French, though to mouth the word "dard" surely calls the English word "dart" immediately to mind. More viable is his assertion that he did not know of the three erotic objects until after the early Targets were completed. To be sure, there is the matter of Johns's personal acquaintance with Duchamp, a detail that must be accounted for, or even the access to Duchamp's mind and persona transmitted to Johns through Cage.

Be this as it may, the artist's mind, unlike that of the historian, does not thrive on niggling one-to-one details, but on making imaginative leaps and playing sudden hunches that throw the origins of the feat into relative unimportance. Even were Johns not fully cognizant of the potential of these three erotic objects in 1955, surely he was aware of some of their implications. What better confirmation of his fascination than that by 1960 he had personally acquired these works.

The intention of the cryptic *Female Fig Leaf* becomes clear on learning that it was modeled against the pudenda of the violated female figure of the *Etant Don-*

nés, on which Duchamp had worked so long in secrecy. Modeling against anatomy or anatomically suggestive fragments is a central feature of Johns' work that begins in 1955, and continues to this day. The *Target with Plaster Casts*, 1955, for instance, supports a register of boxes filled with colored anatomical fragments—lip, nose, ears, fingers, male sex organ—cast from the body of a friend of the artist.

The use of the body fragment, an essential reliance on graphic values, and an insistent intellectual clutch of paradox indicate that Johns, like Duchamp, evolves from the principles of French Symbolism. As Duchamp was the spiritual heir of Mallarmé, so Johns derives from Odilon Redon, in whose charcoal drawings and lithographs we find both the inspirational matter of Johns—fragments of human imagery, especially the floating or severed head—and his richly self-elaborating graphic technique. But beyond these similarities of image and drawing is Johns' consistently ironic attitude toward such subject matter and technique. As interesting as it may be to note formal connections between artists, the issue is more resolved by the texture of Johns' mind itself. Who but Johns so consistently insinuates, so perversely warps the known?

Johns' relationship to Duchamp is one matter, and widely accepted. It serves to establish a model against which a wider and more contemporary mode of art can be discussed. Three aspects of Duchamp's work found response in the ranging horizontal and emotional climate of California art: (1) personal mythology; (2) a punning focus; and (3) modeling or casting itself as an irony as well as a method. The absorption of the folksy and homespun pun as typified in the Bay Area work of several artists, particularly Fred Martin, Jeremy Andersen and William Wiley, is the facet from which derives, in the first instance, Bruce Nauman's introduction to the pun. From such a local usage it was but one step further to explore the physically referential aspects of Duchamp's art, aspects that had been corroborated in the prestigious East Coast model afforded by Johns.

A telling motif, say, of Nauman's appreciation of linguistic circularity is the neon spiral, a motif employed by the artist in executing the early *Maxims*. Their shape obviously approximates the cyclical nature of the pun, as Johns's *Targets* duplicates it.

While the very title of Nauman's *Wedge Piece* (see fig. 40), inevitably recalls Duchamp's *Wedge of Chastity* (see fig. 39), seemingly the least rewarding of the three erotic objects, its appearance relates strongly to that work. The *Wedge of Chastity* presents a ragged metallic element, the male plug, driven into a matrix of dental plastic, the female receptacle. Nauman's *Wedge Piece* counters a vaginal chamfering (registered during the industrial fabrication of the wedges) against an elongated phallic shape. Moreover, the redness of the wedges corresponds in hue to the pinkness of the dental plastic used in Duchamp's piece. There is, then, a close coloristic and structural relationship between Duchamp's and Nauman's wedge variations.[1] It is also important to note that the form of the wedge had been awarded credentials within Minimalism—the preeminent abstract-reductivist movement of our time—as a form in itself. Among the few alternatives open to abstract-reductivist form is commonly found the triangle—the wedge, the ramp, the corner, the "L."

The icons of Minimalism are few—the square, the circle, and the triangle, as well as each of their spatial projections—cube and oblong, sphere and cylinder, pyramid and wedge. In the many Minimalist pieces executed by Robert Morris and Donald Judd, for example, we find "L" variations, wedge forms, ramps, and architectural elements that negotiate corner and walls. Imagine a situation that combines the circumlocutionary processes stemming from literary conceits, plus a value system primarily supportive of abstract art, and the source and latitude of Postminimalism become clearer.

Recent elaborations of this art manifested themselves in the rise of theatricality—the theater of the conceptual. The problem of drawing a mainstream formalist argument with regard to a conceptual theater, one that acknowledges its elements of dance, music, and behaviorism, lies in the difficulty of isolating those elements germane to the histories of dance, music, and behaviorism themselves, and those which have developed within a more contained view of painting and sculpture.

We witnessed, for example, as part of conceptual theater, work by the so-called body artist, Vito Acconci. He extrapolated the mythical type perfected by Duchamp—the androgyne—onto a behaviorist examination of his own psychology, seen in *Seedbed,* a work developed during the period of 1970–72.

Despite scandalized outcries, *Seedbed* presents a bare *mise-en-scène.* Its setting is a ramp or wedge sloping up the corner of a gallery floor. Certainly it was not the external aspect of the work that proved provocative, but that the artist, fed by airholes drilled into the ramp's surface, isolated himself below the slanted floor and engaged in masturbation. The fantasy accompanying this act was faintly audible in the larger gallery space as it was transmitted through a loudspeaker in the corner of the chamber.

Seedbed takes as its metaphor one that Duchamp earlier had attributed to the *Large Glass. Seedbed,* like Duchamp's subtitle for the *Large Glass,* is "an agricultural machine" —Acconci's seed, so to speak, now being cast upon the floor.

The *Large Glass*—the work must here be referred to by its proper name *The Bride Stripped Bare by Her Bachelors, Even*—records an ongoing series of physical changes effected through the actions of complex mechanomorphic machinery. Owing to the functions of the mechanomorphs depicted on the glass, physical states are at one point seen as gaseous—the cloud, or liquid—the "love gasoline" dripped from the Bride in the upper portion of the glass into the realm of the Bachelors below. At length, the love gasoline falls into the *Nine Malic Molds* and therein presumably solidifies. Among still other possibilities, this altered physical matter may be pulverized by the *Chocolate Grinder,* as it once again may be turned into light energy while passing through the lenses of the *Optical Witnesses.*

In arcane lore, the person capable of enforcing the change of physical matter from one state to another is the alchemist or the androgyne—the latter being a fusion of male and female. He-She corresponds to a notion of God, that is, a coincidence of opposites. Throughout highly disparate cultures, such a person is often assigned the role of shaman or seer, the see-er of the future, like Tiresias of Greek tragedy, or the Seller of Salt, the Salt Merchant of kabbalism and alchemy.

By an exiguous and circumstantial argument the salt merchant appears to correspond to the medieval alchemist, i.e., the person capable of effecting the change of matter from one physical state to another. The "salt" of the salt merchant may well be symbolized by the philosopher's stone of the alchemist—the esoteric catalyst without which such changes in matter cannot be made. The arcane knowledge, the gnosis needed to effect this change—say, for example, the secret name of God—and the actual enactment of these changes constituted for the alchemist, the kabbalist or the magus, *le grand oeuvre*, the great work of magic. Duchamp's *Large Glass* as completed by the *Étant Donnés* is his great work of magic and his life's work as well.

In French the Salt Merchant is called "Le Marchand du Sel," a transpositional pun on the four syllables of the name of Marcel Duchamp. Duchamp knew the name of the androgyne—Rose Sélavy (the secret name of God?) as well as the androgyne's appearance—the artist himself in transvestiture. Man Ray photographed Marcel Duchamp in such cross-garb in 1920, when preparing the punning label for the perfume bottle *La Belle Haleine*—beautiful breath, beautiful Helen. The label displays a photograph of Rose Sélavy, a punning name meaning "life is okay" or, "in the pink," or "life is erotic [rose/eros]." She is the anima, the female side of Duchamp's nature.

All of this background is essential to an understanding of *Seedbed*. Acconci's earlier attempts to deal with the projection of an androgynous personality were realized through performances of such actions as the burning away of the artist's body hair, the tugging at his breasts, and the hiding of his penis between his legs. These performances indicate publicly that Acconci projected a notion of the androgyne that had earlier been set by Duchamp within his conception of his mythical alter ego, Rose Sélavy.

It is important to note the difference between the conceptual theater of Acconci's *Seedbed* and Dennis Oppenheim's *Adrenochrome* of 1973. *Adrenochrome*, like *Seedbed*, deals with the emission of chemicals—in Oppenheim's case, the chemical necessary to reconstitute the normal blood-cell structure of a schizophrenic—in Acconci's work, human sperm. *Adrenochrome* illuminates a particle of the chemical at the apex of a pyramid, while at the same time, a slide of the microscopic structure of the chemical is projected against a gallery wall. Both *mises-en-scène* are lent credibility owing to a parallel support system for abstract forms, the ramp and the pyramid.

While both the above works were generated by personal crises, *Adrenochrome* remains a pro forma work that insists on a one-to-one relationship to the artist's biography. *Seedbed*, by contrast, is a highly nonformal and secretive work whereby the autobiographical element is transposed to the plane of myth on the basis of Duchamp's lore.

The ontological artist, therefore, as Duchamp had anticipated and indicated, is the one whose work is completed in the public psyche. It must be noted that the psyche is primed by a literature of myth. In the absence of this acculturation nothing appears to happen except the work itself and the viewer's subjective experience of it.[2]

The mythical personage of the androgyne, it seems to me, is the exteriorization of Duchamp himself, expressed through the surrogate adventure that began when the Nude Descended the Staircase, became the Bride, was Stripped Bare by the Bachelors—female and male personae who ultimately united in the androgyne as impersonated by Duchamp in transvestiture.

An important "proof" for this, apart from the visual evidence, derives from the French name of the *Large Glass: La Mariée mise à nu par les celibataires, même.* La MARiée mise a nu par les CELibataires—MAR-CEL, the first three letters of the French word for bride and the first three letters of the French word for bachelors comprise the letters of Duchamp's first name.

The by now obvious fact that Marcel Duchamp is both Bride and Bachelor at the same instant allows one to recognize something of a mythical core in, say, Vito Acconci's work, as well as to understand why Bruce Nauman may have used his name as a Readymade—*My Name as If It Were Bounced off the Surface of the Moon* or *My Name Enlarged Vertically 14 Times.*

Similarly, as Duchamp had regarded the three sexual objects in terms of morphological transfer—most particularly the *Female Fig Leaf*—so too Nauman casts against his body in unanticipated ways. It was this aspect of Duchamp's work that licenses for us Nauman's move into behavioristic performance, video work, laser stereoptics, and architectural situations. At first, Nauman's attention focused on the external effect made by his body upon some malleable substance, as in the *Template of the Left Half of My Body at 10 Inch Intervals.* From this, Nauman was able to project an art in which no external object was actually formed but which internalized the process back into his body—intangible substances such as space, light, warmth, acting in time—were now reforming his body.

This shift between the mold and that which is molded has influenced much of the open and often seemingly unpurposeful aspects of the conceptual performance. In such instances the distinction between Acconci and Oppenheim may prevail. Those conceptual performances which allow for the consciousness of the mythic may be of a greater interest than those that are purely behavioristic.

Such a judgment is speculative. To insist on this distinction means that I posit a conceptual theater given value largely through an attachment to myth and legend. The converse may as easily be true. The question is still an open one. Conceptual theater may yet prove interesting precisely to the degree that it detaches itself from a mythological frame of reference.

Since literature of any kind has the effect of diminishing the abstractness of a work, a conceptual theater grounded, say, in myth would necessarily be weakened by this connection. But, in the same degree that myth may devalue abstraction, so too does autobiography. In the absence of myth and autobiography the conceptual performance becomes purely behavioral. This appears to be another reason why, in Conceptual art, the behavioral appears to bridge the ontological and epistemological branches of the movement: behaviorism is abstract conceptual theater.

When Nauman investigated the artistic possibilities of his body or his name as a Readymade, he drew away from an art based on the pun and simple language toward what has been loosely called "phenomenology"—perhaps an abuse of the term, but one that nonetheless has entered art talk.

"Phenomenology," used this way, indicates a kind of physiological behaviorist activity and self-examination. What is it like to be? To do? To sense? To enact certain kinds of experiences and activities? Many of the experiences thus examined tend to be those attributed to inanimate things—residual Minimalism again—an underpinning derived from abstraction. What is it like to be immobile for long durations? To mechanically repeat physical activities? In such ways, artists as disparate as Nauman, Gilbert and George, Robert Morris, and Lynda Benglis can be bracketed, if only momentarily.

Moreover, Nauman regarded his body as a medium—trying to find in his body the very vehicle of his art—in the way that earlier artists had discovered the media of their art in watercolor, gouache, oil paint, etc. This may relate to Johns' connection between seeing and orality in many forms—speaking, masticating, ingesting.

This enlarging episode in recent art tied Postminimalism into a loss of distinct species-types—painting and sculpture became "pictorial sculpture." Postminimalism is marked by a loss of typology—the rejection of stretcher supports, framing edge in painting, of base in sculpture, the loss of facture, and the loss of site. Until Postminimalism, "Art" was indoors and "Nature" outdoors. In this connection Robert Smithson's Nonsites, Carl Andre's floor pieces and Richard Long's walking tours cannot be overestimated. Postminimalist elasticity meant that work could theoretically be placed anywhere.

With the loss of time-honored conventions of this kind—once art became part of an infinite continuum ranging from interior to exterior and species to species— painting and sculpture could quite naturally evolve toward and encompass theatricality. Nonetheless, the enactment, for example, of mechanical and repetitive actions and gestures still points to a formal continuity from Minimalism, despite the theatrical nature of such activity. To the painter or sculptor theatricality offered itself as an alternative to the loss of belief in facture, in species-type, in retinality, and in site that had taken place.

Certainly, the *sine qua non* of art—traces of sensitively stroked surface executed with a paint-loaded brush—has been fundamentally undermined, perhaps irrevocably. While such activity is, can, and does remain art for many, other artists feel impelled to investigate looser modes and media, such as laser beam photography, video and film, behavioral phenomenology, the dance, story writing and telling. The latter are all being explored as viable in their own right as alternatives to sensibility drawing and sensibility painting, and even as an alternative to the structures of thought of the pure Conceptualists.

In part this is why there has been such a resurgence of dance. Not necessarily dance practiced as a classically defined discipline, but rather as an art of rudimentary movement: walking as dance, amateur as dancer, another way of painting and sculpting—an alternative. Painting without painting, sculpture without sculpture. This may be a polemical generalization. That today we happen to see many dancers performing in ways suggestive of modes of painting and sculpture does not necessarily mean that the dancer is a painter or sculptor. When dance—and music too, for that matter—engages a wide reach in relation to painting and sculpture, it is tacitly assumed that this kind of dance or music is in some sense an expression *formed* by painting and sculpture rather than one that is *formative* of painting and sculpture. This is by no means a clear question today.

Robert Rauschenberg's connection as a dancer and stage designer to the Merce Cunningham Company is well known. Much of Robert Morris's early career was spent as a dancer working with Yvonne Rainer. Certainly, the prestige of Yvonne Rainer among Postminimalists is high, both as dancer and filmmaker. Similarly, Trisha Brown's "Accumulations" dance of simple abstract movements is suggestive of many of the visual properties of our art. Yet despite such superficial bracketings and circumstantial inferences, the real question remains unanswered: Does recent dance come out of painting and sculpture or does sculpture and painting come out of dance?

In a parallel vein, about which I feel more equipped to speak, I question whether the emergence of "story art" evolves from the Happening, as a surrogate expression of the conceptual performance, or is informed by the abstract qualities of visual art. John Baldessari presents bitter parables, the morals of which ironically underscore the hollowness of art. Lawrence Wiener, like Kienholz before him, presents statements which are themselves projects and works. Vito Acconci and Dennis Oppenheim, among many, present strong performances in the contexts of behavioral phenomenology. Bill Beckley tells shaggy dog stories, while William Wegman opts for a clear, ironical humor. It is possible to see "story art" as a post-conceptual theater.

However, the methods of "story art" use modes still related to abstract form—halting speech, as if something solid and blocky were being formed in the mouth—terse, iconic words, stubby and solid; non sequiturs abound, breaking down the idea of story as narrative; memorization is used as a means of inducing a sense of rotelike immutability; repetition is used to establish a format of constant structure. These are some of the methods by which "story art" announces its connection to an abstract pictorial and sculptural mainstream, rather than to literature.

What of the artists who had typified the pure Conceptualists, the epistemological mainstream? Oddly enough one is witnessing a growing tendency toward more traditional conceptions of art typology. Even those artists who in the past exemplified research into the quantifying elements of art, who questioned the actual physical species of art through borrowed structural systems of knowledge—such artists now appear to be opting for an art of more familiar typologies. Ratification which once came from systems of mathematics or philosophy, is now deriving from nonverbal theories of structure, in which credibility becomes an act of faith in taste and sensibility rather than in cerebral verification systems.

The reintroduction of material processes in the work of Bochner and Rockburne, for example, may indicate a return, but to what? To the conception that art is not necessarily made with notions, but with materials—a position that parallels Richard Serra's notion of sculpture as a distinct species type. This has always been true, but the shift is one of emphasis and context. It may be that such a return to the investigation of material may have been spurred by the open-endedness of theatricality itself, thus ratifying the cerebral radicality of this position.

Most important, this change or alteration may mean that the most forward and intellectually grounded choice in art may now opt for "granted," tangible aspects of painting and sculpture, choices made within typologically defined species. This, in turn, surely indicates that Postminimalism as a movement has come full cycle— from species, to loss of species, to species regained—and in so doing, that a certain period notion style in American art may have ended.

Notes

1. In Germany, Nauman found two red wedges and inscribed the English word "like" on them. Our word for "like" has the same number of letters and incorporates the same letters but in different sequence as the German word for wedge, *Keil*. On the basis of this "likeness" Nauman formulated the palindromic relationship between the words and shapes of the wedges.

    This material was presented in my "Bruce Nauman: Another Kind of Reasoning." In a recent essay on the artist, this interpretation was rejected. Jane Livingston protested that at the time of the *Wedge Piece*, Nauman had never heard of Duchamp (Jane Livingston and Marcia Tucker, *Bruce Nauman: Work from 1965 to 1972*). Even were this assertion remotely possible, it is unacceptable because no serious art student glancing at the illustrations or reading the commentaries on Duchamp's work—rife in both specialized and popular magazines—could remain unaffected by Duchamp. In addition, Nauman worked in an atmosphere in which a multitude of Duchamp-inspired variations and dilutants were to be encountered in studio conversation, gallery cant, and media dispersal. An artist does not have to "know Duchamp" to know Duchamp's ideas. How many persons familiar in a general way with the notions of Freud or Marx have ever read Freud or Marx?

2. The recognition, therefore, of "public psyche" does not take place as a mystical necessity—the overtones of Jungian archetypes—but as a conclusion drawn from a liberal education. Were this not so, then I would be sponsoring an art of mysticism and intuition, qualities, if they exist, that are the paths of madness.

Michael Hurson:
A Fabric of Affinities

Scarcely older than my students, I met my first class in the Ryerson auditorium of the Art Institute of Chicago. It was the fall of 1961. The memory is still fresh—an academic rite of passage. In that survey of 19th-century art were several young artists who would continue the history of The Chicago School, and through this local attachment, widen the issues of contemporary American art. The most singular, perhaps, was a quiet plain boy, Michael Hurson. As I watched him grow, he reshaped this shyness into an ironic ambiguity, into art that now seems a real alternative to the prevailing formalist hegemony or, at very least, to promote access to unexpected critical issues.

There was some priming. While a graduate student at the University of Chicago, I boarded with Thomas Lyman, the medieval art historian, and Mollie Michala, the painter—"Mr. and Mrs. Young Chicago" with at length six kids (they now live in Atlanta). They were enthusiastic about Hurson, whom they had met shortly before at the Oxbow Art School in Saugatuck, Michigan, and who, by his funny manner, had become a friend of Burr Tillstrom (the originator of Kukla, Fran and Ollie), then also summering at Oxbow. This connection would have considerable effect within Hurson's work, since for several years he earned his way assisting Tillstrom in the peregrinations of the Kuklapolitans. Much of the jokey private imagery which once seemed so peculiar in Hurson's work (when meaured against Jansenist formalism) can be traced to this source—for example, the suite of blocky furniture, a take-off on the ranch style house in which he then lived, in the *Ballet of the Left-Handed Piano.*

Stories abounded, earning Hurson a grudged local celebrity. He had already appeared in the 1961 Annual. Through this exhibition, the artist met Henry Geldzahler, then a lion of Pop, recently appointed to the staff of the Metroplitan Museum of Art, and on tour looking at art across the country. Struck by Hurson's 1961 painting, he contacted the artist, then a sophomore at the School of the Art Institute of Chicago, and purchased a drawing from his sketch book. Hurson was just a kid

This article originally appeared in *Arts Magazine*, June 1976.

without standing in the rigid hierarchy of the Chicago scene. Geldzahler's modest purchase added notoriety to the growing awareness—at least in art school—of Hurson's off-the-wall sensibility.

In my own way, I was also seen as an outsider, having come to the University of Chicago from New York City, interfacing my studies in the heartland with annual fellowships that took me to Paris, and, for a while, art dealing as Iris Clert's American assistant (Yves Klein, Takis, Tinguely, etc.) to flesh out the meager international fellowships. In the meanwhile, the School of the Art Institute had set up a new program: the advanced students' final year of painting or sculpture could be spent working alone with a single instructor. It was assumed that a painter would choose to work with a painter, a sculptor with a sculptor. Hurson asked to work with me, the *ausländer* art historian, a choice that rankled in a faculty that on the one hand stressed a retrograde Abstract Expressionism—Tenth Street on Michigan Avenue—and on the other, the ethical pretentions of Bauhaus refugees come to Chicago to begin again in the shadow of big Bauhaus names—Mies van der Rohe, Laszlo Moholy-Nagy, and the like. Both these factions, it went without saying, were distressed by one another; the Bauhaus group—headed by Paul Wieghardt, a respectable painter—feeling their ethos violated by the academized Abstract Expressionists—led by Charles Steegman, "Visiting Instructor" that year—and vice versa. Both were appalled—and thus momentarily united—by the ironies of the nascent Pop movement whose values were then being absorbed by a new generation of art school students.

What did Hurson do that senior year? His major effort was a suite of Barcelona chairs made out of schlock chicken wire and papier-mâché, somewhat akin to the early work of Claes Oldenburg. Since I was "just an art historian" and green, I was not asked to sit on Hurson's "Graduate Critique Committee" even though I was his "advisor." The popular imagery of furniture was anathema to the aniconic pretensions of the die-hard expressionists, and worse—that the exquisite chair of 1929, epitomizing so many of the ambitions of the Bauhaus enterprises, should have been guyed (or so it was thought) in the work of this suburban boy was felt to be an affront to lives shattered by the advent of Naziism. Of course that now lost work was none of these things. Hurson simply loved the Barcelona chair—it and other chromium designs have long functioned as preferred imagery for him—although he is not insensitive to the fact that the Mies look (consecrated by the Museum of Modern Art and Knoll International) was to emerge in the burgeoning steel and glass of the 1950s and '60s as the essential style of corporate identity.

Among my papers I find a carbon of an angry letter to the committee that had diverted attention from Hurson's work to the broader and ambiguous problem of what was then being called "New Realism": "should the Critique Committee force Michael Hurson into more conventional and pedantic channels they would not only be harmful to [Hurson's] artistic development, they would also reflect badly on the School of the Art Institute of Chicago, an institution traditionally above petty insularity." What fawning cant. It wasn't. They weren't. Hurson was put on probation, but with the possibility of an eleventh-hour reprieve: a new group of senior projects were to be made based on works in the collection of the Art Institute. I remember when Hurson showed me a dumbly beautiful self-portrait based on the Fantin-Latour portrait of Manet. He would be redeemed. He had painted himself, replacing Manet's natty and glistening top hat with a folded paper hat, a child's party memory—a fool's cap—that since then still looms large in his iconography. Its connection to the costumes of Picasso's *Saltimbanques* is here maintained, and across these acrobats back through Daumier's theatre scenes of the *commedia dell'arte* to Watteau's portrait of *Gilles.*

Last year, after a stint in the army, working as a draftsman in Maryland and Thailand, and a checkered sequence of addresses—New York, a return to Chicago—Hurson once more took up quarters in New York, a tiny, sky-lit studio space in a brownstone on East 10th Street—the type of building, classic to New York life, beloved of Henry James. Here was Michael again, a bit more scruffy and bunny-like, whose work continued to elaborate the complex imagery of fundamental social exchanges in generalizing, nonillustrative ways. In this theme, Hurson's work seems to key into facets of the broad range of meta-sociologies differently inflected in such work as Scott Burton's behavioral tableaux or Joel Shapiro's monumental dollhouse furniture. Hurson's work, however, is not party to the crypto-mannerist and archly intellectual rejections of High Abstraction through conceptual theatrical exercises such as one finds in, say, Lynda Benglis or Robert Morris. It is also free of these accentuations as they inform many of the more photographic and conceptual manifestations rooted in the abstract principles of the later 1960s, although he is among the first to have used photography in just this way—for example, the eight-part paper hat photographs dating to 1962. In short, Hurson's work is not critical stimulus/response art; rather it deals with a constant imagery that at its core is curiously uninflected and behaviorally neutral, white-bread—WASP, spearmint, if you see what I mean—New Yorkers would think of it as Midwestern, down home. For the first time, Hurson's work which hitherto seemed will-o'-the-wisp and arbitrary, is keying into modernist history; that's when the art may become important because it can be accounted for critically. Of course, such changes are in me; my stress on theory can now gather in an oeuvre which has always been organically whole, in touch with itself, and well able to survive according to its own light, with or without any critical prejudices.

What is equally clear is that the intentionist argument (art as a suite of conscious critical strategies) is not really opposed to sensibility art (at least not in the way it had been in the 1960s through the early '70s). Indeed, neither manifestation is possible unless it grows from an organic center. In the end intentionist art becomes sensibility art—and is subsumed into the succession of historical styles—to which new intentions are attributed anyway as the work recedes further and further back from the present. Ironically, the real task of art history is to reconstruct the lost sense of intention pertinent to any given work.

Hurson was completing the last of his scrupulously made boxes, curious anonymous rooms made of balsa wood, this one based on the skylight structure of the very studio in which he lived. "Did you notice that the skylight shape is something like a paper hat?" This was the most recent of the rooms in a succession of constructions first shown at the Museum of Contemporary Art in Chicago (1973), and subsequently as one of the Projects series at The Museum of Modern Art (1975).

The Projects show further revealed the cryptic and biographical interlace of Hurson's work, culminating in his most elaborate and thwarting box, *Thurman Buzzard's Apartment* (fig. 56). I reviewed these constructions, trying to introduce the spectator to some of Hurson's elaborate built-in references. To pick up on the references in no way "explains" their fascination or effectiveness, just as knowing who Marie Taglioni was does not "explain" in any great degree the Joseph Cornell box in which references to the celebrated dancer are made. This kind of information is fascinating because it is embodied in art and suggests a direction for appreciating it; but it doesn't explain the art:

> The current works are miniatrue crafted sections of rooms, walls, window frames, and stairwells, although I still regard Hurson as a painter and a draftsman. Some balsa rooms are devoid of passing incident, while others are replete with bicycles, television sets, sofas, and evocative trappings. The most ambitious place, *Thurman Buzzard's Apartment,* addresses the psychic and physical space of an imaginary personage, an avatar of the artist, part fantasy, cryptogram and free association. Loosely speaking, Hurson equals Thurman and Buzzard equals Burr Tillstrom, a reference to Hurson's professional association with the celebrated puppeteer; the two r's in Burr equal the two z's in Buzzard, and so on.
>
> Implicit to the problem of miniaturization and the psychic paths that led Hurson to it, is a mindset derived from Marcel Duchamp. Remember that Duchamp made a tiny replica of his *Nude Descending a Staircase* in 1918 for Carrie Stettheimer's dollhouse. And surely the Thorne Miniature Rooms at the Art Institute of Chicago provide an unexpected regional model for Hurson's constructions.
>
> What intrigues me in Hurson's constructions and his paintings is the interplay between an overt ordinariness of imagery and a covert system of logic. One without the other is merely neutral; together in Hurson's work, these impulses produce among the most intriguing art I know being done today—even more striking for being couched in such plain terms. (*Artforum*, December 1974, p. 78.)

The review brings to mind that Hurson is, above all else, a painter, and like so much painting today his is realized in activities still assimilable to sculpture, or photography, or theatre, or even commercial art. In the early 1960s, Hurson's paintings were marked by an expressionist purposefulness linked to sensibility, translations of the midwestern landscape—oil painting muddied by charcoal drawing, typical, say of the Oxbow work. Still, certain personae began to appear at this time, anonymous figures, chunky furniture, or more autobiographically, the artist revealed as a paper hat or a polka dot tie. I appear as a mortar board—regional and attenuated versions of Duchamp's *Cemetery of Liveries and Uniforms* (1915), still sensible in a sociological identification through sartorial accoutrement.

This student period was followed by his military service, travels in Europe after his discharge, and still later, his first long sojourn in New York. This period (ca. 1964–66) is marked by little actual productivity, a certain dysfunction, a sense of dislocation, and the death of his father, "the person I most wanted to prove myself to." By 1967, a body of painting based on television imagery and associations emerges. Hurson had already been assisting Tillstrom, touring throughout the country—the Hollywood Palace, the Johnny Carson Show, then originating in New York. Hurson's preferred format became a long horizontal frieze, interspersed with benign Joes stretched out watching the tube. "I couldn't understand the notion of good composition. I had to figure out a way to make compositions that I could change easily so that I could correct them easily and figure out good compositions that way; so I shellacked the canvas. Working on it in charcoal I can easily correct them like a blackboard."

The desire to shortcut and circumvent standardized notions of good composition led Hurson to make silkscreens of new images so that he could quickly squeegee them onto the canvas. "The subjects never changed; the composition did." Surely Warhol's and Rauschenberg's expressionist use of the silkscreen as a constant imagistic device is paralleled by this procedure in Hurson. Between 1969 and 1971, Dancing Eyeglasses and Pencils appear. The Pencil is the director marking locations where the actor should stand on narrow platforms; the Eyeglasses are the performers. Between 1971 and '72 the Palm Springs Swimming Pool emerges—four large panels depicting the image in twelve variations. The figure lying by the pool is Burr Tillstrom. Still executed through screens, these works invent visual parallel effects—locatable to television lininess—not dissimilar to certain hatchings seen in more recent painting by Johns.

Hurson's paintings to this time locate figures in physical settings that literally are the canvas grounds. By contrast, the balsa rooms emerging in 1972 are free of personages although, as we have seen, they are conceived of as places in which avatars and personae live. These psychological surrogates such as the 1974 *Portrait of Edward and Otto Pfaff* (fig. 57). These portraits, like the other work squeegeed through screens, are a depersonalization—neither expressive nor illusionistic.

In the Pfaff portrait, "closest to Burr's ideas," two puppet-like characters, Otto and Edward, are distracted by some event. The full sequence leading to this momentary lapse of attention is absent. Only two frames are depicted—chosen from an elaborate now-abandoned jokebook-cum-storyboard (a TV and movie method) that dates from Hurson's student days. Edward is probably Edward Albee, whose early plays established short, prototypic expositions of social exchange. Otto, by simple letter substitutions, is the puppet Ollie, although physically he favors Kukla. Pfaff, the perfect name—those double l's and f's recalling Duchamp's attraction to the double r for his alter-ego Rrose Sélavy, because of his delight with the double l's in Harold Llyod's name—appeared on a sewing machine company's sign directly across the river from one of Hurson's Chicago studios.

The theme of absent personae continues from the Pfaff portrait to *Thurman Buzzard's Apartment,* and informs a set of portraits currently being executed of the artist's friends as anonymous puppet-like figures. Hurson's system of reference, while it explains nothing of the art, still indicates much of a method through indirection that parallels through thought an expressionist system of mark, alteration, correction, and remarking. Hurson works out of this painterly methodology, throwing into its mechanism these memories and associations much as he might toss in a little more paint, a little more charcoal. In this sense, Hurson's fabric of affinities functions as one more tone, one more color on the painter's palette.

Figure 56. Michael Hurson, Installation View, 1974
On right, *Thurman Buzzards's Apartment*, 1973–74.
Balsa wood, 8-5/8″ × 69-1/2″ × 25-3/4″.
(Photo courtesy Paula Cooper Gallery)

Figure 57. Michael Hurson, *Edward and Otto Pfaff*, 1974–75.
Oil and silk screen on canvas, 36" ×96".
(Photo courtesy Paula Cooper Gallery)

Maximalism

Introduction to Maximalism

The criticism said to matter in our time skims style from theory, skin from bones. The model, no matter how often denied, is Clement Greenberg. It was he who first promoted a set of conditions for painting or sculpture predicated on values exclusive to painting and sculpture. He saw that one defined the other as separate but equal entities. What painting was, sculpture was not; what sculpture was, painting was not; and taken together, all that painting and sculpture were, was not anything else—neither literature, nor politics, nor psychology; nor did they play themselves out in time.

The honing of these perceptions—those interminable discussions about planarity, frontality, edge tension, and on and on—came to be what we call Greenberg's "modernism," a machinery, at length, ratified by a selective reading of the history of European and American art from Manet on. But Greenberg himself was indifferent to certain conventional methods of art history, especially that area of speculation connected to the non-formal meaning of images, iconography.

While, for sure, perplexing contradictions remain—as when, say, sculpture aspires to a pictorial condition (the work of David Smith) or when he talks about "quality" (a kind of inescapable result when all components are in proper mix)—still, Greenberg's great achievement was not the designation of a diagnostic profile of modernist desirables, but in his having pointed to the artists who really mattered to his generation. His methodology conferred on his perceptions an acute percipience. Though he would not say it this way, Greenberg, the formalist, really mattered because he pointed to shifts in style and these recognitions had the effect of even further intensifying such dislocations.

By the late 1970s, it was thought that the time for the application of Greenberg's methodology had passed, that successive waves of second and third generation formalist art simply failed to obtain, failed to be interesting. But it was the painting and sculpture themselves that were uninteresting, not the critical theory which believably corresponded to the values of the first generation. When latter day formalist art was finally seen to be the academic thing that it was, we were at a moment when all the other stuff being made at that time came to be interesting, if only through negative definition. Whatever it was, and it was many things, at least it was said not to be formalist art. But that it is the Pluralism it is said to be is also in doubt. Still, what this art (whatever it is) lacks is the critical muscle tone that Greenberg's formalist theories gave to the first generation.

There is a ten year interregnum, 1966–76, between the disintegration of a formalist art and the art of our own moment. I tried to account for this episode in *Postminimalism*. Here is postulated the possibility of an osmotic interface between a collapsed form of painting and sculpture deemed "pictorial/sculptural"; the emergence of an abstract, information-based epistemology; its ontological counterpoises, body art and the conceptual theater. That these three modes roughly emerged in so chronological a sequence is seriously doubtful. Though of one thing we can be sure: when one wants to find something, when one knows what one is looking for, for sure one will find it.

It would be nice were one able to postulate such a gremlin-free mechanism at work in the years from the middle of the 1970s to the present moment. Yet one sees that this is hardly the case. Among the reasons militating against so positivist, un-nuanced a reading is that the ingathering, embracing character of Postminimalism led to an even more open vanguardism—so much so as, in the end, to defy categorization.

In the absence, then, of a credible theoretical correlative to the art following the mid-seventies, an art shruggingly identified as pluralistic, baffled criticism fell back upon the very methods which Greenberg proscribed and circumvented—especially iconographic analysis, though Wöfflin-derived formalist analysis had never really been dislodged as a component of the task.

With Pluralism then, if it is Pluralism, many novel features emerged: a refreshed emphasis of Wöfflin; a stress on iconography; the emergence of a neo-formalism based on structuralism and linguistic master-texts; and finally, the chronicle (to which I attribute, at this moment, a value quite beyond the reaches of quotidian journalism). That the chronicle will maintain a heightened value beyond this moment is doubtful—something in our culture today has sent a certain weight to a journalistic exercise.

It is not that I am out of sympathy with the desire to formulate a linguistic theory of contemporary art. The bankruptcy of a specious and sentimental romance of art and its concomitant maintenance of the sanctimonious status of artists, as if they, unlike anyone else, are above discussion, is a salutary demythification. That these desentimentalizations are desirable is unquestioned; to assert that they would occur anyway as a function of an inescapable force of history—some kind of manifest destiny against which free will is powerless—strikes me as specious, and in the end arbitrarily determined.

Also, there is my distaste for the formalist pose itself that makes it seem as if there is a specific content to art, a final and absolutely correct reading. I do not see how this can be since, after all, we are dealing with the imperfect world of experience as well as with the fact that we really do not know what art is; and, in the absence of such knowledge, how can we ever speak of a proper reading for it?

Last, all this is undermined by a simple pragmatic fact—critics are not as good as their methods, no matter how refined these methods are. Their worth, instead, is measured by the art they choose to defend, and whether that defense is made early enough. Greenberg's gift did not consist of the invention of a yeasty set of modernist desirables—nor was it a function of simply writing well. Greenberg's achievement resided squarely in the fact that while thinking well and writing well, he was pointing to the significant artists. And if you don't do the last thing best, the first two just don't matter.

I see the critical task as being essentially that of pointing to the new, and if these gesticulations thrust me into the position of having to call upon dubious art historical methodologies, well then so be it. I prefer to call up those time-honored modes aligned with the freshness of chronicled experience. The real issue at hand is not new modes of criticism, but what happened to painting and sculpture during the last few years. Sculpture had the edge on painting in the late '60s owing to David Smith's early use of a pictorial vehicle of sculptural expression. By the end of the '60s, pure painting was hobbled by its bondage to formalist values insofar as it irresiliently carried the values of first generation Abstract Expressionist painting through a second and third phase. As this shrivelling occurred, so did sculpture flourish. Concurrently, all the unsatisfied need to experiment was cut away from the easel enterprise and was manifested as some kind of sculptural polymorph.

Although less liable of conventionalization, the appeal of a pictorialized sculpture began to fail of late, and sculptors sought a more intense sculpture by reverting to the latency of Constructivism, Constructionism. An unapologetic construction of rigorously architectural character received particular emphasis through the end of the '70s. The Constructionists—Hall, Aycock, Ferrara, Acconci, Oppenheim, Armajani, et al.—did much to preserve the syntax of Minimalism. Apart from the feeling for the elemental character of the substances they used (which would relate them to figure like Serra and Andre), their work also went far to foster a taste for architecture-as-art.

This largely happened for two reasons: the blueprints or working diagrams for Constructionist sculpture demonstrated a high degree of preexecutive awareness and, as such, sought the diagram, the hand-drawn blueprint, as a central expression of the style. This condition is also true of Minimalist arts generally, with the following warning: the Minimalist blueprint is essentially scaleless and placeless—it is a purely refrigerated abstraction ratified in the mind as a Platonic ideal. By contrast, the Constructionist diagram or blueprint is specific as to scale, specific as to site, and generally invokes an impure pictorial metaphor rather than the pure geometry of Minimalism. The aberrant element in all of his is the metaphorical mutant, since what it does is to value those literary and psychological qualities presumably expunged from Formalism. Thus, the metaphor of the Constructionists allowed for a revived interest in architectural drawing at the turn of the decade, and architects-as-artists benefited from this skewing of esteem (from sculpture to their work), provoking an essentially architectural polemic focused on what has come to be called Postmodernism.

All this, and more, is confounded with several colliding streams that originated in quite different spheres of activity. Where Constructionism comes from is easily grasped; architectural style less so. Simply, the latter is reacting to the rejection of applied ornament to architectural problems germane to the International Style Between the Two Wars. Instead of viewing ornament and applied design as taboo, recent architects began to see ornament as a manneristic means of generating forms that answered functional requirements. Thus began a celebratory and eclectic pillage of the history of art for design-cum-functional motifs by a group of architects reacting against the crisp and clean machine forms of a precisionist International Style, a style loosely referred to as "modern"; hence these architects were called "post-modern."

Their eclecticism, on one hand, coincided with the personalistic metaphor of the Constructionist sculptors, fusing these two strands. On the other hand, these snowballing options all feed (as they are being fed) the neo-Primitivistic Expressionist positions in painting which contemporaneously emerged at the turn of the decade, deeply stirred by recent developments in German and Italian painting.

A rough outline of art that emerged between the American Bicentennial and the turn of the decade continues forward from the three elements of Postminimalism, to the advent of Constructionism, Architecture-as-Art, and finally, neo-Primitivism and Expressionism. All this latterly development I am calling Maximalism. With these developments, the reign of sculpture, dominant in the 1960s and '70s, appears now to have been superceded by the successful reemergence of a new Primitivistic painting as the fundamental vehicle of expression of the present, with all that that signifies as regards the appurtenances of painting such as the value of facture, the return to allegory, etc.

The democratic vision of contemporary history, still colored by the ideals of John Dewey, has made a case for egalitarian Pluralism out of all of this. Such a view seems ill-advised since the character of all of these recent modes is an intense awareness of the history of modern art. The essential premise of Pluralism is the separateness of the art experience from the desire to make art imbued with a sense of historical continuity. But, in the absence of an art made in a state of historical awareness, the art experience is no more than mere neurological stimulation. Indeed, Dewey's term "art experience" is a contradiction since "art" implies historical awareness—hence criticism and history—whereas experience may exist free of such attachment.

For the Pluralist, the essential antagonist is nature; for the contemporary artist, the essential antagonist and malleable form of art is the very awareness of art history itself, an awareness most often encountered as an irony.

One of the things that goes unnoticed in the so-called Pluralist position of the present day is just how much of it is merely a Philistine backlash against Postminimalism. In terms of many painters, though not all, this has sanctioned an academic figure painting with a concomitant reliance on the illusionism derived from the Renaissance and the Baroque—the space box of the one, the chiaroscuro and tactile appeals of the other, and the emphasis on figure composition of both. Alone, these issues remain moot; but allied to an ironic awareness of the history of contemporary art, ignition occurs.

Not that all contemporary figure painting is bad; indeed several of its most positive properties have contributed tellingly to the current mood. Figure painting of interest today has stressed the private talisman, a sign of an intensely peculiar personal episode. Perhaps the success of feminist art occasioned this. In so doing, the stress on the private talisman has been allied to the revived Abstract Expressionism focus traceable to the sculptural/pictorial collapse typical of early Postminimalism. Thus, the pictorial properties of Abstract Expressionism—space defined through the gestural allover or blurred optical fields—assert themselves over the academically derived illusionism of Renaissance and Baroque art. Still, the sources for this possibility synthesize private impulse and psychology with such formal properties, resulting in a neo-Primitivism, a new Expressionism which is an ironic commentary on the history of art, though nonetheless masterful for all that.

A paradox: The confines of Maximalism are smaller and tighter than those of Postminimalism. Under the latter's sway, a loss of species occurred—no more painting defined conventionally, no more sculpture defined conventionally. Instead, a broad spectrum of open type was invented in these species—earthwork, say, as sculpture; arithmetic and grammar substituted for painting; performance or story art for either—a vast berth the understructure of which was set in language.

But now, with all that past and under a Maximalist banner, we find that painting and sculpture, for all that seems gratuitous and thrown-in with the kitchen sink, is once more a closed species returned home to normal typology. Thus, Maximalism, despite its brave name, is perhaps a more conservative artistic consciousness—let's say it, style—than its predecessor.

Style, for me, is the ultimate residue of art; it is the intellectual construct, the fiction, that allows for, accounts for, infra- and international transposability. All this points to the fact, however shocking it is to read, that what one ultimately seeks is "signatures"—talisman/objects of the art-experience. But discussion of the experience details self-important lists of enthusiastic response or argues for a transcendental defene of art, that is, "art-as-religion," something one either believes or does not. It is a matter of faith. I do not say I lack this faith. I only say it is futile to pretend that articles of faith can rationally be discussed in other than an historical way, as a branch of the history of religion. All transcendental defense, like religion, ends up with the belligerent "my book is better than your book."

I am aware of the rationalized character of this outline. Its real justification is far more skeptical and fatalistic than those indicated in a specious mechanic of stylistic evolution. Ultimately, we can never know what one ever says about art is true. So, if sheerly factual writing is doubtful from the outset, then for sure speculative histories are even more suspect. My skepticism, then, must reject the formulation of a closed theory of history, including my own.

With this in view, it is gratuitous to broadcast a new "ism" of the kind found in Postminimalism, Post-Modernism, Pluralism, or even Maximalism. If a so-called archaeology of contemporary art, the excavation of straight fact, is not apt to be true, then how much more false would a theoretical mechanism be?

But one mode of discourse in the arts is least liable of untruth—the chronicle. In it, one is really recording what one is thinking or feeling, though the facts may be wrong and the feelings unwarranted. To say all this, to note that they may possibly be wrong is no demonstration that they are wrong—nor, for that matter, right. Statements of right or wrong function outside both the history of art and criticism. Morally, they appertain to law; as abstraction they are a function of logic.

Thus, I view the chronicle—the record least liable of incorrectness set into a cultural matrix of absolute ambiguity—as a literary effort convergent to the art-work of the turn of the decade. In *Postminimalism*, the reprinting of essays sought to capture the discourse of the artists in question; the republication of essays that form *Maximalism* is spurred by the parallel status of these chronicles to the art which provoked them. While not being art, they are perhaps not artless.

New York City
Summer 1983

Entries: Palimpsest and Pentimenti

7 February 1980

Let me try to be more precise as to what I mean by style. Style represents a moment of freeze and shrinkage, an instant when artistic intuitions are perceived as possessing a consistent diagnostic profile. Indeed, it is the overlapping, repetitious character of such diagnostic elements that makes it seem that there is, after all, such a thing as style in the first place. To be interested in this notion of style as generalized phenomenon in no way precludes my greater interest in "pre-style," that is, those moments and expressions of artistic intuition risked even prior to shrinkage and freeze.

23 March 1980

A certain kind of problem continues to nag at what we tend to consider by now a provincial preoccupation—the problem of "quality," in the straight Greenberg use of the word. Astonishing as it may be, many people still haven't gotten around to admitting that "quality" most often means the attribution of a specious transcendency to work that merely corresponds to an *a priori* set of features concerned wholly with formal components. More, such attributions are probably no more than a nostalgic sentimentality inescapable to dying bourgeois aestheticism.

The beginning of the eighties is marked by a rejection of the open modes that had been sponsored and favored throughout the seventies. As always, when this occurs, smug status-quoers (who never flirted with, let alone abandoned, unstable modes) act either as if they had been right all along not to have done so; or, even more gratingly, as if the open modes just never happened in the first place.

The smug entrenched formalist ethos of our Eastern seaboard is a function of the history of more than two and a half centuries of painting here. Thus, Smibert and Blackburn and Copley form a root layer of loam nourishing formalist prejudices favoring painting as a stable and closed species. The historical couche of the West

---

This article originally appeared in *Arts Magazine*, June 1980.

Coast, behavioral and performance oriented, is scarcely twenty years old. That means the local formalist bias is rooted far less securely. But where will it lead? Even on the Western shore today, a fatigue with performance and open modes is sensed.

6 April 1980

A reception to mark the opening of a group show of "Boonies"—Ross Bleckner, Julian Schnabel, and David Salle. The latter's work somewhat resembles that of Eric Fischl (fig. 58)—they were former California schoolmates—whose show opened that day across West Broadway at Thorp's gallery. One could easily add to this list the name of Gary Bower, now with Max Protetch (indeed, Max is showing the important trends: in sculpture, the architectural constructionists; in painting, the contradictory evidence of the figurative disjunctionists). Schnabel is perhaps the strongest painter of the new stylistic coalition and he tells me about his imagistic snatchings—spolia, as it were—from the films of Jean Vigo—Atalante, Zéro de Conduite. Fragments of images from these films supply Schnabel with subject matter.

The key to the work of the "Boonies" is something that escaped my notice recently. And that is the problem (indeed, for them all) of the overlap, the superimposition, the palimpsest (fig. 59). These transparencies and superimpositions allow for a figurative painting denying narrative all the while. In this way, the essential weakness of representational painting is eluded, namely its inescapably illustrative properties. As always, when one thinks about it, models suggest themselves—among them the expressive "Transparencies" of Picabia painted after 1926 (fig. 60) and, more magically, the pile-up of image on image found in cave painting.

I am hounded by a concern that notions of quality in art are merely nostalgic and sentimental hangovers—a kind of grief—associated with a perhaps moribund, certainly threatened bourgeois culture. I worry about the mesh of culture in the art of the eighties, that sieving warp and woof. Can it be that all the "Boonie" painting, all that palimpsest and pentimenti, New Figurative expressionism still represents only the drag of old ideals (which in part it surely does)?

But perhaps rising in this couche is a sprinkling of young artists who do point the way. They most likely deal with photography or photographic notions in their work though they are not necessarily photographers. I suspect that in some way they are photographic collagists though the collaging may occur in an environmental way. Their work derives meaning from the fine-grinding Marxist machinery of Walter Benjamin's The Work of Art in the Age of Mechanical Reproduction, intuitions, it would seem, refurbished in the phenomenology of Adorno and the Frankfurt School and in French Structuralism, especially Foucault.

Of course, what I am alluding to is, yet again, a rigid theory of pure Formalist inevitability. Still, whether one likes it or not (and I hate it), there is the fascination of such a possibility, though one balks at all the tailoring and pruning necessary to demonstrate the validity of such a principle. But this idea does render impertinent many simple, received ideas about style, sentiment, personalistic iconography, the capitalist myth of a great hero, the morphological-similarity of Wöfflin as demonstrating content-similarity, iconography as a literary discipline, etc. The notion that we are just flotsam and jetsam of larger controlling forces of destiny like the one I drew renders all the above and more just so much sentimental rubbish, to be finally relegated to the dust-bin of history.

On one hand, all this then might be viewed as an updated Greenberg-like formalism. On the other hand, such an idea supplants morphology and iconography as the conventional methods of stylistic and/or art-historical method. What I'm talking about then may be a post-Marxist, post-phenomenological, in short, post-Structuralist methodology—as others claim it is—just out there in the world whether one likes it or not, supplanting willy-nilly through its sheer essential force these earlier attitudes and methods.

I would like to be able to believe the above easily, but can't. Mostly I've just recast the general drift of the arguments put forth by the critical "heavies" today. What they won't see (won't let themselves see) is that ideas are as subject to style as forms are. So all this post-modernist inevitability is as locked into bourgeois history as anything else—despite the delicious self-delusion that post-modernism eludes bourgeois history.

24 April 1980

Early modernism is an argument essentially conducted between representationalism and abstraction. Indeed, early modernism is itself the exact embodiment of this discourse with, ultimately, the gaining of the upper hand by an abstraction that had placed representationalism *en jeu* in the first place. What is most rarely noted in this idea of early modern is that, in answering the conditions imposed through the inevitable application of abstraction upon representationalism, form destroys itself, self-destructs. Take a simple example—Analytical Cubism. As a style it is defined, at least partly, as a geometrical analysis of natural form. Fernande's forehead then may be rendered (as indeed Picasso rendered it in 1909) as four rectangular planes. Yet in honoring the principle of analysis in Analytical Cubism, these planes might further fracture into eight facets and these, in turn into sixteen and so on, so that in the end these fractures and facets—if honored as structural principle alone and then carried to a logical conclusion—would ultimately destroy an essential term of the argument, namely its representational quotient. Hence early modernist discourse was made only through partial discussion, through reticences and hesitations that, by and large, maintained the representational term placed *en jeu* by abstraction. With a few exceptions—Malevich, El Lissitzky, Rodchenko, perhaps Mondrian (begrudgingly)—do we find the representational term truly or fully capitulated to the sheer press, to the *force majeure* of abstraction.

Late modernism does not even admit the terms representational versus abstract as being pertinent any longer. They both are indicted terms. Our argument is said to be taking place somewhere else out there. But where? And how?

Modern method is born of a need to reify speculation. Such speculation is reified, is transformed into "real" observation and perception, that is, into "things" liable of discussion. Modern historical method then becomes one in which the following question is posed: What are the models for this *reification*? Hence, modern method—as distinct from those applied to or in the culture of earlier epochs (they were generally formal or iconographic)—is fundamentally linked to criticism, critical observations, and critical speculation.

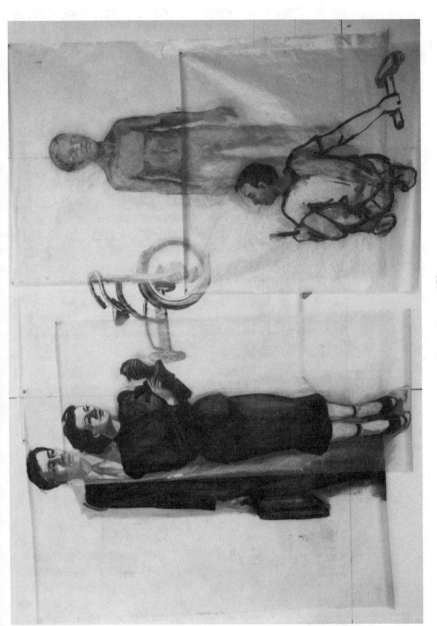

Figure 58.   Eric Fischl, *Critics*, 1979
Oil on glassine, 72" x 121".
(Photo courtesy Mary Boone Gallery)

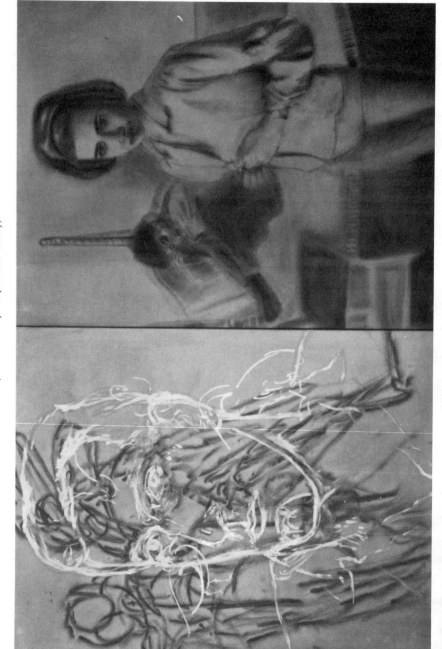

Figure 59. David Salle/Julian Schnabel, *Jump*, 1980
Acrylic on canvas.
(Photo courtesy Mary Boone Gallery)

Figure 60.   Francis Picabia, *Helias,* 1929
Oil on canvas, 32″×28″.
(Photo courtesy Mary Boone Gallery)

Entries: Maximalism

Paris–New York: the failures of both cities are so manifest that they appear almost to mirror one another. Paris works insofar as the city is still respected: its public spaces are, to all intents and purposes, little abused while ours are, by contrast, in frightful disarray. We are witness to the destruction of our parks, our public transportation systems, our libraries, our very walls; the air we breathe is polluted by chemical fumes and tapedeck soundspill.

All that is absent, in certain measure, at least, from Paris. But there, there is only a sense of looming hopelessness. To earn one's daily bread, even for the bourgeoisie, simply means to tread water; and to do that is more than even the French have come to expect as *raisonnable.* All around, the city already aged and decayed, ages and decays even more, providing yet a new burden—the baleful weight of its own history and urban mores. By moments, things get patched up, refurbished—changed *quartiers* and the like; but such changes, while they preserve the city a bit longer, also create the new preserves of the rich.

Bohemia positive and productive, creative Bohemia rather than picturesque poverty, that kind of Bohemia has ceased to exist in Paris. Instead, one gets urban Bohemia, a new type where there is only changelessness, no originality, and a marked absence of choice typical of an urban peasantry.

17 October 1980

Ours is so utterly a cinematographic culture that the pleasure afforded by a painting is, at best, that given when it is regarded as a kind of still photograph. Beyond this, this "still" is just another frame in the larger film sequence. Can this intuition connect with the curiously frozen-frame character of much New Wave painting—Robert Longo, say? Ironically, the term "New Wave" has itself an additional cinematographic association insofar as it was first applied not to the contemporary punk style at our

---

This article originally appeared in *Arts Magazine*, February 1981.

turn of the decade but to the young European film-makers of the post-Naturalist moment, Godard especially, in the late 1950s.

12 November 1980

Helen Winer (ex-Artists Space) and Janelle Rearing (ex-Leo Castelli) open Metro Pictures on Mercer just below Houston . . . the space originally an after-hours disco club—very *Saturday Night Fever*—for garage mechanics—so, in a certain way, Metro Pictures is a bar with a gallery for a back room.

The evening essentially a happy but disquieting one: it definitely marks the death of the '60s. Henceforth, we of the '68–72 set, no matter our good will, are of another, older generation. In the juke box light of the dance floor lit from below I could feel my laughing crow's feet deepen into wrinkles. This is no *plus ça change* moment but a different era, even if it's little history compared to big history. As 1922–25 was to 1912–14, so are the '80s when compared to '68–72. But how can one say this without appearing condescending?

I'm repeatedly being fingered to pull together an exhibition of all the truly innovative artists, including the young Italians, from all the stables. If I do it, I'll call it Maximalism to make as strong a differentiation from the indurated and academized sensibility Minimalism of the '70s as possible.

27 November 1980

Anina Nosei, Helene Winer, Janelle Rearing, Mary Boone, Robert Miller, Angela Westwater, Max Protetch, Holly Solomon, Miani Johnson, Edward Thorp, Hal Bromm—the young dealers sometimes seem so much more interesting that the art they sell. The present scene is much changed, yet fully crystallized. The Italians quite different from the Americans—the former with their intense and acute sense of modern art history; the latter largely indifferent of this history but not necessarily ignorant of it. Rather, the Americans connect to the all-star mentors of a preceding generation. The young New Yorkers defiantly continue to admire Oldenburg and Warhol; the young Californians William Wegman, though he is scarcely older than they; and for them, too, Warhol still casts a long shadow.

The current American mode "hypostatizes," "icon-icizes," "freezes" fleeting memory images of real people in real actions in real settings; in short, much of the American mode derives from the traditions of performance art, that is, the eccentric marginal art of the 1970s—a decade preeminently Sensibility Minimalist in flavor.

The New Wave Americans utterly reject the quietistic monasticism of Minimalist Sensibility painting (though they are, for all that, painters) and link up their work with transient glimpses of artists caught in performance activity during the '70s. But we are in the '80s, after all, and the '80s will be the decade of New Figuration, certainly the first few years of the decade and that's what counts. As the late '60s define early '70s, so do the late '70s determine the early '80s.

Entries: Two Voices

There is a primordial content, a basic content to brute matter, to raw substance. But to say what this content "is" —other than itself—is impossible. More, that this "brute content" denotes an "art content" is disputable even when embodied in objects or things called art. The denomination "art," the very cognomen, is a source of its content—not its brute molecular existence.

Art content is not embodied in the object—at least in any way that can be elucidated—but in its having been assigned to a category. The designation imbues matter with certain value: but nothing can be said about "brute content" except perhaps to name it—if the name is known—and beyond that, perhaps to note that one may experience "brute content" in some way, as weight, say, or mass or color—experience it at some purely retinal or tactile level, as a function of our sheer neurological circuitry. But this is true of all matter whether or not it is said to be art. Thus, the "brute content" argument of a Rembrandt is exactly the same as the one for a Duchamp, or a shoe, for all that. The art is not in the object except through its assignment to a category—and the ultimate source of such assignments and designations still remains unclear although they are made an infinite number of times daily (and it would seem correctly, for to repeatedly assign things to incorrect categories is another way of describing the condition of insanity). It goes without saying that emotional response is a function of the experience of "brute content" of matter.

All other arguments, the myriad arguments (except that of "brute-content") that surround the art object are the art-content—the content of art is all of the arguments surrounding the sheer experience of brute matter. But sheer experience is itself not an argument; it is the bedrock. Art-content arguments are historically embedded functions of prevailing social values, the *Zeitgeist,* they are *dans l'air.* The attribution of argument, that is the making up of the content of art, is historically linked and sets up a chain reaction of seemingly unbearable equations (for the artist,

---

This article originally appeared in *Arts Magazine*, April 1979.

at least): the content of art = the argument surrounding the brute matter of art = an historically embedded content = style, since style = the number of arguments imaginable at any given moment. And style, like water, like any natural resource or organic thing, gets used up.

Style gets used up. The artists who persist in "using up" a certain style are sanctioned in this exhaustion only by the fact that they were the ones who more or less synthesized the style in the first place. All latecomers or diluters are not sanctioned in this waste. (Caveat: this is only an argument. Criticism functions in the realm of the general. Art—well, painting and sculpture—functions in the realm of the specific. Art = practice; criticism = theory.)

Is this why abstract artists of epistemic persuasion are angry with me (for the moment?)—because I hinted that their style was used up. Small matter—the inceptors of the style always will be seen as major figures. Their followers, modifiers of the style—if all that their synthesis amounts to is just another modification of someone else's given—will be viewed as little or lesser figures. Greatness, that heavy word, is only accorded to artists who create a new style—an achievement probably effected in concert with a still larger group of other, like-minded figures.

9 March 1979

No amount of argument can every *fully* explain anything, be it a person or a work of art. The only argument that can fully explain anything is the object itself—*das Ding an sich.* Yet, since period determines argument, there are only so many *salient* arguments that one can append convincingly to works of art at any given moment—though how many one cannot say.

6 April 1978

Being in touch with a stylistic *dernier cri,* with the last word in style, is no guarantor of art (though it shows at least a sense of historical awareness and a certain gift for rapid cultural assimilation). Similarly, a dedicated commitment to earlier stylistic premises—essentially those of Renaissance space and Baroque tactile illusionism—is no guarantor either. Paradoxically, such intense revivals may be viewed, in their way, as ruses and political acts within the contemporary art world. The dedication to an earlier style—even an earlier "abstract style"—does reveal that there are broad reaches of artists who feel alienated from, cannot believe in, the art arguments of their own times. And in their alienation from such arguments they are motivated by them through what might be termed negative definition.

When artists revive earlier principles of style they show that there is something in the art of their own time in which they cannot believe. Such argument is, for all its backward-looking, a contemporary argument and possesses its own contemporary art-content—despite all the negative terms of reference. Among the things revivalists say (that is, through their art) is that they cannot believe in an art-content which they haven't invented (or so they imagine). This need to invent style forces a recapitulation of the history of art. They are saying that if one has not invented "it," one cannot believe in "it." And the revivalists possess no belief-system for ratifying the arguments of contemporary art-content. Mostly, this belief-system is a function of a close knowledge of the history of modern art. And for all their protestations, I find that so-called modern artists are often woefully lacking in a sure-footedness of the history of modern art. So, I suppose, they didn't need to know it after all.

11 December 1977

There is a powerful connection between sculpture being the leading art of the sixties and photography that of the seventies: they both address the empirical fact. Sculpture is real, tangibly real; photography records, peels the skin off the real, steals its outermost membrane—the film of the real. Obviously they both trade in the literal effect of light upon object, of things illuminated or in darkness. One proceeds from the other and painting—that orphan of abstraction—is left out in the cold.

In our arts the avant-garde quotient is always a function of, indeed is measured by, the familiar, the known. Presumably, the audience for avant-garde painting and sculpture is acquainted with the conventions of representational art. Likewise, we assume that the audience of vanguard theater—the Dadaist or Futurist theaters, say, or the Pop Happening—is aware of the conventions and traditions accruing to a naturalist proscenium-arch theater.

1 January 1978

Realist art (and literature, too, for that matter) is marked by a sequence of highly specific detail, believable empirical detail, real data—yet each of the details of realist art must engage the spectator's belief in its ability to function on a symbolic level, each real element must suggest or infer the possibility of symbolic function, even if this is not the expressed intention of realist art. If the details of realist art are unable to invoke symbolic value, then they are no more than lists of things—sequences of mere literal happenstance, statistics into which one is hard pressed to project one's interest. It is the unspoken, frequently unwanted, muddying symbolic function of realist detail that transforms realism into art. This transformation can only occur as the result of an act of faith, primed by acculturation. It cannot happen unless the belief is there that it may happen. Hence, all "symbolisms" are mystical at core, impervious of analysis, functions of attributed content. This does not mean that the artist should strive for a symbolist look—nothing kills or cheapens realist work faster than an obvious striving for the symbolist aura.

16 April 1977

Mistrust my own polemic against representationalism: if one can build with the theoretical template of epistemology, then one ought to be able to build with an actual model in nature. What I suppose I object to, then, is the ignorance of representational artists who work with nature because they know so little of the history of modernism, at least that part of it which could have provided them with the sense of an alternative ratification to nature. Representationalists behave as if there were no available ratification system to deal with the advent and development of the conceptual movement. Thus touch-based painting and sculpture is always there to function as the cultural bedrock. And because it always *is* there, it eventually comes to seem as if it were the only thing that ever *was* there.

20 January 1979

Crafts ratify the culture, are continuous with it. Art, by contrast, is incompatible with, disruptive of, the culture. Art is capable of moving the culture toward new paths. When (and if) this rerouting succeeds, then art begins to ratify the culture and in so doing becomes as crafts are, becomes crafts. The major artist is a demolitions expert always functioning beyond the culture's capacity to absorb and to tame, to "co-opt" (as we used to say), to transform arts into crafts—crafts are socialized arts.

26 January 1979

A peculiar problem: the conceptual artist is in a bind on completing a body of work—since the subject of such an artist is inorganic to the hand (though it may be organic to thought and thinking), what to do next becomes the problem. With conceptually-based arts there cannot be the clear evolution built into hand-based, touch-based, touch-sensitive arts. With these, the evolution of style is built, as it were, into the very muscle fiber of the artist. But what of the conceptual artist? Here there is no "next work," no "next step" built into the hands' development. Rather, the conceptual artist faces the search for a proper subject on completion of work rather than the mere maintenance of a certain range of muscular impulse and consequent retinal stimuli.

The effects of this dilemma have been enormous in the history of conceptual art. "Proper subject" or "good subject," as a photographer might say, accounts for much of the setback the conceptual movement has incurred recently. In periods of "conceptual retrenchment," touch-based arts look for all the world like the "winners," as if they had been there all along. And for a simple reason: touch-based arts never came to grips with the dilemma of the subject, always refused to deal with the advent and development of the conceptual movement. Thus touch-based arts are always there, a cultural bedrock. And because it is always there, it eventually comes to seem as if it were the only thing that ever was there. All this is bound up in, and inextricable from, the problem of representationalism. It too seems so solid, the most granitic stratum on which we build our culture—for better or worse.

1 February 1979

Either/or: what is clear now is that my development as a critic in moving from a formalist premise to a diarist bias allowed me the luxury of possessing two voices. One is the echoing, mimicked voice of the artist whereby the critic soothes and ratifies—the critic as advocate. The other is the voice of the critic-as-adversary. In my writing there are now two voices present—the artist's and the critic's. In earlier formalist writing there was only one voice—one person, really—the artist, though to say this of course invites the very natural protests of artists. They would surely say that the formalist voice was not their voice—but insofar as the formalist voice rejected privileged biographical detail and exacted the suppression of the critical personality, it was indeed the artist's voice, his surrogate.

Entries: Sheer Grunge

5 April 1981

SoHo in a state quite as if tom-toms were beating, the tattoo intensifying as one approached 420 West Broadway for the Julian Schnabel show installed jointly at Mary Boone and Leo Castelli. In the latter gallery, *The Exile* (fig. 61), a gold-ground antler-painting with the quotation of Caravaggio's *Boy with Basket of Flowers,* seems the most brilliant piece—despite a derivation from Rauschenberg's combine-paintings tantamount to homage. In Schnabel's work, the antlers seems as much the symbols of male genitals as do the stuffed birds of Rauschenberg's *Odalisk* or *Canyon* (fig. 62), not to mention the long-haired ram of *Monogram*—one is tempted to say "Monog*Ram.*" Then, too, there is the boy-love Ganymede subtext present in *Canyon* (the black eagle of Jupiter carrying off Ganymede) reiterated as the homoerotic paean of the Caravaggio still life—*basket* of flowers, get it? For me, *The Exile* is perhaps Schnabel's single finest work, though the public, I hear, clamors for more "plate paintings," as that body of his painted assemblages is coming to be called.

The chief work at Mary Boone's gallery was *Painting without Mercy* (fig. 63), a huge Crucifixion-like "plate painting" à la Beckmann that interpolates quasi-Grünewald School gallows (crucifixes) with portraiture—William Burroughs among the notables—the whole thing very turgid and overburdened with the iconographic *horror vacui* typical of Schnabel at his most Burroughsish *Naked Lunch* aleatory. The label for the work crowed a bit, perhaps forgivably: "Collection Peter Ludwig." The "Ludwig Crucifixion" transformed Boone's small space into a chapel-like arena—Think Deep Thoughts—the sacred effect modified by the two large drawings hanging to the left of the huge altar-piece-like work.

As good as Schnabel's show was in itself, as well as for the artist, so too was it good for David Salle, whose works had been shown in Boone's space just prior to Schnabel's. By now the conventional classic/romantic duality (emblematic for us in the work of Johns/Rauschenberg) characterizes the Salle/Schnabel exchange. Salle,

---

This article originally appeared in *Arts Magazine,* May 1981.

it is clear, is now becoming a deft painter whose progress points up incipient refinements and elegant turns of phrase, seen often enough in the ribbonish lines of the overdrawing, not to mention in sprayed soft-edge imagery and yielding fields of stomped figuration. The whole machinery moves ceremoniously, decorously, each element in place, no matter how complex the disguise sought. Salle now approaches the stately and the seamless, without disruption or disjunction.

Schnabel, by vivid contrast, is all gamble and impetuosity—rejecting at considerable risk all notions of accessibility—flinging shrapnel about in his guerilla-warfare *cum* painting. All this "bad taste" suggests a career of giant unevenness—to moments when his pictures will work in the undisciplined way they do now, and to a time when they will fail on precisely these same grounds.

If nothing else, both artists are obsessed with style, past style, modernist style, no matter. One could almost say that a heightened consciousness of style is the raw material out of which they build their work. Only, to say such a thing suggests the ironic Pop tradition of art about art—and neither artist is especially ironic—though, if one were to point to irony, it is present far more pointedly in Salle. Well, at least skepticism is. Schnabel, by contrast, is all about an unquestioned, regressive love affair with art.

What I like most about Schnabel's work is not the work so much but his sheer o'er-arching, knock-your-eyes-out folly. Would that this statement spoke only to the artist's sense of exaggerated defiance rather than to art, or style, or career. Even Schnabel, I suspect, must find his megalo-romantic theatricalized *kunstwollen* a trifle ridiculous.

But if he doesn't, no matter. Each new work of Schnabel's must be a trifle more "ugly" than that last—"ugliness" as sheer will power—"ugliness," being for us, the surest way to avoid petty mannerism and *belle peinture*—that is, until we grasp anew that "ugliness" is (or can be) its own form of mannerism and *belle peinture*.

I recognize to what degree I personalize when I note my belief that all the detritus in Schnabel's work, all that broken crockery, thrown-out light sconces—all that raw materiel—are indices of rejected lower-middle-class life, its sheer grunge, as it gets lived out in vast stretches of Brooklyn, Queens, the U.S.A. really. Then, too, all the smashed crockery is a scaled-up unifying field that the Cubists invoked when they pasted down newsprint—the cracked saucer in Schnabel's case prefigured in the cropped headlines and graphic subtexts of the Cubist collage.

The bridge, then, between Schnabel's china and Picasso's *journaux* is perhaps not only Rauschenberg's combine-paintings, but the disguised newsprint submerged in the waxen fields of Johns' encaustic paintings of the mid-1950s.

But we have forgotten how theatrical Picasso's choice or Johns' choice once seemed—so classical have these oeuvres become for us. By contrast, Schnabel's protracted-adolescent self-dramatization seems vivifying, "wow," risk-filled in a way that allows for a shared exuberance we are perhaps only too happy to lend ourselves to, a certain-self-deluding collusive participation.

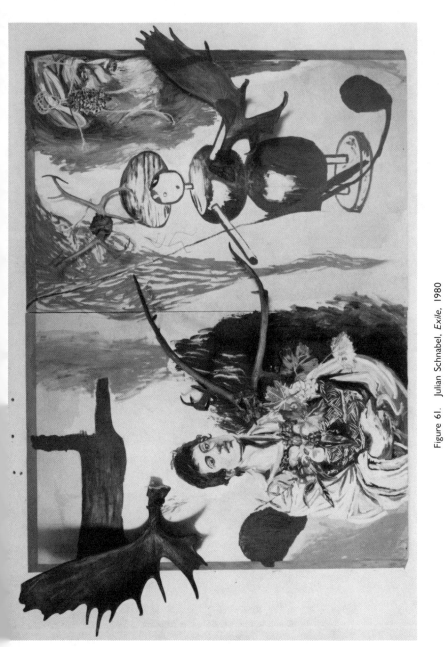

Figure 61. Julian Schnabel, *Exile*, 1980
Oil, antlers, gold leaf on wood, 90" × 120".
(Photo courtesy the artist)

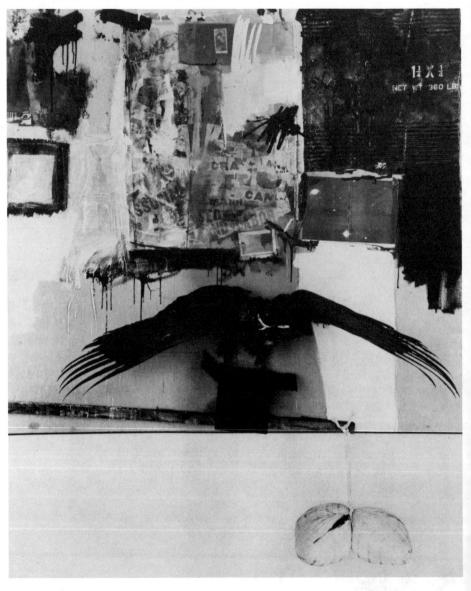

Figure 62.   Robert Rauschenberg, *Canyon*, 1959
Combine painting, 86-1/2″×70″×23″.
(Photo courtesy Sonnabend Gallery)

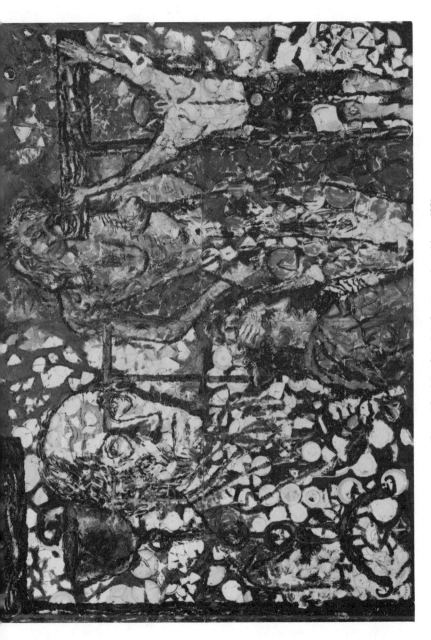

Figure 63. Julian Schnabel, *Painting without Mercy*, 1981
Plates, oil, bondo on wood, 9′×13′.
(Photo courtesy the artist)

Julian Schnabel: Blind Faith

I. The Studio

I September 1981

Talking to Julian Schnabel is a bit like playing snooker: the cue ball scatters the others—some line up sensibly, the rest just go any which way. Schnabel's new life isn't quite so agreeable though it sure sounds it. Reckless comparisons multiply—to Pollock, Rauschenberg, Beckmann, Picabia, whomever, that sort of thing. The snowballing has been hectic, as every reader of art magazines knows.

A few months ago, Schnabel moved into a more or less finished working space—sliding panels, bright responsible young assistants, phones ringing, stacks of carpentered stretcher supports, piles of Le Franc oil paint in pound tubes—an incredible dream of luxury, a monument to painterly orality; in brief, the extravagant appurtenances of overwhelming success. Despite the frenzy, there remains the reticence of an artist who wants to be taken seriously even in the face of a worldly success and reception that is frightfully off-putting, even for him.

It is easy to suppose that Schnabel's art resides in the associative eccentricity of the substances chosen; for sure, there is that. Earlier, one thought that Schnabel's way was just a function of an elaborate personalistic iconography; for sure, there is still much of that. Earlier, one "justified" Schnabel's pictures in terms of a formal continuum with the Combine Paintings of Rauschenberg—appealing to a legitimization afforded by the history of collage and assemblage. Then, too, the "transparencies" of Picabia (from the 1920s) as well as Picabia's "vulgar" calendar art images of the 1940s also provided models (figs. 60, 64). True, there are all of these resurgent iconographic parameters, but now it seems that Schnabel's major impulses are being realized through sheerly assertive surfaces, surfaces that either invoke ironic signifiers of low-class values (the velvet ground as a reminder of "genuine hand-painted velvet ties"), or specific cultural invocations of powerful ethnic identities even if, albeit, "colonized" ones.

This article originally appeared in *Arts Magazine*, February 1982.

Huge rolls of outdated kitchen linoleum—signifying marginal apartment life, say—await their transformation into supports for paint. New pictures are painted on grounds of broken Mexican ollas and clayware or short-order souvlaki amphorae, desert buffalo horns and leather, and the like. Still, with regard to these new works, by no stretch of the imagination can Schnabel be taken as a Mexican or Greek or laboring-class apologist. Indeed, the aggressive presence of these cultural artifacts, if they can be said to "function" at all, do so from a position of ironic indifference—Degas and the laundresses—subject matter viewed *de haut en bas*. Schnabel is hardly a popular propagandist, though acutely he has no aversion to his work being perceived along these lines. And in the end he cannot control this anyway. Anything ever said or written about art is its content—though maybe not its "art-content."

So, do not be misled when Schnabel says that "art is not painted for an informed public." He certainly does not mean by this the popular ethnic illusionism of the *sans-culottes*. His corollary quite properly continues that "art is received by an informed public." Schnabel's primary formal concerns address the question of how to apply paint to disruptive and "sociographic" surface—art for art's sake. All of his "iconography" or "iconology" is pretextual. Nor is this necessarily a failing. Such matters are purely neutral.

Take, for example, those clay elements dispersed in plaster. Schnabel paints for all the world as if there were no disruption at all, as if the support were smooth. The brush turns only when it bumps into some large blockage so that it can no longer assert its original directional impulse. There are constant dual, even triple, readings: a pretended uniformity of surface countered by the ructions occasioned by the relief elements. There is the difficulty and disagreeableness of illegibility of image, the disjunctive and near-haphazard character of the work; then again, there is the conjunctive character of a visual intelligence which is capable of mixing—as an act of will—two layers of visuality. The "support" may more properly be seen as a kind of "depth of field." And painting becomes not an action on a surface, but actions perpetrated within an arbitrary relief-like corridor of space.

Though the fields of broken crockery are in some measure composed during their initial placement in plaster, the final compositions do not necessarily derive from these placements. Often, the painted parts of the compositions run counter to the natural placements of the relief elements, indeed violate them.

On occasion, an exchange takes place between Schnabel's observation of an ornamental motif (found ready-made, pre-existing upon some straight element). He then might visually isolate it and stress the subsequent rendition as a prominent pictorial element of the newly painted composition. This expanded, blown-up decorative motif, image derived from isolated pattern, is particularly characteristic of the new "Mexican" works, *The End of the Alphabet, The Beginning of Infinity* (fig. 65), say.

This attitude of extreme disjunction—big to small—is a working method also seen earlier. In the "drop cloth paintings," enormous painters' drop cloths—what else?—were placed on the ground. Upon these large surfaces very small images—

say, the famous self-portrait of Antonin Artaud, one of Schnabel's heroes (reproduced from a photo in the *Paris/Paris* catalogue)—were scaled up by a rendering of minute features with three-foot brushes. Or, "big to small" might be occasioned by Schnabel's examination (while it was held in one hand) of a small primitive or religious carving, a Santos, say; with the other, he rendered this small devotional object with the obdurate and reluctant tool of a three-foot brush. But it was the process that counted, the way of deriving the image, not only the resulting image.

Granting conditions such as these, it would be absurd to anticipate a cohesive, seamless spatial illusion and one doesn't. The space depicted becomes in a manner of speaking—the artist's speaking, at least—"indigenous" to the material (as well as one invested in the image); or "indigenous" at the very least to the wide discrepancies between depiction and that which is depicted. This need not be surprising. Artists' talk has long sanctioned, say, the notion of color as indigenous to shape. Why, then, not see these other "indigenous-es"? Schnabel speaks with remarkable acuteness, though his sentences are so finely honed and deceptive that to miss a word is to often gainsay meaning. Of the processes noted here, he observes that as his work "becomes a painting, it becomes interesting as painting."

II. The Loft

10 October 1981

Schnabel doesn't paint where he lives anymore. The works at home are now the pictures of changing date that may have come back from an exhibition, or may be en route to yet another, or pictures he has decided to keep, or new work that he is just thinking about. Indeed, the work is here mostly to think about—where it came from and what did it point to in terms of the artist's very rapid evolution.

An extravagant spacious disorder about him, a growing collection of unmatched furniture by pioneer designers of the 1920s through the '50s—Breuer, Aalto. A more recent acquisition—Max Beckmann's portrait of Wolfgang Frommel.

On the wall hangs the old picture (well, 1979), *Procession for Jean Vigo* (fig. 66), just back from somewhere. The T-form, that gallows/crucifix shape so often seen in Schnabel's work, derives in this case from a memory frame of Jean Vigo's film *Zero de Conduite;* while the motif resonates with Danube School crucifixion memories (as do very many others), the structure more specifically images Schnabel's memory of marauding school kids/ "gallows for dry fart," that strange frame with lanterns dangling from the crossbar that the school kids erected to torment the sleeping monitor. Of course, its triune associations are inescapable and its Germanic symbolism invokes as much of Schnabel's fascination with primitive crucifix imagery as the antlers used in many of his combine paintings invoke the legend of Saint Eustace in which as apparition of the crucified Christ is borne upon the antlers of a stag. Then, too, the loping interlace, the triple helix, updates Picabia's *LHOOQ,* itself a paraphrase of Duchamp's celebrated altered ready-made.

In the *Procession for Jean Vigo* there are just some holes sprinkled about the picture. "The holes are there to disregard," the way all the relief detritus in the more recent painting is "just there to disregard," as if one could. Then, too, granting that one can't, it orchestrates its own system of cryptic association.

Schnabel speaks of this meandering conflation as the meeting of "different temporalities," a contemporary fascination with "simultaneity." But it is hardly the "fourth dimension" of the Cubo-Futurists, the introduction of a specious sign-system for time, that Schnabel aims at. Instead, he hopes to stimulate a sense, perhaps, of time list, of introspection and meditation.

"Different temporalities," then, may be likened to those simultaneously presented frontal zones one finds, say, on the walls of Italian churches. These fragmented discontinuous layers of image and relief incorporate unexpected juxtapositions and associations: a Baroque memorial tablet fits into fragments of late medieval fresco edged by plaster and exposed brick and upon which may be pinned votive offerings of all kinds; not to mention the vast religious paintings from the Renaissance through the present. This, too, presents a kind of simultaneity rendered reasonable owing to our acute sense of history and connoisseurship and the renewed vigor of our visual appetite.

Schnabel wants to speak so simply and reduce his creative experience to as clear a phrase as possible that often his sentences seem cryptic or evasive; in fact, they are straightforward descriptions of precisely what he is doing.

Remember the holding of the small object in one hand and the recording of its features with "inappropriately" scaled tools on "inappropriately" scaled surfaces or colors? This notion is continued when Schnabel says that "my shapes are found by concentrating on another shape," by a kind of "looking here but painting there. Blind Faith." In this way, "the shapes arrive at themselves." And they do so through a transformation in which individual status may be suppressed; or, as is also the case, rather confusingly imposed. "I like shapes, simple shapes. I like their breaking down and their breaking up. Like torsos. They are like poplars or mummies or trees . . . ." Now Schnabel is free-associating: "They relate to nature, to leaving off a line, to cutting a statue in half, where the veins in the leaf become cracks."

This elaborate synecdoche contrasts not only legitimate parts of the wholes—for example, leaf for tree, tree for nature—but it obtrudes as well onto yet more extensive areas of substitution, the leaf for statue, say.

Still, Schnabel's intention does not favor ambiguity. If anything, Schnabel dislikes ambiguity as being a place "where artists hide out." Instead he seeks clarity and concentration of emotion, despite the immense ambiguity of the image one is given to digest. What the emotion is, of course, is difficult to pinpoint; but for Schnabel it represents a "certain kind of feeling, the feeling of a certain kind of claustrophobia."

I am reluctant to allow Schnabel to fob off what all too easily might pass for a sentimental piety. I press him to be more exact as to what he means by "claustrophobic feelings." Schnabel would have us see the work as more than its inescapable material presence. Despite all the perhaps excessive hyperbole of his work, he would have us "remove the painter from it, remove 'me' from it. All the works are made to be seen without sensing the artist around." Then maybe you can get what he sense as an ambivalent exchange between "intellect versus madness," a flirtation with the acceptance of death."

One sees how easily, from this viewpoint, Antonin Artaud could become the culture hero he has to Schnabel. The artist wants to retrieve for painting "the idea of death, the void, the abyss. We are responsible to these unspeakable things even if we cannot name them." But Schnabel acknowledges fully that "what I say may be very different from what one gets from the painting."

Figure 64. Francis Picabia, *Adam and Eve*, 1941–43
Oil on wood, 41″×29-1/4″.
(Photo courtesy Mary Boone Gallery)

Figure 65. Julian Schnabel, *School for the Deaf* (formerly called *The End of the Alphabet, The Beginning of Infinity*), 1981 Plates, oil paint, Mexican pots on wood. *(Photo courtesy the artist)*

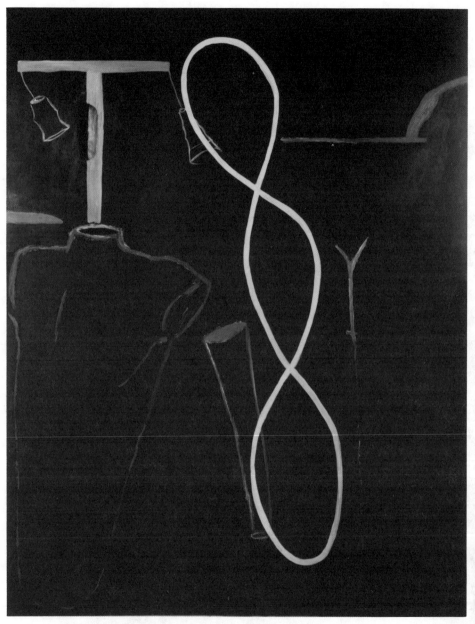

Figure 66. Julian Schnabel, *Procession for Jean Vigo*, 1979
Oil on canvas, 110″×96″.
(Photo courtesy the artist)

David Salle: Holiday Glassware

3 December 1981

Complex David Salle—lean of face, tense, dark hair on a sharp cartilaginous profile—the unflinching gaze of the contact-lensed. A cigar-smoker (by way of affectation?) and a just-audible William Buckley-like speech pattern. Earlier on, I was unduly cautious (as we all were) of what was perceived as Salle's careerism (and Schnabel's too, to be fair—all of "New Wave" careerism, really); while fascinated, I modified support in ways that emphasized Salle's critical/analytical faculties—what he calls, self-deprecatingly, "my criticality, such as it is." Recently, when asked what the "ism" of the '80s would be, I replied "Careerism." While lecturing at the Hartford Art School were Salle once "stinted" as instructor of painting, I spoke to Salle's paramount critical/analytical gifts, scanting in so doing his authentic role—that of a painter born. So in Salle's case, the moral of the tale no longer applies.

The Salle studio is in that row of buildings in which Stanford White—shot by Harry Thaw—died; raking views of the Flat Iron Building, Madison Square Park, and the Metropolitan Insurance Tower. Originally a living loft, the duplex (anomalously redone in the '50s) now serves as painting studio, complete with a *de rigueur* young assistant. A spiral staircase, rooms furnished with examples of '50s furniture once more *en vogue,* a pair of pickled oak fake-Archipenko lampbases, works in progress, finished works being wrapped in plastic sheets about to be sent hither and thither: large rectangles, powerful erotic shots, isolated abstract images, stomped passage-work, cartoon-fragments, scumbled impulsive areas, varied-scaled abutted rectangles, some colored, others not.

First formulations of arguments that trailed away. Salle has extraordinary gifts for cautious postulates so considered in their turning that they are apt to simply fade: "Conceptual art allowed my painting to exist. . . . My work is simultaneously itself, its own representation, and the idea of itself. . . . I am not really interested in the referent, nor to deny the reference—but I am caught up in the way the works

---

This article originally appeared in *Arts Magazine,* April 1982.

are left to stew without being watered down. I am interested in the specificity of their presentation."

Salle's not talking so much, I suppose, about what the image depicts, but somehow of the gravity, the weight accruing to the image, "And I don't see my work as some kind of bridge out of Pattern Painting to Punk, though there may be patterns; I see my painting as emphasizing a dysfunctioniing network of references that establish possibilities outside themselves." Of course, Salle is right. So aware is he of his "critical intelligence," he could allow for the ambition to gratify a functioning system of inferences. After all, "critical intelligence" establishes the logic of references and the perimeter in which these references function.

Still, as it happens, Salle's painting also appears to embody the entire opposite of this ambition. "Sign, symbol, metaphor—all that only matters insofar as one holds it together all at once at the same time. Never losing sight of any of the permutations, the overtones—that is the nature of the experience I want." In short, Salle's imagery is never resolved, only "over" when one turns one's glance away.

Nor is there an aesthetic hierarchy of images; nor one of touch. One gesture serves as well as another; one color as well as another; one impasto frosting as well as another kind of surface; matte or glossy, small or large, sexy or bleak, clichéd or novel; none of this matters except as it functions within a potential for constant conflict. And then, only as it matters in the most conservative way imaginable; that is, only Salle's work can be sexy or bleak in just that way: or granting the chameleon-like myriad options of touch, still only Salle would make the touch that way. So, in the end, despite the myth, the vehicle does remain *faktur,* touch, only his touch, and, in just that way, in just that place.

— "Why are you so combative? Why is your art so contentious? What is being defended?

— "My sensitivity. That is always under threat. More, the specificity of my sensitivity is always in danger."

— "Are we speaking of the defensiveness of the aesthete who, in order to hide, is often a most public chameleon?" It seems the psychological terms of Salle's strategies contrast the chameleon-like aptitude of the aesthete with what passes for the engagé, in present terms, little more than a code word for slob. All that's mental, of course, The outside remains urbane, if a mite dour, a logo on a split-timber fence.

— "What is the counterpoise to the sheer selfishness, the egoism implicit in the aesthete's désengagé position?" I wonder aloud. (Probably exhibitionism and narcissism, the essentially untreatable inversions or denials of the necessary masochism built into the very neutralization of the aesthetic condition.)

Salle comes from an unexpected place—Wichita; Dad from Ohio, Mom from Oklahoma. Salle's escape was through art. That's banal enough. Rescue came in art school: William Dickerson and Karl Nordfeldt, characteristic painters of the broad Art Institute of Chicago manner of the 1920s. His folks wanted to be "modern," did the house up in what '50s suburbia was meant to look like, rented abstract paintings from the local museums. All this and more—the touch, the imagery, the anomaly of the suburban '50s—concerns the "new painting." In Salle's case, its pictorial terms are all rendered perfectly.

Fodder for the New Art—not just Salle's (and to be fair, rather little in his case) but an entire generation's come of age—Suburban Beautification. Looming behind are the turreted Hansel & Gretel castles of Disneyland, Disneyworld—orange & aqua plastic shakes, prefab distress and weathering, the Howard Johnson Shingle Style. Daylong, lifelong exposure to TV cathode rays have burned out the color cones of the eyes; nuanced discretions are in the balance, must go, have gone. Smart conversation as sitcom one-liners, gags or the dutiful, portentous banalities of the soaps, six words strung in a row if even that. Art imitates Life. "Bad" is good, better, best.

3 February 1982

Of course, the Maximalist New Wavers Down at The Clubs are all inventing art out of the conventions of middle-class popular culture. Minimalism (epistemic abstraction and sensibility minimalism included) was perhaps the last cohesive style to emerge from the stimuli of High Art—the art of the text rather than the TV sitcom. And as is always the case with fresh cohesion, symbiosis is in the air. Though, after the fact, one sees that the emergent individuation was present from the beginning, especially in artists as challenged as Salle—or Schnabel.

"We projected different sides of one thing, not that we shared it." "It" remains a vague intangible of concern to the cheez whiz values of the soaps or the more sinister appeals of B-movie stills and the films noir of the 1950s and '60s.

"Julian says to himself, 'I can do anything I want,' an essentially egoistical position. The result is a body of work that is radically uneven." Salle's perception is correct but one that obtains not only in Schnabel's case but in all o'erarching Romantic effort. These always call for heavy pruning, careful editing, to achieve a body of work that appears even-textured, convincingly seamless. The injunction obtains in Salle's case, too.

"For me," Salle goes on, "the meaning of style is *use,* the instrumentalization of style." He differentiates this from "the instrumentalization of the motif," one which leads to "iconography," however neutrally or indifferently employed. Iconography, of course, indicates choice—no matter how unconsciously motivated that choice might be. The appropriation of image, the current despoliation of art and culture, always invokes the specter of specific interpretability. If only one can find the key. Once it was provided by psychoanalysis. Such procedures seem frightfully outmoded today. Marxist dialectics? Frankfort School phenomenology? Poststructuralist semiology? Yawns.

Salle promotes his case as "an instrumentalization of style." This leads to "the meaninglessness of touch," an irrelevance that impinges on "the parameters of painting or something called painting." Salle's distinction between the instrumentalization of style and that of motif is meant to point up the difference between his work and Schnabel's. It all is purely theoretical, as there can be no mistaking the two anyway. But his view of the matter allows him the comforting belief that his work maintains modernism's dialectical shuttling, one that runs counter to a fixed Expressionism that demands no internal dialectic for combustion—Schnabel's art, say.

The whole mechanic seems too pat and programmatic. One has been there before. Substitute terms. Classicism (read ratiocination, dialectic, modernism) versus Romanticism (read revivalism, Expressionism, stuck). Useful, yes, but too wanton and too specially plead. They both are wonderful. They both know it, and none of this says anything about art. Individuation.

17 December 1981

Continue to talk to Salle at the studio and ask, "When do you know the work is finished?"

—"When what I have talked myself into for two weeks falls away." Then, again by way of locating him to his Cal Arts Baldessari-like origins, I questioned him about the role of the conceptual in his painting.

—"You don't have to paint. To paint is a piety I would like to keep alive, though the culture probably won't let me." It has, what with the unquestioned return to painting all about us. The canvases in the studio present startling discontinuous abutments of images spurred by a highly personalistic choice. There is a stomped, Jackie-like head that looks derived from the notorious image of a Vietnam execution—but still Ron Galella for all that. (Actually it is from a French photograph of children bound to a tree.) This image counters a broad, sparkling dark canvas based on Derain (fig. 67). Another canvas takes off on Félicien Rops—the coquettish domino-buttocked woman; a large older photograph of a nude woman with dunce cap on head and two cones extending out form her breasts awaits being incorporated into a still larger composition (fig. 68).

We are sitting in front of a large still life still in progress, based on the slick, sparkling newspaper illustrations published by Lord & Taylor in the *Times*.

—"I was drawn by the malevolence of cut glass. This panel is painted on photosensitized canvas. You may make a mark on it, but you can't make a recognizable image because of the photo-sensitivity. And if you make too many marks on it, it all goes black. Then, I started to paint the look that rhymed with the newspaper illustration—Holiday Glassware" (fig. 69).

—"To be honest, David, I don't really think you successfully caught the slick skills of the department store illustrator; so as a diversionary tactic, you added the little green figure, a pentimento, a throw-away, as a kind of deceit in the margin. Of course, it doesn't really matter that you are not a skilled newspaper illustrator, since, after all, it all ends up as 'just painting' anyway."

—"You know, I have this revulsion of saying things over, and I act out my dissatisfactions with the picture as I paint it."

—"I admit that the failings of the passage are obviated in the very act of describing the scenario of the painting."

—"But," Salle interjects, "my painting is not about Abstract Expressionism's 'natural error.' There are fundamental distinctions between verbal and pictorial recognition. Because I got to it emotionally while talking to you about it doesn't mean I knew it visually when I painted it. Everything that is felt or perceived can be verbalized, though," and here we both agree, "the verbal only may be—probably only is—a descriptive catalogue without affect."

Figure 67. David Salle, *The Old, the New and the Different*, 1981
Acrylic on canvas, 96" × 150".
(Photo courtesy Mary Boone Gallery)

Figure 68.   David Salle, *Autopsy*, 1981
Oil, acrylic on canvas, 48″×112″.
(Photo courtesy Mary Boone Gallery)

Figure 69.   David Salle, *Holiday Glassware*, 1981
Acrylic on photosensitized linen, 91″×91″.
(Photo courtesy Mary Boone Gallery)

Entries:
I-Know-That-You-Know-That-I-Know

16 October 1983

I was describing an artist's new paintings to a friend—how, for him, they represented an authentic vision of transcendent beauty, one I could even share; but how, at the same time, you could sense his unease about them, perhaps a certain shame. The sheepish greeting, deferential body talk, the flaring defensiveness, rapid conversational shifts to a common experience, and cynical-sounding art banter—all spoke to a feeling of raw exposure, anxiety, bad faith, at least with someone who knew something about painting. The shuttling awareness is very painful—for artist and viewer both.

My friend immediately thought of other new work she had seen and her companion added still another example. He spoke to honest effort spurred by an appreciation of Giotto; but, so far as he is concerned, the one real lesson to be derived from the Arena Chapel is to not make art based on the model it provides, but to experience pleasure solely in the Giotto itself. These are but transient examples of an infinite list. How he underestimates the artist's compulsive need "to be creative," no matter the debris thrown up, despite whatever better judgment they are able to make, ought to make, but simply cannot bring themselves to make.

This double-mindedness is marked in older artists, perhaps is only open to them, rendering the pain of indecision and/or failure even more acute. The "I-know-that-you-know-that-I-know" aspect of it all demands some experience of the world. Hence, young artists are singularly free of the malaise and explains why, apart from their age, they seem young in the first place: their narcissism, their state of "being creative" is so naked, so unrepentant, so free of shame.

27 August 1983

Examined the transparencies taken of Julian Schnabel's new work, the relief paintings that I saw quite by accident affixed to a link fence surrounding a private tennis

---

This article originally appeared in *Arts Magazine*, February 1984.

court in Bridgehampton this past summer. Unbeknownst to me, Schnabel happened to be renting the house. I was walking the adjacent land, caught sight of the paintings, and trespassed. Since my examination of this work was rapid and scanty I first misjudged them, at a distance, to be by a follower, not the master. "How amazing," I thought, "Schnabel already has sanctioned a generation of ambitious imitators." Surely he has, but on close viewing I saw that this was his work, not that of some art-school follower.

The new pieces continue to project a crackpot ardor that makes the work seem difficult to take seriously, work made, that is, as if by an enthusiast. Still, they insist upon being taken seriously partly because of the enormous machinery of esteem already set in motion on his behalf, more so because of his rather special crude and cranky intensity. One takes him seriously for two reasons: because of what his work looks like and because he is already in the history books, despite his relatively recent emergence. A good deal of the unpalatability of Schnabel's new painting stems from his reliance on stain method. Vague, curdled puddles often pool on antipathetic plastic surfaces. Express intention to the contrary, this work will be seen as ugly (that is, if one accepts the premise that somehow curdlings are in and of themselves ugly; that the oozings somehow are ineptly congealed; that the plastic surface is ignoble in and of itself; granting all this, then, perhaps one has leave to refer to this work as ugly).

Surely, one values Schnabel's work within a mechanism of season-to-season stylistic or reflexive critical strategies. Such a formalist mode of appreciation plays in Schnabel's favor (as it favors any artist whose career is, in some sense, public: we have to know where he's been to know where he is). Still, it seems that the new work is "ugly" and, having said this, is credited with a great deal, the continuing gift for affront. It takes a lot to be ugly. I'm not talking about some piddling momentary blow to middle-class taste, like graffiti art, say. I'm talking ugly, like Pollock.

Schnabel's new work also possesses all the ungainly power of innocent art, the effort of a naif autodidact, like that put forth, say, by Simon Rodia, whose Watts Towers, with their encrustations of ceramic fragments, have already been drawn into the discussion of Schnabel's sources.

All that granted—if it is—Schnabel still wants to be seen as painter in the high European sense, as *un maître*, not just as a painter in some broad application of the term. In particular, he would like to be seen in terms of the esteem that has accrued to German painters today, to Kiefer, to Baselitz, even to Lüpertz. In some strange way, Schnabel has been done in by them, by Kiefer, perhaps by Baselitz; or, if not done in, then, at least one must, to be fair, acknowledge a sense of competition, as revealed even by the very ambitious scale of Schnabel's paintings.

These big paintings are also marked by a kind of surrealist inkblot discovery of Oriental cast—a semi-sumi wash-like figuration, the touch of which is execrable (a judgment permitted because one so easily perceives the model behind the effect). It is the model that establishes the value system for judging the picture (even

as his assimilation establishes a new value paradigm), not Schnabel's acute appropriation of image and brushstroke. Among the more portentous appropriations are the
references to Victor Hugo as a draftsman—the kind of amoebic Rorschach fantasy
that earlier French poet-draftsmen, from Baudelaire to Redon, adopted as well.

The worst aspect of Schnabel's new work is his ponderous rendering, specially
antipathetic when he sets out for straight transcription—when he is painting directly
before a sitter or more likely from a photograph of the sitter, in his portraits, say,
of Mary Boone and Andy Warhol (the first I saw in transparency, then hanging chez
Boone; the second was in the Klaus Kertess realism show at the Parrish Museum
this summer). Another would be the striving *Ithaca*, a double portrait of the painter's
mother and father, also shown recently in the Boone back room (fig. 70). These
abominable pictures will be salvaged for sure by their historical sequence within his
oeuvre, by the interlocking teeth of the wheels of his evolution, and not least of
all, because of the celebrity of the sitter. The Warhol portrait recalls the notorious
Richard Avedon photograph of the artist, President Johnson-like, showing his scars
(fig. 71).

All this is of scant import if Schnabel's case is one of "genius," as genius lies
beyond the reach of fatuous carping. Schnabel's work from 1979 to 1983 already
has legitimately gained ascendance in the textbooks—at least, by my account. And
to be great one needs to be great only once—and that Schnabel has been, as he
may continue to be. Let grandeur, as a phrase, osmose into genius. We no longer
bother about the membrane, much. All this shows once again that, in art, rank is
partly a function of vaulting ambition and, as long as we accede to a modernist agenda
that demands a sequence of historical styles, even these recent failures of Schnabel
pass muster brilliantly. They are, after all, "failures" of taste and appetite—Pantagruel's
to be exact—not those of petty nerve and niggling ordinance. And beyond this first
moment they too will take their place in the Schnabel canon.

All this is exceeding ruthless for, after all, what should be one's reasonable expectations of a Schnabel? My personalization is only to the point if I can be said
to have a disguised program in my writing, one that (if it is there) may be outlined
as follows: Compelling painting today works within the limits established by Constructivism, however paradoxical. There is an abstraction derived from collage experimentation. This path of originality is already venerable, dating back to Picasso's
achievements of 1912 to 1914. In certain respects, Schnabel may be seen as presenting recent convincing work within this tradition. The problem, despite the plethora
of invention within the mode, is that there is really very little in that vein which
is original, despite the fact that the mode itself flashes the signal reading "original."

By contrast, straight painting, or sculpture for that matter, that chooses to veer
away from being original (that is, from working within the constructivist collage tradition) ends up being either an academic form of abstraction or an academic form
of representation. In short, not particularly interesting. Such aspiration really opts
out of the modernist arena. It doesn't participate, doesn't want to. Often enough,

it doesn't even know that it ought to. The most pathetic condition occurs when it knows that it should but doesn't. After all, "the public really wouldn't understand anyway." So it pitches to consensus. Art that pitches to consensus is crafts, and if it isn't it is probably kitsch. Whatever it is, it is not a sufficient interest to merit the name of art, despite its often very real virtues—refinement of touch, of color, anything.

So, in the end, there is only a choice between the first tradition, Constructivism, a row difficult to hoe; or the second, which amounts really to not participating at all. (There is, I suppose, a third contemporary option, the fashionable Metro-Picture/Real Life syndrome, an art that somehow derives its rhetorical existence from photography or photographic incursion; mind you, to be fashionable is a fundamental *lettre-de-patente* for art—not the whole story—but essential nonetheless.)

Thus, my strong adjuration of Schnabel's new work results not from any pettiness on its part or on his part. It remains ambitious within the sector worth being ambitious in. This moment may represent a respite, *un recul pour mieux sauter,* a moment perhaps when he may be trying to deepen his iconography, say. So, after all, Schnabel has very little choice, for if he wishes to remain an artist of serious concern, to remain important, then I suppose he could not do anything but paint these rude and ugly pictures after all.

11 November 1983

Visiting David Salle in his new studio and living space on White Street, part of a building he shares with Bryan Hunt. (The sculptor has taken the main floor so that access to the loading dock is facilitated, a move necessitated by the difficulty of getting his large works up and down stairs.) Salle's studio directly above Hunt's and his living space, directly above that, are almost finished—having been worked out in collaboration with the taciturn architect Christian Hubert. The living loft is impeccably, unflappably post-modern *qua* style (which is what I thought would happen when all the inflated philosophical claims died down)—a spine of almost Minoan inverted shafts by way of transforming the usual cast-iron column of the loft building divides the space. Even more astonishing is the fifties flagstone terrace that climbs into the wall, incorporating a free-form bench and table—a kind of being outside while sitting inside now loft-dense Tribeca.

As it happens, Salle's new work reveals the rather public impress of an immense referentiality to Jasper Johns. Tentatively taking note of some cheap cutlery hanging from a work in progress, I thought to broach gingerly the meaning that Jasper Johns holds for Salle. My first impulse was intended to be protective of the artist's feelings, reminding Salle that to dangle forks and spoons from a painting would, for the informed viewer, inevitably lead one to postulate an unwarranted affiliation with Johns. Then I looked around the studio again and realized that my caution was quite ill-placed, beside the point, as so much of the new work through indirection or explicitness courageously spoke to the issue of Johns—bearding the lion, but not quite in his den. There are works, for example, incorporating body parts, carved wood elements, hands or ears and such, akin to those that Johns began to include in works even predating the great *Targets with Boxes* (ca. 1955) (fig. 72). Johns is inescapable, too, in a large painting of a nude superscribed with the name Tennyson (fig. 73), alluding to Johns' great gray painting of that name (1958). In short, the Johns connection and citations are hardly inadvertent.

Salle, in response to my cautionary questions, said that he viewed his works as "self-sufficient," as "having transcended the model." He reaffirmed his "primary interest in classical painting," but said that new painting today allowed us to see in a fresh way "the increased specificity of classical painting" and to sense an increased "feeling-tone" before it, noting that Johns' *Tennyson* was already a quarter-century old. "It is as distant from us emotionally and visually as Gericault. Johns' early paintings are as historical as anything in the lexicon."

Of course, Salle is also facing the fact that he views Johns—as does his whole generation—as an emblem, quite in the same way as he (and it) views Rauschenberg. Indeed, Johns and Rauschenberg are now seen to represent an emblematic dichotomy of such big mutually self-defining halves as classical versus romantic, or system versus instinct. Thus, in that sense, Salle's embrace of Johns must be viewed as a conscious "device" (to employ that most Johns-like term) by way of dissociating himself from Schnabel whose work is in many respects understood as a morphological extension of the Rauschenberg combine-paintings.

Naturally, Salle is no "groupie," nor just a painter of no mean gifts, so to point to iconographic connections to Johns may seem to inflate these literary strategies beyond the self-evident splendor of the visuality of his paintings. What Salle would like (as indeed I feel before his work) is that such easy (or attenuated, for that matter) iconographic affiliation to Johns (or any other artist) be experienced as an enhancement of the formal. His paintings, of course, have their own pristine character as painting which, in being perceived, is its most central content just as one recognizes that iconography is employed to play a role as a transformational enhancement of feeling.

Ultimately Salle is wily. He may scatter clues, say those I note in relation to Johns. In his paintings, the clues are not there to shuttle within a logical iconographic continuum—back and forth *ad infinitum* between model and post-model—but to function as his option for multiple and variant brushstroke function. Iconography is essentially neutral for Salle (absolutely not the case for Schnabel). As Salle says, "any move is neutral." Thus, whatever one chooses or opts to image is neutral; and the "categorizing of image" is as radical an activity as the brushstroke employed.

All this is eminently cagey. While it speaks to only an apparent neutrality, as Salle insists it does, any move is neutral (that is, neither right nor wrong), it is only today that someone as keen as Salle may perceive that in neutrality he still risks being right or wrong: "I'm banking on apparent neutrality."

I remind Salle that the notion of neutral category allied to a presumed neutrality of touch derived from mechanical processes (as distinct from Salle's neutrality of touch as derived from a non-hierarchic spectrum of brushstroke) has already found an historical precedent in the work of Warhol. "Ah," Salle counters, "there is a confusion in the public mind that equates neutral with loss of affect." Though attempting to be a neutral painter, so too is Salle attempting to paint pictures that are totally specific as to their emotions. Unfortunately, the convention persists whereby we confuse sincerity with only those aspects of painting that appear expressive. On one hand, Salle is exploding the myth of expressive brushstroke as a vehicle of sincerity, quite as he is expanding for the public eye the range of brushstroke which will inevitably be seen as sincere. While acknowledging Warhol's emblematic role as the neutral artist par excellence—as we both do—it must also be admitted that Warhol is the blank screen upon which is projected an infinity of meanings, even as we recognize that Warhol's recent painting is inefficient, mentally and neurologically. That mutual agreement allowed Salle his greatest artist-flourish of the afternoon: "These are paintings," he said, pointing to the works in progress in the loft, "that will make people stop thinking about Warhol." And I think he is right.

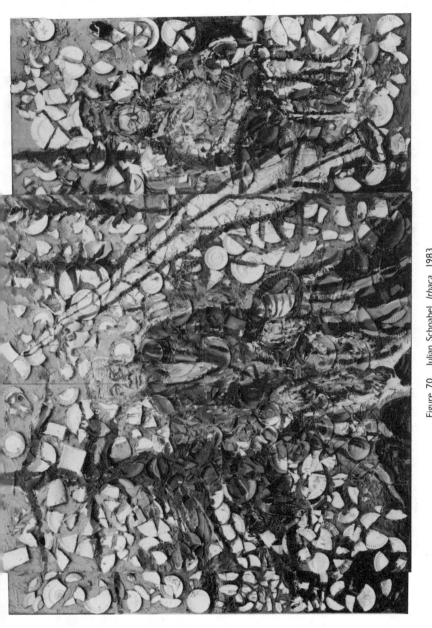

Figure 70. Julian Schnabel, *Ithaca*, 1983
Oil, plates, bondo on wood, 9'×7'.
(Photo courtesy the artist)

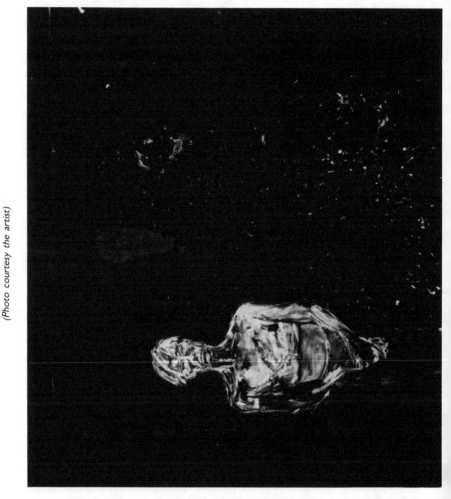

Figure 71. Julian Schnabel, *Portrait of Andy Warhol*, 1982
Oil on velvet, 108"×120".
(Photo courtesy the artist)

Figure 72. Jasper Johns, *Target with Plaster Casts*, 1955
Encaustic on canvas with plaster, 51″×44″×3-1/2″.
(Photo courtesy Leo Castelli Gallery)

Figure 73. David Salle, *Tennyson*, 1983
Oil, acrylic on canvas, 78" × 117".
(Photo courtesy Mary Boone Gallery)

Eric Fischl: Freud Lives

10 May 1981

A complex and rich panel discussion at S.V.A., organized by Joe La Placa and Randy Black with Tim Rollins, Diego Cortez, Jenny Holtzer, Barbara Kruger, Allan Moore, Julian Schnabel, Ingrid Sischy, and Carol Squiers. Rollins and Cortez the most impressive. Rollins' essential point was that artists must hang on to controlling the meaning of their work for as long as possible. If artists cannot state what the meaning of their work is, then they have that much more rapidly lost control over it; for if they cannot say what this meaning is, someone else surely will. Artists must exercise vigilance with regard to this statement so as to forestall meaning from inevitably being misrepresented in weak, sentimental, or just plain wrong terms.

In a capitalist bourgeois world, painting is inevitably reduced to its decorative common denominator which, after all, just may not be so terrible as all that. The forestalling of this inevitability can only be achieved through the artist's control over meaning.

This startling and fresh idea was seconded by Barbara Kruger, whose artful critical lingo was as striking as her unsentimental way of handling a barrage of clichés about art offered up from the floor by the poet-cum-critic René Ricard.

As striking as Tim's insight was, so too was Diego Cortez's burning anger. Cortez spoke after Allan Moore personified the effects of a lingering flower-childhood, Jenny Holtzer that of maternal openness, and Carol Squiers that of hyper-personalistic professionalism: "I will try to be at least as interesting as the last three speakers," Cortez said facetiously.

Cortez has grown more punkishly anti-liberal in the degree that he has come to be perceived as a certain kind of New Wave artist and animating force. Feeling ripped-off, pragmatics suddenly concern him. Cortez is interested in "worth efficiency." After the immense social success of the P.S.1 New Wave show, which he organized (and which will travel), and angry at the "exaggerated factionalism" that the very success of the show generated, and bored by "the exodus of artists into the music scene," he now rejects out of hand: Robert Longo, *Semio-Text(e)*, *Soho News*, Pattern Painters, most "groups," Metro Pictures, Stefanotti, "Energism," alter-

This article originally appeared in *Arts Magazine*, September 1981.

native spaces, the Times Square Show, etc. etc. All in all, the list was hilarious in a *dernier cri* in-group sort of way, but at length despair and frustration sparked Cortez and he walked off the panel.

Something of his anger was rooted in a thwarted awareness of all the mileage accrued to the rest with no fallout for him. New Wave as a style is merchandisable. And yet, at its inception (as if one could ever locate such an instant), New Wave was militantly anarchic and anti-careerist, But that was a long time ago. Now, I suppose, after there's been so much cashing in, Cortez wonders where his share went.

Tellingly, Cortez worried at the most exposed nerve of the evening. An unlistening crowd responded negatively to Julian Schnabel's remarks. After all, though his appears to be the most violently successful and sudden emergence, it's really not been roses all the way (It should be noted that the broken crockery of Schnabel's so-called "plate paintings" may take heightened cue from the grimy years he spent as a dishwasher in crummy SoHo eateries.) "How many of you," Cortez asked of the resistant crowd, "are just plain jealous?" For sure, many; for sure, most of the hostility is rooted in this emotion.

Then Cortez scatter-shot. If in his poverty he has found a way of self-presentation with great flair, then why deny this possibility to Tim Rollins? Cortez should have seen that Rollins' red jumpsuit was just common duck worn by a kid with an innate sense of style. Rollins, authentically stylish and authentically activist, spoke of Group Material and P.A.D. (Political Art Documentation/Distribution), noting that the former was not a "vanity co-op" on 13th Street but a form of "organic democracy" that seeks neither to "fetichize Hero or Collective."

But Cortez is sharply cynical and viewed the 13th Street effort along with, say, Fashion Moda or Co-Lab as yet another form of "racist colonization," despite all claims to the contrary. Joe Lewis, a dreadlocked artist from Fashion Moda, questioned from the floor about the possibility of "New Wave Quality." (Imagine, the sanctions of Greenberg's aesthetics of privilege called up in the most unlikely place!) Then, he offered a deeply convincing definition of that same quality as being the evolution of "something you don't know to something you really don't know."

3 June 1981

A compelling deception inhabits Eric Fischl's suburban world. One is thrown off track by his skillful faux-naif execution and a skewed expressionism intensifies a cunning iconography exactly suited—image to image—to a classical Freudian skin-flick.

A so-so loft on Reade Street, up five flights and an occasional chair covered with cat hair. Several large canvases still being worked on. The first, *Bad Boy* (fig. 74), represents a boy-child rigid at the sight of his mother's (?) large, dark genitals. The scene is seen from behind and we gaze as he gazes upon this Oedipal trauma. His right hand is placed behind him, entering a purse (penetration/violation?), stealing money from mom's store of bucks, if I may phrase it this way; Freud lives. Two forbidden acts: theft/the view of the genitals. The hand slipping into the purse signifies the Oedipal fornication that psychologically precedes all others.

I am of two minds about a second large canvas which may be, perhaps, even finer were it not for a certain willed awkwardness in execution that is hard to get by. This canvas, *First Sex*, is even more cinematographically framed than the first. In it, to the left, sprawls an immense earth mother (Gaia?), legs akimbo, tantalizing and receiving an erect little boy (Gaia's, copulation with her son Uranus from which union sprung the father of the Olympian gods, Cronus?) Toward the left a genital-cupping clothed celebrant may signify carnal knowledge and as such, may be the boy's father (Cronus, father of Zeus?); if so, scale-wise he is either too small or the boy is too large. In the far background scumbled into the grayish paint, a camp-fire dance of Bacchic initiates.

The most impressive painting, *Time for Bed* (fig. 75), depicts suburban frenzy. A drunken mother (?) madly dancing on a glass-top coffee table spills a cocktail across the polyester-like summer togs of a maimed father (?). He has lost his left arm, a slack sleeve tucked into his pocket. The lost appendage, for sure, signifies castration. This lost arm invokes, say, Kirchner's handless wounded soldiers and still other examples of the Freudian awareness of much German Expressionist painting.

Risking rebuff, I jump ahead by two steps: "When did you discover Beckmann?" I ask, the stylistic connections between Fischl and Beckmann amounting almost to homage. "*Departure,* that big painting, taught me how to look at painting again."

To the left of this scene of suburban carnage are two children, a skinny boy-child in Superman p.j.'s (the emblem shield "S" is inscribed backwards). Is Fischl a touch dyslexic? It seems so. "I know it takes me a very long time to read things through." Superboy's ungainly kid sister is seen from the rear, her hair towel-turbaned for quick drying. Her awkward dislocation echoes Mother's expertly rendered high-heeled shoes.

Fischl's uncanny eye builds from detail to detail in an unnerving way. "I work with single events; I just go with images. I had to get over my own sense of embarrassment." On the patio seen through the "walk-through windows," the neighbors (?) dance wildly, a reprise of the dancing figures in the beach firelight. To the left of this scene, a large black idol—middle-class primitive art—asserting through its presence the whole myth of black sexuality as counterfoil to Father's impotence.

Contrary to my snotty expectation, Fischl is not a Long Island Jew, but a cautious, taciturn 33-year-old Protestant who hails from Port Washington. On the death of his mother (the drink-spilling lady?), he moved from Long Island to Phoenix with his father (the man with the injured arm?) who remarried there. In time, Fischl went to Cal Arts. Indifferent to that school's heavy emphasis on the West Coast conceptual tradition, he stayed close to the traditions of refined minimalizing abstraction, studying mostly with Paul Brach and Allen Hacklin. Still, the paintings reveal West Coast fascination with camera technique, parallax distortion, Mannerist scale differential, pan shots, and the like.

The actual application of paint itself is rooted in a loose gray-scale painting, a grisaille permeated with chromatic hue—but in itself not naturally the color of a native colorist *au bout des ongles*. But it is not arbitrary color—if there ever can be such a thing. Indeed, another work, *Birth of Love,* transforms this grayness to a kind of glaucus chlorinated light, almost yellow-green rather than sea-green. At poolside, a naked boy-child massages the thigh of his naked mother—Gaia again? On the water's surface float two great vinyl beach balls—by Fischl's own account representing the testicles of Cronus, those hacked away by his son Zeus. Remember, these mutilated chunks of the Father's body when thrown into the sea churned up the waters occasioning the Birth of Venus, Venus Anadyomene, Venus born of the froth or the foam.

At Cal Arts, to judge from slides, Fischl was a competent abstract painter of minimal orientation with just the barest suggestion of a personalized iconography breaking through a hard reductivist shell. The abstract image is that of "a house in which the Blindman lived" (Oedipus? Oedipus blind equals Oedipus castrated). "My abstract paintings were brought up to a certain level of competence. They had a certain presence. Then I reduced the image to that of a house, an object. The house I saw as a shield, a protection. From here I could go inside the house and abstract the table and chairs. But such objects were insufficiently ambiguous. So from here I began to deal with the figure, if even crude or primitive, and I began to work the glassine figure drawings one on top of the other. From here came the Blindman."

About five years ago, this substitutive process, suburban imagery shot through with classical iconography, freed Fischl from continuing on in a tradition of merely tasteful abstract painting. "I wanted to tell the story of the picture but without recourse to codified and analytical literature." Indeed, Fischl has not studied either analytical literature itself—he was not a "psych" major, nor has he been on the couch—nor is he particularly expert in classical legend. Yet his images never fail. He's not been analyzed, is not a great reader; yet this self-absorbed "conversion process" outlined in the preceding paragraph led him back to figuration.

Figure 74. Eric Fischl, *Bad Boy*, 1981
Oil on canvas, 66"×96".
(Photo courtesy Mary Boone Gallery)

Figure 75.   Eric Fischl, *Time for Bed*, 1980
Oil on canvas, 72"×96".
(Photo courtesy Mary Boone Gallery)

Entries: Analytical Pubism

14 March 1984

To David Salle's studio to put in my two cents prior to his show that opens next Saturday. The work continues at breakneck speed, skimming across the extraordinary plateau where all he touches succeeds. Salle still heavily references Johns, this time through the use of lead sheeting beaten around forms lying below, a gin bottle for *The Miller's Tale*, a saxophone for the huge Ludwig Collection picture. The latter's "lead" painting is called *Fromage*, a work far more concerned with the American condition under late capitalism, that with cheese, despite its name. The title, inscribed in the painting in Salle Sans Serif, recalls an exchange he had with the painter Eric Fischl; the latter, once wishing to employ the expression *c'est dommage*, uttered instead *c'est fromage*, a lapsus that remains a private joke between friends, till now, anyway.

Salle's use of beaten lead refers not at all to Saul Baizerman's Maillol-like reliefs—except as antecedent—and has all to do with Johns' sculptmetal paintings quite as the glancing light of the metal sheets reminds one of the shimmer of Johns' encaustics. Apart from these visual effects, the single image alone would still reference Johns.

A large portrait of Asher Edelman is double-paneled in structure and reveals the most elaborate Johns-like ruse of all. The right-hand panel paraphrases Johns' cross-hatching though Salle used cheap dinner cutlery to do so—a brilliant transformation that Johns himself never saw (fig. 76), but which Salle carries to obsessive perfection. The Japanese stainless steel dinner service in fact is not the original cheap forks and spoons, but is a set the artist had cast into lead and then mounted on the panel, slightly melting them at the surface through direct application of the blowtorch. Painted on the cutlery is a casual pentimento, a yellow sketch, scarcely recognizable as depicting a poster matador.

Historicism is the key, perhaps even far beyond Salle's guile. A fallen woman (pun intended), legs akimbo, is placed in a room full of fifties furniture. Her de-

This article originally appeared in *Arts Magazine*, February 1985.

meaned position visually puns with the Saint in Caravaggio's *Conversion of Saint Paul.* Later, I notice Howard Hibbard's classic text on the Roman artist open for study on Salle's desk.

In another painting, a nude woman is seen from below, her breast pendulous. Above it, on another panel, a copy of a Bart van der Leck geometric emblem (fig. 77). The van der Leck inescapably associates to the work of his De Stijl companion Van Doesburg and, from there, the rapid chain of associations calls to mind the latter's most famous work *The Cow,* which in its abstract geometry symbolically evinces cow-ness. And so, emblem equals abstraction, equals *The Cow,* equals the woman as bovine, equals the breasts as udders, equals painting as a system of self-concealing, constantly mutating iconography.

27 August 1984, Sagaponak

Easily the most beautiful day of the year. I prophesied a future exhibition at Guild Hall in East Hampton to be called "The Pubist Epoch," of which David Salle will be *chef d'école.* Later, I retell the pun to Eric Fischl. "Analytical pubism," he says. "Not to put too fine a point on it," I add, "not to split hairs, that is."

5 October 1984

Tremendous show of Eric Fischl opens. In a giant *Vanitas,* a nude woman examines her face in a mirror that blocks our sight of her features (fig. 78). On the ground between her legs is an open magazine in which is reproduced a small illustration. "How daring you are, Eric, to paint a self-portrait staring right at the woman's vagina. I take it back, you're the analytical pubist. " We laugh and walk around the exhibition.

The father in *Daddy's Girl* (fig. 79), suddenly Fischl sees, really looks like he is hugging a huge sex organ to his body, as the buttocks of the little girl daddy is hugging to his chest in a visually rhyming way form the volutes of the head of an erect penis. The sensational painting of the pool rescue is exhibited as it had first been conceived as one canvas above the other; the three characters—black man, white woman, daughter—poolside, now made cinematographic sense as events played out in time. This is the first Eric had ever seen the work together as a vertical arrangement of two paintings, since his own studio ceiling is too low to have allowed the work to be set up properly.

In another time-sequenced mother-daughter painting, the mother is terrifying because of her near-masculine Gorgon-like power. *Birthday Boy* could be retitled *Bad Mother. Sisters* (fig. 80) is a magnificent and ambiguous bidet scene depicting two women. Then, why the bidet? And the sister who wears the open black shoes, she has the presence of a Balthus sleeper.

14 March 1984 (continued)

This afternoon it begins to snow, so that dinner at Raoul's (sounds rather like a movie title) with Lucio Pozzi proved unduly warming as we went for the bourgeois cooking while the city seemed to shrink the way it does when under a heavy blanket of snow. Lucio may have bitten off more than he can chew in his forthcoming three-gallery manifestation. Huge paintings refer to Last Judgment iconography and pitch towards a mannerist/early Baroque scale.

Pozzi's anxiety revealed itself in defensive pronunciamentos. Pozzi's paintings of these past years, while rejecting a simple theory of causality, were still considered "painted" and there was a certain degree of materiality to the surface. But in the new works the huge circles, squares, and triangles are so thinly painted as to verge on watercolor and, for my taste, are too quickly abandoned. Lucio rationalizes the work by calling up sixteenth-century ceiling decoration, a creditable association—fused with his unshakable faith in arbitrary decision-making as taking precedence over refinement of execution. All this stems from his belief in the power of the unconscious, a virtual volcano—and his will to instrumentalization as the central aspect of his mentality. He argues that all forms in themselves are somehow obsolete. Yes? Why, then, the three Platonic shapes? He prefers an automatic method (perhaps Picabia-derived) of "reading into stains," as he puts it. "I trust that I am clear," he asks, referring less to his argument, more to the light rapidity and self-generating calligraphy of the last works. As Pozzi combines both representational and abstract forms in his painting, the flat and the illusionistic, so too is he cavalier about the fraternization between the just and the damned in his *Last Judgment.* It all comes down to *la voglia,* as he says—will, desire, appetite, caprice, all thrown into one.

As I wanted only to stave off any disappointment the painter might feel when the shows open without traducing my own views, I noted the rapid elaboration of stain as perhaps less gratifying to me and more immediately surrealist-derived than the more cautious build-up of painted surface in the previous year's work. "You know, Robert, you remind me of an academic professor of painting arguing for the use of thick paint. In Italy, we made fun of them. They really are saying, 'Why not shit farther?' "

Figure 76. David Salle, *What Is the Reason for Your Visit to Germany* ["*Fromage*"], 1984 Oil, acrylic, lead/wood, canvas, 96" × 191-1/2". (Photo courtesy Mary Boone Gallery)

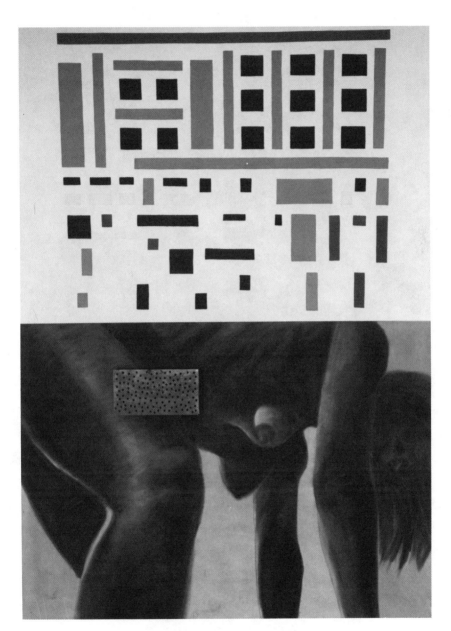

Figure 77. David Salle, *The Greenish-Brown Uniform*, 1984
Acrylic oil on canvas, wood, 120"×84".
(Photo courtesy Mary Boone Gallery)

Figure 78. Eric Fischl, *Vanity*, 1984
Oil on canvas, 108″ ×96″.
(Photo courtesy Mary Boone Gallery)

Figure 79.   Eric Fischl, *Daddy's Girl*, 1984
Oil on canvas, 78"×108".
(Photo courtesy Mary Boone Gallery)

Figure 80. Eric Fischl, *Sisters,* 1983
Oil on canvas, 108″ ×84″.
(Photo courtesy Mary Boone Gallery)

Pure Pinter:
An Interview with David Salle

RPW: Do you feel that there are important areas of issues and perceptions of criticality to read into your work which are simply not being addressed in the discussion around your work? Are there areas that you feel have somehow been misapprehended or insufficiently discussed?

DS: Well, you can't expect commentary to keep pace with the work, but let's say that the lag, it's like a rubber band: the slack gets very great and we just take it out. The commentary advances, closes the gap, and the work advances, and there's a big gap. It's chess, or marching, maybe. Well, actually neither. Maybe the work is different in feeling, in tone than it was a couple of years ago.

RPW: In what sense?

DS: It seems to be classical.

RPW: Too big a term.

DS: I don't really know what that means; it's just the way it comes to mind.

RPW: Could I, may I suggest something?

DS: Yes, of course.

RPW: I don't know that I would use the word classical. Do you mean something like the work is less immediately perceived in its connection to its conceptual origins?

DS: Its so-called origins have always been an area of great mystification. I would say that the work is less immediately perceived in connection to anything else around it.

RPW: You mean, there's nobody working like you.

DS: Right. No one's making work similar to mine, but everyone says that, or thinks it, and it's probable that it's the way this will be misread.

RPW: But there are devices, pictorial, small single . . .

DS: Oh, sure, devices.

RPW: . . . devices out there in the world which, in fact, people are making a good deal of . . .

DS: Dozens.

This article originally appeared in *Arts Magazine,* November 1985.

RPW: They're making rather doubtful claims even. In a certain sense aspects of P&D [pattern and decoration] are now being legitimized through the critical issues embodied in your work as a way of giving muscle tone to . . .

DS: Sure. Sure.

RPW: . . . aspects of P&D . . . at the Whitney.

DS: . . . an accident . . . overlap things, images . . .

RPW: Yes, it's that sort of thing.

DS: But there is a murky, misunderstood area—the notion of popular culture. It's assumed my work is a commentary on popular culture, you know. For years I have been saying the opposite. At least in my mind, my work has absolutely nothing to do with popular culture. Not only does it have nothing to do with popular culture in any kind of didactic, deliberate way, it simply doesn't have popular culture on its mind.

RPW: Is it because what is presented is not a reconstruction of popular iconography, but in fact is an aesthetic and autonomous abstract experience, which is, which has always been available to "an elite," but never been available to popular culture?

DS: Something like that. But who it is available to is less interesting, although connected, to what is being made available.

RPW: It's a kind of false signal, but what you're really getting is some kind of eternal, formal . . .

DS: Yes.

RPW: I'm beginning to see what you mean. One can look at your paintings and isolate out recognizable references to popular culture, while, in fact, one is dealing in the creation of an authentic and isolated aesthetic world.

DS: Okay.

RPW: Something like that.

DS: Something like that. The other thing is that, within that idea, there are very few real references in the work; and the references are not to popular culture or to art, but perhaps to art-like things. I think there's confusion between an image that comes from somewhere and a reference. I don't think of things as references unless they're really something referring to something else. I can think of a few references in my work, but they seem to be rampant for others. That discrepancy itself should tell us something.

RPW: You're not speaking of the indexicality of the work in terms of some sort of popular deconstruction?

DS: I think that the way to look at my work is some other way.

RPW: Can I suggest . . .

DS: Yes.

RPW: The information that one picks up, the references to art and references to the movies, what-have-you, are emblematic relationships; and an emblematic relationship to the movies as distinct from a lived relationship to them. Let's say that they are false clues as distinct from specific clues. It they were specific clues one might be able to construct a narrative layering in your paintings, whereas the lack of specificity in the clue means that one really cannot make a narrative out of your pictures.

DS: Right. There's no narrative. There really is none; there isn't one.

RPW: There's no story.

DS: Right. None at all.

RPW: You see, my way of thinking keys into your notion of the autonomy of the work—its abstractness.

DS: I think about a couple of different things which appear, which have lived out their lives in the arena of popular culture, but I don't think of them as popular. One is a comedy, the other is pornography. Those are two things that are important to me . . . for themselves. Not as a comment on the society that produces them, but in their own mechanistic ways, you know, how they operate.

RPW: In a detached mechanistic way, I think that's what I was saying when I was saying emblematic . . .

DS: Yes?

RPW: But emblematic suggests that it's an index, that is is an emblem of something.

DS: I would say mechanistic.

RPW: Mechanistic is better than emblematic. So, you know you have, say, the mechanism of comedy, the mechanism of eroticism, even pornography . . .

DS: Yes.

RPW: The art references are largely, it seems to me, references to ironic detachment. The movies would be another mechanism.

DS: But the art mechanisms are always about one thing. About how an image is simultaneously some molecules in paint that congeal in certain patterns which at a certain distance appear recognizable as a painting. Are recognized as a painting.

RPW: That's an argument for pure painting somehow.

DS: No, it's an image of reciprocity. There is no such thing as pure painting—or, rather, it's just uninteresting painting; you know, the French avant-garde.

RPW: Which French avant-garde—the early modernists, like Picasso, Matisse?

DS: Do I strike you as a Picasso cultist? No, like Manet.

RPW: Oh, like the 1860s, the 1870s.

DS: Yes, early.

RPW: The Manet-Monet.

DS: The Manet-Monet. The wavering. You know, the just-barely-held-together nature of Manet's paint. Even the linguistic convention is interesting: "his paint." The fact that the paintings were always—I mean not necessarily to our standards but according to the standards by which they were painted—in danger of falling apart.

RPW: You mean, falling apart as an image that coheres?

DS: Yes. The ambiguity in how the image is contextualized . . .

RPW: Contextualized not socially, contextualized on the canvas, you mean.

DS: On the canvas, but also through the canvas to reach its social dislocation. I think that's art, I mean that *is* art, isn't it?

Basically, there is the reciprocity between the thing and how the thing's represented, but more specifically, the slippery, the congealing into something readable at the same time that it's slipping away or draining away. This is timeless. It's the poignancy at the heart of what I mean by classicism: the draining away of recognition or of meaning even as you look at it, and even as you are using your eyes to focus the marks into an image. It's like an alternating current. It happens very fast. You have a very fast rhythm.

RPW: Can I just follow that through and try to isolate out the conversation to a slightly absurd simplification . . .

DS: Well, let me just add something else. One thing which was on my mind from before is the mechanism of pornography. Pornography is about representing—problems of representation—and very exciting because it takes place on a two-dimensional surface, I mean, photographic pornography, or . . . drawn pornography as opposed to literary pornography.

RPW: I think it's virtually impossible for me to equate visual pornography as equal to verbal pornography . . .

DS: Yes.

RPW: It's virtually impossible for me to imagine pornography in a state other than photographic.

DS: Yes, I think that . . .

RPW: There is, there's something about . . .

DS: . . . isn't that perhaps why photography was invented?

RPW: . . . that's what Nicéphore Niépce was about. He wanted to get the barn *and* the pussy . . .

DS: I mean, why else would they have invented it?

RPW: . . . from Daguerre on, anyway.

DS: Can you think of a better use of it, of photography?

RPW: Well, no. I think that the problem—if there is such a condition, if there is such a class of meaning, or a class of objects, that embodies a meaning that was recognized as pornographic—is that that class of objects in modern culture seems to be a class of objects occupied by things which are photographs.

DS: The great thing about pornography is that something was photographed. This thing you're seeing is not just what you're seeing; it's that what you're seeing photographed. That's the compelling . . .

RPW: Yes, and we know how photography works and we know that somebody did it and another person . . .

DS: Yes, of course, and drawing, you know, is absolutely . . . that's why drawing is just nowhere. There is Egon Schiele, for example, but in the particular non-sentimental eroticism of pornography that we're talking about, the "givenness" of it is so much more confounding than any erotic image drawn . . . but to make a painting that has about it that feeling that you get from pornography. The knowledge that this was, this was actually, seen—by someone (fig. 81).

RPW: Clearly your works must be liberated from the false charge of pornography. If not by virtue of the image, then by virtue of the way that image is realized. What

I'm trying to say is: the very fact that the image is painted means that it cannot be charged with the condition of pornography.

DS: Why do you say that?

RPW: Because we just had agreed that pornography, if it exists, exists in a class which is photographic.

DS: We made an aphorism, not a syllogism. Or, rather, the syllogism is meant to be defeated by my painting. I don't think people are necessarily wildly hysterical or prejudiced or blue-noses or Baptists who take my works to be the real thing.

RPW: People will say that the work is pornographic, but in fact they're trying to locate it in the realm of moral indictment.

DS: Well, what they're saying is that those images have a peculiar relation to the world, because they don't have the same neutrality as they believe other painted images have.

RPW: Yes, but I think that they have also . . . either classicism, or autonomy, or whatever that stuff is.

DS: Exactly. Those are the two poles.

RPW: What are?

DS: Classicism and pornography.

RPW: If those are the two poles . . . your polarity argument, pornography and classicism, is part of this stuff you were talking about in the Manet/Monet , when the molecules sort of congeal, but then they slip away, decompose somehow.

DS: Yes, the gravitational attraction to each other diminishes and they . . .

RPW: . . . they're somehow loosened in the non-magnetic environment.

DS: Right. Somebody pulls the plug on the magnet.

RPW: You know, there are millions of images, in the degree that you have a repertoire of images that you constantly appeal to, as a way perhaps just to paint. I mean, that may be just to keep the painting going, so you don't have to constantly rely on the literal sensation of the motif deeply observed; so that you have a repertoire that you, that this is what you paint. You paint and the repertoire enlarges or diminishes, depending upon the year or the month or the day. The point I way trying to make was that this repertoire doesn't only include images which are conventionally assigned to pornography. There are very highly neutral ones, too.

DS: Oh, yes, highly neutral. But it's really the point that there is a repertoire of images that I can pick from, some of which happen to be offensive to some people. All of the images—the way they are realized and the way they are combined—is all part of knowing what kind of pictures I want to make and that it has nothing to do, really, with *taking anything from anywhere.*

RPW: What you're saying means that we're beginning to speak about the work actually possessing an aesthetic condition. We're commodifying the object and we're mythifying the maker. Those two myths are anathema to broad sectors of the intellectual public.

DS: Oh, well.

RPW: Well, that's how it is. I mean I've certainly participated in that mechanism because I believe in the mechanism.

DS: I have a feeling that there's something that can be said that's more objective, that is, would be parallel to, although completely different from in substance and tone . . . the discussion of work from the '60s and '70s. I found it intellectually dishonest that certain kinds of work could be discussed in a, you know, rational way; but that, for some reason, that kind of relationship to culture is denied my work which only shows the arbitrariness of that construct to begin with. That sounded kind of shrill. How did we get started on . . .

RPW: Don't get paranoid. I feel very secure in recognizing you as a fine painter and that your paintings maintain attitudes inherited from the 60s and 70s. Minimalism and conceptualism were perceived as tools, for example. That said simply acknowledges developmental origins, but does not keep you locked into a style, does not academize you. What you are saying now is that you are feeling more congenial to the image of the painting, not as maintaining the criticality that was germane to minimalism, but as an object which enjoys the perks.

DS: No, I didn't say that. I said that there is a claim to objectivity (as if that is even the desired state) that this other kind of work makes, which includes, which has implicit in it, a notion of quality. That self-conferred status is not extended to other work, which is a bias. An artist may have to do something very different-seeming to establish a relationship to his time parallel to one ratified for an earlier generation by time. There was an assumption, all through the '60s and '70s, that certain artists, and certain people who supported certain artists, were *good*. You get it in the tone of voice that's used even by dealers. (Of course, dealers are like method actors—they fall into the emotive tone of the art they're dealing; it's their object memory.) The tone is one of moral superiority.

RPW: You found it oppressive.

DS: Yes, but I also found it extremely interesting.

RPW: I can remember terrible experiences; with your sense of integrity, you're sort of describing a gross process of reactive history of certain moments of your life. I remember how oppressed I used to be—and I'm a critic—when I would look at works that I knew were empty, boldly empty work, I mean, empty art, and I would be told that Clem liked it. I remember that it steeled me against it.

DS: So, what are we saying?

RPW: Maybe everything is significant in your work now, and it may be a stupendous effort to resist your work being made conventional; you're going to deny, more and more, the information and sources that were available to you before, or early on.

DS: Oh, you're saying I'm interested in a certain period because it's so out?

RPW: Yes, not just that. Like it's one thing to talk about Picabia's transparencies, as everybody does, but now let's look at Picabia.

DS: I feel like a man explaining what he was doing at the scene of a crime. Well, yes, actually we were a tiny bit interested in the ghastly murder. I never really talked about Picabia except as a kind of passive-aggressive oddball. The way in which I related to Picabia has not been understood at all, because no one has described the peculiar character, I would say doomed character, of his late realist paintings. It's really about night becoming day; it's about something being the opposite of what it appears to be, but looking exactly like what it appears to be. It could have been anybody. I mean, it just happened that he did something that was parallel or interesting or similarly hard to place in terms of structure of intent. My work never had anything to do with Picabia stylistically. It should be so obvious. It would be like using a double negative. If I were interested in getting to Picabia-*feeling*, I couldn't use Picabia-means *now*.

RPW: And what about the fact that he painted overlapped paintings (see fig. 60)?

DS: The cross-examination. They never interested me. They look like old painting to me. It's the late kitsch paintings that cast a spell (see fig. 64). What I think is interesting about late Picabia is simply subject matter.

RPW: But the transparencies have subject matter, too.

DS: But not interesting subject matter as choices of subject matter. No nudes and bulls, you know, nudes and statues and Greek; I mean just really kinky . . . emblematic.

RPW: Emblematic?

DS: Along the path from kitsch to emblematic lies beauty of a liberating sort.

RPW: What else is kinky and emblematic?

DS: There are, there were, many examples to be found in student art, and the point is that art like that usually doesn't survive. That's what's interesting about it. I don't see it any longer.

RPW: I see lots of it, all over the country, you know, all of the time.

DS: I don't see it anymore.

RPW: You mean you think that everybody's no longer making student art?

DS: No, people are making student art, but I don't see the student art participating in this kind of self-destructive, self-righteous kind of crybaby , bad-person sensibility. Why am I talking about this?

RPW: I see it all over! One of the central features of student art is that it is identified as significant through its virtually immediate appropriation of last year's avant-garde, which is a very important achievement for a student.

DS: Well, that's not the student I'm talking about. The central dadaists, the kamikaze self-haters, do-anything-for-art types. When I was in school . . . [there] was a friend of mine who made films, Chris Langdon.

RPW: I don't know him.

DS: Of course you don't. He transformed himself into a Cajun squeezebox player. But back then his films were hilariously funny, they were outrageously funny, but some people didn't think so. Some people thought they were offensive. He made a film called "The Last Interview with Pasolini" and it was shown at the old Artists Space. Naturally with that title they sold out the house. The image was a man seen from behind; you couldn't see his face, actually, you just saw his arm and shadows of his head. This guy, a friend of ours who was also very funny, played the interviewer; he asked these incredibly obnoxious questions in a flat nasal voice, like: "Mr. Pasolini, it has been said that your audience is the young. Do you feel you are addressing the youth of today?" etc. A very complicatedly accented kind of voice answered in fake Italian—Italian doubletalk, just to talk—and the interviewer would nod his head as if in rapturous communication. This goes on for about 45 minutes and then the words would be inserted in the text such as 'cowboys' and 'pussy' and things like that; the interviewer would just smile and go on asking absurd questions.

People were so offended by this that they got up and walked out, which in the New York underground is *never done*. People will sit through the most atrocious *dreck* for hours on end and take it straight; but in this instance, people got up and stormed out and slammed the door and threw their chairs. He had blasphemed. He really was a very bad child. Bad children don't survive as artists, but when they do, they're very interesting to me. Or were. . . .

Figure 81.   David Salle, *Trouble in Routing*, 1983
Acrylic on canvas, 60″×42″.
(Photo courtesy Mary Boone Gallery)

Gary Stephan:
The Brief against Matisse

Gary Stephan, now in his late 30s: steel-rimmed glasses, incipient embonpoint, well-cut tweeds—no longer the appurtenances of a stylish boy, but those of a stylish man. Not gratuitous. Art, for Stephan, represents, at least in part, a conquest of good taste paralleling the adult conquest of infantile neuroses. Yet all this is ambivalent—since his sharp sense of taste is a quality to be subjugated. Stephan, like us all, broods on the unraveling complex formations occasioned by family and upbringing; ambivalence animates his recollections, say, of a Levittown adolescence.

— "What were the '70s about," I ask, "and how did you fit in?"

— "The strengths and freedoms of the '50s led to the narcissism and license of the '60s. This led to a search for structure, for a logic behind the activity on which to base the activity. This belief in logic led to 'flat geometrics.' Soon we saw that flat geometrics were rigid, not optically responsive. Ultimately, they failed, and in failing, we were forced to turn back to appearances."

Stephan trained as an industrial designer at Pratt Institute, but went off instead to San Francisco before completing the degree. He recalls the Pratt formation as essentially Moholy-Nagy and New Bauhaus, very *Vision in Motion*. It was, after all, the prevailing art school mode persisting from the '50s.

Stephan arrived in the Bay Area of the '60s, a period when artists, especially California artists, were trying to draft a brief against Matisse. Ironically, official California painting today is dominated by the Matisse spinoff—a mode instigated by Richard Diebenkorn.

What this case signified for Stephan, at the time, was the frustration felt by painters identified as provincial and who partly believed the tag whether they wanted to or not— "provincials," then, both angry and envious of a formalism, the formalist criticism of a formalist clique, that excluded them: Greenberg and Co. All this is water under the bridge by now, and formalist criticism in the '80s—late semiological analysis, say—by no stretch of the imagination alludes to Greenberg

This article originally appeared in *Arts Magazine*, March 1982.

any longer. Still, San Francisco as a place, as locale, continues to encode, for Stephan, the consequences of "narcissism" and "license," as he called it.

Stephan's departure for San Francisco has all the marks of a sudden impulse, an impetuous fugue. He enrolled at the San Francisco Art Institute, finding himself in the same class with John Duff, James Reineking—strong sculptors—and the painter of masks, Michael Tetherow. Bruce Nauman regularly dropped in on yet another classmate whom they then regarded as their most brilliant peer, a certain Randy Hardy.

Stephan's psychoanalytical bent was sparked by a set of early paintings about which he now feels a strong attraction/repulsion. We see them today as startling out-of-synch premonitions of the current New Figuration, Neo-Primitivism, Maximalism, what have you. Beyond this happenstance, his present masterful painterly abstractions on Christian themes or derived from El Greco's compositions (fig. 82) are internally linked in his mind "to the mad prophecy of these crazy student pictures."

Stephan showed me some black and white glossies of these early works—wide, hilly vistas, ten feet across, depopulated and schematic, chimneyed houses with smoke coming out, all rendered in a dumb sleazy way, more Walter Lantz than Walt Disney. These large overlapped landscaped passages painted on masonite date to about 1964–66 and are punctuated with legible—if un-understandable—shapes, an odd iconography.

—"That 'odd shape'," Stephan says, "means roses that are chipped and wrapped in aluminum foil and then put in an ashtray." See what I mean, legible but un-understandable. Often enough, queer animals bear a resemblance to toilets or chemical alembics. Stephan vaguely recalls these "anthropomorphic toilets" (dumb cartoon flowers stuck in their bowls) as a distant model for the thin-armed "torso-shapes" that emerged in his painting around 1980.

These quirky pictures were shown at the San Francisco Art Institute as part of his senior project. So unacceptable were they to the professoriate that he was obliged to take them down; only after protracted insistence that they were, after all, really meant to be "paintings" was he permitted to put them up again. (Well, a history of affront and contretemps attaches itself to the "M.F.A. Show" or the "Senior Crit," so ubiquitous has the degree become, that practically every artist nurtures a favorite horror story.)

On showing these works, if even in student circumstances, the question was at last asked if the artist, "Have you ever heard of Carl Jung?" Its reply led him to analysis and the belief in the insights available to painting that analysis provided.

These paintings are now stacked inaccessibly in the New York studio, but Stephan can get to at least one of them—*The Magic Motor Boat* (fig. 83), a scratched water view, a few scattered islands forming a narrow channel through which a motorboat passes, some lightning, a deformed horizontal shape.

— "The odd shape 'objectifies' the painting more clearly," Stephan says. Nailheads protrude from the scratched surface; again "greater objectification." Like a stiff altar cloth, the picture is hung in relief from an old bent curtain rod. "The curtain rod indicates the use of rejected cultural artifacts as an art strategy."

On leaving the cloister of the San Francisco Art Institute—its local quasi-paranoid tradition of the Transcendent Morality of Pure Painting still intact—Stephan returned to New York.

Of course, he had been picking up real-life clues all along, School of Hard Knocks—funnier perhaps in the retelling. It was 1968, and Kynaston McShine was installing the Smith, Irwin, Davis show at the Jewish Museum, back when the Museum had defocused from ethnicity for awhile. (Alan Solomon's first surveys of Johns and Rauschenberg are the now legendary inaugurations of this period.) Stephan and Neil Jenney worked on the installation. Jenney had heard Germano Celant's Art Povera book "chatted-up" in McShine's office, and knew that the future was in "The Conceptual" —dirt, plants, wrapped earth—you remember. So they made some Art Povera—I was calling it Postminimalism—and Jenney called Richard Bellamy to come down to inspect the stuff, with an eye to inviting them into the Green Gallery, then a leading avant-garde locale. A moment before Bellamy's epiphany, Jenney showed up in Stephan's studio to borrow some geranium plants for his installation. Stephan lent them; and Jenney gets taken by Bellamy—with no follow-up visit to Stephan's studio, "though my work used geraniums too!" "It is not who does it first, " Jenney later explained by way of exculpation, "it is who gets it first to the store."

But, it was not all self-service. Later, at an art party, Jasper Johns had asked John Duff to become his studio assistant. Duff, having sufficient funds on which to get by, recommended his classmate. "Johns," totally neutral and taciturn, "is the absolutely perfect Freudian analyst."

— "How much do you want?" Johns asks.

— "$3.50 an hour," the salary he had been earning as a part-time art therapist in a clinic on the Upper West Side. Johns nods assent.

— "And when can you come?" Stephan indicates the hours and the days. Again the nod.

For nearly two years, 1969–70, Stephan worked for Johns during period of the painting of the second version of the Buckminster Fuller Dymaxion Map, arguably Johns' least agreeable work. Stephan gets to luncheon daily with Johns and his intimate circle, this by way of having invented the studio chores—sorting the mail, feeding the cats, stretching the canvases, and reserving the table at old Signor Ballotto's restaurant on Houston Street.

Such recollections are keys to work shown at the now defunct David Whitney Gallery. Whitney, a close friend of Phillip Johnson and Jasper Johns, had once worked for Castelli uptown. During the colonization of SoHo, Whitney had opened a gallery midway down in the then Terra Incognita—4th Avenue and the low 20s—more or less diagonally across from the old Max's Kansas City, then a preferred watering hole for artists. True, not SoHo—but not upper-Madison Avenue either.

The gallery partially reflected the combined tastes of Whitney, Johnson, and Johns, and can now be seen to have had its moments—especially the sponsoring, say, of the early Duff/Stephan experimental work and the early Neil Jenney installations. These high points were countered by much late formalist expressionism then called "lyrical abstraction," an abstraction I obtusely insisted upon calling "fat field." Set upon the gray industrially carpeted floors and walls of the top floor of a small loft building, the mix was novel and anomalous. Whitney's "go-fer" was David White, who also had started out as a Leo Castelli assistant, and the warm secretary was Jeanne Blake, who first "gal-Friday'd" in the old Richard Feigen place just off Madison into which Bykert eventually moved.

Of all the artists who exhibited with David Whitney during the two years of the turn of the '70s, Stephan was shown the most frequently, three times; and at length, he closed the gallery. His work, then similar to Duff's, experimented with rubber, latex, plastic, and free-process—a kind of constructed painting strongly marked by an awareness of pictorialized modernist sculpture. His works, at the time, offer no particularly lovable resolutions, though they were, for Stephan, highly therapeutic.

— "Being back in New York, getting rid of all that weird California shit, I tried to make the paint structural, to make the paint itself into the ground I was painting on. I see them as plastic paint."

My description of these paintings makes them sound too reliant on an admittedly self-evident expressionist bias— "pictorialized sculpture" —suggesting, in this way, that the paintings were worked in the absence of a specific set of informational cues. Quite to the contrary, numerous formal concerns are noted within this group. For example, any pictorial element that carried color was meant to be a specific formal cue. Such colored shapes, for example, always occur as "negative shapes" — though they are afforded an unusual assertiveness since they hold the strongest positive colors. The areas of the plastic paintings that were executed in black and white (or which were piebald or parti-colored) conveyed a sense of field or "spread." These "striped" areas, loosely speaking, connected up with one another across the shape interruptions that held the primary one-colored shapes together. Such stripes did not always take horizontal configurations either; at times they occur as radiating patterns. Last, a kind of order was imposed through the sense of symmetry occasioned by the strongly inflected bounding sides.

But, as Stephan notes, "To match these figurative cues is to deprive it of other things." In short, the paintings of circa 1969–70 attempted (through the application of an exiguous argument) to embody Stephan's desire to "circumvent style." Style, at the time, capital 'S' Style, was torn between the East Coast hegemony (a mode Stephan was, in some measure, attempting to accommodate) and West Coast latitudinarian laissez-aller (the dopey private mythologies he had abandoned).

With noteworthy Jesuitical reasoning, Stephan reduced this antagonism (purging from it its geographical references) to an argument in which Manet is pitted against Cézanne; or in an even larger context, Culture versus Perception.

How can this argument be schematized? Manet, for Stephan, emerges as a student of Spanish painting, meaning for him that Manet viewed historical issues as stylistic questions. "These issues seen this way engage the artist's technical ability at reproducing the diverse, smooth, or rough brushwork of his chosen models. A skillful adoption then allows the artist to be judged as either good or bad; and attendant historical issues then become conventionalized to those called up by iconography or iconographic interpretation."

Duchamp, in substituting mentality for retinality, rerouted this tradition through the introduction of paradox and irony—a content whose recognizability has scant shelf life. While the "thing" remains, the painting I mean, paradox and irony rapidly grow invisible.

Making a rather broad and pointed argumentative leap, Stephan sees this aesthetic curve-ball as a form of latent suicide, a self-destruction with regard to meaning in contemporary high formalist painting (especially that of marked iconographic profile—such as is now being made by Julian Schnabel and David Salle with whom, for better or worse, Stephan's present career is inescapably linked).

The warping of culture is countered in Stephan's argument by "perception," that is to say, by questions concerning what it is that one is seeing. Such straight observations lead to instrumentalization, to the tool rather than to stylistic questions. For Stephan, Cézanne inaugurated this aspect of the modernist tradition (as we all believe anyway), not Manet. Much of what Stephan calls "the perceptual tradition," we call straight formalism. Stephan considers an artist like Ellsworth Kelly, say, to be an exemplar. "Culture, leading to Duchamp, leads to the consequences of 'reading'; whereas, perception leads to the consequences of sensory data."

Culture, then, leads to irony, and as Stephan notes, "Irony is a way to do what one does without assuming responsibility for the action"; or stated even more bluntly, "Irony is visual cowardice."

Stephan admits there is no pure case, though this really may represent an attempt to slip off the hook, for, granting his hyperbole, Stephan also believes that "the social question always goes away. It always evaporates. The only things that have any chance of survival are the things that *remain,* remain, that is, *neurally,* not *socially.* That is where Piero is critical, and that is where Manet's occasional optical struggle to organize the spatial picture leads to less than authoritative spatial discrepancies.

— "What about quality?" I interject, "or our predisposition toward classicism over the long haul? Doesn't the inescapable binding of the notion of quality and the notion of classicism amount to an almost mystical connection in our culture?

— "I don't believe in the question of classicism at all. Quality, for me, is neural, and the neural avoids the shoals of quality. Paintings do something. Like cars, they do something. And this 'doing' is perceptual and neural. Paintings operate. Something happens. That is why painting is a radical activity. It finally is anti-culture. It is in here (he says, pointing to his temples). It is in the engrams. It is purely Darwinian. Our receptors are set up through genetic encoding. Trial and error only help or hinder the process."

— "No," I interject. "That is too positivist a model, too materialistic. It's got no nuances."

— "Look, genetic shuffling brings the syntax flat up against evolutionary limitations. We're on our own. Shuffling occurs within us and within the limits of the enterprise, especially within the limits of the tools used."

If from the vantage of the early '80s the wacky mythologies of the California work, or the degraded rubber and plastic pictures, are perhaps more congenial than the informational aspects also present in the latter group, then the body of work of the early '70s is perhaps the most displaced. In the measure that an epistemic argument for the arts of the turn of the '70s took hold, Stephan's paintings were thought to reflect this tendency, one that favored information. In the degree that Stephan rejected confusion for simplification, the marriage of incipient minimalism to a waxing sensibility became evident (fig. 84).

It is, of course, the classicizing element of Stephan's work that would carry him through this moment despite his disavowal. His first successes were appreciated by a circle of artists and connoisseurs deeply associated with epistemic abstraction. Surely the soundest advice Stephan received in the early '70s came from Richard Serra (advice tendered during the group show of new tendencies organized by Jay Belloli for the Contemporary Arts Museum in Houston, Texas, September–November, 1972): "In a work, never do anything more than once."

This minimalist maxim helps explain the reductivism of Stephan's work throughout the decade. All the consonances and dissonances of shape, scale, and color relationships separate out; relationships simplify, providing only sufficient compositional fodder for single organizations, when previously such material had served as units of far more complex, polyphonic structures.

Two elements, reduced dualisms, now suffice to justify the organization. Briefly, composition became that of a reductivist formal strategy: How does one scale or locate a figure? How do you validate a figure in its place? And how can the artist continue to reduce the number of pictorial elements from picture to picture? The answer to these questions at least led to the emblematic gray square that haunted minimalist painting during its sway, and eventually occasioned the sense of the utterly contrived and academic which sounded the death knell of the style.

Stephan bridles (as any artist would) at this formulation of minimalism's evolution. He would point instead to the "neural" validation of shape and form. Shapes were thus and so because they inescapably had to be that way, not out of any accommodationist tactic to a larger controlling *Zeitgeist*. For the public, though, Stephan's pictures at the time were seen as the chief representatives of a minimalist gradualism, the vague coloristic and tonal aspects of which continue to place his work outside the theoretical pale of the absolutist "heavies," a gradualism that continued to speak for pictorial qualities then seen as of dubious consequence. Among these properties were Stephan's "designerish" organization (from Bauhaus graphics, say) or a color connoting a broad range of evocative association. These were regarded as sentimental hangovers that fell outside the pervasive minimalist context. It is precisely in the degree that these works do fall outside the precinct that they are today able to be seen quite freshly.

Naturally, for Stephan, the whole issue of color and formal connotation is false. His view of color at the time was one of neurological absolutes: colors had to be (and are what they are) not because of a palette predicated on association, but because of a concentrated focus, a bearing down on the issues of pure abstraction. Then, if one speaks of a Mediterranean palette, or delicate ranges of *greige* or flesh, or refined hues as indications of a drained and tasteful imagery, such associations are made on the viewer's account, not the artist's.

All this nuanced color is countermanded, as it were, by essential geometrical configurations based on simple weight displacements—a circle placed against a triangle, a semicircle against a rectangle. Such compositions are rendered in an equally reduced palette, one that seeks to establish no more than figure-ground relationships despite the unswerving delicacy of the colors assigned to the figures and the ground. In this way, one may continue to make dubious bracketings between the pronounced sensibility minimalism of the '70s and Stephan. Figures like Brice Marden, or Ralph Humphrey, or Doug Ohlson, or Doug Sanderson, or Susanna Tanger all come to mind and all are, quite naturally, wrong in varying measure.

In truth, the minimalist graphic attachments of Stephan's work of the early '70s represented a return to painting itself, if only by fits and starts. Naturally, there had been the example of Ellsworth Kelly whose work—though reductive and itself even attached to the prevailing epistemic enthusiasm of the mid '60s—grew out of an abstraction grounded in distillations of landscape and architectural motifs. This abstraction as an essence of nature is, for the modernist, its most venerable form.

Still, for all that, the period is marked by a hostility towards an overt and unapologetic painting. Indeed, painting itself was taboo, and even as they painted, Stephan (and many others) regarded their work as akin to the analytic reduction of the clear informational structures of early minimalism. In short, they worked from a hobbled and apologetic stance. It was not until the middle of the decade that the need to rationalize and justify the very fact that one was painting faded. Work, as it were, stood on its own, freed from the highly referential systems imposed by epistemic abstraction.

The Garden Cycle, a group of ten approximately 44-inch square canvases, is characteristic of the shift. The paintings were shown at the Bykert Gallery in 1975. They may be understood as demonstrating elementary figure/ground relationships rendered ambivalent through spare illusionistic bends. This reading of convexity was occasioned by applications of denser pigment. At this moment, Stephan's characteristic impasto, a build of graduated crust along a slightly scored edge, becomes quite incisive; equally marked is his still somewhat apologetically adduced historicist iconography and associative color. The instances of powdery brickish colors were specific to Stephan's art book study of the program for Giotto's Padua Arena Chapel, the fresco cycle depicting scenes from The Life and Passion of Christ.

The very use of the word "cycle" in the Garden Cycle was triggered by this connection. Not only did fresco technique provide a range of chalky color relationships; it provided, as well, an isolated focus on curious architectural settings and motifs to be seen throughout the program. For example, the section depicting Anna and Joachim (the future parents of the Virgin) meeting at the Golden Gate—Giotto's imaginary Jerusalem—provided a set of architectonics which, when even further reduced, appear in Stephan's pictures as abstract figure/ground relationships emblematic of the distilled architectural motif.

Occasionally, the shapes are not modified at all; rather, they are "lifted," traced from the compositions reproduced in glossy picture books or popular guides to religious art. Thus the figure/grounds, on a certain level, may be read as excised turret or fortress dentellations. In certain ways, bold elements were meant to transfer the massive sack-like figures invented by Giotto suggesting, to Stephan, "the human plus its metaphor in architecture." All this *italianismo* came to a head in 1975. Not only had Stephan visited Venice, California, in that year, he also made his first trip to the "real" Venice, sojourns that had the effect of confirming the incipient Italian connections—associations, like particles of metal, that came to adhere to the magnet of minimalism.

So excited was Stephan at this discovery, he communicated it to Bryan Hunt, then beginning his own career in California. Hunt, excited by Stephan's discussion, literally built a model of the Golden Gate at which Anna met Joachim. Surely for a Californian, erstwhile or otherwise, the coincidence of "Golden Gate" and Golden Gate would be very striking, as is the parallel Venice/Venice equally arresting.

Thus the Garden Cycle is a culminating effort for Stephan. Each element encodes highly conscious choices for the artist. Its shape, for example, purposefully equivocates on the format issue, being neither vertical nor horizontal. The implication of the square format was first guessed at during the Venice summer. A vertical format, Stephan suddenly grasped, invoked a mimetic "other person," a peer and equal out there in the world. By contrast, the horizontal format came to conjure the spectator who looks out over the terrain. In this sense of inspection, the "voyeur" (too erotic a notion) or the dutiful Christian (associated with a reconstruction of the lost earthly paradise) was invoked. But the square itself waffles. Stephan's perceptions were, of course, part of the growing awareness of the pronounced iconographic classicism that attached itself to minimalist logic—Ellsworth Kelly's spare balances and swells born of an acute appreciation of classical epigraphy and letter forms, Bochner's *sinopia* and dry pigment fresco technique, Rockburne's golden sections and her own version of *Maestà* imagery, Marden's Fra Roberto Caracciolo of Lecce, Mangold's Albertian church facades, Novros' *predelle*, etc.

Behind much of this Pre-Raphaelite overload is to be found the neglected figure of Gordon Hart, who, like many before, had been stimulated by Cennino and the recipes necessary to early Renaissance painting—grinding one's own pigment, setting down one's own perfect gesso ground, burnishing the hand-set gold leaf, rediscovering the lost techniques of egg tempura, studying the magical ratios of polytychly subdivided surface, and on and on. Hart's career, though checkered, was pervasive in the '70s, a prestige heightened through his friendship with Barnett

Newman. "While he didn't get to run with the ball," notes Stephan, "he was the one who made the connection."

The use of gold leaf in Lynda Benglis' sculpture, for example, may be traceable to a residual connection to Gordon Hart. On her arrival in New York from New Orleans in the late '60s, Benglis associated with him, a point of some interest insofar as it was across Hart that Benglis first met Klaus Kertess, the director of the Bykert Gallery, with whom she entered a friendship that spanned the decade.

Briefly then, at the very least, Sensibility Minimalism of the '70s may be viewed as The Bykert Problem, insofar as Kertess' highly sensitized taste brought his gallery to the pivotal place it enjoyed at the time. We have already traced Stephan to the closing of the David Whitney space on Park Avenue South; indeed, it was on the closing of that gallery in 1972 that Stephan joined the Bykert stable. Before 1972, Kertess had been installed in a small office-like space on West 57th Street. Stephan remembers visiting him there, sitting at his makeshift cardtable desk with these "self-conscious mauve boxes posed on the floor," wondering, "What is all this shit?" From there, Kertess moved up to 81st Street, settling into the old Richard Feigen quarters and remaining there until the gallery closed in 1976. The move uptown was made during the summer of 1968. Stephan, by way of supplementing his still uneven income, worked as library cataloguer for Feigen in anticipation of the latter's installation in an elegantly renovated 79th Street townhouse. Gallery chores were shared with Frederica Hunter, who would shortly open the Texas Gallery, still one of the better galleries devoted to reductivist minimalist taste. Need one add, by way of noting the extraordinary network of apprenticeships, that Kertess' last gallery assistant was Mary Boone, whose early taste as a dealer was initially formed by the gallery and by her strong personal relationship with Kertess, Benglis, and Stephan.

"The thing about Klaus that was so striking to artists," Stephan notes, "was this unnerving ability just to look and look at a work, for a long period of time, staying with it longer, even, than the picture itself worked. Klaus, in a way, could watch a picture end. I think that is why," Stephan continues, "so much of the art shown at Bykert was tinged with melancholy. They were seen through."

Kertess' most profound friendship from among his roster of artists was with the young Brice Marden. In a certain way, Kertess can almost be said to have been under his emprise. The intensity of the connection inescapably marked the gallery's orientation. Stephan's belief in the neural engrammatic character of painting, its sheer essential quiddity as deriving from Cézanne (not Manet), was shared by Marden.

This staying with the work, Kertess' way, Bykert's way, Marden's way, may be taken to be yet another facet of the strong rejection of Greenberg's modernism felt at the time. Greenberg had postulated the original sanctions of the modernist dialectic as stemming from Manet. An essential character of modernist painting at the moment of its failure in the mid-70s was its presumed instantaneity of perception. Painting, by way of differentiating it utterly from sculpture, had to be accessible within a single glance. This way of seeing equally was countered by a then contemporary reassessment of the work of Reinhardt, in whose painting glossy instantaneity was replaced by time-consuming, long looking. Thus it dislodged painting from its role merely as a screen of delectation to become, instead, one of meditation, as Reinhardt would have it. Need one note, then, that among the canonic field painters as determined by Greenberg—Newman, Rothko, Louis—Reinhardt's name does not appear.

Indeed, Stephan's first memory of a significant art experience is intimately allied with Reinhardt, but much before this date, when he was a callow mid-Long Island teenager who had been taken to see a Reinhardt painting, part of an exhibition organized by Vincent Price for the New York Coliseum; and like the rest of the teen-hoods he was with, Stephan merely laughed as he was paraded through the gallery. An astute teacher knowing him better than he knew himself chastened him and sat him down before the Reinhardt: "You just sit there and look hard," she said, "and you will see something you have never seen before." After a while this black cross jumped out at me from the canvas," Stephan continues, "I was so excited. When I got home, I had to make black on black pictures; and I had just seen Jackson Pollock on a talk show, too," which means this memory dates to 1956 or earlier. "The point was to make fun of his 'dripping,' because they put him on with this jerk—WOW—who made a pair of wings to fly with. I put Pollock and Reinhardt together, mixing gravel and paint and throwing it in the form of a cross on my father's shirt cardboards. Then I made these crosses mixing Karo and chocolate syrup on the cardboard. They were slow gravity pictures and had to be turned once a week or else the stuff would fall off onto the floor. And my parents turned them faithfully once a week without complaining. They never really impeded anything that had to do with art for me."

But instantaneity is but one factor of the modernist problem—its essential question addresses the illusion of flatness. Stephan counters that "painting's true space is all the space it is" —an affirmation of the artist's essentially existential and phenomenological attachments.

These, of course, led to the rejection of the progressive or evolutionary character implicit to Greenberg's notion of modernism, the notion of art as a result of a dialectical process. Of course, to reduce Greenberg's historical machinery, to regard the procession toward literal flatness from Manet through the formalist painting of the '60s as merely a progress from illusionistic space to flatness, is to deprive it of its paramount mystical feature, its tacit acceptance of the condition of "quality," a condition that eludes all mechanical use of history. Even for Greenberg, quality is a transcendent inspiriting force fully palpable to the true connoisseur, but invisible to the laity. It is not so much that two pictures may present concordances of flatness, but that despite this concord, one still may note that one space is "better" than the other or "purer" or "finer" or "deeper."

For Stephan, painting is constantly rejective of notions of transcendence, as indifferent to academic norms as to cultural desiderata. Painters are involved (as are all sensitive artists) in the instrumentalization of their work, another way of saying that they keep their options open; but this in itself may yet prove to be simply an updated reprise of the Marxist dialectic necessary to Greenberg, whether one likes it or not. For Stephan, "artists simply find ways of doing things," admitting all the while "that their work is limited by their personality."

Granting this, they ought not (as the expressed intention of painting) engage in "personal production," ought not make "ego-directed choices," ought not "agonize over how the work will 'look' or worry about 'style'." Instead, the enterprise of painting has a kind of inadvertency attached to it. Things all happen "because there is no way for them not to happen." Through sheer repetition of the activity of painting, "the unbidden subtext will emerge anyway, those formal and iconographic considerations through which we recognize an intelligent work."

In a curious way, Stephan seems to be talking about statistical occurrences as a kind of demonstration of formal and iconographic content. He rejects seeing the intention of painting as merely the forcing of their appearance out into the open. When this happens, he speaks of a manifestly "distressingly subtexted picture." Thus painting for Stephan may become a kind of diffident exercise, a pragmatic activity engaged in without an end in view. As activity, it is all filler material. Formal values and iconography happen anyway, so why worry about them?

But all this has led me from The Bykert Problem. Kertess himself came to outgrow, if not resent, his "helpmate" role—the myriad insistent details of "just running" a gallery were, in the end, inimical to his ambition of being a writer. And he closed. At the same time, his attachment to his artists assumed the demands of their own destinies—in Marden's case, to the considerable glamour of the Pace Gallery and its powerful support system. For others, the situation they found themselves in did not prove so easy. The psychological sustenance of just being able to say that one is represented by this or that gallery is an immense aid; this whether or not one's work sells.

The closing of the Bykert Gallery was coincidental with the incipient, turbulent expressionist resurgence, one that I have come to refer to as Maximalism, much of it stimulated out of sheer despair with so long a diet of Reductivist Minimalism. The bridge to this mode, so characteristic of the present moment, led to Mary Boone who, sloughing off Bykert, continued to enlarge her own taste, at length to support the more radical-seeming palimpsests of Schnabel and Salle and other Maximalist Neo-Expressionists.

Perhaps, by way of conclusion, a word separating Stephan from Schnabel and Salle is in order—especially after having forged so specious a link between them. The fundamental differences between Stephan and the others is primarily one of generational attitude. Stephan's first convincing style comes to fruition within a Minimalist frame of reference, theirs in a Postminimalist. Thus, there must be between them—on an artistic level—a profound antagonism. Stephan, like the other artists who matured when he did, can easily, naturally embrace the history of art.

He can feel his work, in some sense, to be in continuity with it, can feel his work, in some natural way, to continue a self-aware tradition of high art, and can view this continuity as normal, associated with the grand epochs and great figures of the textbooks. In short, he can feel at ease in drawing connections between his work and the artists and heroic "isms" of early modernism—especially Mondrian, Malevich, Suprematism, de Stijl—and so on.

By contrast, generally speaking, this cultural baggage provides a kind of embarrassment, in both senses, of riches and emotional disturbance, to the younger painters. They feel, in some measure, ill at ease, a certain bad faith at the seeming pretensions of such adduced associations. Of course, words like "bad faith" or "embarrassment" say nothing of quality. Both Salle and Schnabel, not to mention other generational compeers, are quite simply superb painters. My words are meant to speak to a certain cast of mind, a position of awkwardness vis-à-vis a cultural history that, after all, has the effect of generating compensatory systems of ratiocination, a need to justify their arts and actions in ways that are far less than convincing than the art itself. By contrast, the sovereign security of their painting is never in doubt.

In further contrast, Stephan does not believe in a generalized imagery of fractured and dispersed subject matter, but of highly specific and reduced information. His painting is not bidden by the democratizing visual gambits ultimately ratified in the Combine Paintings of Rauschenberg. Stephan celebrates his sense of profound continuity with tradition, his emotional ease with the past. "I want to reassert a sense of Mission. They," meaning the Postminimalists and Maximalists, "need to cover their sense of shame about tradition through visual sarcasm. I wish I could feel what they feel. I wish I, too, could feel free of history. But, I'm not free of it, so I have to take it all in and still hope to make 'normal objects'—we call them paintings—objects that sit comfortably with the facts of themselves."

Figure 82. Gary Stephan, *The Agony in the Garden*, 1981
Acrylic on canvas, 90″ × 48″.
(Photo courtesy Mary Boone Gallery)

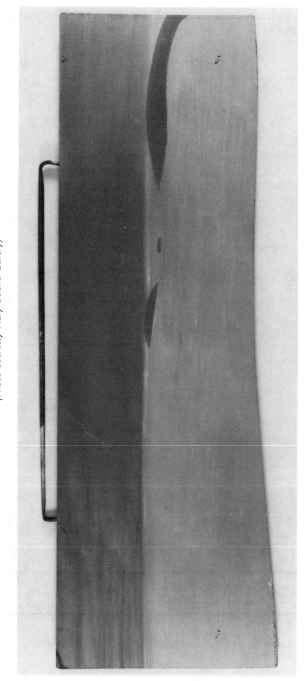

Figure 83. Gary Stephan, *Magic Motor Boat*, 1966
Oil on masonite, 21"×61".
(Photo courtesy Mary Boone Gallery)

Figure 84. Gary Stephan, *Pink*, 1975
Acrylic on jute, 68" × 92".
(Photo courtesy Mary Boone Gallery)

Gary Stephan: The Utopian Paintings

I visited Gary Stephan's studio at the extreme western end of Canal Street. His painting moves from strength to strength. Gary has become one of the few remaining credible abstractionists. In reaction to this isolation, Gary is strongly disturbed—as am I—by the threatened status of abstraction today, especially after what seemed its vanquishing triumphs of only a day before yesterday.

At the moment, Stephan's new work adopts the general Constructivist drift of the 1930s. After the initial struggle-to-purity from their impure cubist origins, both analytical and representational, the Constructivists (particularly in the USSR and in the work of their enthusiastic Italian and German followers) came to see that their work signalled a utopian vision. This was a far richer signification than the hangover aestheticism from before World War I critically allowed for—though clearly 1912–14 is the source as much for them as it still is for Stephan.

The origins of Stephan's new constructed canvases, the Utopian Paintings, derive from small watercolor drawings based on the shape of a tumbler that for all the world look as if painted by Malevich in his allogistic phase (1913–14) or by Alexandra Exter or Ivan Puni. When Stephan extrapolated these watercolors into large scale, he discovered them to be paintings through their very making. In so doing, the primordial cubist motif of the container all but disappears, enlarges even to include the utopian referentiality to the period Between The Two Wars. Prampolini gets dragged in, El Lissitsky, Domela, Moholy-Nagy. You see the stylistic idiom (fig. 85).

As always, Gary is a superb colorist. Before, I naively imagined that it was possible for a painter to be a bad colorist and still make good paintings: Munch, say, was the paradigm. Now, with the Utopian Paintings under my eyes, I see that if the painting was good, the color had been good all along—no matter whose. Even Munch's.

An irony: we took up the case of Mondrian. Presumably, Mondrian is an anticolorist, a murderer of color—a view drawn from the inexorable conclusions of an exigently applied reductivism which at length resulted in Mondrian's acceptance of only the primary triad. This paring down to red and yellow and blue (plus black

This article originally appeared in the catalogue for the exhibition, *Gary Stephan: Recent Painting and Sculpture* (New York City, Marlborough Gallery, September–October 1984).

and white) permitted Mondrian to resolve the issues of color on a practical level since all color theoretically exists in permutations of the primary triad. In Mondrian's work, then, color functions as theoretical signifier of a range of transcendental subject matter while it avoids the mine-field of color perceived as associative stimuli.

Yet, Gary's engrammatic commitment to color (as to all visual elements) allows Mondrian to be perceived as a colorist, even in Gary's sense because, after all, *De Stijl* color "works; it does the job." For Gary, color remains the organizing force of the picture, as color is "also productive of the picture space. If things don't work out, aren't 'operational' then you're screwed; you're making flat pictures, designs."

Of course, by now, Gary's early coloristic gifts have been modified by the sheer evolution of his painting, and for the moment, everything he touches succeeds. Early on, Stephan's evocative color signified ranges of sentimental association—the early Mediterranean palette. But now he is no longer working with a "psychology that permitted the shape to sit there. Now, the beauty is to open up the color" whether the range is dank and murky or lurid and technologically pearlescent. In any case, his work no longer addresses color as a sign system for nostalgia.

I suppose this change occurred with the advent of the dark pictures a few years ago, the ones he calls the "torso paintings." (ca. 1980) when, "in darkening down," he realized that he could "drain the color cues out."

Now, Stephan's Utopian Paintings are pieced-together canvases, abutments worked out naturally while painting, that one could call sculpture/paintings—reliefs. One must never forget that, despite his mind-set as a painter born, there is built into Gary's pictorial evolution a compelling body of sculpture. The problem of sculpture, particularly as it is informed by pictorial issues, is part and parcel of Gary's concerns (fig. 86). Though discreet in number, one could without misrepresentation meaningfully survey his sculpture from the earliest hand-hidden talismans to the large expositiory constructions that keep pace with his recent paintings.

In this loss of discretion between painting and sculpture, Stephan asserts affiliation to all utopian ambitions, especially when the utopian and the visionary are experienced in a continuum. This assertion is as true for van Gogh as for Moholy-Nagy despite their clearly antithetical purposes.

That's one argument. Another would be the pettiness of the commitment to formal species for the modernist—as arbitrary for Matisse as for Picasso. Naturally, Clement Greenberg would have it otherwise despite even his purist capitulation in the case of David Smith, but Greenberg's bluff (if I may thus characterize it) has already been called in Stephan's painting and has been amply challenged by Stephan's work.

Last, the conflation of painting and sculpture—its telescoping into a single pictorial/sculptural presentation—is one hallmark of early Postminimalism, the banner under which Stephan first emerged. For sure, the Utopian Paintings are the neurologically convincing works, the engrammic canvases of the deep brain waves that Stephan defended in the "Brief against Matisse." They are, that is, "totally convincing objects, rendered events functioning in space whose timing is right." As a result, "you can't escape the color."

In part, Gary traces the history of his color to what in the nineteenth century was called "normal" painting—well, he calls it that—the local color of the depicted elements of representational painting. Within the abstract tradition, let alone its Constructivist update, there is no word for this kind of color, for color used this way, though "operational," the one suggested by Will Mentor, his studio assistant, will do as it conveys a sense of the instrumentalization of color.

Gary has a gift for the pedagogic; he's a born teacher. His conversation is a suite of astute aphorisms. For example, he contrasts "the optical tradition" (of which he sees himself a part) with "the cultural tradition," a contrast he esteems as being "incredibly simple." The former he traces back to El Greco (and now with the new work making references to Carpaccio, I expect he'll extend it back to Venice and the 1500s).

El Greco to Goya to Picasso—all that is made in easy conversational leaps. All he wants to say is that these painters "slightly screw things around; they made the shadows too big or they lighted things evenly." He is just talking studio talk, verbalizing impressions garnered helter-skelter from just looking at things and trying to convey quickly the impressions thus gainsaid. He might as easily refer to any formal detail, but at this moment, these are the ones that came to mind. Such stimuli are, for him, countered by "how an object sits in culture, the cultural tradition." This latter mesh of clues infers issues which are not formal; that is, those that reference all the ironic codes of civilization, perhaps even the unconscious and the psyche. In short, he draws a contrast between the effects of seeing and those of reading. Those of seeing are "operational" and, for him, represent the neural tradition. The other clues, the cultural clues, derive from reading. They lead to irony.

Gary seemed pleased with my attempt to place him with a kind of pragmatic latter day de-aestheticised Cubism. And beyond Cubism with Surrealism, though the reference may seem startling. Owing to the intellectual force of Greenberg's proscription of Surrealism from the presumably mainstream formalist agenda, the movement was stigmatized for nearly forty years. As a result, one failed to see that Surrealism—at least, that part of it signalling social liberation in the manner of Trotsky (according to Breton)—and Cubism already had fused in the 1930s by way of fortifying one another in the struggle against Fascism. This amalgam forms the historical model against which Stephan's fresh reassimilation of these positions may be measured.

Little did I guess that I had stumbled into a pet three-part categorization he uses to discuss painters. The first type are those whose work signifies the past: "pictures of desire and longing for a lost beauty" —Morandi, say, or Balthus. Then, there are the painters of the present who "paint their time," such as Rosenquist or Lichtenstein: "They are looking for the texture of how the world feels now." Last, there are the painters of the future, the Utopians, "the painters of the visionary. The importance of that vision lies in the attempt. It is the attempt that counts, not necessarily the success." Stephan believes, and so do I, that "painting can take us forward. The big American paintings of the fifties are like that, optimistic."

Figure 85. Gary Stephan, *Where the Animal Can Go*, 1984
Acrylic on linen, 84"×144".
(Photo courtesy Mary Boone Gallery)

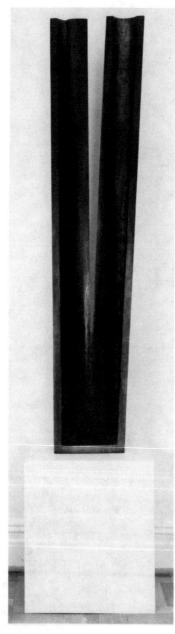

Figure 86.   Gary Stephan, *Untitled #1 Cast*, 1982
Aluminum, 72″×14″×5″.
(Photo courtesy Mary Boone Gallery)

Lucio Pozzi:
The Continence of Lucio

13 November 1977

Pozzi = wells; Pazzi = Crazies. The Window Series of P.S.1 = Lucio (light), Pozzi (wells) = Wells of Light (Lucius Wells?); or are these wells of light a crazy version, a spectacular Pazzi Chapel (figs. 87 and 88)?

Born to a family of the high bourgeoisie whose now-reduced fortune originally was based in North Italian textile production. Four generations of Ajroldi-Pozzi forebears: his great-grandmother wove beautifully and set up a single loom. She took on a girl and a second loom; at length, six girls, six looms, and then a dozen of each. During the grand paternal generation, industrialization. In a short decade, Pozzi's grandfather on his mother's side rose from sales representative to administrator (among other things) of the Teatro alla Scala in Milan, dying before the war and the destruction of the opera house during the Allied bombing of Milan.

An isolated, awkward teenager, the artist first saw himself as a poet in the manner of a bilingual Verlaine; there was a lot of il-pleut-dans-mon-coeur-stuff, and the ardent, if blaspheming Catholicism typical of the style—lyric, ejaculatory appeals to Gesù Gesù.

Pozzi's mother Ida, deeply artistic, perhaps was embarrassed by her gifts and, as a good bourgeoise, while dissipating energy, always made substantial contributions along the way. She founded, for example, a circulating library, Il Carosello, in Milan following the war, bringing home a wide circle of literati who encouraged the youth to continue on as a poet.

Lucio Pozzi's studies were disastrous. For all his denials, though, the humanist traditions of North Italy are still the bases of the artist's wide-ranging cultural referents. The dormitory of his boarding school is still clear in his mind and remains a kind of Pozzi *in petto*—a room of a nineteenth-century villa in the Renaissance style, a bare room; outside the window stands a mimosa tree, brilliant yellow in its springtime bloom—and beyond that, the blue Gulf of Genoa. All simple, direct, urgent. Like

---

This article originally appeared in *Arts Magazine*, March 1980.

a Pozzi. On one wall of this room are the art postcards published by the Galleria il Milione, after the work of early twentieth-century European masters—as you might expect, but Arthur Dove and Marsden Hartley, too—abstract, ideogrammatic, compelling scrupulous examination from the young boy.

Pozzi's first pictures were made during a childhood quarantine when downed with scarlet fever. His nurse, by way of diversion, showed him how to paste collages together and to paint in watercolor, the latter a medium he has never abandoned.

Then, too, there was the extraordinary sideswipe of the Scottish sculptor, Michael Noble, the artist's mother's second husband. Noble opened the family's villa in Lago di Garda to friends from his Paris days, friends from the Diaghilev circle and the ballet generally—Russian emigrés such as Igor Markevitch or Boris Kochno. Pozzi remembers his first abstract gouache attempted an ideogram of a ballet dancer, abstracting along the simplifying lines to be seen in Noble's sculpture. This ideogrammatic side of things also has a curious connection to Balla, a not gratuitous linkage as will be seen.

Noble's associations with Italian art, too, brought Pozzi into intimacy with the traditions of Italian Modernism. Especially close to the household was Noble's dealer Ghiringhelli, then the director of the Galleria il Milione. On one hand, the latter defended the traditions of classicism associated with the Scuola Metafisica—at this date Morandi was its great exemplar, having supplanted the vulgar late de Chiricio (fig. 89). Ghiringhelli championed the experimentalism of Futurists of all stamp, Sironi say, or Magnelli, even late Severini—the latter phase of Futurism so contrarily and perplexingly absorbed into the classicistic character of Italian art of 1920s through the '40s, into the work of the *Novecentisti,* that is the "Painters of the 1900s" (as Sironi and his colleagues were called by the Fascists); or even more importantly, the great sculptor Arturo Martini, whose work afforded Noble a model for his own fusion of Moore and Giacometti; a not antithetical mix, when you think about it. Then, too, Ghiringhelli was aware of aspects of the *informel* developing in Paris following World War II, leaning more naturally to De Staël rather than to the Fautrier side of the question but *informel* for all that.

Ghiringhelli always found an hour to visit the young painter, telling him how he remembered Kandinsky would move a brush— "like so," doing it Kandinsky's way (since he had been a friend as well as a painter in his own right); or how Morandi would put down a color or make a line— "like so." All this was un-self-consciously performed, just part of the distractions of the household, slightly amateurish even, if you see what I mean.

Still, in all of this Chekhov-like indolence ran a serious strand. Noble and Pozzi's father, after whom the artist is named, believed in the supremacy of drawing (for quite different reasons), of the importance of conquering anatomy and perspective, that kind of thing. Thus, for all the advancement of the experimental espoused in the villa, there would also be that solid understructure so typical of an early Modernist view of abstraction—its derivation, that is, from a design-oriented simplification of nature strictly observed. The traditional strain of a businessman-father naturally would lead him to believe that his son's development as an artist should also be made along conservative lines. So Pozzi, ardent in everything, lived with a human skeleton in his bedroom, drawing the bone structure and inventing the concomitant musculature.

As a young man then, Pozzi's cultural fusion was that of all high *liceo classico* culture, one marked by a lyric expressivity far deeper than that permitted by the social norms in which it was set. This "Leopardismo," if it may be called this, is shaped by the recalcitrant tradition of Pozzi's Lombard forebears; culture was humanist, understated, liberal, consciously resisting the ultra-montane traditions of Catholic Letters. It maintained a quasi-heretical stance, blonde in its darkness, Protestant, Arabizing (in the manner of Averroës) if not even a kind of Hebraicising Catholicism. (That Pozzi's son—he also has a daughter, Eve-Anna ["Nina"]—would one day be called Giordano after Giordano Bruno is what I mean—classical, mystical, heretical; it's all there—the spiritual forebear of Spinoza martyred by the Church for what we today recognize as an early expression, however mystical and heretic, of the modern tradition of philosophical inquiry.)

At twenty, Pozzi began to break from his family, enlisting in officer's training school, a choice based on class and costume—officer's white gloves, you see. His military service enlarged the range of his national awareness, lessening the emphasis on the Lombard and the Milanese, pushing him into the Roman arena. It was necessarily South Italian too, a kind of inescapable earthy testing that the experience of the military reinforces.

Since officers were allowed greater freedom, Pozzi's architectural studies began at this time as well. They were highly colored by the nascent *Partito Radicale,* a movement particularly felt in the Italian architectural schools of the day. The *Partito,* to all intents and purposes, directed the national student movement. It was in the architectural schools that the early rebellions—culminating in the uprising of 1968—were first manifested. An early student rebel, Pozzi and a fellow architecture student once refused, for example, to execute a simple Beaux-Arts rendition of a column in a Greek order. Pozzi and his comrade insisted that the social symbolism of the exercise be disclosed prior to making the drawing.

During the years of his architectural studies, Pozzi was a founding organizer of a co-operative of graphic designers whose ambition was to improve society through the solution of graphic design problems—the models of Werkbund, Bauhaus, not to say Kelmscott and Jugendstil run before him in this systematic utopianism. Pozzi grasped his elitism a bit better when the text of his first poster (one set upside-down) was merely shorn off by the socialist cadres to which it has been sent. Pozzi had intended that, when inverted and alternated, the poster would form a new coherent mural-like sequence. The Socialists merely thought that the line of propaganda had been incorrectly set and printed.

In Rome, too, he discovered that he was persona-grata in the city's literary and artistic community—Moravia, Elsa Morante, the young Pasolini. Pozzi's first wife's family, distant Sicilian nobility, moved more or less in the same social sphere of his own, and the marriage, though it at length failed, was at first thought to be quite perfect.

His mother-in-law, Topazia Alliata, had opened the Galleria Trastevere, one of the period's most advanced galleries. Ambivalent about the Italian *informel*, she went so far as to scandalize her artists by showing, say, the young Piero Manzoni, just beginning an intensely iconoclast career, one that in its own way despised painters and painting, that is, despised all that Pozzi was drawn to and believed in—as he continues to believe—despite all his curious philosophical detachment from conventions surrounding painting as an end.

It was the Trastevere that Lawrence Alloway, then the ambitious director of the Institute of Contemporary Art in London, brought the young English painters who worked around William Turnbull—Marc Vaux and Gillian Ayres among others—painters who had absorbed the influence of Rothko, Newman, and Kelly before Italian painters had availed themselves of these now preeminent models. Pozzi's lean and simple solutions led him directly to Kelly's work, because they were both working at a point of extreme simplicity, though in disparate ways; and when at last in the United States, Pozzi sought out Leon Polk Smith, still one of the least appreciated American abstractionists, though one always championed by Alloway.

Pozzi's world then was curiously schizzy. On one hand were the literati whom he frequented—naturally dominated by Moravia. The latter intensified the artist's social conscience, informing Pozzi, as best he could, of the Italian role in the Holocaust. The literati all read Wittgenstein and Adorno. Then there were the architects: always sloganeering, theoretically and philosophically inclined. Their catch-phrases of Heisenberg's indeterminacy and the mathematics of Gödel also provided for a new emphasis on aleatory structure. But architecture then mostly meant "urban design," while aleatory meant music.

Through all of this Pozzi intensified a penchant for all things American. Always a passionate enthusiast of jazz, he now discovered the "indeterminacy" of Cage, which he regarded as a type of "indeterminate seriality" (if there can be such a thing) paralleling the musical seriality of Karl-Heinz Stockhausen. He recalls an under-populated Festival di Venezia when he was one of the rare audience members to remain to the end of David Tudor's and John Cage's concert of the latter's music. He realized then that his lot was to be cast with the Americans, slowly abandoning a community and a society that he came to recognize really had despised painting despite lip service. By 1962 he had tentatively set himself up in his first New York studio on 4th Street and Second Avenue.

The earliest work Pozzi felt secure enough to exhibit publicly was painted at the end of the fifties. These works, large by contemporary Italian standards, hence "American," were broadly brushed simple arrangements. Often as not, these emblemlike configurations were so thinly painted as to reveal bristly striations of stroke and wash. In this sense, they are not without a certain oriental cast.

At the time, Pozzi was committed to a bright, emblematic figure, so large a figure in fact, that the even larger format of the canvas seemed to cut the compositions arbitrarily. The painting is marked by a sense of scale, a flat designer-like configuration, an impertinent color, and in an occasionally soft-modulated profile, an organic connection. Works of this type were shown in 1963 at the Galleria l'Indice in Milan. Oddly, had these works any creamy thickness they could bear comparison with contemporary paintings by Al Held, those swelling variations on geometric shapes that occupied Held until he forswore the use of color in 1967.

A curious subtheme of Pozzi's essentially Abstract-Expressionist position at the turn of the decade is to be found in simple constructions based on prefab-modular components, cast-iron pipes, say. Presciently, Pozzi sought to contrast "very much of something"—that is, the big painterly canvas—"against very little of something else"—the painted pipe sections. And in so doing he stumbled, as it were, into a kind of talismanic minimalism, the private reductivism of, say, certain very early objects of Judd, LeWitt, even Bochner, not to mention even more obvious affiliations to Tuttle. All of this will be clearer much after the fact; at this point, I believe these odd private objects serve a kind of neutralizing, even possibly curative role vis-à-vis the public, clamorous character of the artist's preeminently painterly concerns.

In 1964, the year Pozzi definitively settled in New York City, the abstract painting continued apace, scale and tart color anticipatably still in the forefront. At this point, the first biomorphic stirrings adumbrated in the earliest shown paintings become a fully-explored, even intentionally vulgar transposition of Surrealist biomorphic accretions, ranging in character, say, from the high art associations of Arp to the down-home biomorphic aggressiveness of Walt Disney (or earlier, the animistic cartooning of Charles Burchfield) (fig. 90). This shift was facilitated by the period's most characteristic change of medium—the giving up of oil paint for acrylics, the physical properties of which allowed for the broad biomorphic resurgence in painting at the time.

By 1968, impeded by the despairing turn taken in the world at the time, Pozzi, like many, abandoned large-scale painting, giving over most of his energies to teaching and to the small, notational watercolors he had always kept as a kind of picture album of his life. In the last months of the year, the scale of Pozzi's work diminished radically. Rejecting acrylics as somehow basely materialistic and inculpated by the Failure of the American Imperial adventure of the day, Pozzi's last works were tiny gouaches whose shapes were somehow lost in gray fields. These feckless, vestigial elements were "left-over" after the "very little against very much." In a certain sense, as the imagery had diminished to near nothing, so too had Pozzi's idea of painting itself. But if diminished, it was still there, near dormant. The painter had not really fully accepted the prevailing studio cant of the day, one that precluded painting at all.

It can hardly come as a surprise to those who follow the sequence of contemporary art that 1968 represents a most novel and critical fulcrum for the shift in priorities of sculpture and painting—as important as, say, 1912 or 1947. It is then, and for the subsequent four years or so, that the classical figures of Postminimalism were producing their most recalcitrant and unyielding work. At this most critical juncture, Pozzi too felt that painting as it hitherto had been known was somehow ethically inadequate, an insufficient position. And like most, he too has by now returned to a less distressed anxiety about painting as such, so that what is presented in his paintings today seemingly may be assessed according to more conventionalized systems of appreciation. The widespread resurgence of painting that we associate with the present moment, though, is of a quite different order in the case of artists of an initially conceptual bent from those paintings which derive in an unbroken line from the easel conventions of modern formalism. The latter stand quite nakedly as merely a new academy; the former must be seen as an expression of a continuing if deeply modified organic relationship to its conceptual origins, rather than as merely more "painted things" in the world.

Among the provocations so indicative of the post-minimalist break of 1968–72 is the emergence of a behavioral and performance-oriented manifestations. By April of 1971, Pozzi found himself at the turbulent center of this startling development.

In connection with an exhibition of paintings held in Italy, Pozzi created an aesthetically polarized situation. Six close-valued taciturn works were countered by six strong declarative performance operations in two adjacent spaces at the Galleria dell'Ariete in Milan. "I don't mix incompatibilities—I just juxtapose them."

Whereas the New York vanguard had already been startled by a wide array of performance-oriented art (Vito Acconci above all, which in part continued the submerged tradition of the Happenings of the 1950s), Italian manifestations had lost touch with the protean originator of the Happening, the Futurist performance. Perhaps the need for Performance Art in Italy, that is, from a certain ironic viewpoint, unexpectedly had been answered by an intense political life played out in the street, workers' manifestations of all kinds, not to mention the linked kidnappings— political or brutishly extortionary—and in the end the assassinations. Nothing like this disturbed the admittedly jarring streets of New York.

As it happened, Pozzi's performance pieces in Milan coincided with the first judicial assassination there (fig. 91). Pozzi's personal, even quietistic, performance (suggestive perhaps of the role that George Brecht played in contemporary *Fluxus* performance in Germany and France) was announced as a public execution, a civil killing symbolized through the modest gesture of dropping a red carnation after an actor/victim was shot with a blank cartridge. Needless to say, the agitated state of the police led to Pozzi's arrest and jailing. After two days of friendly phone calls between family friends, Pozzi was released and he resumed the announced performance activities—to paint in the gallery "on order" and to sell the results for a dollar apiece; or, in homage to Hans Haacke, to request gallery visitors to fill out questionnaires about their attitudes toward Nature, Art, Politics, and Sex. All this activity and its considerable multiplication over the next few years was part of Pozzi's need "to do as many things as possible different from painting—to show painting as just another thing—yet always to refer to painting."

Truthfully, the juxtaposition of performance and straight academic abstraction was not especially popular at the time. It still isn't, since the work was neither sanctioned by painters nor the nascent conceptualists either in Europe or in New York City. Pozzi's dismissal by these various groupings, the condescending silence that marked the reception of his work, further intensified his commitment to a perhaps untenable position, merging also, perhaps, with a certain undertone of reactive criticism that marks his work to the present. That painting and performance-type activity did not seem to marry well in the studio context and not at all in the gallery—this confrontational mésalliance—perversely was agreeable to the artist in the degree that he felt that "Things just belong to each other without having to worry about whether they ever did."

But the irresolution nonetheless sparked a period of retrenchment, even a kind of continence during the very period of the most radical art activity in New York, an activity of which Pozzi's work is a very natural product and expression. In 1971 Pozzi, who had been teaching at the Cooper Union, organized a structured performance activity of 29 nude models. The work, played throughout the institution, was highly nervy and set up in a gamelike way with Pozzi calling the shots. If Duchamp's *Nude Descending a Staircase* is annunciatory of the death of painting, as it is said to be, then *"'29 Models' Descending an Art School Staircase"* (fig. 92) is an even greater multiple of calamitous absurdity. At length, Pozzi was asked to leave the faculty, though he now teaches in the perhaps more anarchic ambience of the School of Visual Arts. These encounters with the conceptual granted, Pozzi's main preoccupation remained dedicated to a kind of painting in which aesthetic decisions could be so systematized as to be the source of aesthetic itself.

It sounds as if I'm making Pozzi out to be a Heisenberg-derived epistemologist. Certainly something of the case is true, but at the same time far off course. Pozzi's work insofar as it has been a source of controversy was taken to be a function of reductivist sensibility marked by a personal color and small talismanic organization.

During the early '70s when Pozzi unrepentantly resumed a painting that had paralleled his other work all the time, he was taken to be part of a vague coalition of quasi-unreconstructed painters who, after having been told that painting was dead, continued, for all that, to paint, admittedly in a flat, self-effacing, quietistic way. Several artists belonged to this group, insofar as it ever was a group. Michael Goldberg, the elder figure of this loose coalition, talked about the group as a group, but Pozzi, having experienced first-hand in Italy the twisting to self-service of Marxist idealist architectural theory, felt the incipient move to institutionalize was coercive. Pozzi is a Marxist but not a populist. Not that he would not contribute to a public awareness of this new, scarcely viable position. Writing for the Italian art journal, *Bolaffi Arte* (under the pseudonym Peter Licht; Peter the stone, Licht the light—the reversal of his initials), Pozzi contributed three important, lavishly illustrated articles during a short career as a critic. The articles, published over a three-year period, 1972–75 addressed the three main trends that Pozzi thought the most emblematic directions to have emerged in painting following the ructions of the '60s: the advent of Photo-

Realism, the flat painters (who largely formed the circle of his friends and closer acquaintances), and a last one dealing with certain eccentric, non-flat painters with whom he was also associating. In a sense, these articles were written from a position of self-defense, insofar as they went against the still prevailing notion of painting's demise as incipient or as a *fait accompli.*

Among the figures of the amalgam were Ron Gorchov, Pozzi himself, Michael Goldberg, Paul Mogenson, a smattering of the younger painters from the Klaus Kertess stable—Lynn Umlauf, Judy Rifka, Doug Sanderson, Susanna Tanger. Since the exact nature of the correlations between the members remain irretrievable, except insofar as they believed in painting, however vestigial a painting it may be— one really can't see them fully as a distinct stylistic group, certainly without stretching credulity. At least some of them were drawn to the elementary logic and dualistic structures of the axioms of Bochner and Rockburne; but they pondered why these propositions had to be applied at the expense of the hand. (Indeed in the end they weren't.) This vague sense of community led to the opening of links with a broad set of artists bridging out from a scarcely definable core. Pozzi, showing at Bykert, was introduced to Paul Mogenson and Eve Sonneman (the photographer). Lynn Umlauf, then supplementing her income through cooking in the burgeoning bars and restaurants of SoHo, drew in the younger figures of the 112 Greene Street Co-operative—Richard Nonas, Jene Highstein, Suzanne Harris, and Gordon Matta-Clark of the Anarchitecture group. There were others too: Denise Green, Jim Bishop, Joel Shapiro, Marcia Hafif, Jeremy Gilbert-Rolfe. For sure I miss some. In short, taking into account the broad network of SoHo gallery and social affiliations, Pozzi found himself, for better or for worse, at the center of what was taken to be a nexus of sensibility-oriented epistemologists—or, if you like, of a yet more recent school of information-oriented abstract painters, whose work was marked by the modest scale of Tuttle's personalistic ineffable art. By 1975, all of this opened up, boomed as it were, and it is scarcely possible, even at this short remove, to imagine that so divergent a group of painters, sculptors, and even photographers might have thought themselves to have formed even a transient coalition. "Look Robert, the sequence is so," Pozzi says to me about his work, pushing his closed hands forward across the table top. "Until 1975 it looked like this and then, after 1975," —opening all his fingers— "it looks like this."

For all the eccentricity of Pozzi's career, there is an artist who might serve as emblem—Giacomo Balla (1871–1958). Like Pozzi, Balla's career also seems a suite of brilliant disconnections, even more surprising for its antedating World War I: *The Stairway of Farewells, The Young Girl Running on a Balcony, The Path of Swifts,* the full abstraction of the *Iridescent Interpenetrations.* Naturally, a cohering thread runs through all of this, the search for a Futurist Sign of Energy in an Environment. But, taken as a whole, Balla's work appears to lack an organic growth toward consistent manual felicity (often misconstrued as the touchstone of art). Instead, Balla offers the constant thread of style as inconsistency. Pozzi's art is also marked by his horror of formula, a distaste for what he calls the "bureaucratic" character of style manifested through "predictability" and/or "precodification." Relentlessly William James-like, Pozzi deducts empirically from experience, rather than from any larger metaphysical or abstract ambitions. Despite this, Pozzi admits that this kind of empiricism also invokes "an order of approach, that of change even, which is itself capable of becoming its own kind of norm." Such "norms" signal, for Pozzi, moments of "cultural alert" because they so easily play into the demands and appetites of the publicity media. In reacting against these "norms," fresh artistic moves are postulated—else the artist achieves no more than the shoring up of a merely normative or frozen style. The norm then may be seen as a kind of rule that in turn indicates the tool, a methodological mechanism or a path of discovery. In acting on the fresh impulse provoked by the norm, the utopian dream of public and private reintegration once more may be affirmed in the artist's work: "With rules come the state of emergency; with tools come the state of discovery."

Still, intentionality—even when expressed as an intention to reject style—is no guarantee of art, though in the end it may be all there is to Pozzi's art. Said simply, Pozzi views art making as "just doing," granting the continuing examination of the basic experience of the visuality we call painting. But we misapprehend Pozzi when we do not perceive the links binding Pozzi's art episodes together—however distant one component may be from the others. These bonds may take the form of

> . . . imitation; force of gravity; the incorporation of accidents and context; dualisms, simple or multiplied; adding; removing; translations or transpositions from one medium to another, the six basic colors of painting mixed or alone; the arranging of information in clusters and series (progressive or constant); patterns, either regular (grids) or irregular (textures); and an awareness that any elements can be combined so that density, distance and contrast, both within and without, are detectable and describable. These mechanisms are the base from which fantasy, intuition and experimentation can start off in unpredictable directions.
>
> (Lucio Pozzi, "Letter to Peder Bonnier," 28 July 1979; edited by Peter Zabielskis)

Pozzi's definitions of painting are exemplary for an absence of metaphysical posturing; for example, "Color transforms something which is something else and makes it look different"; or, "Painting is something that makes sense but is not logical." Of course, the absence of expressed intention may be, in its most extenuated sense, a form of intentionality leading to no error, no mistake, no slip-up, everything as it happens, hence on purpose.

In the degree that such a philosophical premise is even possible, Pozzi may be said to embrace, as Balla had before him, unintentionality as a model. Yet to call upon historical models or artistic paradigms abrades Pozzi's nuanced views. Rather, he seeks reconciliation with a certain strand of indecision and ambiguity in Modernist history. For Pozzi, the drift toward sheer ambiguity in art-making begins in the first assemblages, in the initial pictorial-sculptural conflation that took place in Picasso's painted constructions of 1912–14. This episode is uniquely heroic for Pozzi. The Synthetic Cubist assemblage—an addition to what it does do—also stresses elements that escape artistic control and volition. This places art-making in a position open to "deconditioning forces" or "uncontrolled properties." Thus, it is easy to grasp Pozzi's view that the Synthetic Cubist assemblage generated, in large part, the automatism of Dada and Surrealism. This "other tradition" of 20th-century art is the one to which Pozzi feels drawn, though never in an iconographic sense, only in a process sense. This evolution, strung out to the present, goes far in explaining Pozzi's identification with the elaborate paradoxes of John Cage and Jasper Johns.

This last development toward the third avenue—that of Johns, Cage, Rauschenberg, Cunningham, etc.—is far more culturally linked in Pozzi's case than might be expected. Pozzi arrived in the United States as both European and pilgrim. As the one, he is marked by a liberating nostalgia for something given up, eschewed— and in being given up, being liberated; as the other, that is, as pilgrim, Pozzi actively, participationally, sought the new condition of exile—one that studiously rejected an inquisitory Marxist stance—especially that of a declaration of intention enunciated prior to invention. Not only did Pozzi's ingrained Marxism fall away from him here, but so too did the Futurist-Marxist model of perpetual revolution—since, for example, the Futurist manifestos jumping the gun on their superannuation had become for Pozzi merely a new set of encyclicals.

Four culprits of rationality stand indicted in Pozzi's fine-slicing shredder: Modern novelty, Romantic object making, the Renaissance commodity fetish, and, in the grandest indictment of all, the broadest plaits of European rationality, be they Socratic, Aristotelian, or Platonic. All this was shucked off in the name of another rationality perceived by Pozzi, one that seeks a more authentic level of visuality, form in its more pristine expression.

This, of course, brings one full cycle, to those very qualities that mark Pozzi's work as being so thoroughly "European": its richness of contradiction and incongruity, its Mannerism and the concomitant sense of elegance germane to mannerism. Elegance implies, more than anything else, an awareness of the contradictions and paradox inhering to all human activity. Still, though the sensibility may be European, its self-evident pragmatism is utterly rooted in the traditions of American philosophy—in short, the work could only have happened here, in New York, at a certain compelling moment of recent New York history (fig. 93).

Of course, it is impossible finally to say how or why it is that artists might find themselves in such a position. Little trite phrases disguise or minimize Pozzi's obli- quity: he "feels good" in paradox, he "feels authentic" in it. Mind you, Pozzi is marked by the heroic years of the American hegemony; and emerging in the salad days of early Postminimalism, "elegance" is a difficult term of admission for him despite the manifest elegance of his work. Still, we can stay with Pozzi's evasive conversa- tional gambits a bit longer, since the sentiments of "feeling good" and "authenticity" in Pozzi's usage are liable of yet greater repercussion. Such existential clichés in his terms imply an historical assessment. The artist—Pozzi really—is "a fine instrument in the culture who disallows the norms that play into the media." From 1965 on, then, one sees how clearly Pozzi evaded the pre-digested cliché insofar as there appears to be no formal consistency locatable to a coherent methodology. Yet the method for all that remains consistent. So too does the infinity of corollaries—Pozzi's art, that is—that forms the fallout of this syllogism.

Figure 87. Lucio Pozzi, *Four Windows*, Detail, Installation at P.S.1, 1976–77
Sheetrock, wood, 4 chairs, paint, 12′×28′×12′.
(Photo courtesy the artist)

Figure 88. Lucio Pozzi, *Four Windows*, Detail, Installation at P.S.1, 1976–77

Figure 89. Giorgio de Chirico, *The Return of Ulysses*, 1968
Oil on canvas, 23-1/2" × 31-1/2".
(Photo courtesy Robert Miller Gallery)

Figure 90.   Lucio Pozzi, *Moon's Hook*, 1967
Acrylic on canvas, 77-1/2"×64".
(Photo courtesy the artist)

Figure 91.   Lucio Pozzi, *Shootout #1 (Execution)*, 1971
Performance, Milan.
(Photo courtesy the artist)

Figure 92. Lucio Pozzi, *29 Models Descending an Art School Staircase*, 1971
Performance, New York.
(Photo courtesy the artist)

Figure 93.   Lucio Pozzi, *The Migration*, 1981
Oil on canvas, 124″ ×108″.
(Photo courtesy the artist)

The New Irascibles

Defenestrations:
Robert Longo and Ross Bleckner

4 March 1982

Imagine, people believe in the difference between Modernism and Post-Modernism. All bright young sets claim a difference from preceding gospel—it's truistic. Modernism is an open caliper taking the measure of all within, even Post-Modernism.

Still, that young artists may feel, do feel, different from past artists is important. If they believe in their peculiar focus, say the way the Metro Pictures group refers to their receptivity to an awareness of urban terror, well, fine, even if the dread they point to has a venerable name, paranoia.

The sense of differing consciousness, hence of altered choice, that young artists mouth as a matter of course, and ultimately promote, is a component of all style shifts. *Plus ça change . . .* to invoke the old saw is not waving a flag of obdurate hostility or indifference (as is often the case when an oldtimer appeals to the jaded view). Indeed the belief in the difference is thrilling even as the difference has all the distinguishing features of a conventional avant-garde posture.

It seems little different if Minimalists point to Suprematism as their paradigm and the Metro crowd points to B-movies, *films noirs,* or TV sit-coms from the '50s. Both groups remain the same in that they seek (or is it that it has been sought for them?) earlier sanctions—the one in high art, the other in popular media. In any case, an acute awareness of difference (even when unfounded) does effect style change—if only in this linear way.

31 March 1982

A visit to Robert Longo's loft on South Street, near the Seaport. The loft somehow hangs on even though all around, the city is being dug up or restored, archaeologically excavated. The loft was taken when Longo was part of the Hallwalls crowd (working out of Buffalo)—so many of whom have now begun strong careers in New York: Cindy Sherman, Michael Zwack, et al.

This article originally appeared in *Arts Magazine,* November 1982.

Longo is more rumpled than I imagined he would be, a genial dumpiness that the '50s d.a. haircut does not belie. The Kosuth-like black shirt and pants don't ameliorate this affect. The loft is tightly organized, revealing a tough-minded professional sense of what his work is about and how it will be promoted. Fliers for a yet-to-be-completed movie are available; photographs and slides are quickly accessible. The tall, 8-foot-high drawings upon which his first success was so strongly built are set about, taxing in their close observation as in their execution and very impressive.

Longo's new ambitious sculpture is made of plasticene awaiting its casting in aluminum, perhaps bronze (fig. 94). The plasticene substance is less repellent than usual as the arms and faces of the enormous figure composition have been polished, shining, with a water wiping—indicating a contrast between glossy and matte surface.

The relief is astonishing. About 12 feet wide and 8 high, it fits snugly just below the low loft ceiling. The figures crowd (some 15 or 16 of them) and are engaged in a frozen-time fall and struggle as if they had been "lifted" or extracted from a photograph or film frame. The relief, complex and technically demanding with passages often in full relief, invokes civic architecture of a conservative stamp, of a kind once conventional to academic sculpture. Indeed, ironies about academicism are endemic to this *Real Life* magazine mode. References range from motion pictures to the early Michelangelo battle relief, the Raphael and Caravaggio *Deposition* figurepieces. Not just a lucky guess—Longo mentioned them in conversation.

He has been sweating, at work three months now without break, in order to finish the model in time (the very next morning), for it to be sliced into thirds and cast for a photo-finish inclusion in this year's Dokumenta 7.

The relief, wildly virtuoso, is based on a neighborhood stroll—street smarts—Longo often takes to the Stock Exchange. There he watches the daily Battle of the Business Men as they violently elbow one another on the Exchange floor. It became Corporate Man's Battle of the Centaurs and Lapiths—a fascinating spectacle Longo views from the spectator's gallery. Baroque warfare. Many extravagant passages—a female figure borne aloft in the upper left; a gesticulating kneeling figure in the left; a business man duplicating the Christ of the *Deposition* in the center; the double vertical freestanding arms of combatants in the lower left; violently groping figures wrestling slightly to the left. For sure, spatial and anatomical impossibilities abound and in their excess a Mannerist model is alluded to.

A paperback of New York architectural sculptural ornament is open nearby for easy reference. Longo acknowledges his appreciation of Noguchi's Associated Press Building aluminum relief in Rockefeller Center.

Longo's battle relief is to be set into complex flanking elements—Deco-like views of raking office buildings. The violent perspectival foreshortening suggests not only the Art Deco, but also views of buildings as if seen by someone falling from them, businessmen suicides.

Visiting the hyperbolic Ross Bleckner. A fascinating morning marked by the artist's brilliant rushes of insight and arching metaphor. Bleckner is a crisp assessor of the scene. His art begins to impress itself, to succeed, though often *à rebours*. His is a painting (and a painterliness) that, in a certain sense, may be said to want a certain naturalness, an ease, a fluency. Of course, I'm wrong. It's not that Bleckner wants a gift for painting (he has that in abundance), but, rather, one for color—a quality, not incidentally, characteristic of most painting today. So, in this absence of a natural ease with color, Bleckner is by no means unique. It is a reason why his work reminds one, say, of Edvard Munch, who proves anew that one can be a great artist without, in fact, being a great painter. Do I have to flail you? The difference I'm drawing is between art and painting. Beckmann's awkward grandeur often shows this, too.

To note these comparisons is not to suggest that Bleckner is anywhere near genius—it is simply to make a point that obtains as well in the cases, say, of Pollock, Schnabel, or Salle. None of these painters has a gift for color, but for painting—yes. By contrast, Stephan, say, has a gift for color.

Bleckner, 33, can be witty about the literal situation in which he finds himself: "Look, I had to do painting with bars because I lived right next to the jails; and I had to do New Wave painting because I live over the Mudd Club."

Since Bleckner lacks (presumptively) a genetic coding for color in the DNA spiral, he craftily transformed anemia into strength, addressing himself to painting in black alone and/or ironic commentary upon Op Art—yes, Op Art—yet another 1950s signifier and middle-class revenant that young artists are exploring today (fig. 95). Of the blackness of his work Bleckner notes by way of countermand: "When I close my eyes I don't see color. Yet my black-and-white paintings are completely fused with color. They're tinted."

Bleckner's "opticality" also disguises a verge-imagery which just may be there, perhaps isn't. "Each painting randomly mutates. Op is a kind of failed imagery. The pictures appear to have iconographic interest, but then don't. There's a level of randomness. Simultaneously you want different things to happen."

This multiplicity and ambiguous richness struck him as a potential at his most recent show but one. Instead of a monolithic Minimal clarity, "I wanted the show to suggest at least five different branches of meaning." With the Black Paintings, Bleckner realized that "I could have what I wanted and I could have what was supposed to be identified." The earlier work, to be sure, had been marked by a stress on specific image. The image bank is Picabia/Man Ray—that is, New York and Paris Dada, especially Man Ray's *Revolving Doors*. "So now, at least, there's an image. The Black Paintings are a kind of veil, a layer leading to an afterimage. Only it really doesn't mean afterimage."

"How can I have just one thing? How can one image really suffice?" the artist queries. "The problem is to define yourself through your production." Hence, "A lot of artists spend a lifetime to find this equivocal image. But no sooner than found, it 'deconstructs' [destroys?] itself—as it really couldn't possibly be a carrier of so rich and important an intention. Iconic abstraction can't be glommed onto iconic experience. It's just too complex."

"Moreover, my sensibility is essentially not a formal one. My narrative is personal and disjunctive. The objectives of one's scrutiny don't make themselves known in a logical sequence" —this perhaps by way of refuting a widespread belief that all painting can be seen as possessing logical verbal meaning.

In these ruminations and self-doubts, these expressions of a belief in an important newness and existential enrichment, Bleckner shows himself still to be a committed and elemental Modernist. Against all reason, his is perplexed by Quality—that bugaboo—for without "quality," credible transcending presence, Bleckner's tantalizing self-doubt would be quite beside the point.

Conversation, though easy, ignited when I spoke of artists whom I saw as emblematic of specific movements because they are so stylistically hidebound in a way that Bleckner's diverse intentions would never allow. It matters little whether they continue to grow (as indeed they give every indication of doing) as their essential contribution is measurable in their determining relationship to the sense of the immediate. The point of their work is to be frozen and stabilized. As artists, Bleckner called them "Open Signifiers." (This is in no sense a statement of quality though I can see the horror registered by readers of these notes. I am the culpable party, not Bleckner.)

Bleckner and I were strolling now with mutt Renny (Renaissance), partaking of the noontime sun with the office workers of his Foley Square municipal neighbors. Bleckner carried "open signifiers" further. Referring to those artists I had casually savaged, he continued that they (and many others) were artists "whose work was immediately subsumed into the conventionality of the discourse."

Bleckner is, of course, ambivalent about his own rejection of, or anxiety over, meaning—assuming all the while that the "quality" of the paintings nonetheless warrants this search. In his evolution Bleckner identifies three central events, *just* events. The first is *just* becoming an artist, *just* going to college," to NYU Washington Square where, it so happens, he took a B.S. in art. Chuck Close, he recalls, was a rare "positive source." "The second event was the experience of *being* an artist, not just *becoming* an artist." The third, which took place in '75, functions as a complex symbol. "I saw a dog fall out of a window. Maybe it was thrown out."

Figure 94. Robert Longo, Corporate Wars: *Wall of Influence*, Detail, 1982
Aluminum, 7'×9'.
(Photo courtesy Metro Pictures)

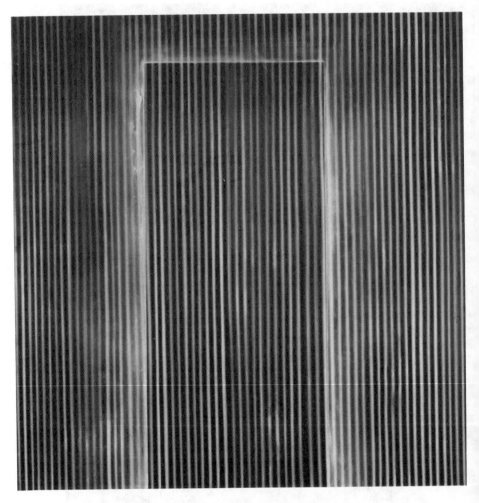

Figure 95. Ross Bleckner, *The Door to Last Year,* 1981
Oil, wax on canvas, 90″×88″.
(Photo courtesy Mary Boone Gallery)

Donald Baechler:
Increments of Inaccessibility

12 May 1982

. . . ran into the hardnosed sculptor Arman. We drove to his two floor studio near Canal Street. He continues to churn out his easy works. They remain "accumulations." Still, as a pioneer figure of *Nouveau Realisme* he merits the status of a modern master, at least in Europe.

Later, told Donald Baechler of my meeting with Arman. Baechler said something fascinating. He spoke to Arman's "artlessness," by which this very young and ironic artist did not mean something positive—the "artlessness" of something novel and freshly left. He meant instead something hackneyed and untranscended, with regard to the use of brute material, as indicating a condition of artlessness. His literalist irony, at that instant anyway, employed the term in a flat-footed way, meaning that the "accumulations" were not art. I appreciated the irony and the deadpan use of the word, and was struck by the fact that Baechler saw Arman as devoid of historical couche—the New Realist tag—which entirely colored my perception of him.

. . . Baechler is arresting, oblique, cryptic. His paintings appear to fall within the iconic new image context. His isolated motifs of high culture (Le Corbusier's *Chaise Longue*, say), are centered against backgrounds of modernist allusion—Stella stripes, Johns' hatchings—all rather suavely and richly painted.

2 November 1982

Among the obligations of an Indian summer day is a visit to the meager fifth floor studio walk up on lower Broadway of the artist Donald Baechler. Baechler has had the recent visit of the German painter Dokoupil—a good friend.

How is it that he would know Dokoupil? Baechler's mode of discourse seductively meanders. He was Hartford bred, born there to Quaker parents in 1956. (It's that Quaker idealism that still comes through in Baechler's irony.) He grew up somewhere in the middle of four kids—among the only whites in the city's North

This article originally appeared in conjunction with a Donald Baechler exhibition (New York City, Tony Shafrazi Gallery, March–April 1983).

End. But, at length, even they gathered that Idealism sometimes takes its toll, and settled for pink-house subdivision in suburban Connecticut. This was followed by Quaker boarding schools and summer camps. Though it sounds privileged, it was not. It's the reserved Spartan side of Quaker formation, though, by 15, Baechler knew that he "wanted to be a rich and famous artist."

Art training was a succession of first year basic programs, "False Starts," to invoke the Johns metaphor: he was at the Maryland Institute of Arts, the Cooper Union, etc., jumping bail, as it were, when the tuition promissory notes fell due.

The most influential class at Cooper Union was that of Hans Haacke, whose politicized art provided an open conceptual model. And, too, some of the younger German artists would visit Haacke's classroom, including Dokoupil. This was in 1977. By '78 Baechler was working in Frankfurt at the *Kunsthochschule,* in the independent *Frei Malerei* course. Among the works he produced were his "Meaningful Activity Drawings," which activities included waiters carrying trays, tourists snapping pictures, etc. The conceptual loam is *selbstverständlich.*

Baechler has a very characteristic face with a high forehead, resembling Debussy's. His conversation is inflected with facial mannerisms. His gaze averts as soon as the conversation gets personal. Then again, so does everybody's. But with Baechler there's a studied increment of inaccessibility.

Baechler is no longer painting in the enamel substance he had worked with, as it was poisoning him; instead he is now making painting/collages of canvas and cloth, depicting simple motifs—three men, four trees—a coloring book landscape the pieces of which are held together by Rhoplex and glue (fig. 96).

I wish I had chatted with Baechler before "Defenestrations" appeared. He is an obsessive. Working in isolation and filled with angst he revealed that by moments he fears he may hurl himself through the plate glass wall of his working loft. In a depression marked by an inability to paint he passed long hours abed watching daytime T.V.; weeks of this diet ensued. In a fever-dream he imagines that he is hurling the television set through the glass and awakens in terror. The next morning he steels himself with a view to act out the impulse suggested by the dream and in so doing, be "cured" of the fantasy as well as liberated from the depression. And the work-block would end too.

But he reconsiders, thinking of all the waste, and instead gives the television set away—only to regret, even more, the unrealized beauty of the act, had he in fact done it. It's a god-myth, of course, life, death, resurrection, allied to Gide's *Acte Gratuit.* And now he's got no T.V.

28 January 1983

Yesterday to Donald Baechler's studio over Broadway in the Wall Street area. I admire Donald's dedication and the furious freedom that his isolation imposes. There's no sense of the mean or the poor in him. It also allows for independent art decisions.

The work as it develops is abandoning the Rhoplex collages, favoring a new drawing/painting—works that seem, in their making, discovered and unpremeditated.

The paintings depict isolated pictorial fragments in turbulent grey fields. Each element is rehearsed over and over, though painted in ways to suggest a clumsy freshness and sense of adventure. Spiral-topped heads, pipe faces, singing faces based on Oum Kalsoum, the wailing Soul of Egypt—faces resembling opera singers and large breasted maternal fetishes.

These iconic types are almost scribbled. The surface is thickened by consideration and reconsideration of the motif. Each time the image is set down in relation to another, it may suggest a too cohesive composition, one that hangs together all too well. It is the "too well" that discomfits. So, Baechler paints it all out, again corrects it, so as not to postulate a too logical or a too narratively credible space. Baechler is a classicist outlaw: the deftness of touch, the grisaille, the willed aestheticized gawkiness refer to Twombly and to Johns.

Figure 96. Donald Baechler, *Schwarzwald*, 1982
Acrylic on canvas, 105"×152".
(Photo courtesy Tony Shafrazi Gallery)

Entries: Peter Schuyff, Anamorphic Distortion and Stretch

28 June 1984

More light on the struggle between formal content and stylistics, a particularly grinding issue vis-à-vis Peter Schuyff and other pretenders to East Village royalty—David Wojnarowicz, Keith Haring, Mike Bidlo, Don Baechler, etc. (Chatting with Schuyff, I find him shrewd about Bidlo, recognizing in the latter's resurrections of Pollock and Warhol another form of Sherrie Levine. Levine's photographic facsimiles are credible in terms of "deconstruction," though her watercolor work lacks authority insofar as her hand seems insecure when inventing fakes after famous modern painters.)

Schuyff's work advances the cautious maintenance of high modern information—shallow depth of field, frontality, equality of surface emphasis—combined with a tamed Surrealist automatism, which speaks to a filiation with Pollock's allover however different each artist's work appears at first sight and all proportion guarded. This formalist background sounds official (if not even dreary) but Schuyff's work is vivified by his keen awareness of a dandy mannerism-as-style, a consciousness that forms the core of much East Village aspiration. Of course, Schuyff's credibility is reinforced through East Village demography.

I first met him as a sinister youth hanging back at the margin of a Baechler party. The introduction was made by David Kapp—he's quite another kettle of fish; royalty for sure but not so clearly of East Village ilk. Subsequently, Gary Stephan pressed for Schuyff's work at the time of the opening of Pat Hearn's gallery, a somewhat more pulled-together space than most of the storefronts opening as part of the East Village phenomenon. Stephan was struck by Schuyff's kidney-shaped Fifties amoebas (right out of Dali's protoplasmic harps), painted over weekend motel art and blue collar department store kitsch.

Schuyff filled in on the myth. Of Dutch origin, he arrived in Vancouver, Canada, at the age of seven, his father being a Dutch governmental employee. Schuyff stayed

---

This article originally appeared in *Arts Magazine*, September 1984.

in Vancouver until he was 18, a self-conscious *enfant terrible* taxing the patience of a provincial situation but, according to Schuyff's telling of it, one that embraced the going cosmopolitan avant-garde, inviting, for example, to the Vancouver School of Art (from which Schuyff is becoming a noteworthy drop out) the influential Niçois Conceptualist, Ben. By degrees, Schuyff and his art school cronies, the most notorious being Richard Hambleton, saw themselves as comprising an art movement parallel to what was going on in Berlin or Cologne. In short, they saw themselves as the New Western Front.

Schuyff's studio is on the second floor of a anomalous building just across the Williamsburg Bridge, part of disputed Brooklyn turf—the Hasidim versus the Hispanics. The studio is of modest dimension and messy though finished paintings are neatly angled and layered into a corner by way of saving precious space.

The new paintings continue to examine suave contours of automatic stamp—pudgy templates of Etienne Hadju and the occasional Brancusi invoking Cycladic carving. Worked in acrylic paint on linen, certain patterns recalling linoleum motifs cause stripes, say, to be subject to anamorphic distortion and stretch (fig. 97).

The more recent work maintains Schuyff's motival obsession, though the scale is smaller and marked by a kind of optical blur through which one perceives the influence of Ross Bleckner, a regular hero to Schuyff. Cryptically paraphrasing Bleckner, he said of the latter's stripe paintings of a few years back that "the light came from the eye"; with regard to Bleckner's last show, that "the light came from the stomach"; and of the new paintings, that "the light came from the book."

Amid the studio disorder there is a pile of small wooden panels, some seven by nine inches each, old cheese box faces. He remembered that these panels, when first exhibited, were arranged in permutable grid formation—pointing to a source in Minimalist Conceptualism. This student-like work constrasts Ambrogio Lorenzetti-like heads against tubular macaronic abstraction à la Picasso, ca. 1932. A large repro-duction of a heroic Picasso head of that vintage curls up on the wall. Passing on iconographic information: the Yellow Man, found in many Schuyff titles, refers to the famous albino reggae star and Mr. Cool is the name for Schuyff's self-beautifying alter ego.

11 May 1984

I am struck by the amount of painting today marked by an emphatic visual conges-tion, a quality seen in young painting from Schnabel to Brett de Palma. I take this visual indigestibility as a progressive index. It tends to recast the role of the ground in the figure-ground relationship from that of passive receiver into one of visual equivalent to the figure. This has the extravagant effect of impacting the narrative elements of a painting (usually the figure) against the abstraction (generally the ground). The venerable cliché about this dualism, this dialectical honing, speaks of form versus content.

Today perhaps this development may allow us to pit process against image; with this further admonition: now that both components are so active and accident so instrumentalized, one is hardpressed to say where it is that process begins and iconography leaves off.

Figure 97. Peter Schuyff, *Bride of Yellow Man*, 1984
Acrylic on linen, 90″×66″.
(Photo courtesy Pat Hearn Gallery)

Entries:
The Scene That Turned on a Dime

28 November 1985, Thanksgiving

Peter Schuyff's new paintings at Pat Hearn are politically brave, formidable canvasses based on staggered sequences of optical luminousness rooted in Albers and a sign for mysticism, but underplaying for all that the Surrealist illusionism that so abruptly catapulted Schuyff to front rank (fig. 98). I take the move to be spurred by an acute reading of the scene rather than premised in aesthetic demand or felt necessity—though, after all, so sharp a political act is, in its own way, an aesthetic one, too. Despite reservation this still is a big statement just when the small and easy to place would have done as well, even as it had passed before.

7 January 1986

Touch-sensitive art looks tired. In the air, the Photographic Conceptual is taking hold though it has kicked around since the Conceptual Sixties; and a certain kind of Conceptual Painterly too: Peter Halley, Jeff Koons, Ashley Bickerton, The Nature Morte set, Jay Gorney, International With Monument. I sense it. Emily Spiegel, too. I met her by chance today and with astonishing prescience, or so it seemed to me, she tells me of the numerous studios and galleries associated with the resurgent genre she had recently visited. It is the cold absence of touch that once more pleases, though not the jejune arguments in favor of a factitious political deconstruction. From the concentrated abstract icons like the ambiguous highway directions of Peter Halley to the multi-signaled supergraphics of Barbara Kruger, the separation of the signified from the signifier is still said to encode a critique of Capitalism. But can that also pass as encoding support for Socialism? Now that The Collectors are there, Radicality is usurped. When Money Flies In Through The Window, Commodity Comes In Through The Door. That's Infotainment. Cindy and the Cindycalists. Scratch A Socialist, Find A Capitalist.

This article originally appeared in *Arts Magazine*, April 1986.

2 February 1986

This past Friday afternoon, I run into the lean, the thoughtful and efficient Philip Taaffe who, taking me aside in the Pat Hearn Gallery, where once more I had gone down to think about his work, inquires, after I had used the word "stylistics" several times in conversation, "Well, Robert, just what does it mean?" To be sharply brought up marvelously focuses the mind, f/16, and without skipping a frame, I reply "Politics." Politics corrupt and absolute Politics corrupt absolutely.

We both draw in air at the chilling concision seeing as how we are also forever slogging through the Jell-o of the Art Long, Life Short aspic, even granting the disparity of age between us. Of course Art is one and Life the other, but before they got to be those things they were "political," functions of "stylistics." Thus, when others, not Taaffe this time, respond "And, in six months? . . . " I am compelled to think if not answer aloud, "So what?"

Such cynical observations play preamble to The Scene That Turned On A Dime which despite its shiny thinness was fully measurable last night. Ross Bleckner, whose brilliantine Neo-Surrealism should render him anathema to the Neo-Opticians, remains more fully mired in the momentary stylistic crosscurrents than ever before. Bleckner's optical field paintings of a show or two back have become model for the Op Art revivals of Taaffe; the optical glow of Schuyff is also connected to Bleckner, who even earlier than Taaffe had accommodated the suave glow of Bleckner's operatic chandelier paintings to his own work, a subject matter that continues to be explored in the recent group of Chandelier paintings and Iron Grill Gates (figs. 99 and 100).

Schuyff, in disaffiliating himself from the neo-Surrealists and pulling Taaffe-y, made one of the savviest style moves, read political moves, in recent memory. This happens organically in the work as a function of thinking about the scene. Artists! It's your Industry. You've got to know the competition.

For the painters, the motival pillage of history leads to iconographic reformulations; for the conceptual generation, be they painters and/or photographic constructivists, to a revival of conceptual iconographics. So, the Neo-Opticians are really part of the Neo-Conceptual revival going on all about us and which is perhaps the key feature of the Changed Scene.

All these groups and affiliations of the youngest generation treat the past as if it were a five-and-dime counter imagistically sectioned into leitmotifs to be appropriated at will. Naturally, such motifs are not devoid, for them at least, of the anguish felt at their discovery by their original creators or that authenticity of reeling that the originators of the motif felt in finally mastering it. But it is equally true that by appropriating the earlier motif, the young artists today, just like those of the past, also feel sensations and emotions of anguish and mastery in bringing their work to happy end. Which confounds the marble coldness and cynicism of the scene far beyond any of my voyeuristic distancing. Taaffe revived Bridget Riley (fig. 101) and appropriated Newman Zips renaming *Vir Heroicus Sublimus* the parallel *Homo*

Fortissimus Excelsus. Meanwhile Schuyff leapt picket fences from Neo-Surrealism over to Taaffe, the Neo-Opticians, or as I think I'll now say, the Neo-Conceptualists. Goodbye Condo. Goodbye Dokoupil. Goodbye Nouveau Bohème.

Ironically, for all of his earlier optical paintings, Bleckner returned to Neo-Surrealism in these new Chandelier and Iron Grill works. Bleckner, in straddling the interests of junior camps, plays the role of older brother to his compeers—not quite being of an age for the avuncular let alone the paternal. It was Bleckner who pulled together the Taaffe catalogue and never has the menu in a Greek Short Order Hash House—for such is the origin of the printing—looked more beautiful.

Nor should it be forgotten that Bleckner emerged in the generation of Salle and Schnabel, his black paintings having close formal affiliations with aspects of early Schnabel, and he remains steadfast to both, no mean trick considering that Salle and Schnabel have by now sharply individuated. It is even difficult to remember that their work was once perceived to have been painted by an emerging Female Talent, a certain Sally Schnabel.

Imagine, Salle and Schnabel together again at a dinner to fête Bleckner's opening at Boone, a putative First anyway since the Schnabel defection to Pace. Schnabel behaved with model decency at the festivities, looking neither to the right nor the left, and never in the direction of the Boone table. Her back was set toward him throughout the meal, doubtless a sheerly fortuitous seating arrangement. Schnabel sat upon the arm of Ross, who had appeared but shortly before, garbed in a particularly dishevelled and unshaven deshabille, a reverse snobbery that only Clemente can carry off, cackling a happy giggle by way of acknowledging the rounds of applause that greeted his entry into the subsequent suite of toasts.

The Conceptual Revivalists included Peter Nagy, whose show had opened that evening that evening at International With Monument. Nagy's logo-like isolations of image in stark black and white brings to mind Bob Stanley's illustrative graphic pop paintings shown when O. K. Harris first opened, though it is far-fetched to imagine that Nagy was reviving that aspect of things if even he had ever heard of Stanley, which I doubt. But you never know. If Taaffe can rethink Riley, Stanley isn't entirely out of the question.

Anyway, International With Monument is up there for the nonce as purveyor to the court of the Neo-Conceptual and its dealer/artist sullen Meyer Vaisman, having pioneered with Peter Halley, Jeff Koons, etc., and had something to smile about at last.

At my table, conversation was centered on The Dance. I sat to one side of Karole Armitage, David Salle on the other. The dance/choreographer was distressed at not yet having found a name for the new ballet that she has choreographed for Mikhail Baryshnikov: Brancusi's Head? Giacometti's Dog? Barbara Jakobson observed that such names needlessly oversituate an audience into a set of expectations that, in the end, might not be satisfied and thus work against the ballet. But Karole protested that there still was something Slavic about the dance, perhaps inspired by the dancer himself. I suggest Tirgu-Jiu, the Brancusi park in Romania with the monumental *Gate of the Kiss, Endless Column, Table of Silence.* Barbara polishes the idea; she submits The Park at Tirgu-Jiu. Taking another tack, I suggest Mischa/Mishima. General consternation and repulsion.

The rolling beneath the crust has now broken through. David Salle and Julian Schnabel are justifiably taken to be historical figures. The kids hone in, misperceiving Bleckner as a Generational Comrade rather than as a Mentor. Peer Pressure. Am I so overly preoccupied with stylistics that the sense of the sharp displacement of Neo-Surrealism on one hand and of high modernist abstraction on the other smarts rather? For all that, Mary appears, in Bleckner's case, to have been the loyal dealer who stayed with the artist through thick and thin—Oh, these dull clichés—though another interperetation, not necessarily the truth, is also germane: when it's hot it sells itself. This is a lesson learned through a lifetime of obsessive dealer watching and though platitudinous, it still is a lesson not so immediately evident to the laity.

Figure 98.   Peter Schuyff, *Untitled*, 1985
Acrylic on linen, 90″ × 66″.
(Photo courtesy Pat Hearn Gallery)

Figure 99.   Ross Bleckner, *Chamber*, 1985
Oil on canvas, 87″×60″.
(Photo courtesy Mary Boone Gallery)

Figure 100.   Ross Bleckner, Gate, 1985
Oil on canvas, 14"×18".
(Photo courtesy Mary Boone Gallery)

Figure 101.   Philip Taaffe, *Brest*, 1985
Linoprint collage, acrylic on canvas, 108″×108″ (Diagonal).
(Photo courtesy Pat Hearn Gallery)

Entries: David Wojnarowicz, Myth in Formation

David Wojnarowicz, 28, is lean and angular and is brilliantly gifted, though in ways difficult to pinpoint. Much of his visual semiotic is shared commonly by other artists today—generally of East Village stamp—and if not his semiotic, then for sure his apparently liberal politics. His work is marked by the use of stencils and occasionally slick, commercially graphic passages, large sectioned horizontal or eccentric formats (garbage can lids, beach logs), and the use of commercially related preexisting graphic material—supermarket sale signs, world maps, and the like (fig. 102).

To build a sociology around him is awkward—to infer it, easy—as the few facts offered up are of such high profile. I don't for a moment doubt them, though scads are glossed. He's been on his own since childhood, rejected by a New Jersey family at nine. From what little he says (that's a problem: he hints, not to be flirtatious, but to maintain distance), he had no use for them and they apparently had even less for him. Survival was contingent upon itinerancy and vagabondage. Apparently, even as a child, he had the presence of mind to register in public school, receiving a desultory education and a grand love of letters—not to mention an intimacy with the urban netherworld in which he survived in the street. A reasonable model is Genet. François Villon is equally apposite, as William Burroughs notes in an introductory blurb to a volume of monologues of boys in bus stations, and on the road which Wojnarowicz, in his capacity as writer, has published. The tone remains very Beat.

Such stray biographical detail serves to point to meanings within his spattered Third World stencils. Central American references, Vietnam imagery, glimpses of prison life, and upfront homosexual motifs about which he is never apologetic. Still, direct questions are replied to with evasions: "I used that map because I liked the colors." Such answers don't get one very far if one hopes to illuminate meaning in Wojnarowicz's important work beyond that of mere neurological stimuli. I like to converse with artists but balk at interviewing. Guarded discourse enforces the latter mode.

This article originally appeared in *Arts Magazine*, November 1983.

A stray reference was very rich, to a passage in Yukio Mishima's *Confessions of a Mask* as a source for his stencil paintings of Saint Sebastian. The memory allows for the following collapse: the arrows of the Christian martyr (long a homosexual icon) may be surrogate for the junkie needle. In Mishima, the sight of a Sebastian by Guido Reni reproduced in one of his father's Western art books inspired the author to a passionate first masturbation, as I discovered in looking up the passage, and occasioned a magnificent description of his first ejaculation over his student desk—lesson book, inkwell, his father's art book just saved from soiling by a judicious reflex gesture. Mishima continues to develop into a grand sado-masochistic obsessive (ultimately a ritual suicide in the rite of Seppuku) dedicated to the caprices of his "toy" as he called it. And Wojnarowicz?

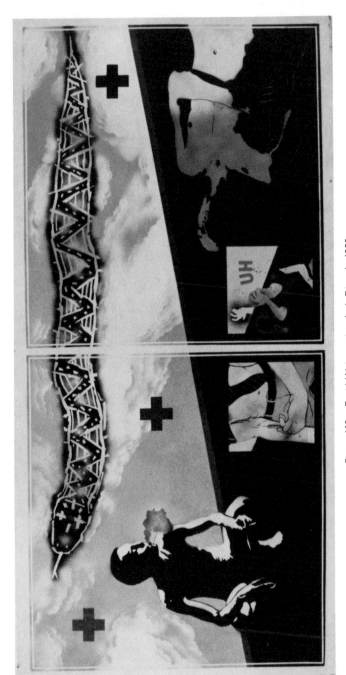

Figure 102. David Wojnarowicz, *Junk Diptych*, 1982
Spray enamel on masonite, 4'×8'.
(Photo courtesy Gracie Mansion Gallery)

The New Irascibles

A retrospective viewing of the East Village Bubble can hardly be deemed an original inspiration. The phenomenon has been repeatedly examined, both superficially and in depth, as it will continue to be with surveys proposed for cities as distant from us as Tokyo. At first, the appellation East Village Art had the effect of demarcating geography and mode, both vague as to actual limits and to the specifics of style, though the East Village green, Tompkins Square Park, has evolved in three years from junkie, bongo, and barrio blaster-heaven to a quasi-Regency Parc Monceau and by now is far safer by night than the abandoned ranges and rambles of Central Park.

Still, the vague sense of East Village ghetto, promoted, for the nonce, a sense of confinement, of stylistic consistency and reification. East Village became tag, handle, and lever—a tag of easy appeal; a cognomen akin to the heroic self-invention, the names of the graffiti writers; a handle that allowed for local, national, and ultimately international transposability, in short, for commodification; a lever whereby a broad, wildly disparate set of options could be pried free from other contemporaneous avant-garde episodes, be they ongoing or incipiently moribund.

But first there had been a depressed area, albeit in Manhattan, populated by generation upon generation of solid ethnic blue collar workers, as well as, of late, a sprinkling of artists in need of the cheap living space that once it offered though hardly the large working space of the Soho loft. For several years too, it served as litter ground of the wrappings of the Great Society Candy Bar—the sociopathic detritus of urban society, the street corner drug dealer as purvey to the court of the disaffected junkie. Here was the burned-out, cold water tenement, its ironstone sink/bathtub as the main feature of the makeshift living room; here, where greenhorns once extended meager incomes through the preparation of piecework for the neighborhood sweatshop, the ambulant psychotic (abandoned by public institution and welfare surveillance) now roamed; here was human graffiti—the wino, the junkie, the bag-lady, and a growing number of young artists, really their clubby hangers-on who took stylistic clues (quite as they tried on the old clothes of the Retro boutiques) from this farrago, heartlessly seeing it as all too punkishly glamorous for words.

This article originally appeared in *Arts Magazine*, September 1985.

Then came the club-cum-gallery, and a constellation of mutually interdependent elements—artist, dealer, alternative space, collector (uptown, out of town), critic, hanger-on, etc.—a scene that finally imploded into some vast culture, a mushroom bomb.

Alert young dealers West of Broadway in Soho extended antennae into this nutrient mass, absorbing back into their more conventional venue the talisman of the yeastiness, further legitimizing it as art—as if it ever needed legitimacy. This percipience was also shown by young European dealers, especially in Germany, who saw in the East Village counter-culture a parallel to their own fragmented city-against-city-competition, class against class, their *Stilkrieg*.

There has been an immediately preceding migration, not westward across Broadway into Soho, but northward up across Houston Street—from the old Lower East Side to the new Lower East Side—from teeming tenement streets of ironically cruel bucolic and anglophilic names to the numbered streets and alphabet soup avenues of New York in its post-Civil War expansionist boom.

This drift, for East Village Art, registered shifts in class character, from the *Lumpenprol* to that of a proletarian consciousness and, as it shuttled back and forth between the East Village and Soho, brandishing those letters of patent, finally achieving the bourgeois commodity status of "real art." But it was along Ridge and Rivington, Norfolk and Suffolk Streets, where the Eastern European pushcart gave way to the Hispanic shaved ices vendor, that the earliest generation of East Village artist first emerged from the primordial grunge.

Next came the astute curator who grasped that a historical overview of the East Village would provide an occasion for the "scientific" study of a closed model while it vouchsafed the host institution all the glamour accruing to so novel an enthusiasm. Indeed, in this respect, the museological effort has been preeminent in validating the East Village. The catalogues, say, of the overview held at the Institute of Contemporary Art at the University of Pennsylvania (in 1984) or "Neo York," the survey presented at the Santa Barbara Museum the same year, are central reference works—all the dates are there, the firsts, the bios, the bibliography.

Hard upon the museum survey came the brief group exhibitions of established dealers who, sensing the displacement of excitement from conventional spheres of influence, reinvigorated their polite turf through the presentations of smaller versions of the museum survey. As icing came the commercial flip book and hip guide—ready reference, fast info, like the columns of East Village newspapers such as *New York Talk* or the *East Village Eye*—and the notion of the East Village as citadel of art was flyingly buttressed.

Truth is, walls are crumbling and what we have now are mounds of fallen stones; the original matrix has not held. Well, that is overstated. Rather, what we have now is another level, another mesh, another scene built on the earlier foundation. Archaeology. But the mastic whereby early work was experienced as talisman of a set of commonly held aspirations, that period is over. The sweet, the idealistic, the green are gone.

Style, like all natural resource, gets used up, gets absorbed. An obsession with stylistics lets one know whether new art is good or bad; surely all art is good at the beginning, good, that is, if you are predisposed to the new (however long the new may last and acknowledging all the while just how manipulated this predisposition is—but so are all prejudices); bad, if you are for the old.

Artists who make bad art know it and hope for an audience deaf to the mechanistic hum of the machinery of style. But, even bad artists, in that sense, may have been good artists for a while if they were participants in an adventure of the new. To have been a participant confers a momentary patent of excellence. Time will tell if the warrant holds.

Why then this album? Precisely because the East Village episode, even if far from over, has transformed radically. This was the last moment whereby it was still possible to assemble a photographic record of the early participants. As such the album is a valedictory effort, marked by the sense of nostalgia and rue occasioned by such adieux (figs. 103–8).

18 April 1985

Visit Timothy Greenfield-Sanders yesterday. We worked through the first lists of The New Irascibles, a project addressing the artists (first, second, and third generations), the art dealers (first and second generation), and the art critics (sufficient for one generation)—granting, as we now do, the notion of generation as encompassing September–June, like an academic year, or a season in the rag trade.

Greenfield-Sanders wants to document the art world participants of the changing neighborhood where he and his family have lived a decade now (in the rectory of Saint Nicholas, the old German Catholic Church, now razed), through a reconstruction of "The Irascibles," the celebrated photograph taken of the Abstract-Expressionist group by Nina Leen in 1951. (All of this, mind you, must be done with a minimum of fuss; no social secretary rescheduling. One accepts; one doesn't; that's it.)

"The Irascibles" stands behind much of Greenfield-Sanders' efforts as a photographer, perhaps most—the series of portraits of the Abstract-Expressionist painters Thirty Years Later, for example, or the Art Critic Series, etc. "The Irascibles" is both talisman and paradigm for Greenfield-Sanders, who is, after all, the son-in-law of Joop Sanders, a painter from the Leen years.

Understandably, Greenfield-Sanders thought that Hans Namuth had taken the original photograph, a natural error considering Namuth's intimacy with the Abstract-Expressionist circle. But the photograph, as noted, was really shot by Nina Leen, a *Life* magazine staff photographer, which explains perhaps why Hedda Sterne, then Mrs. Saul Steinberg, the lone woman in the famous photograph, is so prominently situated, standing just off center right. This positioning may be construed as an act of gender solidarity, a political gesture, expressed between the photographer and the photographed.

Half-jokingly I opted for the Hedda Sterne spot as we worked on the lists and locations. We decided against informing the artists, dealers, and critics what the origin of the arrangement is lest they jockey for key positions. To play down the inevitable gossip and self-service, we will say the project is a commission.

Numerous details remain as we plan for a portfolio as well as an inexpensive give-away that will reproduce all the images and, in so doing, answer the East Village appetite for the free and the cheap. If we can swing this latter detail, reproductions will in due course be rendered valuable because they reproduce Greenfield-Sanders' photographs and vice versa. So much for The Work of Art in the Age of Mechanical Reproduction. Instead of devaluating the original, the photographic reproduction both valorizes and commodifies. Reproduction succeeds in ways opposed to the contentions of collegiate theorists, supposedly in the name of Walter Benjamin. After all, the reproduction is an image in a stamp album. As such the collector is obliged to fill in the page with the original (which even in the case of stamps remains a problem in graphics, like photography).

2 April 1985

The dissolution of the early East Village continues apace. Run into Steven Adams—originally of Limbo Lounge—on a brilliant Sunday. "Last year at this time we were having fun. Now it's just business," meaning the fantasy of art dealing in the East Village has moved from a profession of solidarity to that of *sauve qui peut.*

The pizza can only be sliced so far.

The art shows this, too. It is no longer brash, unmanageable, and unsalable. In short, the art has improved, has *become art,* and in its evolution to a commodity status there has been a concomitant devolution in energy. Only beginnings and ends are interesting.

Economic necessity rears its head. Once was that those god-awful storefronts didn't cost much. Within three years rents have rocketed. So the art *must* sell if only to cover expenses, though mostly it still doesn't. Thus fun becomes work and work becomes art and/or toil.

Minutes before I had run into Dean Savard, co-founder of Civilian Warfare, and he is opting out. The New Civilian Warfare has just not panned out, what with David Wojnarowicz gone to Gracie Mansion and Judy Glantzman too. Both began in the old Civilian Warfare 11th Street storefront. Gentrification and institutionalization.

Talked to Gracie Mansion about The New Irascibles. She remembers the first generation of artists as being of just small enough number for a Conversation Piece, like an 18th-century painting—the subjects of which could all appear identically "in basic black and pearls"; but, she admits, that at last count, the third generation crowd might well be shot from the air as they spill out over the edges of Tompkins Square Park. Can it be only two years since Nicolas Moufarrege first walked me about the neighborhood? Or that the P.S.1 Studio Selection Committee awarded so many

East Village artists studio space? Or that the first Wojnarowicz's were ever sold? The worst rumor of all is that Moufarrege has succumbed to a terrible pneumonia.

17 June 1983

Yesterday Nicolas Moufarrege walked me up and down Tenth Street, Eleventh Street, around Tompkins Square, introducing me to the emerging East Village scene—the Fun Gallery, Patti Astor, Bill Stelling, Gracie Mansion, the New Math, Civilian Warfare, Nature Morte.

Moufarrege would like me to like the art as much as he. The new entrepreneurial mode and unrepentant careerism are appealing. The scene is a kind of feeder to the developed Soho situation, especially of the younger dealers there like Tony Shafrazi and Hal Bromm, who, in comparison, represent legitimacy and solidity. The young East Village dealers are carving out a sector for themselves, and in so doing, gentrify both art and neighborhood. They begin with Untouchables like the graffitists and a machinery is set into motion that transforms detritus into treasure.

The socially motivated art of the urban guerilla such as that made by Mike Bidlo and David Wojnarowicz is perhaps the most interesting but one sees how the smallness of the scene, the minute working space of the old law tenement flats, and the impossibiity of privacy all conspire to underscore a myth of communal exuberance.

This enforced fraternity argues against private development and reinforces the notion of a shared iconography—the Basquiat distillate, the Garet knock-off, the Scharf imitation, the Barbara Krugerands, and on and on. These are some of the East Village versions of *Köln Freiheit*. The work of art here is a talisman of common experience, not art as a thing in itself, not yet the commodified signature work of Soho or Uptown; but it functions as art in the degree that it is able to invoke a novel sense of community. I take this to be true of all art at the beginning, since all art begins with a consciousness of style.

Naturally, this communal vision of art argues against personalistic theory enforcing a fictional bonhomie and easy access. It justifies the shared iconography and reifies a sense of a mindless absence of theory; it devalues verbalization quite as it promotes a facticious hedonist pleasure. the garden in the slum, the flower in the brick, the non-biodegradable blossoms, erase (in theory at least) distinctions felt between artists as to success and class. If these distinctions are still present, then they have at least been temporarily glossed and the public face of such matters is veiled.

Naturally, much of this has happened because economically it had to. Even these slum alternatives are expensive to come by. Fun Gallery, for example, has to scrape together $1,200 a month and it is virtually the oldest gallery here except for Rich Colicchio's 51X. Space for each new gallery grows more and more expensive as newer dealers compete to enter the scene.

In the East Village, Nicolas Moufarrege's embroidery and tapestry work (fig. 109) can pass for art insofar as no received opinion downgrading crafts is at work here.

If graffiti is accepted as art, why not *grospoint?* This democratic view won't wash west of Broadway. Were, however, Moufarrege to suddenly take up painting, as a critical strategy that is, he probably would spark an appetite for his early needlework.

27 April 1981

A small, sweet Lebanese Christian in exile, polyglot, studied chemistry at Harvard, who having read the "Entries: Maximalism" dogged me until I looked at his embroideries. His work is based in a colliding iconography—Pop comix plus the *gnudi* of Michelangelo meet Owen Jones' *The Grammar of Ornament.* It seems Moufarrege, that's his name, has already shown with Jacques Damase in Paris. First he must pay his dues. He thinks the collision of images represents a natural dialectical argument.

7 May 1985

Dean Savard, on a sabbatical from art dealing, has returned to his folks. Judy Glantzman's cutout portrait filled in for him today during the shooting of the first Dealers. Glantzman's cutouts honor Alex Katz though his portraits are flat, while hers are vivified in simple constructivist relief (derived from Picasso). Her painting remains trim and with all she is very funny, employing a hoarse comedic banter, a spiel, that puts one in mind of Joan Greenwood.

Moufarrege won't make the critics' shot. His condition has worsened and I fear these notes may become a kind of dedication to this first East Village Cicerone, its Salomon Reinach, whose essays on "The Mutant International" make for a basic primer of East Village aspirations [Nicholas Moufarrege died June 4, 1985.] How to represent Nicolas in the art critics' shot? Through the inclusion of one of his embroideries?

I come to like the phrase "New Irascibles," with its internal rhyme calling the word "rascals" to mind, and its memory of the Depression short subjects, *The Little Rascals.*

5 February 1985

Some sitters have guessed that the organization of The New Irascibles loosely follows Nina Leen's photograph, one might say "deconstructs" it—a double deconstruction insofar as the photographic mode and its duplicate are further distanced and rendered ironic through videotaping of the latter photographic event. Irony as an anti-bourgeois mechanism, hence as deconstruction.

Mike Bidlo grasped the paradigm immediately and loved filling in for the artist whose work he has so brilliantly impersonated.

But the presumed ambitions of deconstruction are utterly inverted in this event. Out of unexamined convention, deconstruction is tagged as positive, intellectually dense, Marxist, while its opposite, nostalgia, is tagged as negative, as neo-conservative pastiche. Can we really know? It's the old problem of seeming and being. The distinction is invisible—though for sure, the distinction between these attitudes does lead artists to imagine that they are making hard art versus soft or easy art—thus fortifying in their work a system under constant threat, arming them with a belief in the quality of what they do. All to the good—but, in the end, the nostalgics can lay as legitimate a claim to this conviction as do the deconstructionists.

Poor Peter Nagy and Alan Belcher of the conceptually-oriented Nature Morte were visibly perturbed by the sitting and tore out quite as the other dealers relished reliving the experience in real time video. "But who is Hedda Sterne?" Gracie piped up in her high rushing voice, unwittingly wearing a perfect Hedda Sterne costume.

20 April 1984

Each moment seeks two polar exemplars—one movement, two poles; one moment, two poles. This is the natural result of cultural *embourgeoisement*. In the big world of art this means Salle/Schnabel, Kiefer/Baselitz, Polke/Richter. Earlier examples would be Rauschenberg/Johns, Mondrian/Van Doesburg, Matisse/Derain, Picasso/Braque. You get the point. In the little world, the marginal world of the East Village, this means David Wojnarowicz (about whom see "Entries: Myth in Formation") and Mike Bidlo (figs. 110, 111).

Through moral example they divide turf between them and Bidlo's culminating effort, the reconstitution of Warhol's Silver Factory, was shown tis weekend at P.S. 1. Of course, Bidlo's strategies skirt stabilization. First came the tableaux from the Life of Jackson Pollock, as in his reconstruction of the Peggy Guggenheim fireplace episode—Pollock pissing—in "Jack the Dripper." This was part of a replication of Pollock's *Autumn Rhythm, Lavender Mist, Blue Poles,* etc.; and now the Silver Factory—though it came as a surprise to Bidlo's to learn that it was Billy Linnik, one of Andy's alleged junkie squirrels, who first covered the 47the Street loft in aluminum foil, not Andy.

Bidlo made extreme sacrifices by way of demonstrating his dedication to the project such as stripping his hair and bleaching his brows. "It burned like hell for 45 minutes and you have to press your eyes down hard to keep from crying." We were having lunch in a mafiosi waterside restaurant a brief walk from P.S.1. They took Bidlo for some kind of rock star.

Bidlo knows better than anyone else that should he continue in this vein of mock culture, his work threatens to become as academically stabilized a form of conceptual performance as, say, Lichtenstein's art-about-art is as painting. (Only Lichtenstein is ahead, since he makes paintings as commodified objects from the outset that are viewed commercially. Not so Bidlo—who sees his Pollock copies as underscoring the absurdity of the inflated value of the original Abstract Expressionists. My sanguine view—that's what a Pollock costs; that's what a Monet costs; in time, that's what a Bidlo will cost.) Yet Bidlo begins to see that despite earlier justifications (Conceptual Art as anti-capitalist analysis), all that must capitulate before the *force majeure* of the return to conventional typologies, the return to painting, taking place all around us, and with it the return to commodity.

Bidlo was exhausted by his Silver Factory bash and depressed by the uncleared-away mess. Of course, Bidlo identifies partly with Warhol because of his Czech background and, I suppose, because of the Warhol-like careerism that so inflects post-conceptual culture.

"What do you really want now?" I asked.

"Oh, you know, Fame, Success, Beautiful Lovers."

I don't know what Bidlo's work was before the rehabilitation of the Pollock Estate. Did he even paint? And, if so, how? Because if he did it is there in the early painting that one will find a clue toward an instrumentalization of the past. For the moment what particularly fascinated me is how he coopted P.S.I, turned it into a stage, a loading dock upon which he unloaded his careerism. In this he was not alone. He was part of that brilliant late conceptual class at P.S.I that used its studio space as a surrogate gallery.

27 April 1985

Jean-Michel Basquiat balked at our request to appear in the first artist photograph, Keith Haring having reached him first and Haring refuses to appear with Bidlo. "Yes, it's true. I know him." Haring says. "Once we were waiters together but you're falsifying history," Haring correctly accuses. Indeed, all history falsifies history and the falsification issue was taken up by Basquiat. Still, if the documentation is not made now, then for sure the unravelling mesh of the East Village will be totally pulled apart by next year and this tattered fabric will never again be liable of reweaving.

Haring went on: "The East Village artists excommunicated us. We are Soho artists to them now. Okay, I accept the tag. I don't mind being a Soho artist." Despite resistance, Haring, Basquiat, and Kenny Scharf—Palladium as Parnassus—did agree to a separate sitting which we will call "The Excommunicants," situating these alienated artists—alienated through their stupefying success—in the power seats of "The Irascibles," leaving the other places empty.

16 May 1985

Jean Michel "forgot" (slept through?) to appear for the shooting of the Excom-municant photograph and no amount of alert from his "managerial assistants" could stir him. Haring and Scharf made it and would meet again for Jean-Michel. But would I? Yes, I suppose, since after all only the artist is remembered.

Excommunicant strikes me as a preferable term to the Excommunicated. Ex-communicant suggests an active condition that might swing both ways. Excom-municated is a final and absolute condition of ostracism, connoting neither ambiguity nor paradox.

4 December 1983

Basquiat is a fascinating problem. Despite his emergence with and inclusion among the first Graffiti artists, his work possesses an official edge, a painterliness quite at home in today's painterliness so that, at Dolores Neumann's "Post-Graffiti" Show for Sidney Janis, say, his work stuck out from that of his confrères by virtue of its mainstream, not to say European, look. As a German dealer said: "Sigmar Polke is the most important artist. Kiefer copes Polke and everybody copies Kiefer."

Thus Basquiat looks ill at ease amidst a group to which lip service is played while his *Mona Lisa* sits securely amidst the bedrock of the Werner/Boone New Master painting show, quite as his work appropriately adorns the cover of the Beyeler New Expressionist catalogue, an exhibition that ratifies the new expressionism, as is to be expected, in the origins of *Die Brücke* and Max Beckmann.

Mona Lisa, with regard to Basquiat, is concerned less with Leonardo's androgynous Eternal Feminine (though it is partly about this) and more with Nat King Cole's crooning, "Mona Lisa, Mona Lisa . . . ."

Immense social/art voltage around Keith Haring's exhibition for Tony Shafrazi. Like Basquiat, Haring also makes obeisance to an early club world despite a continuing social romanticism. His totems and wall plaques, pattern above and pattern below, his extra space hired for the rock band, breakdancers, and teen-rappers who thronged as his show opened—the black light graffiti, thousands of posters, T-shirts, and work hats—all conspire to keep the work afloat at an unusually high level of achievement and at an extreme edge of desirability.

But a curious disarray seeps through all this. Despite the immense and focused success of certain artists associated with a certain group of galleries, an odd depression and malaise hangs over stretches of a disaffected, brooding art scene including a "why bother" syndrome should, somehow, more serious ambition ruffle the collective artworld brow. This malaise is underscored by the highly visible ascendance of the graffitists and the East Village where the artists, notwithstanding liberal lip service, aspire to a different social paradigm. Time was when, no matter the radicality of the art, artists identified with the disenfranchised and the weak, identified with a clichéd leftist vision. This is not so with the kids whose ironic self-mockery is itself beyond the turf of the left, beyond the pale.

Unexpectedly, Haring's body design in art is closer to the graffiti tradition (despite his Kutztown, Pennsylvania Wonderbread boyhood) than Basquiat's painting which now lays scattered beyond the graffitist precinct. Basquiat's roots now are more readily found in the old Cubist/Expressionist mix despite his authentic development as the Haitian kid in the land of the Subway.

2 December 1984

Saturday, artworld climax. Kenny Scharf at Tony Shafrazi's jammed to bursting with a performance celebrating the facticious "fin-ism" of Scharf's 1960s Cadillac. The room hung in huge empty pictures that gain in meaning in the degree that there is a vast young artworld crowd just out there, in front of them. The thinner the crowd, the emptier the images become. Something of the same drained effect extends to Keith Haring's work.

16 May 1985

During the shot of the second artists group a tense flare-up between Ronnie Cutrone, a gifted cookie who wants to take a Polariod of the event, and Greenfield-Sanders being proprietary as, after all, this is his shot, his art. The artists of course mostly regard him as just a photographer, hence as the ancillary helpmate of their own celebrity, a fame about which they are not a little twin-minded. Grasping the Nina Leen model, the question was posed as to whether Greenfield-Sanders was poking fun. The issue remains unclear as to who then is being mocked, certainly not the original group of The Irascibles, as they were at that time a particularly irate bunch in high dudgeon over a then-proposed survey of contemporary American painting to be organized by the metropolitan Museum of Art that so pointedly excluded the emerging Abstract-Expressionist group. [See B. H. Friedman, "The Irascibles": A Split Second in Art History," *Arts Magazine*, September 1978, pp. 96–102.]

Rick Prol evidently had studied the photo before arrival. For all his slum-lot affectation, he is a very learned painter. At this present show at the B-Side Gallery I refer to an abstruse set of early twentieth-century sex-murder drawings. "You mean by George Grosz?" he correctly adds.

19 May 1985

The critics seating marked by the absences of Diego Cortez, away in Europe, and Rene Ricard who sent the following demurrer: "*Arts Magazine?* My agent advises me against cameo roles." It was Ricard who at the opening of Diego Cortez's exhibition, "The Pressure to Paint," for Marlborough (June 4–July 9, 1982), led the crowd down to the Fun Gallery that opened the same evening. Fun was founded by Patti Astor and Bill Stelling. This fall, Stelling separates from Astor to open with the London dealer, Edward Totah, in Soho. [Fun will close too. Burnout—so apt an idiom for the East Village. Den Mother to the graffitists is a role inimical to Patti Astor's true theatrical gifts.]

The saddest absence for the critics' shot is Moufarrege, who is represented there by one of his Lichtenstein embroideries. So perhaps there is a pattern in the rug. *Drowning Girl*, the Lichtenstein from which Moufarrege developed his work, once served as cover illustration to one of the first *Artforums* in which my reviews appeared. Now, twenty years later, that image reappears behind me to fill in for the missing artist/writer who, like she, is now drowning. Art in New York After the Plague.

Figure 103. Timothy Greenfield-Sanders, *The New Irascibles, Artists I*, 1985
Black-and-white photograph, 13″×13″.
(Photo courtesy the photographer)

Judy Glantzman	I
Rodney Greenblat	2
Richard Hambleton	3
Stephen Lack	4
Joseph Nechvatal	5
David Wojnarowicz	6
Futura 2000	7
Mike Bidlo	8
Luis Frangella	9
Arch Connelly	10
Rhonda Zwillinger	11
Mark Kostabi	12
Craig Coleman	13
Greer Lankton	14

(Diagrammatic key by Mark Kostabi)

Figure 104. Timothy Greenfield-Sanders, *The New Irascibles, Artists 2*, 1985
Black-and-white photograph, 13″×13″.
(Photo courtesy the photographer)

 1 Rick Prol
 2 Keiko Bonk
 3 Peter Schuyff
 4 Louis Renzoni
 5 Jim Radakovich
 6 Cheryl Laemmle
 7 Martin Wong
 8 Ronnie Cutrone
 9 Philip Pocock
10 Peter Drake
11 Philip Taaffe
12 Thierry Cheverney
13 Colin Lee
14 Kiell Erik Killi Olsen
15 Bobby G
16 Kiki Smith
(Diagrammatic key by Mark Kostabi)

Figure 105.   Timothy Greenfield-Sanders, *The New Irascibles, Artists 3*, 1985
Black-and-white photograph, 13″×13″.
(Photo courtesy the photographer)

Richard Hofmann	1
Jane Bauman	2
Kiely Jenkins	3
Huck Snyder	4
Fred Brathwaite	5
Richard Milani	6
Christof Kohlhofer	7
Paul Benney	8
Ellen Berkenblit	9
Guy Augeri	10
Lynn Augeri	11
Barry Bridgewood	12
Will Mentor	13
Brad Melamed	14
Debbie Davis	15
(Diagrammatic key by Mark Kostabi)	

Figure 106. Timothy Greenfield-Sanders, *The New Irascibles, Dealers I*, 1985
Black-and-white photograph, 13″×13″.
(Photo courtesy the photographer)

1 Doug Milford
2 Patti Astor
3 Nina Seigenfeld
4 Alan Belcher
5 Peter Nagy
6 Elizabeth McDonald
7 Bill Stelling
8 Sur Rodney Sur
9 Mario Fernandez
10 Alan Barrows
11 Dean Savard
12 Rich Colicchio
13 Gracie Mansion
(Diagrammatic key by Mark Kostabi)

Figure 107.   Timothy Greenfield-Sanders, *The New Irascibles, Dealers 2*, 1985
Black-and-white photograph, 13″ × 13″.
(Photo courtesy the photographer)

Hal Bromm	1
Barry Blinderman	2
Pat Hearn	3
Penny Pilkington	4
Wendy Olsoff	5
Steven Adams	6
Tim Greathouse	7
Jamie Wolff	8
Jane Gekler	9
Colin De Land	10
Steven Style	11
Deborah Sharpe	12

(Diagrammatic key by Mark Kostabi)

Figure 108. Timothy Greenfield-Sanders, *The New Irascibles, Critics,* 1985
Black-and-white photograph, 13″×13″.
(Photo courtesy the photographer)

1   Robert Pincus-Witten
2   Carlo McCormick
3   Walter Robinson
4   Michael Kohn
5   Nicolas Moufarrege
6   Dan Cameron
7   Joseph Masheck
8   Yasmin Ramirez-Harwood
9   Ted Castle
10 Richard Milazzo
11 Tricia Collins
12 Edit deAk
(Diagrammatic key by Mark Kostabi)

Figure 109.   Nicolas Mouffarege, *Drowning Girl and Wave*, 1984
Embroidery, paint on buckram.
(Photo courtesy the Nicolas Mouffarege Estate)

Figure 110. Andy Warhol, Installation Photograph Ferus Gallery, Los Angeles, 1962. (Photo courtesy Mike Bidlo)

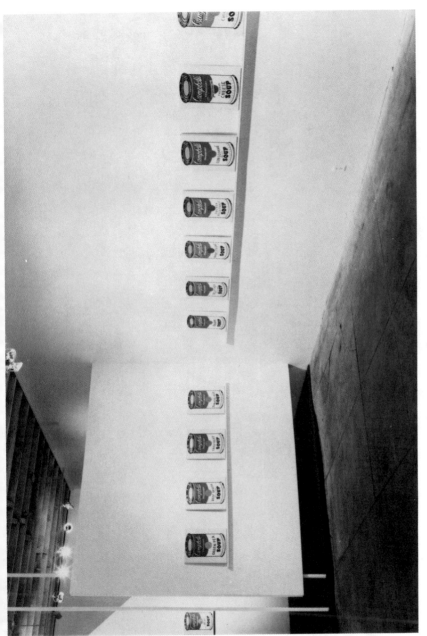

Figure 111.   Mike Bidlo, Installation Photograph, *(Not) Warhol's Campbell's Soup Cans*
Piezo Electric Gallery, Los Angeles, 1986.
(Photo courtesy the artist)

Entries: The Collectors

Who are these people (fig. 112)? They are not especially photogenic. Unlike American sports heroes they have no Instant Recognizability. Nor is there a danger that they will become ciphers, forgotten next season the way sports stars are. For in a certain sense these people are not known. And why is it that were they recognized, they would probably generate a sense of anger rather than one of appreciation? Unexamined prejudices are at work, hardened received values—though cherished ones for all that; artist good, dealer bad; artist good, critic bad; artist good, collector bad.

This suite of clichés grew especially acrimonious when it became clear that the middle class was capable of seeing as art even those objects and artifacts critical of the class itself. This capacity for absorption, even of creations resolutely antagonistic to middle-class perquisites, came to underscore the sentimental aspects of a Marxist-derived criticism, new or old.

While this critical effort purportedly examined the means of production in which the work of art appeared, and in so doing deconstructed Capitalist ideology (doctrine perceived on *a priori* grounds as The Enemy), it never came to terms with the baleful puritanism of Socialism, the real source of the envy (hence of the anger) felt towards the people before you. Free Love—to recall one of the more attractive frivolities of Anarchic Socialism—promised a hedonism rather more honored in the breech (if I may phrase it that way) than in the reality of Red History. Family values of a starchy petty-bourgeois irresilience is more the case. All this remains bad enough in Eastern Europe today, worse in the Far East, and crazed in the Middle East with its admixtures of Kapital and Koran.

This critical mode has grown particularly shrill these past years owing to the continual vitality of a foredoomed middle class (so far as the Marxist agenda is concerned) as it reveals a nostalgia for the transcendent Object of Radicality characteristic of the early modern period. Then it was still possible to believe in Salvation through Classlessness. No such illusion obtains today since the Socialist state has repeatedly

---

This article originally appeared in *Arts Magazine*, February 1986.

shown itself to be culturally repressive and ruled by a class-ridden bureaucracy as jealous of its perks as any of its Capitalist counterparts—in the degree that parity can be perceived.

This recognition goes far in inflecting our despair—deemed post-modern by some—of ever producing an object encoding Utopian signifiers—as if it ever did. That too is mythic. The real lesson of Modern art is that its meaning must always be learned anew and in successive waves.

Still, recent Marxist criticism continues to mouth the clichés of class consciousness by way of appealing to remembered feelings of community. This does not mean that these feelings do not exist—but only that the university classroom is precisely the place in which the realities of class consciousness are most delusionary and self-beautifying. The truth is that the University Marxist is closed out of the struggle, ostracized—not ingathered as he or she would like to believe, or pretends to believe.

While the myth of the object of radicality is at best maintained as a form of nostalgia, ironically it continues to reside with considerable imaginative force amidst the unknown people seen here, The Collectors, perhaps even more than among the artists themselves. Still, to heap irony upon irony, the cumulative effect of The Collectors' exertions has also had the effect of defanging radical content from a work of art even as it transformed it into an object of commodity and its maker into a fellow bourgeois.

The passions and activities of The Collectors have especially influenced the course of immediately contemporary art, a path acutely sensitive to nuanced shifts of pressure. The corroborative impact of acquisition—acquisition often made in virtually paranoid secretiveness—will make a work by an artist thus discovered at least this, as effort perceived as central to an alteration in sensibility. In every likelihood such work will be taken up by a dealer of greater renown than the one with whom the artist began, assuming, if even for argument's sake, that the artist was willing to participate in the gallery system. Mind you, whether he or she does is beside the point, except perhaps for the warm feelings of purity conferred by the refusal to participate in the first place. Mostly such sentiments are used to buoy an artist's faltering sense of protean originality or to bolster a growing awareness of displacement.

The Collectors are assiduous. Even as they are secretive about their own moves, so are they curious as to the actions of the others. Indeed, in the early stages, the multiple ratification of an artist's work adds considerable impact in the resolution of a commonly felt ambivalence and fortifies resolve in the face of everpresent feelings of unease, inadequacy, and disequilibrium. There are, as well, the contrasting emotions of pleasure at the discovery and eventual possession of new work. And there is also pleasure in the recognition of this work's future, its potential for dispersal back into the museum or marketplace, back into the world. Still, even here, at the exchange point of commodity and culture, the gains for art as well as market far outweigh the losses.

Were the toils of acquisition recognized for what they are, one might be less apt to designate The Collectors as a Happy Few. By the same token one is hard-pressed to transform this argument into a source of empathy. These are only neutral observations made from a vantage of privilege.

That these folk are well off goes without saying. They inhabit easily recognized stretches of the demography of the rich though a few have broken through even the roof of the upper-middle-class crust possessing great wealth (or at least having ready access to corporate forms of it). They enjoy what the French call taxable exterior signs of wealth—in the more notable cases, double-lot townhouses or limestone co-ops in that stretch of East Side real estate that members of the Manhattan Old Guard refer to as God's Country, a gentry, by the way, whose values they would find tiresome if not even anathema. Not for them the inert impotent alcoholism of the birthright clubman or the genteel cutthroat good works of his lady. All that is risible when not merely invisible to these high-profile go-getters.

All have collected in some form or another throughout their lives, generally beginning at modest levels of acquisition of work from which they by now largely have grown away—except perhaps for the occasional revenant memento of early passion. What signals them above all other collectors is that consensus "good taste" is an empty question for them while speculation on the possibility of connoisseurship in the history of immediately contemporary art is a matter of considerable intrigue.

As artists and critics are dialectically driven (or so we have learned) to differentiate themselves from one another as well as from their own histories, so are collectors driven by their obsessive appetites. They must know everything or their version of that knowledge—Being In The Know—at least as regards the art world. In the degree that such omniscience is open to them, so are The Collectors armed with a mechanism for selection, drawing from an infinite field of embarrassing riches. I speak now to the art, not to the price of it.

Once choice is conferred, the central myth of modernism—that of the transcendent object embodying a radical consciousness—is usurped, virtually annihilated. Through the actions of The Collector such mythic content is neatly ironed out though its crushed remnants continue to be appealed to in a remembered language of sentimental pieties. Thus in its laundering, the myth is transformed and new conceptions of style and history are formulated. The substance of radicalism is neutered, reduced to style quite as its shadow is reduced to specimen preserved in the formaldehyde of collegiate criticism.

So the effects of the activities of these passionate collectors go far in creating our sense of what is seen as vital, original, and significant. Little History versus Big History. We see and experience stylistic change whether we like it or not. Largely we don't. But we derive our sense of style from the *force majeure* of the history of The Collector Class.

3 October 1985

Today, all caution gone. The most absurdly hyperbolic letter was tossed off on Timothy's Apple II. We have written some twenty great collectors of immediately contemporary art asking them down to Timothy's studio for a group sitting. This is not going to be a portrait shot of individual collectors—of that there are myriad.

"Have you ever seen a group photograph of collectors?" I asked. "No. The reasons are complex.," I went on, "not the least of them being a clichéd vision inherited from a conventional left position. I suspect that we ourselves retain some of this unexamined residue. What has been edited out is your open embrace of adventure, your romantic jeopardy, and your rejection of the stereotypical."

Were the letter made public the Leftists would pillory me even beyond these years of misprision. Why do such a heedless thing in the first place? The perverse imp of self-destruction, I suppose. Or middle-age death wish. Of course I want to test the limits of my own sense of outrage and of the outrageous too. Partly I want to quell a growing frustration in the face of all the reverse snobbery and received opinion that continues to raise its head each time The Collector comes up. What an outmoded cliché—the collector as social undesirable, as greedy self-servant. Enough Already.

I suppose I really wanted to see if I could pull off this absurd coup with only a minimum of fuss. "Be there," I said, "between the salesroom and the museum. No excuses." The brick has been tossed through the plate-glass window.

Figure 112.   Timothy Greenfield-Sanders, *The Collectors,* 1985
(Left to right: front row: Donald Rubell, Martin Sklar, Elaine (and Werner) Dannheiser,
Eugene Schwartz, Adrian Mnuchin; *second row:* Hubert Neumann, Mera Rubell, Martin
Margulies, Jerry Spiegel, Barbara Schwartz; *third row:* Dolores Neumann, Herbert and
Lenore Schorr, Emily Spiegel)
Black-and-white photograph, 13″×13″.
(Photo courtesy the photographer)

Index